Mockingbird Grows Up

MOCKINGBIRD GROWS UP

Re-Reading Harper Lee since *Watchman*

With New Introductory Materials

Edited by Cheli Reutter and Jonathan S. Cullick

The University of Tennessee Press
Knoxville

LIBRARY OF CONGRESS CATALOGING-IN-PUBLICATION DATA
Names: Reutter, Cheli, editor. | Cullick, Jonathan S., editor.
Title: Mockingbird grows up: re-reading Harper Lee since Watchman / edited by
Cheli Reutter and Jonathan S. Cullick.
Description: First edition. | Knoxville: The University of Tennessee Press, [2020] |
Includes bibliographical references and index. |
Summary: "This collection, the first to consider Harper Lee's late novel,
focuses on re-reading *To Kill a Mockingbird* in light of the publication of
Go Set a Watchman. The essays range from evaluations of the characters, setting,
and themes of *To Kill a Mockingbird* through the backward lens of *Go Set a
Watchman* to studies of race, sexuality, and how the characters change in
Harper Lee's posthumous novel. Three essays focus on teaching both of Lee's
novels to students familiar with the canonical *To Kill a Mockingbird* and
to a new generation not yet introduced to Lee."— Provided by publisher.
Identifiers: lccn 2019030992 (print) | lccn 2019030993 (ebook) |
isbn 9798895271018 (paperback) | isbn 9781621905479 (adobe pdf)
Subjects: lcsh: Lee, Harper—Criticism and interpretation. |
Lee, Harper. To kill a mockingbird. | Lee, Harper. Go set a watchman.
Classification: lcc ps3562.e353 z768 2020 (print) | lcc ps3562.e353 (ebook) |
ddc 813/.54—dc23
lc record available at https://lccn.loc.gov/2019030992
lc ebook record available at https://lccn.loc.gov/2019030993

To the memories of our fathers,
Clifford J. Reutter and Isaac Cullick

CONTENTS

PREFACE TO THE PAPERBACK EDITION

Cheli Reutter

Our purpose, when we first published *Mockingbird Grows Up* in the wake of the *Go Set a Watchman* controversy in 2015, was to expand the conversation on *To Kill a Mockingbird* to public audiences and to integrate scholarly and pedagogical discourse with popular and cultural discussions of the book even while also considering *Mockingbird* in the light of *Watchman*. Jonathan and I worked together closely on Harper Lee's oeuvre for five years, beginning when *Watchman* was grist for the rumor mill. We worked with several scholars, writers, and teachers in various corners of the US, from New Jersey to Nebraska, from Ohio to Texas, on its production, and we believe the resulting volume is one worthy of teachers, scholars, and critical readers alike. In 2025, we were still not done yet. We needed to be able to get it into the hands of more people.

On June 11, 2025, Jonathan Cullick and I had an interview with Kate Gibson and her father, retired Good Morning America host Charlie Gibson, and they aired a cut of it on their ABC podcast *The Book Case with Kate and Charlie Gibson* on June 26. It was a lovely conversation, and an opportunity to remember the enduring impact of Harper Lee's most famous work and its much-more-recently-published sister novel while also fulfilling our own goal, with *Mockingbird Grows Up*, of encouraging critical considerations.

While I admit to being star-struck, the four of us had a fluid and energetic discussion about Harper Lee. It was, for Jonathan and me, reunion and remembrance. It is always a pleasure to engage with *To Kill a Mockingbird*—inarguably a brilliantly well-crafted work—even as we hold onto real questions about what personal and cultural work the book does and does not do—and it was important to be able to address the value of the controversial work. Some of Kate and Charlie's questions and comments were particularly grounding, including Kate's pithy question about what *To Kill a Mockingbird* was really about, another question about compassion, and Charlie's about whether we should still teach it.

The podcast also prompted us to resume conversation with our long-time supporter, University of Tennessee Press's acquisitions editor Thomas Wells. We agreed that it was the right time for a second edition, this time in paperback. For us, this meant tracing out what was essential in the volume—including Kate and Charlie Gibson's questions—and how the discourse around *To Kill a Mockingbird* has grown up and still needs to grow up.

Go Set a Watchman sold 1.1 million copies in the US and Canada in its first week of publication back in 2015, and its initial print was 3.3 million books. Pre-sales exceeded any Harry Potter book. Yet—hindered by detracting literati and swirling rumors of author coercion—the discourse has not grown up in classrooms and in scholarly review to the extent we hope for.

That does not mean not at all, though. Jonathan and I are both familiar with teachers and professors who have taught it and book clubs who have read it. My colleague Michael Hennessey, for example, teaches *Go Set a Watchman* in tandem not with *To Kill a Mockingbird* (which still about half of his students have read, in the average year) but rather, with Colson Whitehead's *The Nickel Boys*. A nearby high school invited me into a project introducing excerpts from Ta-Nehisi Coates and Martin Luther King's "Letter from a Birmingham Jail" and *Go Set a Watchman* into a discussion of *To Kill a Mockingbird*, and another local high school teacher I know taught only the *Watchman* novel—to striking effect.

It was the "provenance" question which started us on our *Mockingbird* journey, and confrontation of this topic remains essential to fruitful contemporary dialogue. In 2015, Jonathan researched the provenance of *Go Set a Watchman*, and he delivered a lecture at a local public library just ½ mile from my home in Campbell County, KY. I came because I saw a flier—and it might have been the best whim of my career. After the talk, I asked Jonathan if he would collaborate on a book project with me.

At the time of *Go Set a Watchman*'s release, it became clear that the "ownership" of the discourse on the classic *To Kill a Mockingbird* was at stake. Though early reviewers rushed to protect the reputations of both the author and the novel's patriarch, Atticus Finch (assuming that such protection was necessary), we believe that a novel should belong to everyone who reads it—to the high school student assigned to it as a course text to the casual reader to the scholar—not to those who have assigned themselves the role of honor guard—nor even, entirely, to its author, once released—though of course the author's voice is can be an illuminating intervention in an ongoing dialogue. Yet it became abundantly clear in the release of *Go Set a Watchman* that, despite the efforts of some legal scholars since the 1990s and literary scholars since the 20-oughts, the novel, its hero, and its author were considered sacrosanct, enshrined in national narrative as monuments.

The sheer audacity of Jonathan's original research was like partying with a living monument coming down off its pedestal. For a moment, it leveled the field, allowing us to come together in conversation as we marveled over the new information, even, for some, struggling against what we thought we knew or understood in the face of it. To this day, a library book club discussion we hosted some months after Jonathan's original talk, at which a septuagenarian explained that the book challenged her to reexamine some enshrined racial assumptions she had held onto even while considering herself a progressive person, is seared into my memory. Some version of her experience is what we hope many readers experience with this second edition of *Mockingbird Grows Up*.

The question of what *To Kill a Mockingbird* is "really about"—one of Kate Gibson's lead questions—gave us pause. While dozens of accounts in popular media lead with the claim that it is about Black man falsely accused of raping a white teenager and about the lawyer who defends him in court as told through the eyes of his daughter, many do not consider that Tom Robinson is not even introduced until about ¼ of the way into the novel.

Many people read it, or they are taught to read it, as a clarion of racial justice. My own former high school English teacher reposted something on Facebook in *Mockingbird*'s 50th year in print, calling it the most significant American novel about race in the 20th century. When I wrote something like, "I'm not sure Tom Robinson's family would agree with that assessment," I got a private message saying that comment was "disrespectful," and then he blocked me. Sigh. While I am ashamed to say that my first reaction was something unprintable (and a determination that I would continue to strive to keep my own pedagogical ego in check so I did not ever become like him), my second was to remember that I was a literature professor and not a high school student anymore—and that I had work to do to. This anecdote about a white high male school teacher insisting that the work of a white female author must signify about race in a specific way—and that what it should signify is white superiority in accounting for representations of Black people—is an example of how *To Kill a Mockingbird*—whether it is inherently guilty of racial paternalism or not—has, to some considerable extent, been pressed to the service of it and become a monument of it.

Inherently, it is at the very least an intentional folk story. The book, as Kate Gibson mentioned, offers a history. To explicate: with its blurred lines between history and historical fiction, it is a regional foundation myth, with real-life hierarchical and structural implications. From the first page, we learn of the Finch family's impressive family tree. We hear about Andrew Jackson and Robert E. Lee and how they are connected to the establishment of the main character's family land claim at "Finch's Landing." Within the text, the fictional Finch family is elevated to "Maycomb first family" status–and the common knowledge that the novel is heavily autobiographical deepens that claim.

That Harper Lee's mother's full name was Frances Cunningham Finch adds layers. The Finches, along with the Radleys, are called "regular folks," and thus the top of the town hierarchy Jem describes to his little sister. The Cunninghams are in the next tier, Bob Ewell in the third, and African Americans lowest.

When Harper Lee's book was banned, she defended herself—perhaps surprisingly, to those who ascribe to her the role of champion of racial justice—with a claim that she was a preserver of a Southern legacy in which African Americans are not recognized. She famously wrote in her letter to a school board that, "Surely it is plain to the simplest intelligence that "To Kill a Mockingbird" spells out in words of seldom more than two syllables a code of honor and conduct, Christian in its ethic, that is the heritage of all Southerners." In her words in her interview with Roy Newquist in 1964, she said that *Mockingbird* is about the "soul of the South." Notably, in this single extant recorded interview, she defined "Southerners" as "mostly Irish, Scottish, English, Welsh"—not mentioning African Americans at all. The paradox is notable in context of her own expressed hope to be the "Jane Austen of the South."

The narrative structure, including the framed narrative with a mature Jean Louise vividly recounting her childhood, deeply romanticizes a mythic version of the South in which a family much like the author's own holds primacy. Yet this artistry, including its charming intimacy, plays into the way that the novel is not an agent of but a barrier to social change.

An acknowledgment of this hierarchy puts a different spin on another one of Kate Gibson's questions: Does *Mockingbird* teach compassion? Roy Newquist called it a "gentle, compassionate work," and many remember Atticus's quip about not knowing someone unless you have walked a mile in their skin.

One obvious (though not entirely correct) answer would be a simple "yes." After all, Atticus Finch encourages compassion for Tom in his trial, and for Boo Radley in protecting him from trial, and for the children engender our compassion when Bob Ewell nearly kills them. Yet the whole picture of the role of compassion in Harper Lee's work is more complicated. We as readers are encouraged to limit our compassion for certain characters even as it endures or is amplified for others.

Compassion expenditure in *To Kill a Mockingbird* follows predictable pathways. After Jem Finch explains the stratification of Maycomb to Scout, she responds that "There's just one kind of folks. Folks," and says that if this were not true, Atticus would say so. Yet, paradoxically, the narrator gives us explicit permission to forget about Tom Robinson. Despite what would no doubt have been for them an amplification of the trauma Scout and Jem face with the Bob Ewell scare, given that their father is jailed, threatened, and shot to death, Tom Robinson's children, shown in one brief clip in which Atticus rests his hands atop their heads, are never even mentioned again. The extent to which we are encouraged to feel compassion for the widowed Helen Robinson is work-related only: Link Deas walks her to work every day.

Then, there is misplaced compassion. We have forgotten Tom and his children, and yet we do have misplaced compassion for Walter Cunningham despite, as Malcolm Gladwell says, his homicidal tendencies. Joining a lynch mob is no small thing. And even as we absolve the guilt of Maycomb's entire white community into one person—Tom Ewell—who tried to kill Scout and Jem, the legacy children of Maycomb, and who may have defiled his own daughter—we offer misplaced compassion to his daughter Mayella. Should we have compassion for her as the presumptive victim of her father? Absolutely. Should we forget that this hardship was translated into her own willingness to sentence another man to death? I think not.

Meanwhile, Boo Radley comes to light (literally) as a fascinating study on the subject of compassion. He is the one in the novel to receive the ultimate legal, moral, and sentimental protection. Yet Boo is a much more interesting character than just about any discussion I have been privy to renders him, given his wild days hanging out with the Cunninghams and the moment he thrusts a pair of scissors into his father's leg. Boo has both broken his obligation to behave as a legacy child of one of the two first families of Maycomb ("the regular folks, like us and the Radleys") when he gets in trouble for cutting up with some Cunninghams and other lower-ranking boys in the county. After his father deems him too good for trade school along with the rest of them, and when he is isolated from them, the issue of mental health comes into play. It is not every character in every book who shanks his father with a long pair of shearing scissors, and who is imprisoned in his own home ever after. For bringing in this character and the morphine-addicted Mrs. Dubose, Harper Lee also deserves credit. That Harper Lee's own mother, Jean Finch was alive, but spent most of her time inside, depressed, but alive until the author was 53, furthers interest in this relatively unexplored topic of mental health and compassion in Lee's work.

Compassion, it turns out, is simultaneously overabundant and under-abundant in relation to this novel, and the subject certainly deserves further attention.

The teaching question is also essential. Charlie Gibson asked us whether we should still teach *To Kill a Mockingbird*. My response is a hearty but qualified yes. We must teach it in the context of African American texts, of African American cultural perspectives. While in *To Kill a Mockingbird*, set in the 30s, it is realistic that Scout is not aware of African American leadership or literati, the lack of reference even in *Go Set a Watchman* to any but a vague reference to "NAACP lawyers" leaves a void that needs to be filled by attention to works of the era by Lorraine Hansberry, James Baldwin, early works of Martin Luther King, Jr., and others. It is important, too, to hear from later African American scholars like Malcolm Gladwell, Roxane Gay, and Bryan Stephens weighing in on the enshrinement of *To Kill a Mockingbird*.

Contributors to this volume have raised this point and related ones, all reminding us that we should not just *revisit* Harper Lee's *To Kill a Mockingbird* in light of *Go Set a Watchman*—we should also *rethink* it—both within literary studies and within public conversation. If Leland Person and Jonathan Cullick emphasize Gladwell and King respectively, Adam Nemmers asks us to notice what is present and missing in the Finch family library, and Cheli Reutter asks us consider the irony evident in Bryan Stephenson's *Just Mercy* and elsewhere of a town which enshrines *To Kill a Mockingbird* and its legacy in a museum even while, in the 1980s and early 1990s, a Black man awaited execution on death row by a jury which knows the evidence against him is false.

Teaching *To Kill a Mockingbird* in our time involves an acknowledgement that this novel is unique, even among commonly taught high school books, in its iconic status and in a widespread loyalty among a large swatch of readers to what they believe the text and its hero, Atticus Finch, represent. Readers love *The Great Gatsby,* but no one adores its characters or even jokingly suggests they be nominated for attorney of the year or get a public holiday. *To Kill a Mockingbird* has occupied a place in our culture where many people look to Atticus not to be challenged but rather for comfort and to tell themselves we are okay, we are not racist. Readers often believe that *Mockingbird* is about our own identity, and it tells us who we are or who we want to believe we are. Contributor Patricia D'Ascoli brings Atticus down to a more human size as she compares him to Huck Finn, while Laura Fine, Holly Blackford and Jericho Williams similarly level the field with their attention not on Atticus but on to Scout-as-Jean-Louise, even, in Williams' case, comparing her to Janie Starks of *Their Eyes were Watching God.*

Other contributors encourage perspective shifts addressing the novel's iconic status through review of language and cultural artifacts. Brandie Bohney encourages linguistic comparisons, while Audrey Fisch and Susan Chenelle expose cultural artifacts showing how entrenched stereotypes which may persist without conscientious reflection, and Kwakiutl Dreher offers the shattering reminder, based on a historical postcard, that real-life white girls in towns like the one where Mayella Ewell and Jean Louise Finch grew up may have witnessed lynchings and even smiled at them.

This paperback edition of *Mockingbird Grows Up* presents an opportunity to clarify the purpose of our volume. Several articles in the volume did take *Go Set a Watchman* seriously as a literary work, and these are important. Still, the volume's most important purpose is not to argue for whether *Go Set a Watchman* is a "good" book, to compare its craft to that of *To Kill a Mockingbird*, or to defend a seemingly drastically different representation of Atticus. Rather, reading *To Kill a Mockingbird* in light of the publication of *Go Set a Watchman*—and now, in light of contemporary events—involves an intentional challenge to historically entrenched narratives, common and popular opinion, myth and spin, propelled by generations of readings of *To Kill a Mockingbird*. In the process we may have to conscientiously reject others' readings, as I learned clearly in my interaction with my high school teacher. We may even have to weigh Harper Lee's own words in her public letter and her interview—as discussed above—to explore the contradictions within the comfortable but contradiction-filled worldview *To Kill a Mockingbird* provides.

The issues the volume's contributors bring up are more relevant than ever even as political contexts have shifted significantly in the millennium and even more so in the last five years since publication. Even while Harper Lee herself famously defended *To Kill a Mockingbird* from censoring, influential literary critics did the opposite when *Go Set a Watchman* was set to be released in 2015–ironically asking readers to self-censor by rejecting a perceived "threat" to the "real" Harper Lee and her "real" work. On the other hand, in a recent wave of book banning accompanying the second term of President Donald Trump, *To Kill a Mockingbird* appears quite safe. In a recent article by Chandler Fritz in *Harper's Magazine*, we have learned that certain conservative homeschool group circles are championing *To Kill a Mockingbird* in the canon—even as the author—a teacher as well—attempts to decenter Atticus as a character and encourages students to think more about Tom Robinson instead.

Through this second edition, we urge readers and teachers keep *To Kill a Mockingbird* in circulation—while at the same time urging that they consider these complex contexts. Comparative readings, decentering characters, biographical readings examining Harper Lee's own values and perspectives, and reflection on cultural artifacts are all effective. We also encourage approaches not contained within this volume, such as disability studies reviews offering a collective reading of the widely varying representations of at least five disabled characters in *To Kill a Mockingbird*. This volume can help readers engage with smart new readings even while considering their own. All these readings of *To Kill a Mockingbird* in light of the publication of *Go Set a Watchman* thread through the simple question Jonathan Cullick asks in his "Reconsidering Maycomb and US Populism": was *To Kill a Mockingbird* really the song of innocence many have supposed?

TIMELINE

In the years between the first and second edition of *Mockingbird Grows Up,* we have had the privilege of presenting our scholarship on Harper Lee, individually or in partnership, in public venues and forums, including at a "Six at Six" talk sponsored by the Northern Kentucky University Scripps-Howard Center for Civic Engagement; at a panel at the Harriet Beecher Stowe House in Cincinnati with contributors Brandie Bohney, Kwakiutl Dreher, Monica Miller, Adam Nemmers, and Leland Person; on a Cincinnati Edition broadcast with Michael Monks; and in a *Cincinnati Enquirer* op-ed about Judge Nathaniel R. Jones and wrongfully accused murder suspect Walter McMillan in the context of *Mockingbird.* We've also applied our research in teaching: Jonathan Cullick works regularly with high school secondary English education teachers, including some who teach *To Kill a Mockingbird.* Cheli Reutter has participated in Cincinnati-based high school programs at Elder and Finneytown High School which place Lee's published novels in the context of modern and contemporary African American writers.

Through our ongoing scholarly and pedagogical experiences, we recognized the need for a timeline offering multiple contexts for Harper Lee as a writer and literary figure. This includes information in the public domain as may be expected in a historical timeline, such as the Montgomery Bus Boycott, Brown v. Board, and Dr. King. It also includes related but lesser-known Civil Rights content about the Freedom Riders and other Civil Right activists including Diane Nash and the Ohio-based Freedom Rider David Fankhauser. If Harper Lee's story in some significant ways describes her journey to the North and back, Fankhauser's is the reverse narrative.

While the vector of Harper Lee's public career ends on a nostalgic note, Bryan Stevenson's work and writing indicate there is much to be done so that similar racial injustices do not resume in Alabama even decades later. If Harper Lee's novels suggest that racial problems have been addressed (with *To Kill a Mockingbird*) or that gradualism and love will prevail (as with *Go Set a Watchman*), several African American book and speech writers suggest that racial and social problems need continued attention.

1926	(April 28) Nelle Harper Lee, the youngest of four children, is born in Monroeville, AL to Amasa Coleman Lee and Francis Cunningham Finch Lee.
1945	(September 2) WWII ends.
1949	Harper Lee moves to New York City to pursue a writing career; works as a bookseller and travel agent.
1951	(June 2) Death of Nelle Harper Lee's mother, Frances Cunningham Lee (nee Finch).
1954	(May 17) Brown v. Board decision.
1955–56	(December 5-December 20) Montgomery Bus Boycott following Rosa Parks' refusal to give up her seat to a white passenger.
1956	(November) Lee meets her long-time literary agent and friend Maurice Crain.
1956	(December) Friends of the author give her a gift of one year of wages to pursue writing.
1957	(spring) Crain submits manuscript of *Go Set a Watchman* to publishers on Lee's behalf; JP Lippincott editor sees a "spark" in the manuscript.
1957	(January) Dr. Martin Luther King founds the Southern Christian Leadership Conference to champion civil rights through nonviolent protest and civil disobedience.
1957	Civil Rights Act of 1957 (September 9) signed by President Eisenhower.
1959	(March 11) *A Raisin in the Sun* by Lorraine Hansberry debuts on Broadway.
1960	(July 11) *To Kill a Mockingbird* is published.
1961	Freedom Riders (May 4, 1961-December 10, 1961) Despite laws prohibiting segregated interstate facilities, Freedom Riders in Aberdeen, Alabama are brutally attacked by KKK members as the police officers watch and then arrest the Freedom Riders on charges of disturbing the peace.
1961	Diane Nash, student civil rights organizer, calls for additional volunteers after the first rides end in severe beatings by the KKK.
1961	Nathaniel R. Jones is appointed by Attorney General Robert Kennedy as assistant US attorney for Northern Ohio District.
1961	David Fankhauser, a 19-year-old white chemistry student at Central State College in Ohio, an HBCU enrolling eight white students in a diversity initiative, joins the Freedom Rider movement, stays with Ralph Abernathy, where he meets Rev. Dr. Martin Luther King Jr. Arrested and jailed with other Freedom Riders in Jackson, Mississippi.Robert Kennedy, US attorney general from 1961–1964, agrees to enforce the Civil Rights Act and the Freedom Riders are released.
1961	(May 29) *A Raisin in the Sun* film released.
1962	(April 15) Harper Lee's father Amasa Coleman Lee, for whom Harper had become primary caregiver following illness and infirmity, dies. Amasa

was proud of Harper Lee's *To Kill a Mockingbird* and signed his name "Atticus Finch" on *To Kill a Mockingbird* souvenir items.

1963 (January 31) *The Fire Next Time* by James Baldwin is published.

1963 (February 14) *To Kill a Mockingbird* film released.

1964 (February 19) Harper Lee's interview with Roy Newquist of WQXR, her only known extant and recorded interview. In it, she describes her desire to be the "Jane Austen of the South" and equates "Southerners" with the rural elite of Celtic, Welsh, and Anglo-Saxon origin.

1966 Harper Lee writes an open letter in *The Richmond News Leader* sharply rebuking the Hanover County school board for removal of her book from schools.

1966 (January) Lyndon Johnson appoints Lee to the National Council on the Arts.

1968 (April 4) Rev. Dr. Martin Luther King Jr. is shot and killed in Memphis a day after delivering his "I've been to the Mountaintop" speech.

1969 Judge Nathaniel Jones appointed general counsel of the NAACP; delivers a keynote address including "we still live in the basement of the great society."

1978 Harper Lee returns from New York, where she has been living part-time since 1949; observes the trial of Reverend Willie Maxwell; many including journalist Casey Cep suggest she was working on a true crime novel.

1987 Walter McMillan wrongfully arrested in Monroe County, Alabama (the model for the fictional Maycomb County), for the killing of Ronda Morrison; spends six years on death row.

1988 Walter McMillan meets attorney Bryan Stevenson, who prepares his defense though the Equal Justice Initiative, a nonprofit he founds after the Southern Center for Human Rights's fund for death row inmates is cut.

2006 Harper Lee's letter to Oprah Winfrey, reflecting on her childhood love of reading, is published in *O Magazine*.

2007 (November 5) President George W. Bush awards Harper Lee the Presidential Medal of Freedom.

2014 (October 21) Attorney Bryan Stevenson publishes *Just Mercy: A Story of Justice and Redemption*.

2015 (July 14) HarperCollins publishes Harper Lee's *Go Set a Watchman*.

2015 (July 14) Spiegel and Grau publishes Ta-Nehisi Coates' *Between the World and Me*. (Note that this is the same day as *Go Set a Watchman*.)

2016 (February 19) Harper Lee dies in her sleep in Monroeville.

2016 (April 21) *Go Set a Watchman* is published in paperback with a new preface to explain the book's provenance.

2025 (October 21) *The Land of Sweet Forever*, a collection of Harper Lee's shorter works, set to be released.

RECONSIDERING MAYCOMB
AND US POPULISM

Jonathan S. Cullick

To Kill a Mockingbird never was a song of innocence. Cheli Reutter and I do not find in Maycomb a place where childhood was once idyllic but then disrupted. It was violent at its inception. The novel begins with Jem's broken arm, and the opening paragraphs explain the injury in a regressing chain of causes: the violent attack by Bob Ewell, the children's efforts to make Boo Radley come out, and ultimately, more than a century earlier, Andrew Jackson's actions in the Creek Indian wars. It is a town that can commit a collective act of violence against Tom Robinson. Even Tim Johnson, a dog, gets shot. By the time Uncle Jack strikes Jean Louise in the face in *Go Set a Watchman,* we have become familiar with the pattern.

Nothing about Maycomb was ever quite right. Like a living room painting hung askew, Maycomb County and the town wobble on an uneasy foundation. A wilderness "cut off from the rest of the nation" (GSW 7), the county was named for Colonel Mason Maycomb, "a man whose misplaced self-confidence and overweening willfulness brought confusion and confoundment" to the troops he led. Incompetent with maps and directions, the Colonel made wrong turns and got lost in the woods where he and his soldiers "sat out the wars in considerable bewilderment" (GSW 9). Their accidental settlement became Maycomb County.

The town became the county seat when a tavern owner named Sinkfield used liquor to manipulate a team of surveyors into making his establishment the exact center of the county (TKM 148). The courthouse is an awkward building, early Victorian on one side but Greek revival on the other with columns that "clashed with a big nineteenth-century clock tower housing a rusty unreliable instrument" (TKM 184–185). The building delivers justice about as well as it tells the time.

The town is inhabited by a population whose eccentricities are either self-facing (the heroin-addicted Mrs. Dubose and the reclusive Arthur Radley) or outward-facing (the violent Bob Ewell and the judgmental Miss Stephanie Crawford). Every family, in Aunt Alexandra's telling, has a "streak" of some kind (a drinking streak, a mean streak). Considering that "'our generation's practically the first in the Finch family not to marry its cousins,'" Atticus suggests, the Finches could be said to have "'an Incestuous Streak'" (TKM 147).

The town certainly has a racist streak. Speaking to Uncle Jack, Atticus worries about the children "catching Maycomb's usual disease," which causes "reasonable people [to] go stark raving mad when anything involving a Negro comes up." He can only hope that Jem and Scout will "come to me for their answers instead of listening to the town. I hope they trust me enough" (*TKM* 100–101). Not enough, apparently. The grown-up Jean Louise not only takes her questions to someone outside her home, but she also even takes the Maycomb train all the way to New York City. Her discoveries about her father in *Go Set a Watchman* suggest that she is on the right track.

As easily as Harper Lee rode the rails from Monroeville to Manhattan, Jean Louise's voice travels from her time to ours. Some readers return to *To Kill a Mockingbird* for the reassurance of the putatively virtuous figure of Atticus Finch. Others re-read to revisit the disorder of Harper Lee's fictional 1930's town and the limitations of Atticus's advocacy. Which readers are right? There are fine people on both sides. I say this unironically because the best literature offers comfort and confrontation. The narrative gets complicated, and one finds what one comes looking for.

What I find is that the violent and racially divided Maycomb has a populist streak. Cheli and I are writing this nearly a century after Scout observed the trial of Tom Robinson. In this first quarter of the 21st century, the populist disposition, which for decades had been preserved in the margins, has resurged in mainstream American culture. We are revisiting Maycomb only to discover that we all live there now.

Consider an early scene in the schoolhouse—observed and narrated by Scout—when the teacher Miss Caroline tells the unkempt and lice-infested Burris Ewell to go home and wash. As he exits, he calls the teacher a "slut" and yells, "You ain't makin' me go nowhere, missus. You just remember that, you ain't makin' me go nowhere!" (*TKM* 31). Here this poor white kid insists that he has autonomy against an institution that would govern not only his behavior but also his self-presentation. It's his identity versus the establishment. The pride he asserts is a petulant reaction against all that the school represents—merit, social status, economic success. Whether we're in the 1930s or the 2020s, it's the Ewells against the elites, and it's a short road from calling the teacher a slut to, say, dismantling the U.S. Department of Education.

In the classic study, *The Populist Persuasion: An American History*, Michael Kazin defines populism not as an ideology but as a "language of mass discontent." The rhetoric of populism is an "us vs. them" binary. Kazin identifies two traditions in populist rhetoric, each with a different definition of the *them* group. Civic Nationalism, concerned with economic disparities, opposes a financial elite. Ethnic-Racial Nationalism, concerned with preservation of identity, opposes both a cultural elite . . . and immigrants. (The cultural elite are deemed to be using immigration to displace people in the middle culturally and economically.) For Kazin, a representative of the former rhetorical tradition would be Senator Bernie Sanders, and a representative of the latter rhetorical tradition would be President Donald Trump.

Wherever on the left-to-right political spectrum populism appears, it always performs a key rhetorical and conceptual maneuver: it draws a line between those perceived to be regular or real people and those considered to be the elite. The "people" are authentic, practical, productive, small-town or rural, and powerless. The "elite" are artificial, intellectual, condescending, cosmopolitan, and powerful. When Mayella senses Atticus condescending to her on the witness stand, and when she challenges the "fine fancy gentlemen" to stand up for her, the us/them binary is on display (*TKM* 213). When Jem, in his discourse on the "four kinds of folks in the world," refers to the Finch family as "the ordinary kind" of folks, he shows insight into his own community's social strata (*TKM* 258).

The problem is that ethnic-racial populism usually defines "the people" as white and western European. Uncle Jack in *Go Set a Watchman* articulates an intellectual foundation for this kind of populism. Of Southerners fighting in the "War Between the States" he says, "They fought to preserve their identity. Their political identity, their personal identity" (*GSW* 196). Uncle Jack says, "People's attitudes toward the duties of a government have changed. The have-nots have risen and demanded and received their due" (*GSW* 197), which would sound reasonable enough if he did not define "people" and "have-nots" only as white people. He fears the federal government becoming so large (protective of minority rights) that "the smallest person" (white person) "will be trampled underfoot" (*GSW* 198). "When a man's looking down the double barrel of a shotgun," referring again only to a white man, "he picks up the first weapon he can find to defend himself, be it a stone or a stick of stovewood or a citizens' council" (*GSW* 200).

Or a noose, we might add. Uncle Jack rationalizes the lynch mob in *To Kill a Mockingbird* with the same erudition as the pundits and politicians who defended the mob that swarmed the U.S. Capitol on January 6, 2020, which came to Washington DC with a noose of their own.

Yet, still, as I listen to Mayella up on that witness stand, repulsed by what she is doing to Tom, I cannot ignore her circumstances. Socially ostracized by her community, economically disadvantaged by her birth, sexually exploited by her father—she evokes some compassionate response. Even Tom Robinson feels sorry for her. This is not to excuse her false accusation against Tom. It is only to note that this is not merely a type character in a novel; this is a person. In what I think is a lovely passage in the novel, Scout notices the dilapidated and debris-strewn condition of the Ewell home, telling us: "One corner of the yard, though, bewildered Maycomb. Against the fence, in a line, were six chipped-enamel slop jars holding brilliant red geraniums." Scout can see that someone was caring—"tenderly"—for those flowers. "People said they were Mayella Ewell's" (*TKM* 194).

In the first edition of this book, I pushed against the reassuring domestic scene of Atticus protecting the children at the conclusion of *To Kill a Mockingbird*. There is another ending, I argued, another family across town not experiencing that kind of security. I was referring directly to the Robinson family. Now, with this second edition, I wish to extend my claim. The Ewell children have also lost their father—an abusive father, to be sure—and their lives, already on the margin, are even less certain economically, socially, and emotionally. Teaching the novel today, I want my students to imagine all the missing final chapters.

The Robinsons, the Ewells, the Cunninghams—all of them need better and deserve better from their community. The poor white families would be well served by economic populism, but unfortunately, they are attracted to, yet poorly served by, ethno-racial populism. The same stressors that call for economic remedies make fertile ground for the rhetoric of racist populism, which is divisive and corrosive but also terribly seductive. If Maycomb is a town in which some "folks" win and others lose, then everyone will lose. So it is with all the Maycombs in our own time. My hope for *Mockingbird* to "grow up" is that returning readers and new readers will connect 1930s Maycomb to our current moment.

ACKNOWLEDGMENTS

This volume has been a labor of love and persistence. We would like to acknowledge the efforts of our contributors, our families, and the colleagues and communities who have supported us from the project's inception in 2015 to its publication in 2020.

Of our contributors, we cannot sing loud enough praises. Our call for papers produced many excellent proposals, many more than we could include. And yet we were not prepared for the diverse perspectives, the deep insights, and the vigorous scholarship we received and came together to form this volume.

Our thanks go to our colleagues at the University of Cincinnati and Northern Kentucky University. Particularly, John Alberti and Kris Yohe, of NKU, and Gary Vaughn, of University of Cincinnati, have offered conversation and encouragement. To Leland S. Person, thank you for joining us on a panel at the Society for Southern Literature in Boston in 2016, and, especially, for your pithy contribution to the volume. Gary Weissman, we appreciate your organization and support of our kick-off lecture.

The University of Tennessee Press has been a joy to work with. We are indebted to excellent readers, to our copyeditor, Annalisa Weaver, and to our cover designer, Rickie Le. We especially appreciate acquisitions editor Thomas Wells, whose determination, diplomacy, and encouragement were vital to the project. To local organizations including the Campbell County Public Libraries and the Harriet Beecher Stowe House, Cincinnati, we express our deepest thanks.

We are deeply grateful to our families for their support of this project. Cheli would like to acknowledge her children, Justin and Theo, who remain her inspiration for everything. To our respective spouses, Cheryl Cullick and Keith Whitehead, we owe a great deal. Both of you helped us across many bridges.

We would be remiss if we did not also acknowledge the cats in both of our households, whose demands, antics, and affection forced us to take breaks during those times when we were working too hard.

Mockingbird Grows Up

INTRODUCTION

Cheli Reutter

In 2015, HarperCollins released to press the manuscript of a yet more famous "Harper": Alabama-born and world-renowned *To Kill a Mockingbird* author Harper Lee. The manuscript was to become *Go Set a Watchman,* also set in the fictional town of Maycomb, Alabama, but featuring an elderly Atticus Finch and a twenty-six-year-old Jean Louise just returned from New York. HarperCollins's decision to publish *Go Set a Watchman* without any literary contextualization or definitive explanation of its provenance led to what can best be described as a frenzied legacy-grab. Early reviewers, including Maureen Corrigan, encouraged public outrage about the 2015 text and its publication, indicating that potential readers would meet "Ahab turned into a whale." According to Alex Shephard of the *New Republic,* the reputation of the "noble, high-minded" icon Atticus Finch was at stake—and so was that of its author.

Many Americans, from casual readers and scholars to students and pedagogues, are invested in *To Kill a Mockingbird* and in what scholar Benedict Anderson terms its "imagined community." A Common Core exemplar text in the high school curriculum in many states, including Alabama, Tennessee, and Kentucky, *Mockingbird* continues to impact the education of many students. Between its thirty million plus copies sold, the award-winning film starring Gregory Peck, multiple stage adaptations (most recently Aaron Sorkin's Broadway version), and even Tom Santopietro's 2018 book *Why To Kill a Mockingbird Matters: What Harper Lee's Book and the Iconic American Film Mean to Us Today,* it is apparent that Mockingbird still runs broad and deep in the American imagination. It is no surprise, then, that many wanted direction in their assessment of *Go Set a Watchman.* Given early reports that *Watchman* was a "mess" (Corrigan) indicating the demise of popular and scholastic access to *Mockingbird* (Shephard), many wanted someone to allay their concerns.

Biographer Charles Shields provides some comfort through his position as a familiar biographical authority on Harper Lee. Shields tells Alexandra Alter in an interview that the coming-out of *Go Set a Watchman* changed his view of *Mockingbird,* primarily in that he sees "the influence of her editor, Tay Hohoff, much more now" (Alter). In his 2016 revision of *Mockingbird: A Portrait of Harper Lee,* he opines that Hohoff "must have" told Harper Lee to "improve" her Maycomb novel by writing it from the perspective of a child. Shields calls *Go Set a Watchman* an "important cultural document," but implies a relative lack of literary merit.

Concerning the provenance of *Watchman,* Shields's explanation provides a counterforce to implausible conspiracy theories circulating in public media involving attorney Tonja Carter's supposed authorship of the *Watchman* manuscript. Shields's supposition may quell rumors from the proverbial radical fringe, yet it begs the larger question of how to understand *Watchman* in a broader literary tradition. It also does not address popular understanding and pedagogy concerning Harper Lee's classic novel. Some scholars who have researched *Watchman*'s provenance have arrived at a different conclusion than Shields concerning its value and potential impact.

Joseph Crespino and volume co-editor Jonathan S. Cullick see Lee's own authority in the provenance of both of the novels, likely originating in a six-month timespan in 1957. These scholars opine that these two novels fulfill distinct purposes for the author and the audience. Crespino's reviewer, Howell Raines, reminds us that Harper Lee "kept the rails hot" between Alabama and New York. Cullick imagines a "Manhattan Harper" and an "Alabama Nelle." *Watchman,* these scholars suggest, satisfies the author herself as she comes to terms with her father's racial politics, while *Mockingbird* mounts a defense against the white mobocracy that felt her father was still too liberal leaning.

Each of the articles in this volume proceed from the premise that *Go Set a Watchman* was *not* simply a failed first draft of what was to become the Pulitzer Prize–winning *To Kill a Mockingbird*—nor was *Mockingbird* a mere literary prequel. We might cite significant changes in details of the rape trial in each novel, or we might remark on chronological inconsistencies, for instance. Yet the important differences are of audience, literary style, and the purpose they might serve.

The editors and contributors in this volume recognize common source material but distinctive literary paradigms for each novel. Some of the volume's essays, including Monica Carol Miller's, consider the value of *both* novels in the classroom, in conjunction with popular writing, as means by which students can learn to critically read culture. The nostalgic memory-narrative of *To Kill a Mockingbird* might be juxtaposed with a raw and modern style and young adult appeal of *Go Set a Watchman,* and with the expository writing of Ta-Nehisi Coates and others.

Patricia F. D'Ascoli compares Harper Lee's two novels to earlier and later portions of Twain's *Huckleberry Finn,* which significantly evolves from beginning to end in the presentation of its titular character. As Laura Fine points out, the intensity of Jean Louise's challenge to her father, in *Go Set a Watchman,* is deflected by Uncle Jack. Still, as D'Ascoli explains, Jean Louise's perspective on Atticus bears some comparison to Huck's perspective of his father later in Twain's text.

Also in this volume, Jericho Williams compares *Go Set a Watchman* to *Their Eyes were Watching God,* Janie Starks's coming-of-age story. By considering Harper Lee as a writer with the capacity for a bifurcated consciousness capable of creating both novels, perhaps we can apprehend that Ahab was always also the whale. By assessing both of her texts, perhaps we can come to terms with the "legacy" that, without benefit of the maturation novel (*Watchman*), we might understand only in childlike terms.

The articles in this volume push past a relatively low regard for the literary merit of *Watchman* implied by Shields and expressed by Tom Santopietro. Holly Blackford reads *Go Set a Watchman* as a literary text in its own right—independent of comparison with *Mockingbird* and worthy of a more serious role in the literary tradition. Blackford, whose 2011 *Mockingbird Passing* was the last major single-authored scholarly text to review the *Mockingbird* novel, recognizes the place of *Go Set a Watchman* in the literary tradition through comparison of the *Watchman* Atticus with Willa Cather's eponymous Ántonia.

Collectively, we confront an issue the 2015 novel addresses: the fear held by many white mainstream readers that *Watchman* will make them discover the closeted racism in themselves or a family member they regard as iconic. To this, we can only say, let the *Watchman* be set on each of our own consciences. Let it belie the sanctity of white privilege, white supremacy, and normativity in any form—benevolent or strident—in the courtroom, the privacy of the home, the classroom, the literary tradition, or the popular imagination.

On July 19, 2015, the day Harper Lee's *Go Set a Watchman* was released, Robert McCrum claimed in a review for *The Guardian* that *Go Set a Watchman* is a "literary curiosity" that may not have been "worth the wait" on its own merit. Yet McCrum differs from other *Watchman* naysayers: in the end, he suggests that *Watchman* is worthwhile. McCrum praises *Mockingbird* for its merit as a fictional memoir, remarking on "six-year-old Scout remembering the childhood days that will change her forever." Still, McCrum argues, *Mockingbird* enjoyed an "extra-literary circumstance" propelling its success: the Civil Rights Movement. He claims that, "sometimes, novels have afterlives that no author could anticipate." McCrum then encourages readers to regard *Watchman* in terms of another powerful but darker "extra-literary circumstance," maintaining that *Watchman* is an apt reminder of this "traumatic history of the American South" into which Lee ingeniously taps. In the conclusion of his review, he reminds us that such traumatic history is still being made: "Even after more than six years of an African American presidency, the people of Charlottesville, Ferguson and Alabama know all too well that their democratic republic is still haunted by the ominous tolling of Jefferson's fire bell in the night."

When McCrum mentions unanticipated "afterlives," he refers to textual interactions with current events. Yet the many allusions to *Mockingbird* and the iconic Atticus from celebrities including Barack Obama and Stephen Colbert indicate that the timely events of the 1960s were merely the infancy of *Mockingbird*'s afterlife. *Mockingbird* has also loomed large in the popular consciousness in which texts interact—often engendering feelings of nostalgia. Yet others experience exclusion. Naa Baako Ako-Adjei describes the treatment of *Mockingbird* in her high school classroom as "sacrosanct." I recall this from my own high school years, and I have evidence from my own students that this practice endures. Just after the release of *Go Set a Watchman,* one of my own white students wrote in her first-day writing assignment that Atticus was the "father I never had," and praised him for his effort defending Tom Robinson. (I gave her a copy of *Watchman,* which productively complicated her reading.) On the other hand, one of my African American students reported feelings of great discomfort with every discussion of *To Kill a Mockingbird* in her high school English class. That she took the time to visit my office to tell me about her experience the day after I mentioned the publication of *Watchman* in lecture only emphasized her concern. No doubt this discomfort is exacerbated when Atticus Finch, a fictional character, gets parades (for example, for Brazos County's Annual Atticus Finch Day) and accolades (including nominations to the American Bar Association's Attorney of the Year).

Still, *Mockingbird* has prospered in both classrooms and the national imagination. It even thrives in some niche communities, for example, presenting possibilities for popular and scholarly queer readings. Part of the appeal of *To Kill a Mockingbird* is its sympathetic portrayal of characters who can be read as representing LGBTQ people and communities. *Mockingbird* is listed among the one-hundred best lesbian and gay novels, along with other books, including Carson McCullers's *Member of the Wedding* and Rita Mae Brown's *Rubyfruit Jungle*. Scholars have also specifically commented on the queer landscape, scenes, and settings in *To Kill a Mockingbird*. The neighborhood in the town of Maycomb where Jem and Scout live and where Dill spends his summers nurtures queer children, and even queer adults can sometimes navigate this space. Gary Richards examines the queer masquerade in the penultimate scene in which Scout walks Boo Radley home. Yet Holly Blackford's *Mockingbird Passing* also points out the racial foibles of the book even while offering an intersectional analysis of some of queer scenes and settings.

In the dialogic imagination surrounding novels in the literary tradition, *Mockingbird* creates an extensive cultural event that Leland S. Person compares, in this volume, to the century-earlier *Uncle Tom's Cabin*. Each of these novels may be characterized by a humanitarian appeal that buries inequalities even as the story runs wild in what Benedict Anderson calls the "imagined community" of readers, pedagogues, students, and scholars. Yet Stowe supplies ghosts in *Uncle Tom's Cabin* (in the intertextual gothic parody and the extratextual *Key to Uncle Tom's Cabin*) to haunt this belief. As it turns out, so did Harper Lee. The ghosts of *Go Set a Watchman* haunt populist readings that have gone blithely out of control in the dialogic process spawned in a film adaptation, bookstores, libraries, book clubs and classrooms.

In the final chapters of *Watchman,* Jean Louise herself experiences a modicum of the "traumatic history of the American South" McCrum mentions. Her trauma is physical and emotional, beginning after she severs ties with Calpurnia, whom she admits has raised her—guiding her through the terror, shame, and misapprehensions of kissing, menstruation, and pregnancy. In flashbacks in *Watchman,* Calpurnia is there for Jean Louise through depression and suicidal ideation. Yet even the grown Jean Louise appears either unwilling or unable to take into consideration Calpurnia's own feelings. When Jean Louise crosses into the black section of town to visit the now-elderly, anxiety-ridden and infirm Calpurnia, she disrespects the older woman's privacy as she tries to force Calpurnia to sing Atticus's praises. It appears that Jean Louise only registers Calpurnia's humanity to the extent of her service to Atticus and herself. Here, readers should recognize in their reading of Maycomb an application of Benedict Anderson's principle of imagined community, that, "regardless of the actual inequality and exploitation that may prevail ... the nation is always conceived as a deep, horizontal comradeship" (*Imagined Communities* 7).

Before entering Calpurnia's place, *Watchman*'s Jean Louise apparently believes (as have a many growing up with *Mockingbird*) that Atticus's power as the patriarch of Maycomb stems from moral authority. Jean Louise should have known better. Given Calpurnia's steadfast refusal in *Mockingbird* to let her little charge come home with her, Jean Louise might have considered, at least as a grown-up, that Calpurnia was shielding her from disquieting truths about the nature of relations between the black community and the remnant white aristocracy in Maycomb. She might have considered that black folk did not *enjoy* having to live in a system of white patronage.

As several contributors in this anthology note, Calpurnia also takes a terrifyingly long minute answering Jean Louise's question of whether Calpurnia could "hate" her and her brother. For some readers as well as, presumably, Jean Louise herself, this moment of tense silence signifies the terror of the uncanny. Yet in this terrifying experience of this familiar-unfamiliar, brought to light in this moment of Calpurnia's refusal to speak words of comfort to Jean Louise, the reading audience might also notice in the Maycomb narrative collectively what Mikhail Bakhtin calls heteroglossia. In *To Kill a Mockingbird,* Calpurnia's language, self-determined as it may appear, is still ensconced in a narrative framework privileging Jean Louise's interest, and it is only in Calpurnia's refusal to speak that she can come closest to revealing truth.

The truth is that everything does not have to be all about Jean Louise Finch. It does not have to be about her "kind": making white people feel good about the other white people they wish to admire is not the job of black people. The truth is also that it is not the job of older black women to make young white women feel like favored daughters. This is a truth Jean Louise might have heard in Calpurnia's silence in *Watchman,* but ultimately chooses to reject.

Harper Lee's decision (influenced as it may have been by her editor) to write *To Kill a Mockingbird* through the eyes of a child allowed the author to create a new narrative in which the white heroine could more easily avoid coming to terms with feminine participation in white privilege. In her article in this volume, Kwakiutl L. Dreher describes Mayella Ewell's hyperbolic white femininity. Exaggerated as it may be in the film version of *Mockingbird,* Mayella's white feminine agency is already evident in Harper Lee's book. Mayella Ewell has a power that she wields fiercely and never has to apologize for, because pity generally preserves her from blame for Tom Robinson's blood. Laura Fine suggests in this volume that in *Go Set a Watchman,* Uncle Jack is Atticus's doppelganger, fierce where Atticus is benevolent, but as necessary as Atticus in Jean Louise's maturation. Similarly, in *Mockingbird,* Harper Lee frees the Finch heroine of any negative association with the power and privilege of young white womanhood, instead projecting it onto Mayella Ewell. Scout, who remains a loveable, tomboyish and perpetually innocent white girl-child in *To Kill a Mockingbird,* nevertheless still benefits from her white feminine status.

Yet *Watchman*'s legacy is a reminder of the consequences of denial of privilege. At the point of her leave-taking of Calpurnia, Jean Louise does not want to admit to the actual inequality and exploitation; it is far easier and safer to simply deny. A few of our contributors, including Fine and Jericho Williams, draw out important points about ways in which Jean Louise will be able to use her position subversively, given constraints. Others, however, focus on the ugly side of her compromises.

Jean Louise spurns Calpurnia for the older woman's apparent lack of loyalty to Atticus. Yet it appears she then develops doubts about the idyllic nature of race relations in the town (perhaps as a result of her experience with Calpurnia). She expresses these to her Uncle Jack, who then attacks her, slapping her and calling her a "bigot" when she will not voice acceptance of Atticus's views. The lesson taught by this trauma is that if she (as a female, as a daughter) wants to maintain her privilege as a Finch, she must validate "all sides" of the argument. (Given the violence of this interaction, it is no wonder McCrum thinks of Charlottesville.) By the end of the novel, Jean Louise has also given up her lower-class and single-mothered boyfriend, who is not more racist, but is less pedigreed, than the Finch men. He is not her "kind," she confirms to her Aunt Alexandra. In the end, Jean Louise embraces that she is "a Finch," but it is unclear where that acceptance will lead her, her town, and her imagined community of readers.

In the aftermath of her uncle's slap, Jean learns more about why Hank could never be her husband, as she discovers just how inescapably and incestuously "Finch" she is. The "dark secret" (in McCrum's terms) is that Uncle Jack "was in love with [her] mother" (274). Jean Louise is the sole heir, biologically and sentimentally, of the last two of the Maycomb Finch men. That Atticus, her father (or uncle?) *knew* of this secret and kept it from her should certainly awaken readers to the possibility that there are other "dark secrets" propping up the Finch dynasty, even in the demise of its biological line and aristocratic wealth.

Nostalgic sensibility is not the only thing Harper Lee's two-time heroine comes into possession of. In *Go Set a Watchman,* the incest narrative of southern fiction from Edgar Allen Poe to William Faulkner turns out to be Jean Louise's legacy as well. Unlike Jean Louise, readers might be able to distance themselves from the legacy of Maycomb. Some (like Ako-Adjei) may have always felt distanced by Maycomb's legacy. Meanwhile, readers who recognize and admit that it is—to one degree or another—their own legacy must face their own consciences about what to do about it. What does one do about such a legacy?

This is not the only question a reading of both novels might raise. What if a reader recognizes a family member in one of the Finch men (as happened to two of my own students, who saw their father and mother, respectively, in Atticus)? It is a complicated question, which all who recognize the shared American legacy ought to come to terms with from their own social position. Indeed, Uncle Jack may be reprehensible, but he is right about one thing: "Every man's island, Jean Louise, every man's watchman, is his conscience. There is no such thing as a collective conscious" (*Watchman* 264–65).

We, as readers, collectively should allow ourselves to be haunted because of scholarship such as Naa Bakaa Ako-Adjei's. Ako-Adjei's essay "Why It's Time Schools Stopped Teaching *To Kill a Mockingbird*" posits that *Go Set a Watchman* provides the scholar with further evidence of why *To Kill a Mockingbird* should not be taught in schools. Ako-Adjei's experience of humiliation at the cheers of white classmates when they saw, in a clip from the film, the entire black section of the courtroom stand up when Atticus Finch passed exemplifies the continued tolling of Jefferson's "fire bell." Ako-Adjei urges the interrogation of the racial consciousness and even the removal of *To Kill a Mockingbird* from the high school classroom. In her article in *Transitions* in 2017, she maintains, "It is a testament to how exquisitely unwilling we are to wrestle with the depravity in our violent, racist past that America's most prominent book on racism is a mawkish novel where racist violence against black people is so thoroughly exorcised of reality that the book is remembered more for its sentimental portrayal of life in a small Southern town, its precocious narrator, and the singular virtuosity of Atticus Finch than for the conviction and violent death of an innocent black man" (200).

Jonathan S. Cullick addresses Ako-Adjei thoughtfully in the ultimate piece in our volume, but arrives at the conclusion that *Mockingbird* still *must* be taught. Indeed, the novel is culturally entrenched, even if we cease reading it. As Morrison says of *Huckleberry Finn*, we might not have a choice but to confront the racism in Harper Lee's well-known novel. It is fortunate that *Watchman* gives us further opportunity to do so.

Given *Mockingbird*'s durability in popular and pedagogical venues, our own purpose in this collection is to promote close readings and pedagogical exercises that challenge even high school readers to revisit the landscape of Maycomb not as an ideal but as a flawed and representative community. This purpose includes the introduction of *Watchman,* even in the high school classroom, as contributors including Brandie Bohney suggest. Audre Fisch and Susan Chenelle provide contextual materials and approaches. Ironically, perhaps, we take as strong a stance for *Watchman*'s inclusion in the classroom as Harper Lee herself took in 1966 against *Mockingbird*'s censorship. In a public letter that year, Harper Lee invited readers—Southern ones, at least—to claim *To Kill a Mockingbird* as "heritage." We do the same, in full knowledge that heritage is not always something to be entirely proud of.

The truth that *Watchman's* presence on the literary landscape challenges us all to remember is that *Mockingbird* has its own ghosts of racial injustice. In it, Scout Finch lies in bed at night worrying about racial phantasms, as "Every passing Negro laughing in the night was Boo Radley loose and after us" (57). By the end of *Mockingbird,* Boo Radley is still taciturn but discrete and real, unlike the unnamed and phantasmagorical "African presence" Toni Morrison cites in *Playing the Dark* as a common foible of twentieth century white writers appealing to a "white literary imagination." In *Mockingbird,* Boo is rendered distinct from "the Negroes" he would have done jail time with if the sheriff had not decided to give him house arrest instead. It should haunt us that *Mockingbird*'s Scout feels safe from this imagined ubiquitous black threat only when she fully recognizes Boo Radley's white humanity. It should also haunt us that, despite the novel's seemingly happy ending, Helen Robinson must remain fearful every day as she walks through the white part of town to work. Link Deas's patronage may assuage white readers, but it does not solve the real problem in Maycomb.

In *To Kill a Mockingbird*, white mainstream readers may be captivated and convinced by the innocent-omniscience memory-narrative McCrum praises, while *Go Set a Watchman* is a raw, postmodern tale, told, as Holly Blackford notes in this volume, by a distanced narrator. As such, its readers have the opportunity at times to get outside of the mythic ideal and catch a glimpse of more realistic responses from various characters, including African Americans. In *Watchman*, as Adam Nemmers and others note in this volume, Calpurnia is adamant in her refusal to speak "Jeff Davis's English"—and haunting in her silence. Meanwhile, Jem, the dead brother, speaks in a language from beyond the grave.

"Haunting" is an apt metaphor in *Watchman* because of its ghosts, dead and alive. In *To Kill a Mockingbird*, Jem, from our side of mortality, questions Scout's colorblind assertion that "there's only one kinds of folks. Folks" (138), pointing out that Maycomb is organized as a four-layer hierarchy, with "colored folk" at the very bottom. In the final pages of *Watchman*, Jean Louise admits (in a curiously inconsistent first-person voice) that she has been hypocritical. "Dear goodness, the things I learned. I did not want my world disturbed, but I wanted to crush the man who's trying to preserve it for me" (277).

In plain terms, she recognizes that she is indeed a "bigot," as Jack calls her, in the sense that she has clung to a childish claim of colorblindness that, under scrutiny, indicates her privileged investment in the status quo. By the end of *Watchman*, she chooses to embrace her present circumstances. Despite talk from Aunt Alexandra that she is her own person and from Atticus that she might revolutionize the community, there is no reliable indication in the novel that she will be anything other than a conventional Finch woman interested in having her "world" preserved. Still, she begins to experience her own haunting. "Someone walked over my grave," she says, "must be Jem on some idiotic errand" (278). In *Go Set a Watchman*, Jem, from the other side, haunts his sister with the reminder that she should not be too comfortable with the racial and social hierarchy she has come to recognize and accept.

Provoked by the publication of *Watchman*, Jonathan S. Cullick and I came to realize that it is critical for scholars to do what Alice Petry said in 2007

academics often avoid, whether for snobbish reasons (as Tom Santopietro claims) or for sentimental ones. Harper Lee's *To Kill a Mockingbird* needs to be studied more critically; it cannot be ignored or granted sanctuary. Added to this, the discussion of *both* Maycomb texts should be introduced to a broad public, including generations of popular readers, teachers, and students. If Michael Meyer's 2010 anthology offers some articles keenly aware of *To Kill a Mockingbird*'s flawed logic, especially in terms of race (in Angela Shaw-Thornburg and Katie Rose Guest Pryal's articles in particular), other works, including Santopietro's, still defensively idealize it as a triumph of social justice. *Watchman* needs to be studied carefully alongside *Mockingbird* to effectively change the conversation.

It took eating humble pie for Jonathan and me to realize we needed to be deeply involved in this process. After Jonathan was asked to lecture at our county's public library on the provenance of *Go Set a Watchman* back in 2015 (a lecture I attended out of interest, as I knew Jon only a little then), we decided to go to two more *Watchman* meetings offered by other branches of the local library system. The first of these was a book club, in which I convinced Jon to remain incognito as I was, thinking that revealing our identities as professors would intimidate casual readers. The last meeting was also a discussion, at which Jon gently explained to one of the participants why the conspiracy theory (that Harper Lee had not even written *Watchman*) was not possible. Two women recognized him. The elder, a thoughtful octogenarian, confronted him. "My friend says you were at the last book club. And I was at the lecture. Now we both know you are a professor. Why didn't you tell her, at the book club, what you knew?"

Shameful as the experience was for each of us (and as amusing to our respective friends and family members), Jonathan and I moved to remedy our error. *Mockingbird* is a text that belongs to all readers, love it or hate it, because of its influence. It is up to us to be as relatively frank as we can with our own positions as, post-*Watchman,* we navigate the spaces in which *Mockingbird* lives. This volume, a collaboration of pedagogues and academics, leads the charge our octogenarian adviser gave us: it tells what we and the contributors in our volume have discovered.

The articles in this anthology disrupt, revisit, contextualize, and imagine a different future for readers young and old growing up with *Mockingbird.* While each article focuses on reconsidering *Mockingbird* since the arrival of *Watchman,* and while each is informed by formal and informal dialogue since the arrival of *Watchman,* each is unique in the extent of its focus on one or both of Harper Lee's novels.

In the volume's first unit, "Mockingbird Disrupted," Jonathan S. Cullick and Holly Blackford address essential new understandings of the literary landscapes and publishing contexts in which *Go Set a Watchman* came out. Cullick's "Mockingbird's First Draft: How *Go Set a Watchman* Was Made to Come Out" traces the development of the manuscript, the events leading to the publication of *Watchman,* and the ensuing controversies. It encourages readers to remember the ambiguities and competing interests at work in Harper Lee's novels. Blackford's "*Go Set a Watchman* as Southern Pastoral" positions Lee's 2015 text securely in a rich Southern, American, and even world literature tradition, noting the richness and significance of its literary allusions and machine-in-the-garden metaphors. Blackford's article also places *Go Set a Watchman* within the tradition of American women's literature specifically, offering an extended comparative analysis of the narrative techniques and metaphors of *Go Set a Watchman* and Willa Cather's *My Ántonia.*

In Part Two, "Mockingbird Revisited," Laura Fine, Leland S, Person, Patricia S'Ascoli, and Kwakiutl L. Dreher engage literature, theory, film, and current events to interrogate the assumptions of the past in which *Mockingbird*'s popularity grew. Laura Fine's "Atticus Revised: Race, Gender, and Sexuality" reconciles the roles Atticus plays in Jean Louise's life in *Go Set a Watchman* and *To Kill a Mockingbird.* Reminding us that many readers fell in love with Scout Finch for feminist reasons (appreciating a story focusing on a young girl's happiness and free spirit), Fine follows her navigations of a less ideal adult world which, Fine argues, Jean Louise can make at least partially her own.

Next, Leland S. Person's "How to Lynch Tom Robinson and Still Feel Right" revisits, in Lee's first narrative, a familiar contemporary problem. The article stipulates that reading *To Kill a Mockingbird* and other American literature must not end in normalizing racial injustice. In "Atticus Finch: A Civilized Huck Finn," Patricia F. D'Ascoli presents an original argument revising Harper Lee's icons in comparison with Mark Twain's ambiguous ones. The scope of Twain's maturation novel *The Adventures of Huckleberry Finn* is broad enough to allow readers to identify changes within the character from beginning to end. D'Ascoli introduces the concept of "intertwined narratives" to allow for a comparison of both of Harper Lee's novels with *Huckleberry Finn.* The Atticus Finch of *Mockingbird* is generally interpreted as a stock or iconic character; however, a tandem reading of both Lee novels reveals complexities and competing impulses concerning race and social justice in Atticus familiar from Huckleberry Finn.

To complete this unit, Kwakiutl L. Dreher's "I Got Somethin' to Say!" revisits the Robert Mulligan film of *Mockingbird*. Dreher propels audiences to interrogate white fragility and the stock use of the poor white woman as sentimental victim, challenging even relatively new scholarly writings pitying Mayella. Dreher reminds us that in *Go Set a Watchman* Harper Lee did *not* indulge in this fetish; in *Watchman,* the character is merely "a white girl" who accused "a black boy" of rape, whose claim is invalidated. Dreher makes readers question sympathy for a pathologized and sexualized poor white girl. It pushes mainstream audiences to avoid this pity trap of white female fragility in order to justify retention of racism.

"Mockingbird Contextualized," the volume's third unit, brings readers into language lessons, classrooms, and libraries, and even takes its readers to church. "'With All Your Book Learnin': Ignorance and Literacy in *Go Set a Watchman*" by Adam Nemmers leads us on a tour through the Finch family library. Nemmers reminds us of the role of the literary canon in shaping a white-washed "truth." Yet it challenges us to consider that narratives from outside of this Finch library may be the most enlightening. It is Calpurnia who reminds readers (via her chastening of Scout) that all the books in the world will not educate ignorance.

Brandie Bohney's "'Command of Two Languages': Language Awareness and Acceptance with Calpurnia" pays close attention to Calpurnia's role and voice in Harper Lee's writing. Bohney's concern is for African American students and others who do not speak "Jefferson Davis' English," as Jean Louise calls it, and who may not have a level playing field in the classroom where Harper Lee's work is taught. This apprehension translates into pragmatic classroom strategies. Bohney uses theoretical commentaries by Vershawn Ashanti Young to show how such work is possible in today's classroom.

"Building Context to Read the Relationship between Scout and Calpurnia in *Mockingbird* and *Watchman*" by Audrey Fisch and Susan Chenelle helps us move outside of the *Mockingbird* text. The authors provide us with materials contemporaneous with the publication of Lee's novel to contextualize race and cultural issues. Cheli Reutter's "Queer Absences: Christian Polemics and Boo Radley" concludes this unit with a consideration of religious and political discourses contextualizing Lee's novels. The activism of gay rights spokesman Bill Kraus sheds light on Boo Radley, while LGBTQ exclusion decisions in the 1972 Annual Conference and 2019 Special Session of the United Methodist Church mirror the publications of Harper Lee's two novels.

The volume ends not with a whimper but a bang, in Part IV, "Mockingbird Reimagined." Monica Carol Miller's "Fear/Vulnerability/Anger: Teaching *To Kill a Mockingbird* in the Era of #Black Lives Matter" reminds us that the sacrificial exclusion, degradation, criminalization, and slaughter informing the Black Lives Matter movement are, as Ta-Nehisi Coates suggests, rooted in rhetoric and political practices of the past. Miller imagines using Harper Lee in the classroom critically, to draw college writing students out as they use these contexts to read and discuss racial realities suppressed or only half-expressed in Lee's novels.

"In Spite of Watchful Men: Harper Lee, Zora Neale Hurston, the Limits of Orderly Regionalism, and Feminist Hope" by Jericho Williams offers an intersectional feminist future by studying the feminisms in the seemingly outdated regionalisms of Zora Neale Hurston's Janie and Lee's Jean Louise. These heroines find themselves in the dilemma of navigating worlds unsatisfactory to live in, regardless of their own status or privilege within those worlds—heroines who find parlors or front porches where their stories might continue to be told and discussed. While Janie proves more courageous and eloquent than Jean Louise about the limits to feminist expression, both offer the possibility that their story will continue and that their feminist hopes will be realized.

Jonathan S. Cullick concludes the volume with "Teaching *Mockingbird* in the Post-*Watchman* Classroom," an invitation to renovate pedagogies that have become conventional in the teaching of *Mockingbird*. The publication of *Watchman* is a productively disruptive presence in the classroom, and objections to *Watchman* have become the very reasons for teaching it. Cullick calls upon high school teachers and professors to embrace the potential that *Watchman* brings to the classroom.

Reutter's epilogue, "Revisiting Monroeville, Alabama and Maycomb, USA," begs for reckoning with the detrimental impact that the imagined community of Maycomb, Alabama, has on racial social justice in real life. This epilogue revisits and contextualizes mainstream readings of *To Kill a Mockingbird,* and it encourages the use of *Go Set a Watchman* and nonfictional narratives to disrupt dangerous outcomes and possibilities for unchallenged conventional readings. With a nod to Susan Mizruchi's *Science of Sacrifice,* it critiques American readers' collective desire for sacrifice narrative. Citing Pete Earley's and Bryan Stevenson's books on the 1986 murder of a young white woman in Monroeville, Alabama, for which Walter McMillan was wrongfully accused and sent to death row before Stevenson proved that the (white) witnesses for the state had lied, this final piece articulates the volume's goal of a mockingbird reimagined.

The volume in your hands is a result of years of Harper Lee's choice to hide the *Go Set a Watchman* manuscript, and of her much later choice to bring it to light. The ghosts of *Go Set a Watchman* should haunt all of us growing up with *Mockingbird*. *Go Set a Watchman* is worth reading, and *To Kill a Mockingbird* worth re-reading, from a critical standpoint. Those who read the classic when it first came out; those who are reading it now for the first time; those whose have published scholarship on Harper Lee and American literature or culture; those who spend their days at teachers' podiums or exploring contextual materials; librarians responsible for acquiring and circulating literature, including Harper Lee's writings; those who love (or despise) Harper Lee's writings; and those casual readers who are going back to it for a fifth time might all gain from this endeavor. Those with experience from what Vorris L. Nunley identifies as the hush harbor may already read Maycomb as more haunted than hallowed; yet *Go Set a Watchman* is still worth the read for its additions to this imagined community. Our collection of essays belongs to all Harper Lee readers.

Trends in the years following the initial kerfuffle over *Go Set a Watchman* have indicated that the 2015 novel has mostly receded from popular interest, even while *to Kill a Mockingbird* enjoys an uptick in critical praise. In 2018, Great American Read survey participants voted *To Kill a Mockingbird* America's most beloved novel. The *National Review*'s Great Books podcast of April 30, 2019, hosted by John J. Miller, takes a nostalgic approach to *To Kill a Mockingbird*. Miller's guest, Dedra Birzer, portrays *Mockingbird* as a novel about the innocence of growing up in idyllic small-town America, never mentioning *Go Set a Watchman*. Meanwhile, despite attempted updates in the storyline in Aaron Sorkin's new Broadway version of *To Kill a Mockingbird*, for example, expanded roles of African American characters, reviews indicate that the play has not essentially changed the nature of the conversation about *To Kill a Mockingbird*. John D'Amelio records Jeff Daniels's sentiment that he had "big shoes to fill" in taking on the role of Atticus; D'Amelio also reports on young people praising the play for "life lessons" learned from it. Casey Cep's new 2019 book *Furious Hours: Murder, Fraud, and The Last Trial of Harper Lee* attempts to unravel the mystery surrounding a true-crime narrative Harper Lee is believed to have begun work on. Cep's work is intriguing. Yet neither the appearance of Cep's book—nor even, an actual true-crime manuscript by Harper Lee, if it surfaces—should make readers forget about the literary and cultural contribution of *Go Set a Watchman.* And, they should continue to strive for a more nuanced reading of *To Kill a Mockingbird* and the imagined community of Maycomb, Alabama.

These recent responses to Harper Lee, her work, and her legacy have left unanswered critical questions concerning the imagined community of Maycomb and the development of its iconic hero, its protagonist, and its supporting character Calpurnia. This volume, *Mockingbird Grows Up: Rereading Harper Lee,* attends to these questions on behalf of scholars, pedagogues, and the generations of readers past and present growing up with *Mockingbird.* Contributors address race, gender, language, and rhetoric in Harper Lee's novels, and the literary traditions, pedagogical practices, and the popular imagination into which both of Harper Lee's published novels figure. We hope that this volume serves as a catalyst for further dialogue, on issues thoroughly explored herein, and on issues less fully considered , including queer theory, disability studies, and other intersectional readings.

Works Cited

Ako-Adjei, Naa Baako. "Why It's Time Schools Stopped Teaching *To Kill a Mock-ingbird.*" *Transition* 122 (2017): 182–200. https://www.jstor.org/stable/10.2979 /transition.122.1.24. Accessed 24 Sept. 2018.

Alter, Alexandra. "Harper Lee Biographer Charles Shields on His Latest Edition." *New York Times,* 25 Apr. 2016, https://www.nytimes.com/2016/04/26/books /harper-lee-biographer-charles-shields-on-his-latest-edition.html. Accessed 30 Jan. 2019.

Anderson, Benedict. *Imagined Communities: Reflections on the Origins and Spread of Nationalism.* Revised edition. Verso, 1983.

Bakhtin, Mikhail. *The Dialogic Imagination: Four Essays.* Slavic Series. Edited by Michael Holquist. Translated by Caryl Emerson and Michael Holquist. University of Texas Press, 1981.

Birzer, Dedra. Interview by John J. Miller. National Review Great Books Podcast. Episode 81. 30 April 2019. https://www.nationalreview.com/podcasts/the-great -books/episode-81-to-kill-a-mockingbird-by-harper-lee. Accessed 29 May 2019.

Blackford, Holly. *Mockingbird Passing: Closeted Traditions and Sexual Curiosities in Harper Lee's Novel.* University of Tennessee Press, 2011.

Brown, Rita Mae. *Rubyfruit Jungle.* Bantam, 1977.

Cather, Willa. *My Ántonia.* Houghton Mifflin, 1918.

Coates, Ta-Nehisi. *Between the World and Me.* Spiegel and Grau, 2015.

Cep, Casey. *Furious Hours: Murder, Fraud, and the Last Trial of Harper Lee.* Alfred A. Knopf, 2019.

Corrigan, Maureen. "Harper Lee's *Watchman* Is a Mess that Makes Us Reconsider a Masterpiece." Book Review. Fresh Air. National Public Radio, 13 July 2015, http://www.npr.org/2015/07/13/422545987/harper-lees-watchman-is-a-mess-that-makes-us-reconsider-a-masterpiece. Accessed 15 Sept. 2017.

Crespino, Joseph. *Atticus Finch: The Biography: Harper Lee, her Father, and the Making of an American Icon.* Basic Books, Hachette Group, 2018.

D'Amelio, John. "*To Kill a Mockingbird*: A Story for Our Time." CBS Sunday Morning. 21 April 2019.https://www.cbsnews.com/news/to-kill-a-mockingbird-on-broadway-aaron-sorkin-jeff-daniels-harper-lee/. Accessed 29 May 2019.

Earley, Pete. *Circumstantial Evidence: Death, Life, and Justice in a Southern Town.* Bantam, 1995.

Freud, Sigmund. *The Uncanny.* Introduction by Hugh Haughton. Translated by David McLintock. Penguin Classics, 2003.

Hurston, Zora Neale. *Their Eyes Were Watching God.* New York: J.P. Lippincott, 1937.

Lee, Harper. *To Kill a Mockingbird.* J.P. Lippincott, 1960.

———. *Go Set a Watchman: A Novel.* HarperCollins, 2015.

McCrum, Robert. "*Go Set a Watchman* by Harper Lee Review—A Literary Curiosity." *The Guardian,* 19 July 2015, https://www.theguardian.com/books/2015/jul/19/go-set-watchman-harper-lee-review-literary-curiosity. Accessed 30 Jan. 2019.

McCullers, Carson. *Member of the Wedding.* Houghton Mifflin, 1946.

Meyer, Michael. *Harper Lee's* To Kill a Mockingbird: *New Essays.* Scarecrow Press, 2010.

Mizruchi, Susan L. *The Science of Sacrifice: American Literature and Modern Social Theory.* Princeton University Press, 1998.

Morrison, Toni. *Playing in the Dark: Whiteness and the Literary Imagination.* Harvard University Press, 1992.

———. "The Site of Memory." *Inventing the Truth: The Art and Craft of Memoir.* Second edition. Edited by William Zinsser. Houghton Mifflin, 1995, pp. 83–102.

Nunley, Vorris L. *Keepin' it Hushed: The Barbershop and African American Hush Harbor Rhetoric.* African American Life Series. Series Editor Melba Joyce Boyd. Wayne State, 2011.

PBS. The Great American Read. 29 October 2018. https://www.pbs.org/the-great-american-read/home/. Accessed: 29 May 2019.

Petry, Alice. *On Harper Lee: Essays and Reflections.* University of Tennessee Press, 2007.

Pryal, Katie Rose Guest. "Walking in Another's Skin: Failure of Empathy in *To Kill a Mockingbird*." *Harper Lee's* To Kill a Mockingbird: *New Essays.* Edited by Michael Meyer. Scarecrow Press, 2010, pp. 174–92.

Richards, Gary. "Harper Lee and the Destabilization of Heterosexuality." *Lovers & Beloveds: Sexual Otherness in Southern Fiction, 1936-1961.* Louisiana State University Press, 2005.

Salinger, J.D. *The Catcher in the Rye*. Little, Brown, and Company, 1951.

Santopietro, Tom. *Why* To Kill a Mockingbird *Matters: What Harper Lee's Book and the Iconic American Film Mean to Us Today*. St. Martin's Press, 2018. Shaw-Thornburg, Angela. "On Reading *To Kill a Mockingbird* Fifty Years Later." *Harper Lee's To Kill a Mockingbird: New Essays*. Edited by Michael Meyer. Scarecrow Press, 2010, pp. 113–27.

Shephard, Alex. "The Mass-Market Edition of *To Kill a Mockingbird* Is Dead." *New Republic*, 11 Mar. 2016, https://newrepublic.com/article/131400/mass-market -edition-kill-mockingbird-dead. Accessed 30 Jan. 2019.

Shields, Charles. *Mockingbird: A Portrait of Harper Lee, from Scout to* Go Set a Watchman. Revised & updated. Henry Holt & Co., 2016.

Stevenson, Bryan. *Just Mercy: A Story of Justice and Redemption*. Spiegel and Grau, 2014.

Stowe, Harriet Beecher. *The Annotated Uncle Tom's Cabin*. Edited with an introduction and notes by Henry Louis Gates, Jr., and Hollis Robbins. Norton, 2007.

"Tenth Annual Atticus Finch Day." *Brazos Valley Insite*, Apr. 9, 2018, https://www .insitebrazosvalley.com/lifestyle/food-fun/10th-annual-atticus-finch-day/. Accessed 30 Jan. 2019.

"The 100 Best Lesbian and Gay Novels." *The Publishing Triangle: The Association of Lesbians and Gay Men in Publishing*. http://www.publishingtriangle.org/100best .asp/. Accessed 30 Jan. 2019.

Twain, Mark. *The Adventures of Huckleberry Finn: An Authoritative Text, Contexts and Sources, Criticism*. Edited by Thomas Cooley. Norton, 1999.

PART 1

MOCKINGBIRD DISRUPTED

1

MOCKINGBIRD'S FIRST DRAFT

How Go Set a Watchman Was Made to Come Out

Jonathan S. Cullick

I had never seen our neighborhood from this angle.

—Harper Lee, To Kill a Mockingbird

In the dimly illuminated darkness at the conclusion of *To Kill a Mockingbird,* Scout looks at the street where she lives from the vantage of the Radley house: "I had never seen our neighborhood from this angle" (320). In that single statement, Jean Louise, grown up and narrating her own story, recalls how the familiar world became unfamiliar in that night of Boo Radley's coming out. Twenty years later for Scout—fifty years later for her readers—an unexpected novel, *Go Set a Watchman,* returns Jean Louise to that very same street. This recovered narrative casts readers into a different kind of darkness, where they view from an unanticipated angle the neighborhood that they thought they knew so well.

When HarperCollins Publishers announced the release of *Go Set a Watchman,* loyal readers of *To Kill a Mockingbird* were shocked to receive the news that Atticus Finch would appear transformed in an unrecognizable way. The heroic figure who protected Tom Robinson from a lynch mob and defended him in court would be presented as a racist who had past membership in the Ku Klux Klan and ongoing participation in the local White Citizens' Council. The endearing Scout of *Mockingbird* would be presented as the disillusioned Jean Louise packing her bags to flee Maycomb County. Further exacerbating these reactions to the unexpected plot and character developments were accounts of the novel's discovery, which raised concerns about the chronology of those events and questions about Harper Lee's mental capacity to consent to its publication.

The publisher did not include a preface to the novel, which could have addressed these issues. The task of providing a thorough exposition of the novel's provenance would fall to investigative journalists, who questioned how much of a role the author had in approving its publication. As a result of these literary and ethical concerns, some *Mockingbird* fans might have hesitated to read this newly published book.[1]

Their visceral reactions were understandable. Harper Lee was a beloved author whose *To Kill a Mockingbird* has had sustained success as a treasured book through the fifty-plus years since its publication. In the fall of 2018, millions of Americans voted it the nation's favorite novel on the PBS program "The Great American Read" ("the literary equivalent of 'American Idol,'" in the words of Casey Cep). Many Americans would agree with Oprah Winfrey's calling *To Kill a Mockingbird* "our national novel," and also with a 1999 *Library Journal* poll of librarians designating it the Best Novel of the Century, and with President George W. Bush awarding Harper Lee the 2007 Presidential Medal of Freedom (Puente). As of this writing, more than thirty million copies have been sold, it has been translated into forty languages, and the book's popularity in middle schools and high schools remains strong (Alter, "Second Novel"; NEA, Reader Resources).

Many factors have accounted for its popularity: the engaging voice of its narrator and the accessibility of its characters, its seemingly unambiguous, universal morals about race, justice, and empathy, and its adaptation into an Academy Award–winning film starring Gregory Peck, who created an indelible image of Atticus. An additional factor enhancing the value of this novel had always been its singularity: because it was the only production of its author, *Mockingbird* had the uniqueness of a precious gemstone. We treasured it all the more because, as the decades passed, our hopes for another Harper Lee novel diminished.

Then *Go Set a Watchman* appeared: a new book but an old book, a sequel in the life of its characters but a prequel in the career of its author. In the terms that Phyllis Frus uses to explore journalism and fiction, *Watchman* is the "timely" narrative, embedded in the political moment of the post-*Brown v. Board of Education* civil rights movement; *Mockingbird* is the "timeless" narrative, freed from historical context by its reassuring universality. Mary McDonagh Murphy, director of the film documentary, *Hey Boo: Harper Lee & To Kill a Mockingbird*, observes that "*Go Set a Watchman* is much more forcefully about civil rights. It's much more political, but that tells us what was in front of Harper Lee's brain at the time" (Alter, "While Some are Shocked"). *Watchman* makes Harper Lee's readers aware that as she began writing the novel that would become a classic, she was struggling with the civil rights movement and the push-back it was receiving from states-rights southerners and segregationists. The question facing readers is what to do with that new knowledge.

Go Set a Watchman originated three years before the 1960 publication of *To Kill a Mockingbird.* In 1957, the thirty-one-year-old Harper Lee de-livered the *Watchman* manuscript to J.B. Lippincott Publishing Company through her agents, Annie Laurie Williams and Maurice Crain. (Lippin-cott would later become HarperCollins through acquisition.) The Lip-pincott editor who would work with Lee, Theresa von Hohoff (who went by the name Tay), later wrote in the company's history that "the spark of the true writer flashed in every line," though the manuscript was "more a series of anecdotes than a fully conceived novel" (quoted in Shields 90). The childhood episodes in *Watchman* had the greatest potential. In *Mockingbird: A Portrait of Harper Lee,* Charles J. Shields speculates that "Hohoff must have recognized these gems scattered throughout *Watch-man,* the evidence being that the change in perspective from a twenty-eight-year old Jean Louise to a nine-year-old Scout is what drives the second novel [*Mockingbird*] and creates its charm" (92). Using previously unavailable sources, Joseph Crespino in *Atticus Finch: The Biography* suggests a chronology of both novels being "conceived back-to-back in the first six months of 1957" (xvi). As the publisher considered the manu-script of *Watchman,* Harper Lee was already starting a new novel based on previously written stories inspired by her childhood. "It seems that this second novel, which grew out of Lee's short stories, is the one that would eventually become *To Kill a Mockingbird.* The book focused on the childhood and earlier lives of the characters that she had written about in *Watchman"* (Crespino xv). After she had tried unsuccessfully to merge the two novels, Maurice Crain suggested that she work only on the latter novel, eventually titled *To Kill a Mockingbird* (Crespino xv). Harper Lee and Tay Hohoff worked on the *Mockingbird* manuscript together, closely and frequently, over the next three years, with Hohoff functioning as the "midwife" (Shields 101).

If Harper Lee had any intention of eventually publishing *Go Set a Watchman* after *To Kill a Mockingbird,* she gave no such indication to her publisher, agent, or anyone else. Lippincott executive editor Edward Burlinghame said the publisher wanted another Harper Lee novel ("Lippincott's sales department would have published Harper Lee's laundry list") but "that in his years at Lippincott, there was never any discussion of publishing *Go Set a Watchman*" (Mahler). According to two *New York Times* reporters who investigated the publication of *Watchman*, the archives at Columbia University support the contention that Lee and her agents regarded *Watchman* as a first draft of *Mockingbird* rather than as a separate novel. The available correspondence between Lee and Williams and Crain shows that none of them treated *Go Set a Watchman* as a possible second book even though pressure was on to publish another one. Williams and Crain additionally kept "fastidious" notes documenting the development of the novels, using index cards to keep track of their authors and manuscripts. "The notecard system Ms. Williams used to track individual works bolsters the view that, at the time, Ms. Williams viewed *Watchman* as a first draft. She did not, for example, create two cards for two books, just one that tracks the evolution of *Watchman* into *Mockingbird*. At the top of the card, the original title is crossed out to make room for the new one" (Kovaleski and Alter, "Found Earlier").

The index card for Harper Lee is headed in the upper left corner, "TO KILL A MOCKING BIRD" (*sic*, all in caps and underlined, with "mock-ingbird" as two words) immediately above "GO SET A WATCHMAN" (*sic*, crossed out). Below the titles appears "by Nelle Harper Lee," and below her name appears the word "Novel," with "Contract dated 10-17-57" listed in the upper right. The remainder of the card reads: "Publisher: J.B. Lippincott 7-11-60 / July, 1960 Reader's Digest Book Condensation / Aug., 1960 Literary Guild Selection." The use of the same card with the first title scratched out suggests to Kovaleski and Alter that the editors considered *Watchman* to be a first draft of *Mockingbird* (Shields; Kovaleski & Alter).[2] In Crespino's chronology, *Watchman* was considered not a draft but a separate, first novel that was put aside in favor of the manuscript of the second novel, which would become *Mockingbird*.

Mockingbird hit the bookstore shelves, bestseller lists, book clubs, and classrooms while gaining the notice of the Pulitzer Prize committee and Universal Pictures. As the final product of *Mockingbird* entered public consciousness, at some point, the *Watchman* manuscript was placed into a cardboard Lord & Taylor department store container in a safe deposit box in a Monroeville, Alabama, bank. It remained in storage for fifty years, undisturbed and unnoticed. That changed in February of 2015, when HarperCollins issued a press release:

> Harper, an imprint of HarperCollins Publishers, is thrilled to announce it has acquired North American rights to a newly

discovered novel by Harper Lee, beloved author of *To Kill a Mockingbird*. The novel, which Lee titled *Go Set a Watchman*, will be published on July 14th, 2015.

The deal was negotiated by Michael Morrison, President and Publisher of HarperCollins US General Books Group and Canada, via Harper Lee's lawyer, Tonja Carter.

The press release then included this quotation, attributed to the author:

> In the mid-1950s, I completed a novel called *Go Set a Watchman*. It features the character known as Scout as an adult woman and I thought it a pretty decent effort. My editor, who was taken by the flashbacks to Scout's childhood, persuaded me to write a novel from the point of view of the young Scout. I was a first-time writer, so I did as I was told. I hadn't realized it had survived, so was surprised and delighted when my dear friend and lawyer Tonja Carter discovered it. After much thought and hesitation I shared it with a handful of people I trust and was pleased to hear that they considered it worthy of publication. I am humbled and amazed that this will now be published after all these years.

The press released continued with a brief description of the provenance of the novel:

> After *To Kill a Mockingbird* was published by J. B. Lippincott in 1960, Harper Lee set aside *Go Set a Watchman* and never returned to it. The original manuscript of the novel was considered to have been lost until fall 2014, when Tonja Carter discovered it in a secure location where it had been affixed to an original typescript of *To Kill a Mockingbird*.

The day following the HarperCollins press release, the *Wall Street Journal* (which is owned by News Corp, the same company that owns HarperCollins), introduced Harper Lee's lawyer, Tonja Brooks Carter, in an article titled "Meet the Lawyer Who Found Harper Lee's New Novel." It identifies Carter as an "Alabama lawyer described by HarperCollins as a gatekeeper between the author and the outside world." Carter was an attorney at Barnett, Bugg, Lee & Carter, LLC, the law firm of Alice Lee, Harper Lee's sister and attorney. In declining health, Alice (who died in November 2014), had turned over Harper Lee's legal affairs to Tonja Carter, who would ultimately have power of attorney and become the executor of the estate upon Harper Lee's death in 2016. Hugh Van Dusen, Harper Lee's editor at HarperCollins, calls Ms. Carter "the go-between for HarperCollins and the 88-year-old Ms. Lee, who resides in a Monroeville, Ala. assisted-living facility and, according to court documents filed by Ms. Lee's lawyers, has trouble hearing and seeing." Dusen describes the circumstances of Carter finding the manuscript in a bank safe deposit box: "I don't know this for a fact, but one must imagine that Harper Lee—we call her Nelle—just never told anybody about the book and then forgot it existed. Her lawyer, Tonja Carter, who is also Nelle's very close friend, was apparently looking through this safety deposit box and found [*Go Set a Watchman*]. I guess she then went to her friend and said what is this?" The article notes, "Ms. Carter didn't respond to a request for comment," a statement that would be reiterated in future articles by reporters attempting to inquire into the publication of *Go Set a Watchman* (Gershman).

A wave of questions arose in the literary world and the media. Where did this book come from? Was Harper Lee, in declining health since her stroke in 2007, competent to consent to the publication of *Go Set a Watchman?* Was there any possibility that someone might be taking advantage of her? Harper Lee's friends and hometown acquaintances disagreed, offering conflicting impressions of her lucidity and competence. In 2011, for example, Harper Lee's sister Alice had written in a letter to writer Marja Mills, "Poor Nelle Harper can't see and can't hear and will sign anything put before her by anyone in whom she has confidence" (Kahka). On the other hand, Alabama historian and Auburn University Professor Emeritus of History Wayne Flynt, a long-time friend of Harper Lee and one of the few people who saw her regularly, "insists that she is 'sharp as a tack' and makes her own decisions. 'No one tells Nelle what to do'" (Nickell).[3] Flynt visited Harper Lee one day before the release of *Watchman*, delivered a stack of press coverage to her, and "is adamant that she welcomed it" (Severson).

Responding to an anonymous complaint to Alabama state authorities alleging possible elder abuse, investigators from the state's Human Resources Department and Alabama Securities Commission (which investigates financial fraud of the elderly) met with Harper Lee at her assisted living facility, The Meadows. They interviewed Meadows staff and Lee's friends, the *New York Times* reported. Lee's literary agent, Andrew Nurnberg, issued a statement calling the complaint about elder abuse "shameful" and "sad," saying in part, "Having spent quality time with her over the last couple of years, I can categorically state that she is in full possession of her mental faculties." Ultimately, the Securities Commission closed its investigation, determining that Lee was competent and not being exploited, with this statement: "We made a determination that Ms. Lee, based on our interview with her, was aware that her book was going to be published. She wanted it published. She made it quite clear she did." The rest of the investigation concluded in the same manner ("Harper Lee Agent Says Author Is Delighted"; also see Kovaleski, Alter, and Howard).

Such concerns about Harper Lee's physical condition and mental competency to conduct her own affairs were not new. The *Watchman* controversy was the latest and most widely visible episode in a series of conflicts and litigation surrounding Harper Lee in recent years: a copyright dispute with Lee's former agent, Samuel Pinkus; a trademark dispute with Monroe County Heritage Museum regarding its sale of *Mockingbird*-themed merchandise in its gift shop; conflicting accounts of whether Lee approved of the Penguin Press publication of the book *The Mockingbird Next Door* by Marja Mills. Observations of "the decline of Harper Lee" had been made months before the HarperCollins press release, with a description of the author's "life and legacy in disarray, a sad state of litigious chaos" and the author's affairs being conducted by an attorney who was "making as many enemies as headlines" (Kahka).[4]

Amid all these concerns for the ailing author, in mid-July 2015, attorney Tonja Carter wrote an explanation titled "How I Found the Manuscript," a kind of bookend to the earlier *Wall Street Journal* piece introducing her to the public. In her account, in June of 2011, Sam Pinkus, Lee's literary agent at the time, contacted Lee's sister/lawyer, Alice, requesting to inventory and appraise Harper Lee's literary assets (which included a typescript of *To Kill a Mockingbird*). In October 2011, three individuals met at the bank in Monroeville, Alabama, to open Harper Lee's safe deposit box: Sam Pinkus, Tonja Carter, and Justin Caldwell, an appraiser from Sotheby's. They found the Lord & Taylor box stored within the safe deposit box, containing what Carter describes as "several hundred pages of typed original manuscript." She continues, "After we all read a couple of pages, someone mentioned that the first page was not the first page of *Mockingbird*, but rather seemed to be a later chapter." Carter says she noticed the name "Hank" in the manuscript but just assumed that it was one of the parts of the book that "came and went with an early draft." Carter decided to get a copy of *Mockingbird* to enable Caldwell to compare the openings: "I then left the meeting and didn't return." The next day, in Carter's account, Caldwell sent her an e-mail: "He made no mention of the existence of a second, unknown book." Nor was any mention made in future correspondence. Similarly, "If they said anything to Alice, well, Alice never said anything to me or to Nelle."

In the summer of 2014, at a gathering of Lee's family and friends, talk turned to a "second novel" that was thought to exist. "This was the first time I had actually heard that Nelle had written another novel," Carter said. She remembered the manuscript she had seen in the safe deposit box along with that name "Hank," so she returned to the bank and examined the contents "when I came across a title page that said, '*Go Set a Watchman*, Harper Lee, York Avenue, New York, New York.'" She went to Harper Lee and asked her about this manuscript. Lee told her what it was and replied, "I guess it's finished, it's the parent of *Mockingbird*." Lee approved Carter's request to read and share it with literary agent Andrew Nurnberg. From there, the novel went through the publication process (Carter).

Carter was responding directly to an early July *New York Times* article reporting discrepancies in the accounts of how the manuscript had been found. Those reporters questioned whether Carter had discovered the manuscript in summer 2014. "Both Mr. Pinkus and Sotheby's, however, say Ms. Carter was there during Mr. Caldwell's 2011 review." Sotheby's declined to discuss the meeting in detail, citing client confidentiality, but the literary agent, Pinkus, said, "Ms. Carter was present in the safe-deposit room and, along with Mr. Caldwell and I, read manuscript pages" (Kovaleski and Alter, "Found Earlier than Thought").[5]

Justin Caldwell of Sotheby's has only reported that he was examining the *Mockingbird* typescript when he noticed another typescript similar to *Mockingbird* but with older characters and set later. He compared passages to a published copy of *Mockingbird* and told everyone in the room that it appeared to be an early version of *Mockingbird*. The *Times* reporters continue, "Ms. Carter acknowledged in a statement last week that she had accompanied Mr. Pinkus and Mr. Caldwell to the bank at the request of Alice Lee, the author's sister. But she said that she was sent from the room to run an errand before any review of the materials occurred. She denied ever learning that a different manuscript had been found that day and would not elaborate on whether she had later asked what had happened." The article states that Ms. Carter declined to answer questions from the reporters (Kovaleski and Alter, "Found Earlier than Thought").[6]

Why does it matter when the manuscript was discovered? That question was answered by Joe Nocera, who charged that the discovery of *Go Set a Watchman* was a "fraud." The account reported in the *New York Times* suggested to Nocera that Carter had not discovered the manuscript in 2014, but rather "an alternate scenario: that Carter had been sitting on the discovery of the manuscript since 2011, waiting for the moment when she, not Alice, would be in charge of Harper Lee's affairs." Lee was ill and frail; Alice, her "longtime protector," had passed away, leaving her "new protector," Tonja Carter, "claiming conveniently to have found it shortly before Alice died." With these words, Nocera launched the most direct accusation against Carter, charging that this "constitutes one of the epic money grabs in the modern history of American publishing." Carter's claim that she left the meeting early and discovered the manuscript only in 2014 was, to Nocera, a "preposterous claim," whereas "the others in the meeting insisted to *The Times* that she was there the whole time—and saw what they saw." Thus, *Watchman* cannot be considered a "newly discovered" novel but a draft released by a publisher only trying to sell books. It is a "historical artifact or, more bluntly, a not-very-good first draft . . . a phony literary event" (Nocera).

Phillip Hensher of *The Spectator* struck a similarly incredulous tone: "Lee's lawyer, Tonja Carter, had unfortunately just left the room to run some errands when this announcement was made. No one subsequently thought to tell her of this discovery." Then, three years later, "When she announced it, nobody observed that it had already been discovered. Lee herself had apparently not been told in 2011, and expressed herself delighted with the discovery, and happy to go ahead with publication. This delight was voiced in a statement issued by Carter and attributed to Lee, in which she described Carter as her 'dear friend and lawyer'" (Hensher).

New Yorker staff writer Adam Gopnik offered a summation of the events that began to connect provenance to literary quality. Gopnik allows that perhaps the novel was discovered and published as Carter and Harper-Collins assert; however, if this is so,

> The procurers seem oddly reluctant to be terribly exact about their accomplishment. The finished book that has now emerged . . . has not a single prefatory sentence to explain its pedigree or its history or the strange circumstance that seems to have brought it to print after all this time, as though complete novels with beloved characters suddenly appeared from aging and reclusive and apparently ailing writers every

> week of the year. (This in a book that includes a 14-line note
> on the type.) And then the story that has been offered about
> it in the papers—a story that seems to change significantly
> as time goes by—presents certain difficulties to the reader's
> understanding of the book. (Gopnik)

Echoing Gopnik's call for a preface, Phillip Hensher expressed doubts about the provenance that arose from a sense that the novel was still a draft in need of much revision: "After having read the novel, it is absolutely clear to me that no novelist in full possession of his or her faculties would agree to its publication as a sequel." Perhaps the novel would be useful, he suggests, but only as a curiosity or scholarly edition with a preface to explain its role. As presently published, it is "an interesting document, and a pretty bad novel" (Hensher).

In this manner of linking the book's technical flaws to its unsettled provenance, some reviewers questioned its ability to stand alone as a literary work—even to the extent of doubting that the public should have access to the book. Tyler Daswick of the *Chicago Reader* calls it a "book no one should ever have been allowed to see . . . an early draft" with a narrative that is a "broken, inconsistent, only halfway-to-good effort" that "feels wrong" to read. Adam Gopnik argues that the book lacks relevance without *To Kill a Mockingbird. Watchman's* "emotional force" depends on the reader sharing Scout's shock at finding her father and community transformed, but this shock depends on the reader already knowing them the way Scout does in *Mockingbird*. The problem with the reader getting this emotional effect is that "if you don't know Atticus as a hero—and in this book [*Watchman*], you really don't, except by assertion—why would you care?" "Indeed," Gopnik concludes, "the book as a book barely makes sense if you don't know *Mockingbird*." Randy Dotinga of the *Christian Science Monitor* describes *Go Set a Watchman* as a "talky and preachy" book that "lacks the cinematic power of its legendary predecessor" and is marked by "failures of imagination." National Public Radio book critic Maureen Corrigan of Georgetown University gave an academic imprimatur to these critiques on the nationally syndicated program Fresh Air, calling the book "a mess" and "a troubling confusion of a novel, politically and artistically" punctuated by a plot that has "lots of dead patches." Most recently, Tom Santopietro has posed what may be the most compelling but unanswerable question: "If Nelle had spent the fifty-plus years since *Mockingbird's* publication without ever writing another book, why was she now allowing a first-draft novel to be published to what would prove to be certain worldwide attention?" (203).[7]

Calls for a preface to contextualize the book were reasonable. The publisher could have been proactive in anticipating this need for the issues of the provenance to be addressed in a thorough, forthright preface to provide context for every reader who picks up a copy of *Go Set a Watchman*. Nonetheless, for scholars and teachers and others who read such material "on background" (in newspaper and journal articles in this essay), *Go Set a Watchman* has entered the literary world and is worthy of consideration regardless of how it was conceived. It offers something of interest in its own right, its value not dependent upon the circumstances of its birth. We cannot—we would not want to—ignore the potential of this novel to alter our readings of *To Kill a Mockingbird*.[8]

The exact nature of those alterations is the subject of the essays in this volume and the challenge that scholars, teachers, students, and readers of all kinds will encounter in reading the book. The "coming out" of *Go Set a Watchman* represents a renewed "coming out" for *To Kill a Mockingbird*, as *Watchman's* timeliness, its embeddedness in the sociopolitical struggles of the 1950s, imposes a haunting presence on the heretofore timelessness and seemingly universally uplifting subject matter of *Mockingbird*.

Randall Kennedy, Harvard University Professor of American Law, who has written about the relationship of race and the criminal justice system, says in his review that *Go Set a Watchman* validates earlier claims by legal scholar Monroe Freedman that Atticus in *Mockingbird* "ought not be lauded as a role model," an "impression of Atticus Finch [that] has now been largely ratified by none other than his creator." Although he criticizes the uneven development of the character Jean Louise, Kennedy praises *Watchman* for its "demands that its readers abandon the immature sentimentality ingrained by idle school lessons about the nobility of the white savior and the mesmerizing performance of Gregory Peck in the film adaptation of *To Kill a Mockingbird*."

Mark Lawson of the British *Guardian* calls *Go Set a Watchman* "in most respects, a new work, and a pleasure, revelation and genuine literary event," noting that although it is "a much less likable and school-teachable book, . . . teachers of American literature have been handed a fascinating potential course comparing and contrasting the pair." (He also suggested tongue-in-cheek that *Watchman* might make some readers "feel moved to ask if they can now file an emergency rewrite of their school or university essays.") Daniel D'Addario of *Time Magazine* was also positive: "*Watchman* is both a painful complication of Harper Lee's beloved book and a confirmation that a novel read widely by schoolchildren is far more bitter than sweet."

Many readers and reviewers found new possibility in the revelations about Atticus. They struggled with what Charles Shields calls the "moral fall" of Atticus (2). Michiko Kakutani suggests that we could now turn our attention away from Atticus and re-focus our reading on the character of Jean Louise, as the novel "reminds us that *Mockingbird*, the novel, was more concerned with the day-to-day texture of Scout and Jem's lives and the world of Maycomb than *Mockingbird* the movie, which focused more closely on Atticus and Tom Robinson's trial." As noted earlier, filmmaker Mary McDonagh Murphy finds that *Watchman* offers a new entry into *Mockingbird* because it tells us that the author, as she wrote her classic set in the 1930s, was thinking about the struggle for civil rights as the United States was entering the 1960s.

Many reviewers have noted the book's importance for the way it situates *To Kill a Mockingbird* in the struggles of the nation at a specific period in its history—the *timeliness* referred to above. Atticus is no longer a hero for all time; he becomes a product of a particularly situated time. Dale Russakoff identifies the novel's potential to help readers understand the nuances of a segregated society. Russakoff spoke with Mary Badham, who played Scout in the movie: "We mourned the loss of an icon, but we were not shocked. In 1960's Birmingham, as in Scout's Maycomb, the two Atticuses could coexist, and did." Russakoff concludes, "The whole truth about white people in the segregated South, even the best people, is invariably disappointing."

U.S. Poet Laureate and Emory University creative writing professor Natasha Trethewey, writing for the *Washington Post*, calls *Watchman* "compelling in its timeliness." That timeliness is the book's connection to the post-*Brown* context in which it was written. "In prose less nuanced than that of *Mockingbird*, prose steeped in the political rhetoric after the *Brown* decision, the characters in *Watchman* carry out an ideological debate that began in the South but would come to occupy the national consciousness in the 1960s and 1970s and in many ways continues today." Trethewey finds in *Watchman* a potential for readers to consider the history of the *Brown* decision with "the hindsight to see the larger impact that Lee's characters could not quite see."

The preceding survey of reviews presents only a small selection of representative responses to *Go Set a Watchman*. That so many have reviewed this book, including columnists who are not even nominally book reviewers, attests to the necessity to engage with this novel. Whatever one's reaction to *Watchman*—even if one declines to read it due to unease with its opaque provenance or its tarnished Atticus—it demands our attention. What kind of attention it will receive is now the responsibility of its readers.

In considering *Go Set a Watchman* as a cultural as well as literary artifact, Arifa Akbar of *The Independent* in the UK strikes a nuanced balance. "It is not a finely written story—this reads as a 'good' first draft which Lee has refused to rework," Akbar says, "yet even in its coarse state . . . it is the more radical, ambitious and politicised of the two novels Lee has now published." *Watchman* offers "contemporary relevance where *Mockingbird* is safely sealed off as a piece of American history." *Go Set a Watchman* is the timely text.

In its published form, *Go Set a Watchman* is a manuscript in need of an editor, and it is fortunate that Tay Hohoff stepped into that role for *Mockingbird*. The *Watchman* narrative relies too much on expository speeches presented in the form of dialogue. Some lengthy scenes, such as the children's reenactment of a Methodist service, slow the pace. Occasional plot elements, such as Uncle Jack's third-act revelation, lead nowhere. Characters such as Atticus and Hank come across as flat. Throughout the novel, awkward sentences beg for copyediting, despite the insistence of HarperCollins president Jonathan Burnham that "It is completely finished. It needs virtually no editing. The only editing I think it needs is perhaps a light copy edit" (quoted in Santopietro 201).

Yet this novel contains gems to be mined at depths far deeper than those identified by Tay Hohoff fifty years ago. The vivid scene of Aunt Alexandra's coffee with the local ladies in chapter 13 presents Jean Louise with a virtual laboratory of all that is wrong with race, class, and gender in polite Maycomb County society. The character of Calpurnia is more fully realized in this novel. Jean Louise's reunion with Calpurnia in chapter 12 results in the most powerfully moving scene in the novel. The grown-up Jean Louise is another gem. *Go Set a Watchman* reminds us that *To Kill a Mockingbird* is primarily Scout's story, a fact that is easy to overlook because of the drama of the trial and the cinematic presence of Gregory Peck. *Watchman* invites us to re-focus. We like this grown-up Jean Louise. Going her own way—thinking, speaking, dressing, and behaving against convention—this is the woman her father raised her to become, and we are glad to meet her.

So, it is not just that we must pay attention to this novel, despite its flaws—we *want* to pay attention to it. "Whatever its failings," Arifa Akbar argues, "it has so much integrity that it cannot be dismissed." The narrative of *Go Set a Watchman* is about Jean Louise's return home to Maycomb and reconciliation with her father. But its publication invites us readers to return and reconcile our conflicts with *To Kill a Mockingbird.*

Joseph Crespino in *Atticus Finch: The Biography,* an engaging study of the influence of Harper Lee's father (Amasa Coleman Lee) on the making of Atticus Finch, suggests that both novels emerged as Lee's responses to her own father, resulting in two versions of the same character. The first version, the Atticus of *Watchman,* embodies Lee's ambivalence toward conservative and moderate white Southerners. In creating the second version, the Atticus of *Mockingbird,* Harper Lee defends the moderation of those same Southerners, such as her father, whose values were being attacked by militant segregationists in the South and progressive organizations and newspapers in the North. White southerners such as A. C. Lee, Crespino notes, were the very ones Martin Luther King would criticize in his famous 1963 "Letter from Birmingham Jail." In his review of Crespino's book, Howell Raines locates a psychic division between "Nelle" and "Harper": "[Crespino] links Lee's split vision to the lifelong game of hide-and-seek between Nelle Lee, the down-home fisherman, and Harper Lee, the literary expat who was happiest in Manhattan." Raines's conclusion is golden: "Crespino demonstrates that *To Kill a Mockingbird,* while it is the superior storytelling book, wobbles morally in comparison to *Watchman* . . . Atticus shows them [Scout and Jem] 'how one could be *in* Maycomb without being *of* it.' Atticus may have convinced the children, but if Harper Lee really believed that, why did she keep the railroad tracks hot between Alabama and New York?"

Harper Lee herself was silent on that question. Reticence about the provenance of *Go Set a Watchman*—and perhaps that reticence includes Harper Lee herself in declining interviews—may not have done Harper Lee's legacy any favors. For an author who was herself a national treasure, that is unfortunate. But students, teachers, and readers of all kind are now invited to fill those silences with new perspectives on Scout, Atticus, the town of Maycomb, and the social context of "our national novel."

Go Set a Watchman was officially published on 14 July 2015, selling 1.1 million copies in its first week of release (with many sold on pre-order), sales that launched it immediately to the top of the *New York Times* bestseller list (Nocera). One year after its publication, *Go Set a Watchman* returned to the bestseller lists, with *USA Today* citing the reason for the increased sales: alongside *To Kill a Mockingbird,* the novel *Go Set a Watchman* is now "showing up on high school summer reading lists" ("Paperback Trade Fiction," *NYT Book Review,* and McClurg, *USA Today*). Teachers and librarians are beginning to introduce two Harper Lee novels to young readers who will explore perspectives more ambiguous or more complicated than those encountered by previous generations of readers. These future readers will continue to be inspired by Atticus, but they will also visit Maycomb less with innocence and more with a critically informed optimism. They will consider the neighborhood from new angles, and we may hope, they will watch over Jem and Scout through the night until a new light breaks.

Notes

1. The publisher did include a new "Note from the Publisher" in the 2016 Harper Perennial paperback edition. See note 8, below.

2. A facsimile of the original card may be found in various sources but most conveniently in the photographs section of *Mockingbird: A Portrait of Harper Lee* by Charles Shields.

3. Harper Lee was known by the name "Nelle" to friends and family.

4. The *New York Magazine* article by Boris Kahka, "The Decline of Harper Lee," provides an overview of the copyright and trademark disputes and the other litigation that involved Harper Lee in her final years. For additional information about these legal and publishing matters, I recommend reading pages 246–65 of the epilogue in Charles Shields, *Mockingbird: A Portrait of Harper Lee.*

5. Ms. Carter later fired Pinkus, and Lee filed suit against him, accusing him of trying to trick her into transferring the copyright of *Mockingbird* to a company he set up; the matter was settled out of court.

6. Three versions of these events emerge, as summarized by Charles Shields in *Mockingbird: A Portrait of Harper Lee*: "Carter left because she had to run some errands, and so she missed out on an astounding discovery that Caldwell and Pinkus didn't tell her about. That's one version of events . . . Another is that Carter and Pinkus presented Caldwell with a gift box from Lord & Taylor, inside of which was an item he needed to see for himself on the premises. This suggests the pair had previously found something valuable of a literary nature and decided it was important enough to call in an expert" (260). The third version Shields summarizes is that all three, Carter included, examined all the items in the safe deposit box and noticed that the *Go Set a Watchman* manuscript did not match the *To Kill a Mockingbird* manuscript; the three returned the manuscript to the box and said nothing publicly for the time being.

7. Santopietro's suggestion that "it may just be that Lee looked upon the publication of *Watchman* as one last chance to have her say, a final nod to glory" is speculative. More convincing is his acknowledgement that her "intentions will likely never be fully known." We can hope that subsequent sources will emerge in the future.

8. As indicated in note 1, above, the publisher appended a "Note from the Publisher" to the end of the 2016 Harper Perennial paperback edition. About 1½ pages in length, it describes *Watchman* as Lee's "first novel" and briefly explains how Lee's agent proposed the manuscript to publishers and how other material Lee was working on at the time was completed in 1959 to become *To Kill a Mockingbird*. It explains that the *Watchman* typescript "was put away" and "did not reemerge into public view until 2014, after Harper Lee's attorney discovered the typescript in a bank vault in Monroeville." Then, "after consulting with friends," Lee consented to her agent submitting it to HarperCollins.

Works Cited

Akbar, Arifa. "*Go Set a Watchman:* A Rough Draft, But More Radical and Politicised than Harper Lee's *To Kill a Mockingbird.*" *The Independent,* 12 July 2015, http://www.independent.co.uk/arts-entertainment/books/reviews/go-set-a-watchman-by-harper-lee-book-review-a-rough-draft-yes-but-more-radical-and-politicised-than-10384143.html. Accessed 15 Sept. 2017.

Alter, Alexandra. "Harper Lee, Author of *To Kill a Mockingbird,* Is to Publish a Second Novel." *New York Times,* 3 Feb. 2015, https://www.nytimes.com/2015/02/04/books/harper-lee-author-of-to-kill-a-mockingbird-is-to-publish-a-new-novel.html. Accessed 15 Sept. 2017.

———. "While Some Are Shocked by *Go Set a Watchman,* Others Find Nuance in a Bigoted Atticus Finch." *New York Times,* 11 July 2015, https://www.nytimes.com/2015/07/12/books/racism-of-atticus-finch-in-go-set-a-watchman-could-alter-harper-lees-legacy.html. Accessed 15 Sept. 2017.

Carter, Tonja B. "How I Found the Harper Lee Manuscript." *Wall Street Journal,* 12 July 2015, https://www.wsj.com/articles/how-i-found-the-harper-lee-manuscript-1436740810. Accessed 15 Sept. 2017.

Cep, Casey. "The Contested Legacy of Atticus Finch." *New Yorker,* 17 Dec. 2018, https://www.newyorker.com/magazine/2018/12/17/the-contested-legacy-of-atticus-finch?fbclid=IwARozGrKJ3tLQgTovQ-REZaLGZBzC4_biDvP1EI_Q1NHIn-wh2u61oGcqtX8. Accessed 29 May 2019.

Corrigan, Maureen. "Harper Lee's *Watchman* Is a Mess that Makes Us Reconsider a Masterpiece." Book Review. Fresh Air. National Public Radio, 13 July 2015, http://www.npr.org/2015/07/13/422545987/harper-lees-watchman-is-a-mess-that-makes-us-reconsider-a-masterpiece. Accessed 15 Sept. 2017.

Crespino, Joseph. *Atticus Finch: The Biography.* Basic Books, 2018.

D'Addario, Daniel. "*Go Set a Watchman* Review: Atticus Finch's Racism Makes Scout, and Us, Grow Up." Book Review. *Time Magazine,* 11 July 2015, http://time.com/3954581/go-set-a-watchman-review/. Accessed 15 Sept. 2017.

Daswick, Tyler. "*Go Set a Watchman* Reads Like a Book No One Should Have Ever Been Allowed to See." Book Review. *Chicago Reader,* 3 Aug. 2015, https://www.chicagoreader.com/chicago/go-set-a-watchman-harper-lee-to-kill-a-mockingbird-scout-finch-atticus-finch-racism-tay-hohoff/Content?oid=18504902. Accessed 15 Sept. 2017.

Dotinga, Randy. "*Go Set a Watchman* is an Odd Follow-Up to its Classic Sister."

Book Review. *Christian Science Monitor,* 30 July 2015, https://www.csmonitor
.com/Books/Book-Reviews/2015/0730/Go-Set-a-Watchman-is-an-odd-follow-up
-to-its-classic-sister. Accessed 15 Sept. 2017.

Frus, Phyllis. *The Politics and Poetics of Journalistic Narrative: The Timely and the
Timeless.* Cambridge University Press, 1994.

Gershman, Jacob. "Meet the Lawyer Who Found Harper Lee's New Novel." *Wall
Street Journal,* 4 February 2015, https://blogs.wsj.com/law/2015/02/04/meet-the
-lawyer-who-found-harper-lees-new-novel/. Accessed 15 Sept. 2017.

Gopnik, Adam. "Sweet Home Alabama: Harper Lee's *Go Set a Watchman.*" *The New
Yorker,* 27 July 2015, https://www.newyorker.com/magazine/2015/07/27/sweet
-home-alabama. Accessed 15 Sept. 2017.

"Harper Lee Agent Says Author Is 'Delighted' New Book Will Be Published." *New
York Times,* 13 Mar. 2015, https://www.nytimes.com/2015/03/14/business/harper
-lee-agent-says-author-is-delighted-new-book-will-be-published.html. Accessed
15 Sept. 2017.

HarperCollins Publishers. "Recently Discovered Novel From Harper Lee, Author of
To Kill a Mockingbird." Press Release, 3 Feb. 2015, http://corporate.harpercollins.
com/us/press-releases. Accessed 15 Sept. 2017.

Hensher, Philip. "*Go Set a Watchman* Should Never Have Been Hyped as a 'Land-
mark New Novel.'" *The Spectator,* 18 July 2015, https://www.spectator.co.uk
/2015/07/go-set-a-watchman-should-never-have-been-hyped-as-a-landmark-new
-novel-says-philip-hensher/. Accessed 15 Sept. 2017.

Kahka, Boris. "The Decline of Harper Lee." *New York Magazine,* 19 Feb. 2015
(reprinted from July 2014). http://www.vulture.com/2014/07/decline-of-harper
-lee.html. Accessed 15 Sept. 2017.

Kakutani, Michiko. "Review: Harper Lee's *Go Set a Watchman* Gives Atticus Finch
a Dark Side." *New York Times,* 10 July 2015, https://www.nytimes.com/2015/07/11
/books/review-harper-lees-go-set-a-watchman-gives-atticus-finch-a-dark-side
.html. Accessed 15 Sept. 2017.

Kennedy, Randall. "Harper Lee's *Go Set a Watchman.*" *New York Times,* 14 July
2015, https://www.nytimes.com/2015/07/14/books/review/harper-lees-go-set-a
-watchman.html. Accessed 15 Sept. 2017.

Kovaleski, Serge F. and Alexandra Alter. "Harper Lee's *Go Set a Watchman* May
Have Been Found Earlier than Thought." *New York Times,* 2 July 2015, https://
www.nytimes.com/2015/07/03/books/harper-lee-go-set-a-watchman-may-have
-been-found-earlier-than-thought.html. Accessed 15 Sept. 2017.

Kovaleski, Serge, Alexandra Alter, and Jennifer Crossley Howard. "Harper Lee's
Condition Debated by Friends, Fans and Now State of Alabama." *New York
Times,* 11 Mar. 2015, https://www.nytimes.com/2015/03/12/arts/artsspecial
/harper-lees-ability-to-consent-to-new-book-continues-to-be-questioned.html.
Accessed 15 Sept. 2017.

Lawson, Mark. "*Go Set a Watchman* Review: More Complex than Harper Lee's
Original Classic, but Less Compelling." Book Review. *The Guardian,* 13 July 2015,
https://www.theguardian.com/books/2015/jul/12/go-set-a-watchman-review
-harper-lee-to-kill-a-mockingbird. Accessed 15 Sept. 2017.

Lee, Harper. *Go Set a Watchman.* HarperCollins, 2015.

———. *To Kill a Mockingbird*. HarperCollins, 1960.

Mahler, Jonathan. "The Invisible Hand Behind Harper Lee's *To Kill a Mockingbird*." *New York Times,* 12 July 2015, https://www.nytimes.com/2015/07/13/books/the -invisible-hand-behind-harper-lees-to-kill-a-mockingbird.html. Accessed 15 Sept. 2017.

McClurg, Jocelyn. "*Watchman* Climbs." *USA Today,* 30 June 2016: 3D.

National Endowment for the Arts, Big Read. Reader Resources. https://www.arts .gov/partnerships/nea-big-read/to-kill-a-mockingbird. Accessed 31 Dec. 2017.

Nickell, Patti. "Visiting Harper Lee's Alabama Hometown." *Lexington Herald -Leader,* 9 Aug. 2015, http://www.kentucky.com/living/travel/article44614602 .html. Accessed 15 Sept. 2017.

Nocera, Joe. "The Harper Lee *Go Set a Watchman* Fraud." *New York Times,* 24 July 2015, https://www.nytimes.com/2015/07/25/opinion/joe-nocera-the-watchman -fraud.html. Accessed 15 Sept. 2017.

"Paperback Trade Fiction." *The New York Times Book Review.* Weekly Sales Period of June 12–18, Monthly Sales Period of May 1–28, 3 July 2016: 24.

Puente, Maria. "Mockingbird Still Sings at 50." *USA Today,* 8 July 2010: D1.

Raines, Howell. "Harper Lee and Her Father, the Real Atticus Finch." Review of *Atticus Finch: The Biography* by Joseph Crespino. *New York Times Book Review,* 18 June 2018, https://www.nytimes.com/2018/06/18/books/review/atticus-finch -joseph-crespino-ac-lee-biography.html. Accessed 6 Sept. 2018.

Russakoff, Dale. "The Atticus We Always Knew." *The New Yorker,* 17 July 2015, https://www.newyorker.com/books/page-turner/the-atticus-we-always-knew. Accessed 15 Sept. 2017.

Santopietro, Tom. *Why* To Kill a Mockingbird *Matters*. St. Martin's Press, 2018.

Severson, Kim. "Harper Lee's *Go Set a Watchman* Brings Division and Curiosity to Monroeville Alabama." *New York Times* , 14 July 2015, https://www.nytimes .com/2015/07/15/books/harper-lees-go-set-a-watchman-brings-division-and -curiosity-to-monroeville-ala.html. Accessed 15 Sept. 2017.

Shields, Charles. *Mockingbird: A Portrait of Harper Lee, from Scout to* Go Set a Watchman. Revised & updated. Henry Holt & Co., 2016.

Trethewey, Natasha. "In Harper Lee's *Go Set a Watchman*, a Less Noble Atticus Finch." Book Review. *Washington Post,* 12 July 2012, https://www .washingtonpost.com /entertainment/books/book-world-in-harper-lees-go -set-a-watchman-a-less-noble-atticus-finch/2015/07/11/f72b078a-2756-11e5-b72c -2b7d516e1e0e_story.html?utm_term=.e6d257dc3ec8. Accessed 15 Sept. 2017.

2

GO SET A WATCHMAN AS SOUTHERN PASTORAL

American Literature, "My Atticus," and the Past that Never Was

Holly Blackford

[Jean Louise] was extravagant with her pity
and complacent in her snug world.

—*Go Set a Watchman*

The opening of *Go Set a Watchman* is a train ride back in time, space, memory, and history. Flashes of scenes that preoccupy the consciousness of Jean Louise, as she returns South, are telling entries into the novel that unfolds before us. As in Willa Cather's *My Ántonia*, in which a train takes us into the narrative, the past, and an author's enterprise into American mythography, *Go Set a Watchman* opens by asking us to experience a personal and historical past that is expressly, in the mind of Jean Louise, a timeless past outside of technology and modernity. Jim Burden, the protagonist of *My Ántonia*, takes a parallel journey from New York to the plains of Nebraska, his childhood home, which he views as an authentic American home space outside of the train and modernity, a space of childhood wholeness previous to the disillusionment of modern urbanity and marriage.

Jim titles the manuscript he produces—based on his memories o home—*My Ántonia*, which is a celebration of his childhood in relation to his friend and muse, a Bohemian immigrant named Ántonia. To Jim, she embodies his past and the idyllic landscape of his youth; similarly, Atticus embodies what Jean Louise believes to be her past and her childhood experience of fairness and equality, which is not so much truth as a need to anchor her pastoral visions of home. Just as Ántonia, a living woman, refuses Jim's need to see her as his past, and as the earth mother he needs her to be through his Virgilian lens, Atticus refuses Jean Louise's literary lenses and cannot be separated from the idea of "*My Atticus*," a sort of manuscript of the past that the protagonist Jean Louise writes as Atticus fails her. The decline of the king of Jean Louise's imagined empire gestures to a common literary theme in coming-of-age literature; but as in Cather's masterwork of situating American history and immigration, Lee's *Go Set a Watchman* attempts to situate history and race relations in the mind of a highly literary character—one whose frame of references separate her from home.

Jean Louise struggles with the bed on the train and has to be rescued without her pants on, as they are folded up in the mess. Indeed, throughout the novel, her grapples with technology, such as automobiles and a mower, manifest her inability to cope with change in her childhood world. Although the narrator of *Go Set a Watchman* relentlessly gestures to British literature, with references to Robert Browning, Oscar Wilde, Lewis Carroll, Kenneth Grahame, Sir Walter Scott, William Shakespeare, William Blake, William Wordsworth, and Rudyard Kipling, the structure and integrity of the novel can be squarely situated in American literary history, which seeks to situate the past as pure or pristine, given resistance to modernity and social change.

The Machine in the Garden

As Jim Burden does to Ántonia, Jean Louise ruthlessly applies a pastoral lens to memories of her muse, Atticus, who—like Ántonia after twenty years—has aged and is not the muse she remembers, if he ever were. The Atticus of this memoir cannot hold a fork or eat without making a mess. Also like Jim Burden in *Ántonia*, Jean Louise is sorely disappointed when her muse destabilizes her pastoral lens. When a vision and geography becomes hopelessly enmeshed with childhood, past, and American mythos, the mind memorializes a social structure and a place—the train represents just such a site in these novels. Unraveling the mythology of the mind hurts.

The train is the quintessential symbol of "the machine in the garden," as defined by Leo Marx in *The Machine in the Garden: Technology and the Pastoral Ideal in America*. American authors and images, Marx argues, have traditionally endeavored to exalt the country as a pastoral space even as they embrace a narrative of progress and technological advances, which summon the demise of the pastoral ideal. This tension is most evident in a narrative like Henry David Thoreau's *Walden*, in which he endeavors to create his own pastoral space while listening to the train going by and thinking of the country's greatness. The tension between the machine and the garden—looking forward and backward—manifests deeply in American mythography and often crystallizes around a figure thought to be unpolluted by modernity, as Jim sees Ántonia and Jean Louise remembers Atticus. Truman Capote likewise uses the convention of the journey South in *Other Voices, Other Rooms*, among other literary techniques, to signal the influence of Cather, whom he much admired (see Fahy).

It is particularly ironic to see Harper Lee's use of Willa Cather's conventions and mythologies now, in the twenty-first century, since we are hardly new to the world of the Finches. This journey into memory is therefore the journey of readers into deconstructing their memory of *Mockingbird*. Is the world of *Mockingbird* timeless and static? No. Jean Louise on her train home pretends that it is, just as the publisher of *Go Set a Watchman* pretended the work was just "A Novel," the words appearing on the cover.

Go Set a Watchman was published without any contextualization or scholarly apparatus. An editor's introduction and careful discussion of the manuscript, editorial process, and relationship to *Mockingbird* would have provided the reader with a productive interpretive frame. Without such context, the non-descript two words "A Novel" set on the cover are, in fact, irresponsible and obscure the story of *Watchman's* composition, presumably an early draft of *Mockingbird* that would undergo much collaborative revision for the market. Pretending the past is not a constructed, framed, and biased vision is a mistake, one Jean Louise makes in *Watchman*, one the publisher made, and one many readers who once enjoyed *Mockingbird* make by becoming angry that the characters are not heroic. The latter is, in fact, the plot of *Go Set a Watchman*.

It is almost uncanny to see *Go Set a Watchman* not as an early draft of *Mockingbird* but as a response to fifty years of the *Mockingbird's* influence. In *Watchman*, we find the problems of *Mockingbird's* popularity exposed: without a hero and, more disturbingly, white patriarchy, a novel cannot succeed with the broadest of audiences. However, we also find laid bare a composition and reception process. We can presume that Lee's editors advised the composition of what Peter Pan would call "The Great

White Father" to anchor the interesting persona of Atticus Lee sketched in her early manuscript. We find the dry, ironic, and detached Atticus in lines such as, "Hypocrites have just as much right to live in this world as anybody" (235), articulated in response to Jean Louise's refusal to live with Hank, whom she believes to be a hypocrite. This is an early sketch of a man who takes the spit of Bob Ewell calmly and dispassionately. In *Watchman*, however, Atticus is actively involved in barring Civil Rights, taking a case to prevent the NAACP from getting involved. So we must put Atticus aside, in an assessment of *Watchman*. It is not his story, except insofar as he anchors Jean Louise's reminiscence.

In applying greater focus on a fallen father than a potential husband, *Watchman* thwarts expectation; then, it goes a step further in revealing that it is not even about the fallen father, but, fundamentally, about Jean Louise. Lee's supportive editors must have advised that she alter the setting, which would alter the ages and memories, the amount of space women would occupy, and the male figure of preoccupation for Jean Louise. The movement between New York and Alabama that Lee often traversed becomes the testing ground for a more modern story—not of *Uncle Tom* melodrama (see Williams) but of disillusioned and angry youth. *Go Set a Watchman* is the story of an angry and confused young woman who is much critiqued by the narrator in the same style that young Scout is mocked as the center of consciousness in *To Kill a Mockingbird*. The difference is that she isn't six. Her palpable anger drives the plot and effect of tone. After Jean Louise witnesses the courthouse meeting that destroys her sense of home, father, and pride, she tries to mow the yard and ponders how the course of English literature would have changed if William Wordsworth had a mower: a machine in the garden of the pastoral. The deadpan narrator of *Go Set a Watchman* is familiar as the voice of *Mockingbird*, but the concern is not with providing an eye witness to heroism but to ironize Jean Louise's need for the pastoral: "The course of English Literature would have been decidedly different had Mr. Wordsworth owned a power mower, [Jean Louise] thought" (143). In his *Prelude*, William Wordsworth creates a union between pastoral and child reminiscence contingent upon observation of a rural past. Confronting a world that uses racism to perpetuate its existence, Jean Louise now wants a mower, but she is not particularly skilled at using machines.

We find allusions to so many literary traditions in *Watchman* that we can see an early writer situating herself and finding her own humorous voice. The narrator alludes to American writers—Carson McCullers,

William Cullen Bryant, James Fenimore Cooper, Edgar Rice Burroughs, the Stratemeyer series, Margaret Mitchell—for particularly comic effects. Alluding to *The Member of the Wedding* by Carson McCullers, Jean Louise ponders what it might mean to move beyond a pastoral lens and actually live in the South: "I couldn't possibly bring off one of these [ladies] affairs by myself, and there's Aunty having the time of her life. I'd be churched to death, bridge-partied to death, called upon to give book reviews at the Amanuensis Club, expected to become part of the community. It takes a lot of what I don't have to be a member of this wedding" (173). She also experiments with a double-voiced focalizing technique in the distance between the narrator and the mocked Jean Louise, who is exposed as remembering an idyllic life because she lived in a bubble of haves and have-nots. The narrator espouses, "she was born color blind" (122); but this depiction is inaccurate, as revealed in ruminations that signal blindness, not color blindness:

> You will not believe me, but I will tell you: never in my life until today did I hear the word "nigger" spoken by a member of my family. Never did I learn to think in terms of The Niggers. When I grew up, and I did grow up with black people, they were Calpurnia, Zeebo the garbage collector, Tom the yard man, and whatever else their names were. There were hundreds of Negroes surrounding me . . . but never in my life was I given the idea that I should despise one, should fear one, should be discourteous to one, or think that I could mistreat one and get away with it. . . . That is the way I was raised, by a black woman and a white man. (179)

The emphasis on "they" "over there," in combination with the scene confronting Calpurnia, whom Jean Louise expects to conform to her memories, is enough to make us understand that the past of "separate worlds" is Jean Louise's white childhood bubble, a paradox imploded by the story that unfolds before us as Jean Louise disembarks from the train of her memory. It is not simply memories of Atticus that refuse analysis. What we have is an unreliable narrator with a persistent belief in the pastoral, a fixation that disintegrates, as writers in this collection note, with a visit to Calpurnia, no longer a willing Mammy figure, in the era of Civil Rights. Jean Louise knows enough to ask, "Did you hate us?" (160); nevertheless, her erupting anger should involve her own childhood assumptions and do not: "They as a people did not enter my world, nor did I enter theirs." Jean Louise is only as an adult constructing ideas about race and her own acceptance of segregation, which conflicts with the imagined equality of the last line, "That is the way I was raised, by a black woman and a white man" (160).

The narrator keeps Jean Louise shy of actual insight—even judges her: "She was extravagant with her pity and complacent in her snug world" (118). The narrator's appraisal continues: "Had she insight, could she have pierced the barriers of her highly selective, insular world, she may have discovered that all her life she had been with a visual defect which had gone unnoticed and neglected by herself and by those closest to her: she was born color blind" (122). In *Mockingbird*, Lee's narrator (adult Jean Louise) is subtler about mocking a younger Scout, whom she uses as a filter for processing events.

This more nuanced technique comprises the beauty of *Mockingbird*, which has a sharp female wit and exquisite irony. The childhood sections of *Watchman* provide comic views of religion, school, and peer groups, which would become the Boo Radley material of the *Mockingbird* novel. But tracking the numerous allusions to authors, especially Robert Browning and Oscar Wilde, alluded to several times, demonstrates both Lee's conversation with literary artists and her understanding of conflicts in the South between pastoral and Gothic lenses that increasingly crept into late-nineteenth century literature such as *The Picture of Dorian Gray* and "Childe Roland to the Dark Tower Came." Just as the novel explores the crisis of idealized pasts, the authors and styles through which Lee situated herself enabled her to apply literary techniques to thinking about the past that never was, except in the mind of Jean Louis.

My Ántonia, My Atticus

The opening of *Watchman* represents a reverie in which the train movement reflects Jean Louise's consciousness as she returns home, and the passage culminates in her pastoral vision of a shifting landscape as she moves South. As with Jim Burden in *My Ántonia*, the journey frames Jean Louise as a tourist, now detached from the land of her childhood. Her pleasure in the landscape depends on its unchanging red earth and tin-roofed houses, through her eyes noted as a picturesque with framed spaces. Looking at the movement in the passage, however, we find that the picturesque hinges upon segregation, much as pastoral literature idealizes the rural lifestyle: since Atlanta, she has looked out of the dining-car window with an almost-physical delight. Over her breakfast coffee, she watches the last of Georgia's hills recede and the red earth appear and, with it, tin-roofed houses set in the middle of swept yards, and in the yards the inevitable verbena grew, surrounded by whitewashed tires. She grins when she sees her first TV antenna atop an unpainted "Negro house"; as these houses multiplied, her joy rose (3). The various frames in her vision give her pleasure because the images are, in her mind, "inevitable," and unpainted houses of the African American community are a visual, unexamined part of the idyllic return. The second paragraph of the novel introduces Jean Louise's maturity level as she considers being fair to her father, a crucial element of the novel. However, presenting the "joy" of this picture in the first paragraph establishes *Watchman* as featuring the unfairness of not critically examining the "picture" of "home" in Jean Louise's mind. In fact, the moment that Jean Louise is in the house with Aunt Alexandra, she regresses to a less mature state. The movement on the first page of childhood landscape to Atticus is likewise telling as he anchors her pastoral memories of perfect values and human rights, even as the man we meet in the novel bears no resemblance to this impression.

In the introduction of *My Ántonia*, the unnamed narrator meets Jim Burden on the train; together, they idealize the sensory experience of growing up in Nebraska, which they are passing from the "observation" car (like Jean Louise's windows onto scenes removed from her current self and firmly stored in her slanted memory): "[Jim and I] sat in the observation car, where the woodwork was hot to the touch and red dust lay deep over everything. The dust and heat, the burning wind, reminded us of many things. We were talking about what it is like to spend one's childhood in little towns like these, buried in wheat and corn, under stimulating extremes of climate: burning summers when the world lies green and billowy beneath a brilliant sky, when one is fairly stifled in vegetation, in the color and smell of strong weeds and heavy harvest" (Cather 3). What Jim sees is domination by nature, which is what brings him pleasure throughout *My Ántonia*; what Jean Louise sees is picturesque homes. These visions embody what they need the past to mean more than what the past actually means. Both Jim and Jean Louise mark the sensory nature of childhood memory rooted in the mind. The two characters on Cather's train reconstruct an image of stasis around which nature moves and dominates the individual. This image of stasis anchors the modern self emergent from the train and passing by a prior identity, somehow rooted in weather and agriculture, much like the "inevitable" verbena lets Jean Louise know where she is in relation to home. Jim and the narrator of the introduction are in the observation car peering at some kind of primitive essence, something outside of time, while they, in automated motion, race by. Childhood is paradoxically both regional and unchanging or universal, shared and evoked as if it had materiality and context.

What happens in *My Ántonia* is that Jim and the unnamed narrator agree to write about Ántonia because she, an immigrant who rises from nothing to a successful farmer and mother evoking "the founders of early races" for Jim (186), mythically evokes "the country, the conditions, the whole adventure of our childhood" (6) in Nebraska. Advancing the thesis that childhood and the self are outside of history, Jim and the narrator have become tourists in their own childhoods, which, the passage suggests, are either already quite buried or being further buried through discussion of them. The only way to explore childhood is through *My Ántonia*, much as Atticus becomes the only agent through which Jean Louise can situate *her* home. Much of Jim's memoir of *My Ántonia* involves the erasure of roads he once took with her, and Jean Louise actually vomits after she witnesses the courtroom meeting and finds her original home in town is now an ice cream shop. There is nothing "inevitable" about actual human history, which alters and changes.

Joseph Urgo views Jim in the context of what he names a "migratory consciousness" defining so many of Cather's characters and her own feelings of dislocation in childhood, interpreting this mobility as uniquely American—essentially homeless but always imagining a future home. This liminality is precisely the mental position of Jean Louise, who is contemplating marriage and home. Cather's investigation of characters who migrate heightens the constructive and deconstructive nature of consciousness as the unifying but never stable element of a person. As an unhappily married man whose Western dreams compensate for civilization and its discontents, Jim is a wanderer deeply identified with the generative home spaces into which he can imagine burrowing. He is the archeologist of his own childhood. He needs this childhood to anchor his modern New York existence. Lee's Jean Louise, like Jim, is destined for disappointment because the past and the pastoral are different matters. As Atticus does in *Watchman*, Ántonia, aging but still her own persona, refuses Jim's mythic lens. Where the two novels differ is that Uncle Jack spends an extensive amount of time chastising Jean Louise for treating Atticus as Jim treats Ántonia.

As David Hill argues about Cather's introduction, set on the train, flashes of fragmented objects racing by the observing subject animate how consciousness, in general, operates: "the self comes to know itself in relation to objects perceived as outside the immediately present self—objects which include the products of our autobiographical memories" (10). As a symbol of motion and fractured, modern social relations, the train also expresses how the self is never stable; rather, it must seek stability outside of its own motion. As such, the train symbolizes disappearance even as it symbolizes possibility. Modernity itself is the motion of continual disappearance, whereas the landscape of childhood embodies home, and it "appears" to Jean Louise as if by artistic design. Trains change the individual's relation to the landscape and to time, as Joy Alexander says of the train's impact on Prince Edward Island in *Anne of Green Gables*. Like surveyed highways and roads, the train shifts the unmarked and unsettled landscape in which Jim locates his free-floating child self. Leo Marx analyzes the train as "the machine in the garden," the paradox that America embraced as both pastoral and progressive; similarly, the train as Jim's *consciousness* also symbolizes regression and the possibility of return, a backwards motion into the pre-modern unconscious as it links modern cities (Jim's New York) to small western towns and countryside. Jean Louise wants more than anything else the setting of Finch's Landing, but she does not land her quest there very well.

The Dark Tower

As she delights and then gets tangled in the bed of the train, Jean Louise cannot remember the lines of "To a Waterfowl" (5), a poem about seeing the soul's journey through life. References to literature abound in Jean Louise's mind throughout the novel, ranging from pastoral and romantic to Gothic horror marking the fin de siècle. As a whole, they show Jean Louise's efforts to capture literary meaning in her home landscape, which only further separates her from home. The humorous idea of mowing the "middle landscape" of Wordsworth's poetry is tempered by increasing pressure of references to Dorian Gray and Childe Roland, tales of darkness and corruption in which surfaces and appearances mislead. Southern Renaissance writers increasingly used Gothic tropes dexterously and imaginatively to recast ideas of a crumbling and decaying South. McCullers's *The Ballad of the Sad Café* and *Reflections in a Golden Eye*, much as Capote's *Other Voices, Other Rooms*, investigate the gap between appearances and realities in homes and minds by using motifs of decay, horror, inside and outside discrepancies, and run-down architecture and bodies; in this context, Jean Louise's sense that she and everyone around her look like Dorian Gray or his portrait suggests an awakening to the Gothic in the romantic that she cannot fully process. The search for a remembered Atticus in the aged figure before us is highly reminiscent of Joel Knox's search for a father in *Other Voices, Other Rooms*; his father turns out to be paralyzed in a room upstairs that he does not find until midway through the novel; the decline of white patriarchy in both novels is complementary, although Capote's concern is homosexuality and Lee's is race.

To express nostalgic longing for home, Jean Louise actually references the character Mole from Kenneth Grahame's *The Wind in the Willows*, which is as pastoral and external to modernity as one can get: "This is one good thing about life that never changes, she thought. As long as he lived, as long as she returned, Mr. Fred would be here with his . . . simple welcome. What was that? Alice? Brer Rabbit? It was Mole. Mole, when he returned from some long journey, desperately tired, had found the familiar waiting for him with its simple welcome" (152). Nothing could be less similar to her own journey, but the citation suggests tension between home and open road, which is the primary tension in *Wind* (Mole versus Toad in their sentiments), as in *My Ántonia*, where Ántonia is asked to symbolize home and Jim the open road. Atticus and Aunty anchor the search for home while Jean Louise, toying with refusing the open road, seeks a remembered home that no longer exists. The growing tension of Jean Louise's efforts to reconcile home with racism culminates in her kinship with Childe Roland, which reflects the surreal quality of a dark quest as well as what Margaret Atwood calls "Negotiating with the Dead" in the enterprise of writing and composition. Every writer negotiates with progenitors, literary and familial. In Margaret Atwood's interpretation of the poem, Childe Roland is the poet side of Robert Browning that is fated to encounter what all poets fear—that the quest for the unwritten poem is doomed and that "the monster inside the Dark Tower is Childe Roland himself, in his poem-writing as-poet" (33), who may never see the actual poem but who situates his writing in the context of the dark tower of tradition, to which the poet may make a contribution.

Jean Louise's kinship with Childe Roland is, at its root, a deconstruction of the pastoral and a search for home. Looking for a past home is like searching for the dark tower, seeing the knights hurt along the way, and sensing that one cannot trust the guides along the road, especially Uncle Jack. Comparing him to a nineteenth-century aesthete or eccentric like Oscar Wilde, Jean Louise tries to cope with his smoke-and-mirrors discussion of Europe and feudal systems, which of course evokes the nineteenth-century literary predecessors she keeps citing.

The dominant intertext of Jean Louise's interactions with Uncle Jack, who functions as a strange bard of Atticus's plight, is Browning's "Childe Roland to the Dark Tower Came" because it is the searching and not "the find" that matters. Uncle Jack, who is "mad as a hatter," names Jean Louise "Childe Roland," who, in Browning's poem, is horrified to trust a malicious guide for which road to take, suspects the guide lies or seeks a victim in the knight, and takes the road anyway. The road does lead to the dark tower, and the worthy knights on it are both recognizable and not recognizable in their deaths. Uncle Jack recalls the mad guide to the knight on a quest to find the tower, a journey akin to Jean Louise's shifting view of the South and her father in both personal and cultural time. Browning's poem never explains or describes the tower; the journey itself, and an endpoint to that journey, occupies the narrative poem. The speaker seeking the tower first suspects that the guide lies, but life is never this simple. Duplicity is not really lying, but a way to live and pass in an environment shrouded with mist, as is the tower.

Childe Roland "to the dark tower came" becomes a code between Jean Louise and Uncle Jack, describing Jean Louise's return to the South from New York, in accordance with the poem:

> My first thought was, he lied in every word,
>> That hoary cripple, with malicious eye
>> Askance to watch the workings of his life
> On mine, and mouth scarce able to afford
> Suppression of the glee, that purs'd and scor'd
> Its edge, at one more victim gain'd thereby.
>
> What else should he be set for, with his staff?
>> What, save to waylay with his lies, ensnare
>> All travellers who might find him posted there,
> And ask the road? I guess'd what skull-like laugh
> Would break, what crutch 'gin write my epitaph
> For pastime in the dusty thoroughfare,
>
> If at his counsel I should turn aside
>> Into that ominous tract which, all agree,
>> Hides the Dark Tower. Yet acquiescingly
> I did turn as he pointed: neither pride
> Nor hope rekindling at the end descried,
> So much as gladness that some end might be. (1–18)

The allusion to Jean Louise's journey toward some sort of decisive end—whether to marry Henry or not—situates her relationship with the duplicity she suspects in both Uncle Jack and Atticus—not to mention Henry—who might ensnare travelers and not be what they seem. This is why she keeps seeing Dorian Gray. This poem, which Uncle Jack introduces and challenges her to apply, conveys a labyrinth of meaning because that which is sought is never identical to the point of a journey. Likewise, a road may not seem safe, but one takes it anyway. Uncle Jack seems to be challenging Scout to understand that (in the view of some Maycomb citizens) states' rights supersede all other considerations; she considers this meaning, but in challenging Atticus, her interpretation of the meaning shifts because she has no tolerance for this view. This is when the end of the poem, "*Childe Roland to the dark tower came*" (241), occurs to her to be a metaphor for coming upon the meaning of confrontation rather than a particular interpretation of the racist situation. The line occurs to her again when Uncle Jack explains that Atticus allowed Jean Louise to see him as an imperfect man rather than as an idol, which is necessary to growing up. At this point, the tower becomes a general symbol for ideals that no longer hold weight after the treacherous road is walked.

The tower is the home she wants to find, but it is Atticus who asks to go home at the end, because it is his home and not hers, and the final lines watching him "pass," which reappear in a very different context in *Mockingbird*, are eerie images of fallen knights that perhaps pepper the road to the shrouded tower. Jim Burden's story ends with the hopelessness of communicating "the incommunicable past" after two hundred pages of reminiscence. Lee's reminiscence ends not with command of an automobile but "this time she was careful not to bump her head" (278), I guess because bumping her head on machines in the garden has been an awkward many pages.

Conclusion: Beyond Atticus

Even with this treatment of *Watchman* as a Southern literary pastoral, though, a great deal must be resolved. We need a careful edition of *Watchman*, one that annotates the text, preferably as an electronic teaching tool, and establishes the composition process and relationship to *Mockingbird* revisions and conventions. We need scholars to situate the myriad allusions in *Watchman* and its status as American mythography, pastoral, romanticism, Gothic, feminism, and childhood and queer studies. We need a more honest assessment of racial history in American literature and the tropes that refuse to go away in this American drama. We need further assessment of the collaborative editorial process and how drafts are revised to conform to the broader marketplace. We need more research into *Watchman* as a modern text. In fact, just as in *Mockingbird*, Lee uses a modern stream-of-consciousness style in *Watchman* to depict scenes the protagonist cannot integrate—the scenes of court (109–10), the streams of hatred.

Streams of consciousness enter Jean Louise's head in *Watchman* as courtroom racism. Streams of consciousness enter Scout's head in *Mockingbird* as racism on the porch, as she listens through the window to a potential lynching. In *Watchman*, these streams buttress against the line, "[Jean Louise] knew little of the affairs of men" (110). These streams represent a modern style of narration, which destabilizes the nineteenth-century texts permeating *Watchman*. They embody uninterrogated information that the protagonist cannot situate in literary history. These gaps are the moments inviting scholars and students to enter the text of *Watchman* as well as *Mockingbird*. Shifts in style in both texts exemplify gaps in consciousness that demand analysis.

Perhaps, however, the largest gap we can interrogate is one between the narrative bard sorting literary history and the woman coming of age in *Watchman*. It is in this rupture that *Watchman* resides. *Watchman* needs integration and analysis in our sense of Southern Renaissance style and voice. *Watchman* represents not only our ideas of American literary history but also our inheritance of the problems of the pastoral tropes used to view national narratives. Neither machine nor garden, Jean Louise's Maycomb successfully marks white panic and the problem of unexamined white privilege in the era of Civil Rights, and the application of a literary pastoral is both intriguing and terrifying, as, in fact, it is in *Mockingbird* as well. If this essay represents an excursion into the American mythography that surely influenced the *Watchman* draft, as Lee sorted her literary and familial progenitors, then much work remains in sorting the distinction between "the dark tower" and Mole's search for authenticity in home.

Works Cited

Alexander, Joy. "Anne with Two 'G's: Green Gables and Geographical Identity." *Anne with an "e": The Centennial Study of* Anne of Green Gables. Ed. Holly Blackford. University of Calgary Press, 2009, 41–60.

Atwood, Margaret. *Negotiating with the Dead: A Writer on Writing*. Cambridge University Press, 2002.

Browning, Robert. "Childe Roland to the Dark Tower Came." *A Victorian Anthology, 1837–1895*. Edited by Edmund Clarence Stedman. Riverside Press, 1895. *Barbleby.com*. Accessed 28 Aug. 2016.

Cather, Willa. *My Ántonia*. Edited by Janet Sharistanian. Oxford University Press, 2006.

Fahy, Thomas. "'Obliterating Strangeness': Willa Cather, Truman Capote, and the Influence of *My Ántonia*." *Something Complete and Great: The Centennial Study of* My Ántonia. Edited by Holly Blackford. Fairleigh Dickinson University Press, 2018. 163–81.

Hill, David. "The Quotidian Sublime: Cognitive Perspectives on Identity-Formation in Willa Cather's *My Ántonia*." *Arizona Quarterly,* vol. 61, no. 3, 2005, pp. 109–27.

Lee, Harper. *Go Set a Watchman*. Harper, 2015.

Marx, Leo. *The Machine in the Garden: Technology and the Pastoral Ideal in America*. Oxford University Press, 2000.

Urgo, Joseph R. *Willa Cather and the Myth of American Migration*. University of Illinois Press, 1995.

Williams, Linda. *Playing the Race Card: Melodramas of Black and White from Uncle Tom to O. J. Simpson*. Princeton University Press, 2002.

PART 2

MOCKINGBIRD REVISITED

3

ATTICUS REVISED

Race, Gender, and Sexuality in *Go Set a Watchman*
and *To Kill a Mockingbird*

Laura Fine

Harper Lee's legacy shifted with the publication of *Go Set a Watchman* in 2015, fifty-five years after *To Kill a Mockingbird* was published. Critics and the public alike responded with profound dismay when *Mockingbird*'s beloved father, Atticus Finch, turned out to be an unrepentant racist in *Watchman. New York Times* reviewer Michiko Kakutani writes, "The depiction of Atticus in 'Watchman' makes for disturbing reading, and for 'Mockingbird' fans, it's especially disorienting. . . . How could the saintly Atticus—described early in the book in much the same terms as he is in 'Mockingbird'—suddenly emerge as a bigot?" She adds, "'Mockingbird' suggested that we should have compassion for outsiders like Boo and Tom Robinson, while 'Watchman' asks us to have understanding for a bigot named Atticus." In one of many other examples, NPR's Maureen Corrigan notes, "The novel turns on the adult Scout's disillusionment with her father—a disillusionment that lovers of *To Kill a Mockingbird* will surely share. Reeling from the Supreme Court's recent ruling in *Brown v. Board of Education,* Atticus reveals himself as a segregationist and a reactionary extremist," and "This Atticus is different in kind, not just degree: He's like Ahab turned into a whale lover or Holden Caulfield a phony." Indeed, the racism of *Watchman*'s Atticus is hard for both readers and Jean Louise to fathom. However, it is more accurate to view Lee as reframing her portrayal of Atticus than presenting wholly irreconcilable character portraits between *Watchman,* written in the mid-1950s, and *Mockingbird,* published in 1960. The most obvious change is in the depiction of Atticus, but Lee also reorients her portrayal of gender dynamics and of sexuality.

In *Watchman*, Lee seems to use racism primarily as an impetus for the process of individuation Jean Louise undergoes throughout the course of the novel. In this drama of individuation, Lee portrays Atticus remaining as loving as ever toward his daughter as she angrily confronts his racism and strives to break free from him—strives to view him as a man rather than a superhero. This quick shift from rage to resolution, however, is unconvincing. But perhaps even more unconvincing than its capacity to resolve the father-daughter conflict, *Watchman* portrays Jean Louise in a heterosexual relationship with Henry "Hank" Clinton, her father's business partner. The relationship never feels quite right to Jean Louise—or to readers—and Jean Louise's eventual decision to part from him seems trumped up, for she purportedly resolves to leave him in part for the same racism she has discovered and ended up accepting in Atticus.

Harper Lee tries a new tack in *Mockingbird*, which she wrote after *Watchman*, abandoning her attempt to portray Jean Louise as a successfully individuated heterosexual woman. First, she avoids the marriage plot altogether by focusing on the preadolescent Scout. Next, she projects the anger against the father we see in *Watchman* onto other characters, and, instead of portraying Jean Louise's struggle to stand up to him and his racism and still be accepted by him, in *Mockingbird*, Lee romanticizes the father. In this much-loved novel, Lee provides examples of unconventional sexual and gendered behavior and attempts to write against conventional racism. The reframing of Atticus from defender of the racist status quo in *Watchman*—even as he accepts his daughter unconditionally—to the valiant rebel in *Mockingbird* who actively opposes the racist status quo and accepts many brands of unconventional behavior—allows Scout to imagine life on the margin, to live in a liminal space that will free her to explore unconventional gender expressions and sexual identities.

The Atticus of *Watchman* is clearly modeled after Harper Lee's actual father, A. C. Lee, a newspaper editor. The character and the man share similar views on race, and it is perhaps significant that Lee did not publish this novel until many years after her own father's death. In one editorial A. C. Lee intones, "It is a matter of common knowledge among all informed people that where the federal government directs expenditure of large funds, or supervises its administration, no color or race lines are recognized...The only safe course for us is to insist that the states be not disturbed in their administration of public education" (Qtd in Reeves).

The states' rights sentiment is echoed in *Watchman*'s Atticus. When Jean Louise objects to his having attended the Citizens' Council meeting in which the guest lecturer spewed racist diatribes, Atticus responds, "I can tell you the two reasons I was there. The Federal Government and the NAACP" (*Watchman* 238). In response to his daughter's assessment of race and the Constitution—"Well, in trying to satisfy one amendment, it looks like they rubbed out another one. The Tenth" (*Watchman* 239)—Atticus adds, "You seem to be constitutionally sound so far" (*Watchman* 239). Atticus, like A. C. Lee himself, believes that *Brown v. Board of Education* wiped out the Tenth Amendment in favor of the Fourteenth.

Harper Lee biographer Charles Shields notes that, like Atticus, A. C. Lee served in the Alabama legislature for many years (66). In addition, Shields writes of A. C. Lee, "Like most of his generation, he believed that the current social order, segregation, was natural and created harmony between the races. It was a point not even worth discussing that blacks and whites were different" (121). Indeed, Shields recounts A. C. Lee's vehement disapproval of a preacher he heard whose sermon "disputed impressions about Negroes' desiring to intermarry with whites and about Negroes being intellectually inferior" (122), managing in the end to have the preacher, Reverend Ray Whatley, assigned to another congregation (124).

Atticus in *Watchman* reflects A. C. Lee's sentiments, descending even beyond advocating states' rights to blithely promote his view that black people are obviously inferior to whites. Here is a sampling of Atticus's sentiments: "Do you want Negroes by the carload in our schools and churches and theaters? Do you want them in our world?" (245), and "You do not seem to understand that the Negroes down here are still in their childhood as a people" (246).

Jean Louise responds to her father's racism with righteous anger. Indeed, the plot of *Watchman* reflects a fantasy in which the daughter virulently confronts her father's backward beliefs and finds her anger and resistance met with love rather than rejection, a fantasy perhaps not reflected in the reality of Lee's relationship with her father. There are obvious limits to what outsiders can understand about a family relationship. However, it is clear that A.C. Lee wanted his daughter to follow in his footsteps and become a lawyer, and there was tension when she made it known that she hated law school. Shields writes, "She had enrolled . . . because 'it was the line of least resistance,' meaning that she realized how strongly her father wanted to welcome another lawyer into the family fold. But she was discovering that she hated studying law—and that was the term she used, *hated*" (100–101). She dropped out but then went back to try again, in the end leaving one semester short of graduating: "Over the winter holidays she told her father what her plans were: to drop out of law school, go to New York, find a job, and write. A. C. made it clear that he was prepared to pay for law school, but he was not going to subsidize a pack of daydreams" (109). A. C. Lee also seemed to have dreams that Nelle (Harper) would join him at work on his newspaper, the *Monroe Journal*, but she declined to do that as well (101).

The extent to which Nelle Lee felt free to express feelings to her father that she knew he would disapprove of is unclear; but in her literary fiction, Harper Lee has her protagonist freely express deep displeasure with racist views the fictional Atticus shares with the real-life A. C. Lee. In *Watchman*, Jean Louise derides Atticus with "You neglected to tell me that we were naturally better than the Negroes, bless their kinky heads" (247). She continues by comparing her father to Hitler with the distinction that "You just try to kill their souls rather than their bodies" (252), and ending finally with calling him a *"son of a bitch!"* (253). In the literary fantasy, Jean Louise feels comfortable enough to express this extreme degree of anger toward her father.

Significantly, throughout this long argument with his daughter in *Watchman*, Atticus responds with loving kindness, declining to get angry (249). He simply smiles when Jean Louise compares him to Hitler (252), and when she tells him that she despises him (253), he responds simply by telling her he loves her (253). The argument about race, then, becomes subsumed to a drama of Jean Louise's individuation. She throws everything she has at her father, all the virulence and anger she can muster, and he remains accepting and kind, undamaged by her anger. In fact, he is conscious of leading her through this necessary process of individuation. When she laments to him that he was the only person she really trusted, Atticus responds with "I've killed you, Scout. I had to" (252). In her final scene with Atticus, after he asks if she is ready to leave, she thinks to herself, "I tried to obliterate and grind [you] into the earth, and you say ready?" (277). When she begins to try to apologize to him for her harsh words, he reassures her that he would expect his daughter to stand up to him (277). These sentiments are earlier echoed by Jean Louise's Uncle Jack, who analyzes her recent argument with her father: "He was letting you reduce him to the status of a human being'" (266). As a result of this argument with Atticus, he tells Jean Louise, "You are your own person now" (264). Indeed, Jean Louise is to understand that this entire conflict is actually a good thing because it allows her to end her romanticization of her father, stand up for herself, and—in the process—start becoming her own person rather than an extension of her father.

Thus we perhaps see in this portrayal Lee's fantasy that she could stand up to her own father, show him all the anger she had toward him, and still be accepted by him—something that she may not have believed could happen in real life. Indeed, she did not publish *Watchman* while her father was still living. Connected to this fantasy, too, is the depiction of a disturbing scene in which Jean Louise's Uncle Jack, in order to shake sense into her about her views of her father, smacks her across the face, bloodying her lip (260). Jack seems to be acting as a split-off part of Atticus here. Lee informs us that Jack sees himself as father-figure to Jean Louise and her brother in the same scene in which he also makes the odd disclosure that he was in love with Jean Louise's mother (274). Lee, then, shapes a fantasy in which a benevolent father, Atticus, accepts his daughter's nearly violent wrath with loving kindness in combination with another father-figure, Jack, who responds to Jean Louise's assertion of contrary views with violence and rejection. The Atticus/Jack doubling couples the fantasy of being able to express anger toward the father and be accepted with the fear of violent retribution for claiming one's anger against the father.

Tied to Jean Louise's difficult process of separation from her father is the conflicted portrayal of her separation from her love interest, Henry "Hank" Clinton. This struggle is connected with Jean Louise's trouble with gender norms (explicated in the narrative) and with her unacknowledged resistance to compulsory heterosexuality. Gary Richards's analysis of gender in *Mockingbird* pertains to *Watchman*. Richards uses Judith Butler's contention that gender is a performance to show the ways women and girls in the novel perform gender. He focuses in particular on how Scout's Aunt Alexandra insists on Scout's following traditional gender norms: "Just as Aunt Alexandra subscribes to and performs proper southern white femininity, so too does she demand the same of others—and the transgressive Scout in particular" (123). The novel shows, Richards contends, "through the disciplinary actions and demands exercised on Scout, the punishments for disbelief in the naturalness of the performances of polarized genders. Lee's readers thus have the potential to realize just as forcefully as Butler's that white southern femininity, like any other sort, is but a 'regulatory fiction'" (126).

Jean Louise in *Watchman* struggles, too, with her performance of gender, and in part this struggle troubles her relationship with Hank. Lee presents Jean Louise's reluctance to marry Hank first due to her abhorrence of assuming a traditional gender role in marriage. At one point Jean Louise thinks of marrying Hank and considers, "But I am not domestic . . . What do ladies say to each other when they go visiting? . . . I'd drop the babies and kill 'em'" (80). Here, Jean Louise seems to consider the prospect of her performing traditional femininity farcical. During Alexandra's tea party, she thinks of how stultifying marriage would be: "If we married—if I married anybody from the town—these would be my friends, and I couldn't think of a thing to say to them. . . . It takes a lot of what I don't have to be a member of this wedding" (173). This quotation of course evokes the McCullers novel it contains the title of, calling to mind the unconventionally gendered Frankie's frustrated desire to insert herself into the heterosexual marriage binary. Here, Jean Louise suggests that she does not have what it takes to perform not only traditional gender but also traditional heterosexuality. What feels like an absence in her would have to be filled with a performance of heterosexuality, and the imagined toll of that performance speaks through this line.

This sense of heterosexuality as a performance also emerges in Jean Louise's memory of her high school dance date with Hank when she was fourteen years old. In order to perform the role of acceptable, eligible young heterosexual female, Jean Louise feels it necessary to purchase falsies. And indeed, altering the appearance of her actual body to more closely resemble having conventionally approved breast sizes for women seems to pay off as she notices that several boys attempt to converse with her (*Watchman* 212). However, her performance fails in that Hank spots a wardrobe malfunction: "Her right false bosom was in the center of her chest and the other was nearly under her left armpit" (213). In what is told as a humorous remembrance, Jean Louise recounts how Hank, having convinced young Jean Louise to go without the falsies, tosses them far away—it turns out so far that they end up obscuring the lettering of part of a billboard. When the high school principal attempts to discover the evil doers, Hank enacts a scheme whereby girl students en masse write the principal to accept responsibility for the misplaced falsies. Ironically, more than one hundred girls falsely accept responsibility for the falsification of their actual bodies and for the damage the discarded evidence causes. This incident in effect depicts the performance of heterosexuality as absurd. Moreover, Jean Louise portrays in her response to Hank's insistence on playing the proper heterosexual gender role of protector (he devises the plan to allow Jean Louise to escape punishment) her contempt for such performances: "'I will never understand men,' she said, no longer in love with Henry. 'You don't have to protect me, Hank'" (219–20).

Lee recounts another childhood memory about gender norms in comic fashion, too, but with some serious undertones. Twelve-year-old Jean Louise believes she has become pregnant after a boy French kisses her and her girlfriends misinform her about how a girl gets pregnant. In the course of dispensing the misinformation, they tell her of a girl they all know who has become pregnant with her own father's baby (129). The girls connect the pregnancy to the onset of menstruation, which to her chagrin, Jean Louise has recently experienced. Jean Louise silently concludes that she herself must be pregnant since Albert touched his tongue to her lips. Though she knows very little about the subject, Jean Louise knows enough to realize "if someone had a baby without being married, her family was plunged into deep disgrace" (130). After nine months pass, she determines to kill herself by jumping off of the town water-tank (135). Hank sees her, climbs up, and brings her down, and it is then that Calpurnia sets her right about pregnancy. Though Lee tells the story in a comically melodramatic fashion, the memory makes clear the shame the child Jean Louise experiences in contemplating the violation of gender norms, especially sexual norms. The biological onset of menses is linked to helplessness and shame in Jean Louise's mind. She even deems herself unable to play on the playground: "'I can't do anything any more,' she said, and she sat on the steps and watched the boys tumble in the dust. 'I can't even walk,'" she notes dramatically. Since Jean Louise learns from her friends that one can become pregnant only after she has begun to menstruate, it seems that becoming a woman leads inevitably to becoming the passive recipient of male desire: Albert's kiss ruins her and her family to the extent that suicide seems the only option. Also significant is that the framing story she hears about pregnancy is about a father's shameful impregnation of his own daughter—with the shame being assumed by the daughter. Jean Louise learns to connect moving from the identity of girl to woman with shame and trauma.

The contrived and contradictory reasons Jean Louise provides for not marrying Hank seem tied to her unacknowledged reluctance to accept compulsory heterosexuality. Besides the concerns discussed above about being unwilling and unable to follow prescribed gender norms in a marriage, Jean Louise indicates at other times that the problem is that Hank simply is not the right man for her. She thinks early in the novel, "She was almost in love with him" (15) and considers that if she married Hank, in a few years "the man would come along whom she should have married" (15). At the end of the novel, she tells Hank outright: "'I've never been in love with you, but you've always known I've loved you. I thought we could make a marriage with me loving you on that basis, but—'" (228). While the first quoted lines seem to contain the possibility that a heterosexual Jean Louise simply has not found the right male romantic partner in Hank, the next lines complicate the first ones. These later lines suggest that Jean Louise lacks a certain feeling for Hank—perhaps sexual—but that she is perhaps willing to make do with this lack of feeling and carry on a partial sham of a marriage anyway. The sense could be that she loves him, but not romantically, yet is willing to perform a marriage with him because that is what she feels obligated to do as a single woman.

However, the final and purportedly definitive reason Lee provides for Jean Louise's deciding against a marriage to Hank is completely unrelated to issues of gender norms or compulsory heterosexuality: it is that she is so offended by his attendance with her father at the racist Citizens' Council meeting. Seeing Hank there turns her stomach (228). She ends their argument with "Hank, we are poles apart . . . I cannot live with a hypocrite" (234). Her unwillingness to forgive Hank's racism is odd, given that she has forgiven her father his. Interspersed with these contradictory, unsatisfying expositions are Lee's overwrought attempts to portray Jean Louise's heterosexual desire. "I never tire of watching him move," (24) Jean Louise thinks early in the novel, and also tells Hank "I'll have an affair with you but I won't marry you" (14). It remains unclear at the end of the novel whether she breaks up with Hank because he is simply not the man for her or because she refuses to play the traditional gender role of wife or because she is angry that he attended the racist Citizens' Council meeting. Lee struggles to portray her protagonist as a young heterosexual woman who, for one reason or another, does not wish to marry Henry Clinton, but the portrayal has too many contradictions and contrivances to ring true.

In the book Lee published while her father was still alive, *Mockingbird*, the anger against the father remains but is projected onto other characters, largely through the form of doubling. We see a hint of the doubling of good and bad fathers in *Watchman* in the portrayal of the utterly accepting Atticus and the violently rejecting Uncle Jack. In *Mockingbird,* we see the romanticized father, Atticus, coupled with the monstrous father, Bob Ewell. Robert C. Evans notes that while both men are fathers and widowers, "Atticus is a constant, loving, gentle, and inspiring presence in the lives of his children whereas Ewell is negligent, self-centered, unloving, and hard-tempered" (103). While Atticus jokes about the strain of incest in his family—"Our generation's practically the first in the Finch family not to marry its cousins. Would you say the Finches have an Incestuous Streak?" (132)—Bob Ewell commits incest with his daughter and successfully blames a black man, Tom Robinson, for his own evil actions. Indeed, whereas Atticus himself exemplifies racism in *Watchman,* in *Mockingbird,* as critic Gregory Jay writes, the "racism gets largely projected onto morally degenerate white trash" (506). The righteous racism of Atticus of *Watchman* is here represented through the most evil character in the book, a character Scout—and readers—can freely feel anger toward.

We see another projection of anger against the father in the doubling of the victimized fathers, Atticus Finch and Tom Robinson. Scout herself at least superficially connects the two men as she watches them in the court room: "It occurred to me that in their own way, Tom Robinson's manners were as good as Atticus's" (197). After Atticus chooses to represent Tom Robinson in court, the town largely turns against him, from the mob who threatens to kill him to get to the imprisoned Tom Robinson to the many racist insults Scout hears directed toward him behind his back, such as when Mrs. Dubose shouts at her, "Your father's no better than the niggers and trash he works for!" (106) The most extreme example of Atticus's victimization, though, is the vengeance enacted against him by Bob Ewell himself when he attempts to harm, perhaps even kill, the Finch children. And like Atticus, Tom Robinson is a man with a family who is victimized, in this case by Mayella Ewell, through the false accusation of rape and by the townspeople who wish to kill him for the accusation. The racist legal system traps him, and when he attempts physically to flee after being falsely found guilty of rape, he is shot dead. These victimized fathers, Atticus Finch and Tom Robinson, both must receive the town's unjustified anger; but while Atticus emerges unscathed, Tom Robinson dies. Whereas in *Watchman,* Jean Louise expresses her anger directly at her father, in *Mockingbird,* minor characters express anger at Atticus, but actual consequences of the anger are suffered only by Atticus's double,

Tom Robinson. Significantly, both fathers who act as doubles of Atticus in *Mockingbird*, Tom Robinson and Bob Ewell, come to violent deaths.

The character Boo Radley, too, allows *Mockingbird*'s Scout to avoid directly expressing the anger against her father by projecting it onto this outsider, who, as a young man, stabs his father in the leg with a pair of scissors (15) and is punished by being a virtual prisoner inside his family's home. Interestingly, Miss Maudie makes a metaphorical connection between Atticus and Boo Radley's father. Alluding to Mr. Radley, she says, "You are too young to understand it . . . but sometimes the Bible in the hand of one man is worse than a whiskey bottle in the hand of—oh, of your father" (49). She is here suggesting a reason for Boo's violent reaction to his father at the same time that, in suggesting a (non-existent) reason Scout might feel anger toward Atticus, she calls attention to the possibility of that feeling. At the end of the novel, it is Boo Radley who, in defense of the Finch children, stabs Bob Ewell, the most evil father in the novel, to death. Thus, while Scout romanticizes Atticus in *Mockingbird*, anger against the father still simmers but is projected onto minor characters.

Indeed, Lee's portrayal of Uncle Jack in both novels adds another layer to Scout's anger. When *Watchman*'s Uncle Jack smacks Jean Louise across the face, bloodying her, she reacts utterly without anger, instead accepting the wisdom and necessity of his violence. However, when Uncle Jack again violently punishes his niece in *Mockingbird* after she punches her cousin Francis in the face for calling her father a "nigger-lover" (88), it is an angry Scout who rebukes her uncle. She explains after the spanking that Uncle Jack did not give her a chance to tell her side, and when he hears what provoked her, he regrets his actions as is clear later when Scout overhears him telling Atticus, "'Oh dear, I'm so sorry I romped on her'" (91). While in *Watchman*, Jean Louise accepts her uncle's lesson and regrets her treatment of her father, in *Mockingbird*, Uncle Jack realizes he is the one who needs to learn the lesson. Scout is thus able to own and express her anger against this father double in *Mockingbird*, but again not directly against her father.

Critics, too, have noted a doubling between Mayella Ewell and Scout Finch in *Mockingbird*. Evans writes, "Both girls are motherless, and in each case the girl's father is the major influence in her life. Scout, though, is obviously an embodiment of youthful innocence, whereas Mayella (who in various ways seems a victim of her father) comes to seem a rather corrupt figure by the end of the book" (103). In *Watchman*, Jean

Louise angrily stands up to her racist father; in *Mockingbird,* this anger is projected onto Mayella Ewell, who lashes out incoherently in the courtroom at Atticus during his cross-examination of her: "'Your fancy airs don't come to nothin'—your ma'amin' and Miss Mayellaerin' don't come to nothin', Mr. Finch . . . ' Then she burst into real tears. Her shoulders shook with angry sobs" (190). Moreover, Mayella's fear of her father's wrath—she is so afraid of him that she defends him in court and helps carry out his scheme to blame Tom Robinson for his own actions—suggests another projection. In this case, Mayella's fear of retribution from her father speaks to Scout's fear of risking Atticus's disapproval. Indeed, Scout seems to identify with Mayella as she watches her in the court room:

> As Tom Robinson gave his testimony, it came to me that Mayella Ewell must have been the loneliest person in the world. . . . When Atticus asked had she any friends, she seemed not to know what he meant. . . . She was as sad, I thought, as what Jem called a mixed child: white people wouldn't have anything to do with her because she lived among pigs; Negroes wouldn't have anything to do with her because she was white. (194)

Mayella crosses a strict social boundary in attempting an illicit sexual relationship with Tom Robinson, and Scout sees Atticus come down hard on Mayella for this transgression in his summation: "She is the victim of cruel poverty and ignorance, but I cannot pity her: she is white. She knew full well the enormity of her offense but because her desires were stronger than the code she was breaking, she persisted in breaking it" (206). I have written before about Scout's projection of potential unaccepted desires onto Mayella Ewell given that Mayella desires an unacceptable sexual partner, a black man, Tom Robinson (70). Again, Gregory Jay writes, "Scout/Jean Louise sees in Mayella the mirror of her own codebreaking, and a vague but strong linkage along the axis of 'unspeakable' desires. Mayella desires freedom from patriarchal abuse and to be the active agent of her own sexual pleasure, which significantly targets a forbidden object" (515). Scout sees Atticus express his uncompromising disapproval for Mayella's boundary crossing and may unconsciously fear her father's response should she cross any future sexual boundaries herself. However, though this fear may lurk beneath the surface of the narrative, Lee transforms it through the romanticization of Atticus Finch.

Thus, in *Watchman*, a book not published until many years after Harper Lee's father's death, readers see the fantasy in which Jean Louise directly expresses her anger toward her father and has him lovingly accept it. In *Mockingbird*, the book Lee publishes while her father is still alive, she portrays only the indirect expression of anger against the father through the projection of these emotions onto minor characters—at the same time romanticizing Atticus himself. In *Mockingbird*, Atticus is the voice of the oppressed, marginalized, powerless, and the unconventional, whether he speaks for Walter Cunningham and his lower-class family who pay Atticus their legal fees in stovewood and hickory nuts or whatever else they have on hand (25) rather than money, or for Boo Radley, whom he admonishes his children to leave alone and respect and for whom he breaks the law rather than force through an upsetting public trial, or for the virulently racist morphine addict, Mrs. Henry Lafayette Dubose, whom he labels "the bravest person I ever knew" (116) for courageously beating her addiction before her death. Atticus, seeing Bob Ewell clearly from the beginning, nonetheless condones his breaking the hunting laws since that is the only way Ewell's children will be fed (35). And it is Atticus, of course, who defends the innocent black man, Tom Robinson, from the false charges of rape by Mayella Ewell and her father, Bob Ewell. The racist Atticus of *Watchman* becomes not only the sentimentalized father but also the fearless foe of racists like Bob Ewell in *Mockingbird*.

Not only does Atticus stand up for the powerless who reside outside the Finch family, but he also stands up for Scout and shows her he accepts her just as she is, as unconventional as she is. At one point, Scout overhears him arguing with her Aunt Alexandra over her fondness for wearing overalls (85). When Scout discusses her aunt's disapproval of her to Atticus, she realizes—with typical understatement—"he didn't mind me much the way I was" (86). When at another point Atticus tries to lay down his sister's law to Scout and Jem about "how to behave like the little lady and gentleman that you are" (136), his curt tone makes Scout burst into tears. After burying her head in his vest and asking him if he really wants them to behave that way, he tells her not to worry and to "Forget it" (136). In other words, he tries unsuccessfully to uphold the line of tradition and convention but in the end realizes—and makes Scout realize—that his allegiance is to her, not to her aunt's weathered notions of gendered tradition. Finally, his advice to Scout about having courage when the world is against you is incentive for Scout to find her way in her future years no matter what the odds against her are: "I wanted you to see what real courage is instead of getting the idea that courage is a man with a gun in his hand. It's when you know you're licked before you begin but you begin anyway and you see it through no matter what. You rarely win, but sometimes you do" (116).

Atticus as ally to the marginalized rather than as the open racist he is in *Watchman* provides the support Scout needs to dare to be who she is, even if she is different. Indeed, over the last decade, critics have begun to examine the ways in which Scout grapples with her understanding of otherness, the ways in which she identifies with non-normative characters. Gregory Jay, for example, writes, "The other story is Scout's bildungsroman, including her rebellion against society's norms for gendered behavior, and particularly her groping for ways to connect her experiences of queer folks in town, including the strangely secluded Boo Radley" (508). Another critic, Kristen Proehl, in her study of what she calls "tomboys and sissies" in *The Member of the Wedding* and *Mockingbird*, writes:

> As non-gender-normative children, they are neither entirely of nor excluded from mainstream society, because childhood is a period in which gender subversion is permissible. Through their sympathetic relationships, tomboy and sissy figures present a subversive, hopeful model of social change, as they suggest the potential for marginalized figures to forge alliances with one another and across differences in race, gender, class, and sexuality. (131)

Not only the tomboyish Scout, but many other characters in *Mockingbird* perform non-normative gender roles, from Boo Radley and Dill to the "chameleon lady" Miss Maudie to even Atticus himself, who for half the book does not seem like a real man to his children given that he is more prone to read books than play ball or shoot a gun. Atticus accepts Scout no matter how far she strays from conventional gender roles and accepts the utter outsider, Boo Radley, as well. Richards writes that Atticus, "via privilege conferred upon him by masculine spheres, works publicly for social equality and tolerance. His defense of Tom Robinson is the most significant of these efforts, but Atticus also proves himself equally determined to accord Arthur Radley some degree of communal respect" (135).

Moreover, critics have posited that Lee hints at non-normative sexuality in Boo Radley. Richards, for example, suggests that through her portrayal of the reclusive Boo Radley, Lee

> presents a scenario that obliquely—if not always coherently—parallels ones crucially informed by sexual otherness. That is, because Lee surrounds Boo with so many of the silences and absences that structure the frequent closetedness of same-sex desire, she invites readers to speculate that Boo's reclusiveness is comparable to closeted sexuality and thus explore what bearing this literal representation of closetedness might have on an understanding of the figurative. (146)

That Scout feels connected to Boo, and that she sees her father protect and defend him, even in his otherness, speaks to the real possibility that she will feel her father respect her own potential sexual otherness. To be sure, *Mockingbird* focuses on a pre-adolescent Scout whose future sexual identity remains unclear. It is noteworthy, though, that the adult narrator, Jean Louise, never mentions having married a man or being in a relationship with a man, though Lee could easily have added a line about her protagonist's current husband. Instead, by not mentioning whom, if anyone, Jean Louise ends up being in a relationship with, Lee leaves the possibility of Scout's future unconventional sexuality open.

Thus, Lee revises rather than upends her portrayal of Atticus. The direct anger expressed against the father in *Watchman* is muted through projection in *Mockingbird*, at the same time that the romanticization of the father in *Mockingbird* allows Lee to imagine a more liberated future for Scout. With her father's acceptance of many varieties of difference, Scout is free (potentially) to explore unconventional gender and sexual identities. Like Boo Radley, who remains on the periphery of convention, like Dolphus Raymond, who pretends to be an alcoholic to be with a Black woman, and like the unconventional woman, Maudie May Atkinson, who remains happily single, Scout in *Mockingbird* can remain in a liminal space, exploring the periphery of gender conventions and sexual identities.

Works Cited

Corrigan, Maureen. Review. "Harper Lee's 'Watchman' Is A Mess That Makes Us Reconsider A Masterpiece." Fresh Air. NPR.org. https://www.npr.org/2015/07/13/422545987/harper-lees-watchman-is-a-mess-that-makes-us-reconsider-a-masterpiece. Accessed 7 June 2019.

Evans, Robert C. "Unlikely Duos: Paired Characters in *To Kill a Mockingbird*." *Harper Lee's To Kill a Mockingbird: New Essays*, edited by Michael Meyer, Scarecrow Press, 2010, pp. 101–11.

Fine, Laura. "Structuring the Narrator's Rebellion in *To Kill a Mockingbird*." *On Harper Lee: Essays and Reflections*, edited by Alice Hall Petry, University of Tennessee Press, 2007, pp. 61–77.

Lee, Harper. *Go Set a Watchman*. HarperCollins, 2015.

———. *To Kill a Mockingbird*. Popular Library, 1960.

Jay, Gregory. "Queer Children and Representative Men: Harper Lee, Racial Liberalism, and the Dilemma of *To Kill a Mockingbird*." *American Literary History*, vol. 27, no. 3, 2016, pp. 487–522.

Kakutani, Michiko. Review: "Harper Lee's 'Go Set a Watchman' Gives Atticus Finch a Dark Side." Books of the Times. *New York Times*. July 10, 2015. https://www.nytimes.com/2015/07/11/books/review-harper-lees-go-set-a-watchman-gives-atticus-finch-a-dark-side.html. Accessed 7 June 2019.

Proehl, Kristen B. "Sympathetic Alliances: Tomboys, Sissy Boys, and Queer Friendship in *The Member of the Wedding* and *To Kill a Mockingbird*." *ANQ: A Quarterly Journal of Short Articles, Notes, and Reviews*, vol. 26, no. 2, 2013, pp. 128–33.

Reeves, Jay. "Writings of Harper Lee's Dad Reveal Atticus Finch's Conflict." Associated Press, 19 Sept. 2015, https://apnews.com/7274ad0152e44ac5a37ac0e7e56551b9. Accessed 7 June 2019.

Richards, Gary. *Lovers and Beloveds: Sexual Otherness in Southern Fiction, 1936–1961*. LSU Press. 2005.

Shields, Charles J. *Mockingbird: A Portrait of Harper Lee*. Holt, 2006.

4

"YOUR FATHER'S PASSIN'"; OR, HOW TO LYNCH TOM ROBINSON AND STILL FEEL RIGHT

Leland S. Person

Each one of us needs to try to heed the advice of a great character
in American fiction, Atticus Finch. You never really understand
a person until you consider things from his point of view.
Until you climb into his skin and walk around in it.

—President Barack Obama, January 10, 2017

To Kill a Mockingbird belongs in the same category as *Uncle Tom's Cabin* and *Adventures of Huckleberry Finn*, two other novels that test white writers' ability to write about race. At the same time, it features some of the same blind spots and limitations of those other novels, including an inability to represent African American characters and their experience from anything other than a "white" point of view—a failure, ironically, to encourage readers to "climb into" and "walk around in" the skin of black characters. *Uncle Tom's Cabin* includes many examples of racial essentialism, in which slaves are infantilized and animalized. *Adventures of Huckleberry Finn*, despite critics' efforts to attribute authorial irony to just about every instance of racist language, does not take the fugitive slave, Jim Watson, seriously as an adult human being. An object and plaything for Tom Sawyer during the long, final episode on the Phelps farm, Jim does have one moment—easy to miss—where he expresses his feelings. I want to use words that Mark Twain gives Jim as a kind of chorus for testing Harper Lee's representation of race and racism in *To Kill a Mockingbird*. As Tom Sawyer torments Jim, he decides to introduce spiders and snakes and rats into the small cabin where Jim is being held prisoner. When Jim objects, Tom assures him that if he will play music for them, they will have a "noble good time." "Yes, they will, Mars Tom," Jim replies, "but what kine er time is *Jim* havin'?" (327) Despite the way that Mark Twain silences and marginalizes Jim during the last part of the novel, allowing Jim this one small protest opens a window for readers to view and review events from Jim's point of view. What "kine er time is *Jim* havin'?"—a question that can be useful in responding to other white-authored texts, such as *To Kill a Mockingbird*. To what extent do such novels invite us to consider black characters as subjects rather than as objects? Can reading against the grain—switching our point of view—help us "really understand" what "kine er time" black characters may be having in these novels?

I taught *To Kill a Mockingbird* and *Go Set a Watchman* shortly after the latter was published—in a freshman seminar on the topic "Huck Finn and His Tradition." We came to Lee's novels after reading *The Adventures of Tom Sawyer* and *Adventures of Huckleberry Finn*. All of the students had read *Mockingbird* in high or junior high school. None had read *Watchman,* but they knew enough about it to worry that it would ruin their view of the earlier novel and its hero, Atticus Finch. One student said she was afraid to read *Watchman* based on what she had heard about it. Almost all were afraid they would be shocked and disillusioned. They were. I found that curious, since I see many traces of *Watchman*'s Atticus in his earlier incarnation.

I want to begin with two scenes, one from each novel, that seem radically different from one another, despite their common setting. At a critical moment in *Watchman,* Jean Louise Finch sneaks into the "Colored balcony" of the Maycomb County courthouse to observe a meeting of the Maycomb County Citizens' Council, a group dedicated to resisting implementation of the 1954 Supreme Court ruling in *Brown v. Board of Education*. Interestingly, the Council includes "most of the trash" in Maycomb County but also the county's "most respectable men" (105)—an indication that race trumps class under the pressure of possible integration. Lee invokes this Supreme Court ruling in chapter 2, when Atticus asks Jean Louise "how much of what's going on down here gets into the newspapers." In her reply, Jean Louise also refers to bus strikes and "that Mississippi business'"—that is, Emmett Till's lynching. The "state's not getting a conviction in that case," she observes, "was our worst blunder since Pickett's Charge" (24). The *Brown* ruling, credited with launching the modern civil rights movement in the South, effectively overturned the Supreme Court's 1896 *Plessy v. Ferguson* decision that legitimated segregation and fostered the illusion of "separate-but-equal." The highlight of the Citizens' Council meeting: a speech by Grady O'Hanlon, who self-identifies as an "ordinary, God-fearing man," who has "quit his job to devote his full time to the preservation of segregation" (108). O'Hanlon's speech is comprised of vicious racist stereotypes, white paranoia, and hatred—standard-issue white supremacy. Lee excerpts the speech, providing only key words and phrases, but she certainly registers its full effect on Jean Louise, who feels "sick" and "numb" as she listens (111).

From this same Colored balcony, of course, Scout witnessed the Tom Robinson rape trial in *To Kill a Mockingbird*, and the courtroom's repurposing as the site of a white supremacist, anti-integrationist meeting may shock readers just as much as the presence and active participation of her father, Atticus Finch, and fiancé, Hank Clinton, shock Jean Louise. But it should not. Harper Lee did a lot to cover traces of the blatant racism Jean Louise witnesses in *Watchman* as she revised the novel into *Mockingbird*, but I do not think she was naïve enough not to recognize the continuity of values, social and political systems, and the possibility of racial justice in 1930s and 1950s Alabama.

By removing the setting of *Mockingbird* from the 1950s of *Watchman* to the 1930s, Lee accomplishes one of the Citizens' Councils' goals—turning back the clock on civil rights and integration. As an attorney, civic leader, and state representative, Atticus adapts his legal and social strategies to those different times. Eric Sundquist observes that *To Kill a Mockingbird* "harks back to the 1930s both to move the mounting fear and violence surrounding desegregation into an arena of safer contemplation" (127). Novelist Mark Childress agrees that this change of venue (in time rather than in space) "helped the white Southerner because there was distance between the South she was writing about and the present day when it was published. That allowed them to feel, 'Well, we've moved a little beyond that'" (79). This is not to say that 1930s Alabama was free of racial tension and violence. Citing W. J. Cash's *The Mind of the South*, Claudia Johnson notes that, after World War I "many southerners reacted violently to the multiple threats to order and meaning that they perceived, whether those threats were economic collapse, unionism, Communism, Rooseveltism, or a breakdown of the class and, especially, racial boundaries that defined their society. The vehemence with which these traditional boundaries were maintained is at the center of Lee's novel" (*To Kill a Mockingbird* 4). And Johnson, like several other scholars, asserts the likelihood that the

Scottsboro Boys rape trial of the 1930s provides many details for *To Kill a Mockingbird*. As she concludes, it is "reasonable to believe that the issues in *To Kill a Mockingbird* were shaped by the 1950s when it was written as well as the 1930s chosen for its setting" ("Secret Courts," 130). In a brilliant historical reading, Patrick Chura considers *To Kill a Mockingbird* a "cross-historical novel" (1), by which he means that Lee sublimates 1950s history in her 1930s situation. More specifically, the U.S. Supreme Court's *Brown v. Board of Education* decision (1954) and especially the Emmet Till murder trial (1955) are reflected in the race relations and especially the Tom Robinson rape trial in *Mockingbird*. Even though I think *Mockingbird* can still be read in such a way to reveal its limitations as a progressive race novel, *Watchman* certainly helps, like litmus paper, to highlight those limitations. My goal in this essay, following such scholars as Monroe Freedman, Malcolm Gladwell, and Steven Lubet, is to examine those places in *Mockingbird* where it seems important to look at things from another point of view—particularly the point of view of African American characters and, to the extent that this white scholar can do so, the point of view of African American readers.

What Kine Er Time is Tom Havin'?

> So much was running through my head at the moment
> I stood there, at the funeral home, with A. A. Rayner and Daddy
> and Gene and Rayfield all standing by as I gazed at the mutilated body
> that once had been my son. At that moment I didn't see what I possibly
> could gain from the worst experience anyone could ever have.
> All I felt was the vast emptiness left by what had been lost.
>
> —Mamie Till-Mobley, *Death of Innocence*

I want to begin with a remarkable scene in *To Kill a Mockingbird* as the Tom Robinson rape trial ends. Tom has just been convicted of capital rape. Atticus has snapped his briefcase shut, perhaps expressing his disgust with the verdict. He puts his hand on Tom's shoulder, whispers something to him, and then he leaves the courtroom by the exit that will enable him to take a short-cut home (241–42). "I looked around," Scout recalls. "They were standing. All around us and in the balcony on the opposite wall, the Negroes were getting to their feet. Then she hears Reverend Sykes's voice. 'Miss Jean Louise, stand up,' he says. 'Your father's passin' (242). Given that Atticus has just lost the case, this unanimous gesture of support and respect from the Colored balcony, which gathers Scout into its embrace, seems surprising. Largely a white liberal fantasy, this collective gesture of black respect validates the idea that almost any effort by white people in the direction of equal racial treatment is worth celebrating. In this scene, Harper Lee fulfills Harriet Beecher Stowe's injunction at the end of *Uncle Tom's Cabin*: "There is one thing that every individual can do,—they can see to it that *they feel right*" (404). Feelings speak louder than words or actions. Feeling that Atticus has done his best—that is enough.

The reverent gesture from the Colored balcony in *Mockingbird*, an exercise in hagiography, valorizes Atticus's heroic stature for black people and implicitly honors the role of Southern liberals in the civil rights movement. I think we need to read behind this famous scene—attempting to switch point of view—and ask a simple question about the likelihood that "all" the Negroes in 1930s Alabama would be standing to honor a white attorney who has just lost a trumped up rape case. The gesture is all the more extraordinary because in *Watchman* Lee imagined an acquittal in the case that is the obvious basis for this one. She does not represent the actual trial in that novel; she simply summarizes the circumstances: an "acquittal for a colored boy on a rape charge," in which the "chief witness for the prosecution was a white girl" (109). She does, however, provide interesting details about Atticus Finch, his motives and attitudes, as the defense attorney in that 1950s case. She notes, for example, that he "pursued the case to its conclusion with every spark of his ability and with an instinctive distaste so bitter only his knowledge that he could live peacefully with himself was able to wash it away" (109). Lest potential readers think that Atticus betrayed his race, she even notes that after the verdict he walks home and takes a "steaming bath" (110). Lee covers Atticus's apparent apostasy by having him feel sick at the not guilty verdict he has achieved.

In *Mockingbird* some white characters and readers get to "feel right," as Stowe suggested, because one exceptional white man was willing to defend Tom Robinson—even if he lost the case and thereby consigned Robinson to an almost certain death in prison. Many readers eagerly accept the notion that Atticus Finch is that one exceptional white man. Joseph Crespino observes, for example, that in the twentieth century "*To Kill a Mockingbird* is probably the most widely read book dealing with race in America, and its protagonist, Atticus Finch, the most enduring fictional image of racial heroism" (78). Scott Turow, who considers

Atticus a "paragon beyond paragons," represents an interesting case in point, epitomizing the tendency to give Atticus an "A" for effort. A lawyer as well as novelist, Turow admits being uniquely inspired by Atticus's example: "I promised myself that when I grew up and I was a man, I would try to do things as good and noble as what Atticus had done for Tom Robinson" (196–97). So, what are readers to feel? In *Watchman*, a not guilty verdict makes Atticus feel dirty, although we have to assume that black people feel "right." In *Mockingbird*, a guilty verdict apparently makes Atticus, white spectators, and even black onlookers feel grateful.

Why exactly would all the black spectators feel right when feeling right means tacitly accepting their powerlessness and exclusion from the social, political, and judicial systems that rule their lives? What exactly is there to feel right about? Tom Robinson receives a guilty verdict from the officially impaneled jury on the first floor of the courtroom. Atticus appears to receive a not guilty verdict from the unofficial jury in the Colored balcony. While the guilty verdict has plenty of precedents in Southern society, does the unanimous respect for the white attorney? Surely not. And even if every member of this second-story "jury" agrees, do they still feel that way after Tom Robinson is assassinated in prison? Furthermore, what "kine er time" is Tom having as he hears the verdict and watches Atticus leave for home?

Harper Lee seems determined, however, to demonstrate that black people can be convinced that even the semblance of effort by a white attorney can compensate for an unjust verdict. In the face of Atticus's fatalistic explanation of the guilty verdict—"They've done it before" and "they'll do it again"—he returns home the following day to find the kitchen table loaded with food—gifts from the African American community. He finds salt pork, tomatoes, and beans, some scuppernong grapes, and even a chicken from Tom Robinson's father that Calpurnia has already fixed for supper (244). As she explains, "They—they 'preciate what you did, Mr. Finch." Calpurnia even worries that "they" might be "oversteppin' themselves," but Atticus assures her that he is thankful, even as he wants her to pass along the message that "they must never do this again" (244). Lee confuses things by making the gifts of food a potential issue—a violation of strict race relations and the color line—and thereby distracting readers from the question of why the black community feels so much appreciation. Consider the implications: the color line in Maycomb County is so rigid that black citizens must be careful about showing appreciation to a white lawyer who has just lost a case. But in this scene, too, everyone supposedly feels right even as the status quo remains unchanged and unchallenged.

So, what really is there to celebrate? Well, Miss Maudie explains to Jem that Atticus "won't win, he can't win, but he's the only man in these parts who can keep a jury out so long in a case like that." And for her that they are "making a step—it's just a baby-step, but it's a step" (247). Consider the implications. A racist justice system is so powerful that holding a stopwatch on a jury that everyone knows will return a guilty verdict has the potential to signify progress. At this rate, of course, it will take one hundred years to make real progress. But, in fact, progress will come sooner when black people themselves take control of the civil rights movement and insist on change through boycotts, marches, and other forms of active protest. Furthermore, if you are Tom Robinson and his family, does it really matter how long it takes the jury to find you guilty? What kine er time is Tom havin'? How many of Maycomb's black citizens consider this delay a "baby-step"? And how many of them appreciate white citizens congratulating themselves on such miniscule progress?

As Atticus himself explains, "In our courts, when it's a white man's word against a black man's, the white man always wins. They're ugly, but those are the facts of life" (252). The facts of life also mean that Tom's days are numbered. One way or another, he will die in prison. He dies allegedly trying to escape—shot seventeen times trying to jump over a fence, according to the official story (269). Atticus complains to Calpurnia that they "didn't have to shoot him that much" (270), but is that the real issue? Excessive though the number may be, Atticus's complaint represents another red herring that distracts us from seeing Tom's death as a lynching. They didn't have to shoot him at all. Even Atticus's explanation rings hollow and presumptuous: "'I guess Tom was tired of white men's chances and preferred to take his own'" (270). Keep in mind that Atticus is relaying this story to Calpurnia as well as to his sister Alexandra and to Scout. And immediately after he says that they didn't have to shoot Tom seventeen times, he says, "Cal, I want you to come out with me and help me tell Helen." And just as he finishes explaining why Tom decided to take his own chances, he says, "Ready, Cal?" (270). Calpurnia's feelings about Tom's death do not seem to matter in this scene. Never mind that when Atticus first explains his decision to represent Tom to Scout, he uses Calpurnia as a reference. He notes that Tom belongs to Calpurnia's church and assures Scout that Calpurnia "knows his family well" and says "they're clean-living folks" (86). After noting Atticus's condescension, we should note the emotional connection Calpurnia feels for the Robinson family—a connection that Atticus shows no signs of remembering.

Atticus needs Calpurnia to provide cover when he notifies Helen Robinson of Tom's death at the hands of the legal lynching party to which he and his ineffectual defense consigned her husband. He does not ask Calpurnia to help him. He does not acknowledge her relationship to the Robinson family. He simply tells her that he needs her to do this, and he obviously does not expect "no" for an answer when he asks if she is ready. But that is not the only way Atticus ignores Calpurnia or fails, arguably, to see things from her point of view. As Fred Erisman notes, "in the most telling commentary of all upon the pervasive pressures of the caste system, when Calpurnia accompanies Atticus Finch to convey the news of Tom Robinson's death, she must ride in the back seat of the automobile" (39). Atticus needs her to help him, but he will not give her an equal place as his deputy. And what does Calpurnia think and feel about being put in her place—aiding and abetting this white lawyer who has effectively failed Tom Robinson and then being relegated to the back seat? Furthermore, what do Helen and the other members of Tom Robinson's family think and feel when they see Atticus pull up to their house with Calpurnia in the back seat—a crystal-clear sign that, whatever he may have done for Tom, he still accepts and follows Jim Crow principles. The challenge for readers, especially white readers: trying to imagine how Calpurnia and all the black people gathered to support the Robinson family may feel as they see Atticus arrive. All of them—but especially Helen—are in roughly the same position as feeling subjects as Mamie Till-Mobley, all "standing by" as she encounters the reality of her husband's murder. Furthermore, Lee does not follow this moment to its logical conclusion, especially if the Emmitt Till lynching lurks in the background of her imagination. Does Tom Robinson's body return to Maycomb? Do Helen Robinson and her family have to see what his body looks like after being shot seventeen times? Is there an open casket? Does Atticus have to confront the bodily reality of Tom's death by prison guard? Does he have to deal with the "kine er time" Tom Robinson's family and friends are havin'? Harper Lee does not write the scene of Tom's return to Maycomb or even note its occurrence. She leaves Tom, his family and friends—and of course the readers—in limbo. Can we imagine? What do we feel—"the vast emptiness left by what had been lost," as Mamie Till-Mobley said?

Although Scott Turow asserts that Atticus is "of course, the only lawyer in town who will defend this black man accused of this supposedly horrible crime" (196), Atticus does not volunteer. Judge Taylor assigns the case to him. And Atticus admits he is a reluctant warrior, who had "hoped to get through life without a case of this kind" (100). Moreover, he knows, or predicts, he will lose. When Scout asks him if he's going to win, he replies, "No, honey" (86). When she wonders why he would take the case at all, he explains: "Simply because we were licked a hundred years before we started is no reason for us not to try to win" (87). There is, to be sure, something honorable about Atticus's willingness to take the case—honorable if only because we can imagine so many other attorneys refusing. The bar for honorability is not high. Notice the implications—the reassuring appeal to historical and cultural precedent and continuity. Southern traditions can easily accommodate Tom Robinson's case and Atticus's defense. Even if we consider Atticus a gradualist rather than a bitter-ender, it is hard to see him in *Mockingbird* supporting anything better than a gradualism that proceeds at a glacial pace—in one-hundred-year increments. The segregated structure of Maycomb's social, economic, and political life will remain unchanged. "Remember this," he instructs Scout, "no matter how bitter things get, they're still our friends and this is still our home" (87). As Malcolm Gladwell puts it, Atticus's "hearts-and-mind approach is about accommodation, not reform" (59). Any issue surrounding his taking the case, in other words, is rendered moot. Atticus will conduct the trial in a way that will leave him still friends with all the people who, temporarily, are accusing him of defending a black man—that is, still friends with all of Maycomb's white folks. That reassurance effectively defuses any ugliness in advance, folding it into the process. The accusatory chorus that Atticus is a "nigger-lover" is part of the ritual. The townspeople get to accuse Atticus of racial apostasy, reminding him that defending Tom Robinson threatens his place in a white hierarchy. Atticus gets to do his duty in a *pro forma* way that preserves that place. As he says, explaining to Scout that the term "nigger-lover" "don't mean anything," he loves everybody (124). The goal—the alternative to the lynching proposed by the white mob—is a civilized, legal process whose outcome will have the same result. There is more than one way to skin a cat, or shoot a dog, or lynch a black man.

Although B. B. Underwood, editor of *The Maycomb Tribune*, likens Tom's death to the "senseless slaughter of songbirds," this, too, becomes part of a traditional process that the status quo can accommodate. Mr. Underwood could "write whatever he wanted," the older Scout realizes, "he'd still get his advertising and subscriptions" (276). As she concludes,

Atticus had "used every tool available to free men to save Tom Robinson, but in the secret courts of men's hearts Atticus had no case. Tom was a dead man the minute Mayella Ewell opened her mouth and screamed" (276). Racism and racial injustice trump any and every mitigating circumstance or other evidence. Nothing Atticus does or could do would have changed the outcome—a point he understood the whole time.

A trial whose guilty verdict is known ahead of time and a lynching do not seem that different, especially among friends, especially among black people. Under these circumstances, why exactly would Maycomb's black citizens be so grateful to Atticus? Perhaps because they recognize that, under this oppressive social and political system, any semblance of progress—any "baby-step"—can be credited to Atticus Finch. Except that Harper Lee invites us to take a close look at Atticus's motives. "You know what's going to happen as well as I do," Atticus tells his brother, Jack; that is, they both know what the outcome of the trial will be. What concerns him is what effect the inevitable guilty verdict will have on his children. "I hope and pray," he tells Jack, "I can get Jem and Scout through it without bitterness" (100). With his sense of fatalism, Atticus seems focused on the idea of doing his personal and family duty—doing it for his children. Whatever his sense of responsibility toward Tom Robinson—and he knows the verdict ahead of time—he wants to conduct the trial in a way that will protect his children from feeling any bitterness, ensuring that instead they will "feel right." It is their feelings, above others', that matter most. In identifying the affective power of the narrative and its events with Scout and Jem, Lee invites us of course to read and understand from their point of view. In large measure, events—and especially those that Atticus controls or affects—are enacted for their benefit. What kine er time, in other words, are Jem and Scout havin'. Tom Robinson and any bitterness he and his family might feel do not appear to be part of the equation.

Class differences, furthermore, coordinate in carefully orchestrated terms that help keep Atticus and the other townspeople friends. Atticus wants Scout and Jem to understand, for example, that the racist Mrs. Dubose was a "great lady," who simply "had her own views about things" (128). Racism is just part of who she is—a "view" that does not jeopardize her greatness as a Southern lady. Even Mr. Cunningham, a class above the Ewells, gets a "pass" from Atticus. He tells Scout and Jem that Cunningham, one of the lynch mob's leaders, is "basically a good man" who "just has his blind spots along with the rest of us" (180)—a blind spot, as Monroe Freedman points out, that just happens to be a "homicidal hatred of black people" (70). Lee seems to distinguish between lynching and the legal process based on class differences, but it is a false distinction. Lynching is the province of the lower-class, Old Sarum crowd that includes Mr. Cunningham. The court room is the province of the middle-class townspeople—even though they decline to serve on the jury out of fear that their service will hurt their business and social interests. They enlist lower-class whites in their civilized process—including some members of the lynch mob—thereby deploying economic and social jealousies to drive a wedge between the races. Having Atticus and the children prevent the lynching, then, only seems to represent a step toward civility. Maycomb does not lynch black men accused of raping white women; white folks grant them trials in which a guilty verdict is foreordained and then give them the death penalty.

To Kill a Mockingbird may have sponsored more scholarship from members of the legal community than from literary scholars, and much of the conversation focuses on the tension between legal and moral responsibilities. I do not have space—or the legal expertise—to participate in that ongoing conversation, but I still want to examine Atticus's defense and to speculate on how it registers with readers. I do not think it takes an expert lawyer, for example, to recognize the weaknesses in Atticus's defense of Tom Robinson. Lee has stacked the deck in Atticus's favor by giving Tom a useless left arm that, apparently, no one else knows about. That arm is an ace-in-the hole that, when played, should blow the testimony of Bob Ewell and his daughter, Mayella, out of the water. But it does not. Shouldn't Atticus ask the Ewells to demonstrate how Tom was beating and choking Mayella? Absent the knowledge of Tom's left arm (a weird mystery indeed, given the number of times Mayella has had him do small jobs on their property), both would almost certainly have shown him using both hands to beat and choke her. Instead, using a convoluted argument that requires the jurors to do a lot of mental work, Atticus shifts his line of attack to Bob Ewell, asking him to write his name, which he does with his left hand. Under the circumstances, this effort to shift blame from the black defendant to the white trash accuser makes little sense. It complicates things for the jurors, who must make the connection between Ewell's writing hand and Tom's alleged assault and then decide if Tom could have bruised the right side of Mayella's face with his right arm. In addition, Atticus has to know—in fact, has already said so—that the jury will believe the testimony of the Ewells simply because racial solidarity will trump class disparities. And why does Atticus allow Mayella to have the last word during his cross-examination? Does he recognize that no one believes her anyway, so that aggressively cross-examining her would be perceived as badgering and insulting (as she suggests) and would, if anything, enlist sympathy for her? Or does even a white trash lady deserve this deference in a capital case? Either way, racial solidarity prevails.

In his closing statement, Atticus seems to help the jury by pointing out that the prosecution's witnesses have confidence that they would "go along with them on the assumption—the evil assumption—that *all* Negroes lie, that *all* Negroes are basically immoral beings, that *all* Negro men are not to be trusted around our women" (233). In the hearing, surely the qualifier, "evil assumption," gets drowned out by the series of assertions that the gentlemen of the jury already share. Even when Atticus goes on to qualify these assertions by calling them lies "as black as Tom Robinson's skin"—a trope that unnecessarily reminds them of Robinson's race—he reinforces these claims all over again. The truth, he concludes, is that "some Negroes lie, some Negroes are immoral, some Negro men are not to be trusted around women—black or white" (233). Marginal comment to Atticus: It might be more effective if you changed these negative assertions to positive ones—that is, "many Negroes don't lie, many Negro men can be trusted around women; and, furthermore, Tom Robinson is one of those men." At best, Atticus talks out of both sides of his mouth, articulating and reinforcing stereotypes even as he seems to be denying them. If you are a gentleman of the jury, what do you take away? Atticus, after all, says nothing to place the "black" Tom Robinson outside this spectrum of "black" liars and rapists—nothing to remove him from the categories of "all" or "some." As Eric Sundquist puts it, "Tom Robinson's disabled arm is his legal alibi, but it is also the author's alibi—in the one case useless but in the other, for that very reason, perfect. Atticus must not only speak for him but also appropriate into his own ethical heroism Tom's masculinity and dignity as a black man, his very identity, much as the book itself appropriates Tom's African American world to the ethical heroism of its white liberal argument" (134). Sundquist covers a lot of ground in this comment, but I think he reinforces the idea that Atticus's defense of Tom Robinson is designed to encourage readers—black and white—to see him as a progressive hero.

Atticus also must know, despite the claim that they have a good chance on appeal, that the chances are good Tom Robinson will not survive in prison. Even though in *Watchman* she had reported an acquittal, Lee needs a guilty verdict and, arguably, Tom Robinson's death just as surely as Stowe needed Uncle Tom to be beaten to death by Simon Legree. She is not going to prolong the novel by describing an appeals process whose result is predictable. *To Kill a Mockingbird* is less about Tom Robinson than about the town and its middle-class citizens. Ironically, Tom Robinson's death enables the town to return to the status quo. Robinson's death, reported but not witnessed, serves more to close his "case" than to keep it before the reader's eyes. To help that process, Lee takes lynching off the table—or at least seems to. But in truth, the convicted Tom is still effectively lynched—shot seventeen times by the prison guards who allegedly watch this one-armed man try to leap over the prison walls. As Monroe Freedman complains, "He is shot to death—with seventeen bullets—on the claim that a gentle man with a useless arm, in a prison yard the size of a football field, in plain view of guards with guns, broke into a blind, raving charge in a hopeless attempt to climb over the fence and escape." "You can believe this improbable story, as Finch purports to do," Freedman continues. "But I believe (and Harper Lee appears to believe) that Tom Robinson was goaded into a desperate, futile run for the fence on the threat of being shot where he stood" (72). Whether shot or subjected to the torture of Alabama's convict leasing program, Tom Robinson is a dead man as soon as he is convicted. Scout recognizes this after reading Mr. Underwood's post-trial editorial. Atticus and the reader should know this, too.

And Atticus's role in this process? Not only does he not prevent Robinson's eventual lynching in prison custody, but also his feeble defense of Robinson aids and abets that lynching. Whether by intention or effect, Lee stages a lynching designed to "pass" Northern judgment—to demonstrate that the South has some good men who will come to the defense of falsely accused black male rapists, even if they will ultimately prove ineffectual in preventing the traditional outcome. Atticus Finch is the perfect man for the job. The final outcome of trial, conviction, imprisonment, and death assures Southerners that nothing has changed in one hundred years— that systemic racism still works. When Scout overhears her teacher, Mrs. Evans, say after Tom Robinson's conviction that "it's time somebody taught 'em a lesson," because they were getting "way above themselves, an' the next thing they think they can marry us" (284), she makes it clear that Atticus has been working to preserve the racial and social order.

Did You Hate Us? Anger and Violence

I want to conclude by returning to *Go Set a Watchman* and to a wonderful scene—worth the price of the book—between Scout and Calpurnia. The circumstances? Calpurnia's grandson Frank ("Zeebo's boy") has run over and killed an old drunken white man named Healy. Lee sets up this incident a little earlier in the novel when Jean Louise and Hank are driving back to Maycomb after their near-naked swimming adventure. "Something that looked like a giant black bee whooshed by them and careened around the curve ahead." "What was that?" Scout asks. "Carload of Negroes," Hank explains. "That's the way they assert themselves these days. . . . They're a public menace" (80). Within this context, Frank's accident is likely to be viewed as an example of carelessness, even aggression—a case of asserting himself and his rights. After all, the perception is that driving around at excessive speeds is the way "they" assert themselves these days. Atticus has agreed to defend Frank—but volunteered so that the case does not "fall into the wrong hands" (148), by which he means the hands of an NAACP lawyer who will demand that the case be tried in federal court and will even demand that the jury include Negroes (149). That is, Atticus wants to ensure that this trial will remain under local control and that the jury will include only white people. Lee does not stage this trial in *Watchman*, but she effectively gives Atticus the trial and jury he wants as she transforms *Go Set a Watchman* into *To Kill a Mockingbird*.

Scout's response to the news of Frank's arrest and Atticus's determination to represent him is to drive out to Calpurnia's house. (This scene has its parallel in *To Kill a Mockingbird* when Atticus and Calpurnia drive out to the Robinson place with news of Tom's death.) When Scout arrives, she discovers "Negroes in various states of public attire" standing on Calpurnia's porch (156). "When they saw her," Lee notes, "they stood straight and retreated from the edge of the porch, becoming as one" (156). This is not a welcoming committee but a united front of black people who have every reason to be angry at white folks. "Jean Louise was acutely conscious that the Negroes were watching her" (156), but the tense situation relaxes when Zeebo, Frank's father, steps forward after Jean Louise greets him by name. When she asks if she may go in, the "black people parted for her to enter the front door" (156). Lee obviously uses Jean Louise as the focal character in this scene; but if we reverse our point of view, it does not take much imagination to recognize what white privilege Jean Louise enjoys—how much the white power structure controls protocol and behavior. Jean Louise can do what none of the black people can do—show up unannounced and, while polite, assume that she can enter this house through the front door. Surely every character on that porch—except for Jean Louise—understands this Jim Crow protocol.

As she makes her way through the house, with its "musky sweet smell of clean Negro, snuff, and Hearts of Love hairdressing" (156), to the back room where Calpurnia awaits, she enters a space with monumental symbolic value as an inner sanctum where she may learn the truth of race and race relations. When she assures Calpurnia that Atticus will "do his best" in defending Frank, Calpurnia replies, "I know he will, Miss Scout. He always do his best. He always do right." Scout immediately recognizes that Calpurnia "was sitting in a haughty dignity that appeared on state occasions, and with it appeared erratic grammar" (159). Calpurnia is code switching or "puttin' on ole missus"—sitting and speaking behind what W. E. B. DuBois famously called "the veil."

"[W]hat are you doing to me?" Scout asks incredulously, when Calpurnia seems to shut her out with her "company manners" (159). "What are you all doing to us?" Calpurnia responds, in a statement that echoes Jim's question in *Adventures of Huckleberry Finn*: "What kine er time is Jim havin'?" Harper Lee, like Mark Twain, invites characters and readers alike to switch their identifications and try to see things from a "black" point of view. Calpurnia recognizes what Jean Louise does not—that the white racism that shocked Scout in the court house has widened the divide between races, but the color line has always been there. In the climax of this tense encounter, Jean Louis wants the answer to one question: "Did you hate us?" After some hesitation, Calpurnia shakes her head—presumably side-to-side to signal "no." But we should be careful here—and more careful than Scout chooses to be. Calpurnia's hesitation surely speaks as loudly as her head shake, and the head shake is no substitute for the word "no" that she does not utter. We ought to know signifyin' when we see it—or at least the potential of signifyin'. Hasn't Scout read *Souls of Black Folk*? Hasn't she heard of "double consciousness" and its corollary, signifyin'? Who knows what truth lurks behind Calpurnia's gesture, which might simply hide her longstanding contempt for Scout and her family? Scout does not seem to question this gesture. "She loved us, I swear she loved us. She sat there in front of me and she didn't see me, she saw white folks" (161). A non sequitur. Scout swears that Calpurnia loved them but recognizes that now they are just "white folks." She doesn't make the connection. She does not really—seriously—entertain the real possibility they have always been just "white folks." I think we should. Even though this scene seems to set up a privileged view from inside the segregated Negro world, it does not. Scout would not be trusted. The bitter truth may well be that some Negroes hate some white people—that maybe even Calpurnia hated the white family at whose beck and call she worked for years.

Moreover, when Calpurnia seems to agree with Jean Louise that Atticus will do his best in defending Zeebo, do we, as readers, believe that she does not recognize his motives for taking the case? All readers of *Go Set a Watchman* know this because Atticus has said so, but do we attribute this knowledge to characters in the novel—especially the black characters? Not to do so suggests that we think they are stupid and do not understand the dynamics of Jim Crow racism and the divided society it sponsors. Furthermore, what does this assembly of black folks—comparable to the group that gathers in the Colored balcony in *Mockingbird*, think of Atticus? After all, however dedicated he may be to "winning" the case, he wants to make sure that it will not affect the racist status quo in Maycomb. Surely Calpurnia and the other black people who make way for Jean Louise know this, even if Jean Louise herself seems much more focused on verifying the personal relationship between Calpurnia and her family.

When Harper Lee addresses the question of double-speak, or signifyin', in *Mockingbird*, she has Calpurnia explain to Scout and Jem why she speaks differently in different settings and to different audiences. After visiting Calpurnia's church, Scout wants to know, "why do you talk nigger-talk to the—to your folks when you know it's not right?" This is the adult Scout ventriloquizing her younger self. "That Calpurnia lead [*sic*] a modest double life never dawned on me," Scout admits. "The idea that she had a separate existence outside our household was a novel one, to say nothing of her having command of two languages" (143). This is the adult Scout speaking—the Scout who has read *Souls of Black Folk* and understands the concept of double-speak and "signifyin'." Calpurnia's answer is spot-on: "Well, in the first place I'm black" (143). She goes on to explain that her two languages are a function of segregation and the rules and prohibitions on what black people can say in the presence of different racial groups. White people get to speak one language. Black people must have two in order to get along.

Isaac Saney criticizes *To Kill a Mockingbird* because the "novel and its supporters deny that Black people have been the central actors in their movement for liberation and justice, from widespread African resistance to, and revolts against, slavery and colonialism to the twentieth century's mass movements challenging segregation, discrimination and imperialism" (51). At the wildly uncomfortable coffee that Aunt Alexandra puts on for Scout in *Go Set a Watchman*—in the chapter that immediately follows her visit to Calpurnia—one woman says that "You never can tell what goes on in their heads." In fact, her husband Bill "says he wouldn't be surprised if there was another Nat Turner Uprisin', we're sitting on a keg of dynamite and we just might as well be ready" (173). Reading *Watchman* demonstrates that Lee decided to minimize Black anger when she wrote *Mockingbird*. This invocation of an 1831 slave rebellion to describe the relations between white and black people in the mid-1950s offers a provocative context for understanding Calpurnia's shake of the head. "What are you all doing to us?" she had asked. If we can read backwards from this moment to the setting of *Mockingbird*, we might speculate that Atticus Finch is not the only one who's "passin'" in that earlier novel. You never can tell what goes on in their heads. Perhaps Calpurnia has been "passin'" as a devoted and loving housekeeper. Maybe we're not all friends here.

Oprah Winfrey has awarded *To Kill a Mockingbird* the title of our "national novel." As I noted at the beginning, in the sub-genre of white-authored race novels Lee's two novels deserve to be considered alongside those by Harriet Beecher Stowe, Mark Twain, William Faulkner, and others. Author James McBride (*The Color of Water, The Good Lord Bird*) considers Harper Lee "a great writer" (133) and *To Kill a Mocki*ngbird a "great American work" (135). But he also faults Lee for not interesting herself more in Tom Robinson's story. "She wrote about what she knew, but that doesn't absolve her of responsibility of handling the character of Tom better" (133). As for Atticus Finch, McBride says that he "comes off as a liberal who is trying to do the right thing." "I've had my fill of liberals," he concludes, "who are trying to do the right thing" (138). One test of a great white-authored novel about race in America can fairly be reduced to the question Jim asks in *Adventures of Huckleberry Finn*, "What kine er time is Jim havin'?" Lee offers a variation on this question when Atticus tells Scout, "You never really understand a person until you consider things from his point of view—until you climb into his skin and walk around in it" (33). Scout recalls this advice at the end of the novel (322), emphasizing its function as a governing principle. In his farewell address, President Barack Obama also quoted Atticus: "if our democracy is to work the way it should in this increasingly diverse nation, then each one of us need to try to heed the advice of a great character in American fiction, Atticus Finch, who said 'You never really understand a person until you consider things from his point of view, until you climb into his skin and walk around in it.'" President Obama went on to specify what it means to switch point of view and walk around in someone else's skin. "For blacks and other minority groups," he said, "that means tying our own very real struggles for justice to the challenges that a lot of people in this country face. Not only the refugee or the immigrant or the rural poor or the transgender American, but also the middle-aged white guy who from the outside may seem like he's got all the advantages, but has seen his world upended by economic, and cultural, and technological change." Applied to *Mockingbird*, that would mean building bridges between black people and the poor whites (the Cunninghams and Ewells) that Jim Crow principles and practices drive wedges between by privileging racial solidarity over class differences. And for "white Americans," President Obama continued, "it means acknowledging that the effects of slavery and Jim Crow didn't suddenly vanish in the '60s; that when minority groups voice discontent, they're not just engaging in reverse racism or practicing political correctness; when they wage peaceful protest, they're not demanding special treatment, but the equal treatment that our founders promised." President Obama's sense of what it means for black and white people to switch points of view and walk around in each other's skin has the potential to resonate backwards in time to readers of *To Kill a Mockingbird* and *Go Set a Watchman*. For, as much as the temptation arises, as it did for the president, to see the 1930s Atticus Finch as a "white savior" and to boggle at the racist segregationist he became in the 1950s, it is important to remember that he started his fictional life as that racist segregationist and "evolved" backward in time into the figure to whom so much praise is given. As I hope I have demonstrated, however, I think the 1930s Atticus retains many of the attitudes of his 1950s "father." However satisfying it is to consider Atticus an exceptional white man, looking at things from a black point of view—insofar as this white scholar can do so—reveals a character whose attitudes and actions tacitly support the racist, segregationist status quo of the post-Reconstruction, Jim Crow South. *To Kill a Mockingbird* may be our "national novel," but its claim to fame in my view resides, ironically, in the challenge it offers readers—especially white readers—to take Atticus's advice, as well as President Obama's, and reread the novel from an "other" point of view.

Works Cited

Childress, Mark. No title. *Scout, Atticus, & Boo: A Celebration of* To Kill a Mockingbird, edited by Mary McDonagh Murphy, Harper, 2010. pp. 77–84.

Chura, Patrick. "Prolepsis and Anachronism: Emmett Till and the Historicity of *To Kill a Mockingbird.*" *Southern Literary Journal*, vol. 32, no. 2, Spring 2000, pp. 1–26.

Clemens, Samuel. *Adventures of Huckleberry Finn.* Edited by Walter Blair and Victor Fischer. University of California Press, 1985.

Crespino, Joseph. "Representation of Race and Justice in *To Kill a Mockingbird.*" *Racism in Harper Lee's* To Kill a Mockingbird, edited by Candace Mancini, Greenhaven Press, 2008, pp. 77–88.

Du Bois, W. E. B. *Souls of Black Folk.* Edited by Henry Louis Gates, Jr., and Terri Hume Oliver. W. W. Norton, 1999.

Erisman, Fred. "Southern Values, Old and New." *Racism in Harper Lee's* To Kill a Mockingbird, edited by Candace Mancini, Greenhaven Press, 2008, pp. 36–45.

Freedman, Monroe. "Atticus Finch—Right and Wrong." *Racism in Harper Lee's* To Kill a Mockingbird, edited by Candace Mancini, Greenhaven Press, 2008, pp. 67-76.

Gladwell, Malcolm. "The Courthouse Ring: Atticus Finch and the Limits of Southern Liberalism." *Harper Lee's* To Kill a Mockingbird: *New Essays*, edited by Michael J. Meyer, Scarecrow Press, 2010, pp. 57-65.

Johnson, Claudia Durst. "The Secret Courts of Men's Hearts: Code and Law in Harper Lee's *To Kill a Mockingbird.*" *Studies in American Fiction*, vol. 19, no. 2, 1991, pp. 129–39.

———. To Kill a Mockingbird: *Threatening Boundaries.* Twayne, 1994.

Lee, Harper. *Go Set a Watchman.* HarperCollins, 2015.

———. *To Kill a Mockingbird.* 1960. HarperCollins, 2010.

Lubet, Steven. "Reconstructing Atticus Finch." *Michigan Law Review*, vol. 97, no. 6, May 1999, 1339-62.

McBride, James. No title. *Scout, Atticus, & Boo: A Celebration of* To Kill a Mockingbird, edited by Mary McDonagh Murphy, Harper, 2010, pp. 131–39.

Obama, Barack. "President Obama's Farewell Address: Full Video and Text." *New York Times.* January 10, 2017. https://www.nytimes.com/2017/01/10/us/politics/obama-farewell-address-speech.html?_r=0. Accessed 20 May 2019.

Saney, Isaac. "The Case Against *To Kill a Mockingbird.*" *Racism in Harper Lee's* To Kill a Mockingbird, edited by Candace Mancini, Greenhaven Press, 2008, pp. 46–54.

Stowe, Harriet Beecher. *Uncle Tom's Cabin.* Edited by Elizabeth Ammons. W.W. Norton, 2010.

Sundquist, Eric J. "*To Kill a Mockingbird*: A Paradox." *Racism in Harper Lee's* To Kill a Mockingbird, edited by Candace Mancini, Greenhaven Press, 2008, pp. 123-36.

Till-Mobley, Mamie, and Christopher Benson. *Death of Innocence: The Story of the Hate Crime That Changed America.* 2003. Ballantine, 2005.

Turow, Scott. No title. *Scout, Atticus, & Boo: A Celebration of* To Kill a Mockingbird, edited by Mary McDonagh Murphy, Harper, 2010, pp. 195-198.

Winfrey, Oprah. No title. *Scout, Atticus, & Boo: A Celebration of* To Kill a Mockingbird, edited by Mary McDonagh Murphy, Harper, 2010, pp. 200-204.

5

ATTICUS FINCH
A Civilized Huck Finn
Patricia F. D'Ascoli

Our experience of reading Harper Lee's novel *To Kill a Mockingbird* has been forever altered with the publication of *Go Set a Watchman*. *Watchman*, which seems to defy literary labeling, was written before—but published many years after—*Mockingbird*. It is therefore neither a prequel nor a sequel. The novel is best regarded, perhaps, as an early draft of *Mockingbird*, from which the "best" (at least as determined by Lee's editor) was preserved for inclusion in the novel that would ultimately go on to win the Pulitzer Prize and become required reading in high schools across the nation. With the recent publication of the controversial *Watchman*, it seems likely that English teachers will want to consider the pedagogical implications of utilizing the novel as a kind of "sister" text to *Mockingbird*. I would argue that *Watchman* and *Mockingbird* can, in fact, be understood as *intertwined narratives* because they are essentially manifestations of the same story. *Watchman* is simply an earlier version of *Mockingbird*; as such, one cannot be read in isolation from the other. Although *Watchman* takes place some twenty years after *Mockingbird*, they are firmly held together by the reminiscences of the central character, Jean Louise Finch; while she does not narrate *Watchman*, is it still very much her story. It is, in fact, Scout's childhood memories that provide the structure for *Mockingbird*. The difficulty in reading the novels as one narrative comes from what appears to be discontinuity in the characterization of Atticus Finch; readers struggle to align the racist Atticus of *Watchman* with the morally upstanding Atticus of *Mockingbird*.

There is, however, a literary precedent for this type of narrative conundrum, which can be found in Mark Twain's *Adventures of Huckle-*

berry Finn. What may appear to be discontinuity in the characterization of Atticus may in fact be a result of the fact that, over fifty-five years, we grew used to a single-text Atticus and specifically a larger-than-life hero imagined by a child. Yet if we consider that the two manuscripts by Harper Lee were written only a few years apart, we might more easily reconcile the two. Just as Huck Finn appears in *Tom Sawyer* as a comic foil but as a relatively complicated character with a moral dilemma in his own narrative, so, too, does the Atticus of *Watchman* get "welcomed . . . silently into the human race" after a much more ethically ambiguous performance, despite his heroic status in *Mockingbird.*

Mockingbird and *Huck Finn* have many similarities—written by Southern authors and published during pivotal moments in American history. Both are coming-of-age tales told by young, unreliable narrators that deal squarely with the issue of racism. Additionally, these classic works that continue to regularly appear on high school reading lists are among the most challenged and banned books in America, in part because they are deemed racially offensive. Of particular note is the similarity between the way readers object to the apparent disintegration of Huck Finn's newfound "racial awareness" (through his recognition of Jim's humanity) as he succumbs to Tom Sawyer's demands in the "evasion" sequence, and how *Watchman* readers take offense at Atticus Finch's rejection of the apparent racial sensitivity he demonstrates in *Mockingbird.* Readers will ask: how can *Watchman* Atticus be the same person as *Mockingbird* Atticus? The answer is simple: because, like Huck, Atticus merely represents the racist society in which he lives and does not transcend the prejudices he is invited to share in. Atticus and Huck, although polar opposites in the eyes of "civilized society" (one, an educated, well-respected adult, the other, a barely literate adolescent outcast) are nonetheless equally encumbered by a belief system that regards whites as superior to blacks. Despite their seemingly heroic acts, Atticus Finch and Huck Finn are functionally racist.

Huck Finn and *Mockingbird* are also linked in the way they indict the racism of contemporary society through narratives set during an earlier period in America's history. Although *Huck Finn* was published in 1884, the novel takes place pre–Civil War, some forty years earlier. *Mockingbird,* set during the mid-1930s, was published in 1960, amid the early civil rights movement. While this similarity between the two novels may be coincidental, the net effect is essentially the same—the critique is made in a way that might best reach contemporary readers. For example, it is unlikely that Twain's readers would have connected with a narrative featuring an ex-slave who is denied his civil rights as the Jim Crow era takes a firm hold. Similarly, readers in 1960 might have felt uncomfortable reading a novel that so closely portrays the extreme reaction of white Southerners to civil rights efforts following the *Brown v. Board of Education* decision making segregation illegal. It is important to note that *Watchman* is, in fact, this narrative. While *Huck Finn*, in its final form, is clearly a response to the failure of Reconstruction, it was initially conceived by Twain as a kind of sequel to *Tom Sawyer*. As Jim and Huck traveled down the river into the heart of slave territory, however, Twain was, in fact, forced to set aside the manuscript for three years while figuring out how to proceed with the narrative (Valkeakari 31). His decision to resolve this conflict by returning Huck and the reader to the status quo reflects his ability to *obliquely* represent the racially unjust reality of 1880s America. Lee, like Twain, turned her narrative in an entirely different direction. She did so through extensive revisions to the original manuscript over a two-year period until it became *Mockingbird*. While *Watchman's* transformation into *Mockingbird* occurred largely at the advice of Lee's editor and not of her own accord, her initial instinct was to write a novel that *directly* responded to events happening in the late 1950s.

Lee's motivation is clear, according to Patrick Chura, who argues that *Mockingbird* (the transformed *Watchman*), although set during the 1930s, is best understood as a reflection of the racial events and ideology of the 1950s, particularly the *Brown* decision as well as the Emmet Till case, which involved the brutal murder of a black boy by two white men who were later acquitted. The pre-*Mockingbird* manuscript can also be linked, says Gregory Jay, to Lee's earlier writings at Huntingdon College, particularly a one-act played titled *Now Is the Time for All Good Men*, which dramatizes the "defeat of Southern liberalism by the entrenched forces of racism [thus mirroring] what the nation had seen in the battered face of Emmet Till" (506). The acquittals of Till's killers serve, argues Jay, as the actual inspiration for the defeat of racial justice seen in the conviction and murder of Tom Robinson in *Mockingbird*. As *Watchman* was essentially recast as *Mockingbird*, it is impossible to separate the two novels; they are aligned in such a way that requires us to regard them as interconnected narratives. Therefore, Atticus Finch of the 1950s must be understood to be the same individual as Atticus Finch of the 1930s.

It is difficult to make this connection because 1950s Atticus seems so radically different from 1930s Atticus, just as "post-raft" Huck seems so changed from the Huck who bonds with Jim on their journey down the river. But it is not so much a change in characterization that explains 1950s Atticus and post-raft Huck as it is a redefinition of their original selves. One might consider this a process of ironic "civilizing"—as *Watchman* Atticus is transformed by Lee into *Mockingbird* Atticus, he undergoes a process of refinement: overtly racist attitudes are muted and restrained as he moves backward in time. More useful, perhaps, is to consider the "civilizing" process as it occurs in the natural progression of aging—the younger Atticus becomes more ensconced in the racist attitudes of his community as he grows older; similarly, as Huck returns to "civilization" on the Phelps farm, he adopts the racist attitudes of Tom Sawyer and his family. The process of Huck's civilizing, discussed in detail below, offers a baseline from which to examine the similar refinement experienced by Atticus.

Huck Finn—On and Off the Raft

Readers will recall that during their journey down the river, Jim and Huck become aligned in their efforts to escape (Jim because he believes Miss Watson is going to "sell him down the river" and Huck because he fears that Pap might kill him); they build a real relationship that enables Huck to view Jim not as a slave, but as a fellow human. Jim protects Huck as they encounter various dangers on their journey, in effect acting as a surrogate father. Tuire Valkeakari notes that, although flawed, "their interracial existence on the raft – their oasis – has become something of a semi-democratic arrangement" (37). This is destroyed, however, when the Duke and the King take over the raft, relegating Jim to his former status as a runaway slave. When the con men sell Jim to Silas Phelps, Huck is forced to make a decision that reveals his true moral integrity— although he contemplates informing Miss Watson of Jim's whereabouts, even going so far as to write her a letter, he ultimately destroys the letter and makes the bold decision to "steal Jim out of slavery" (237). At this point, we see him as a hero—he must act to save Jim because Jim is not his *"nigger"* but his *friend.*

> Somehow I couldn't seem to strike no places to harden me against him, but only the other kind. I'd see him standing my watch on top of his'n, 'stead of calling me so I could go on sleeping . . . [he] would do everything he could think of for me and

> how good he always was . . . he was so grateful, and said I was
> the best friend old Jim ever had in the world, and the ONLY
> one he's got now. (238)

Nonetheless, Huck remains "shackled by his society's racist concept of black people" and cannot fully embrace Jim's humanity, argues Valkeakari, which becomes obvious when Tom Sawyer reenters the narrative. Huck defers to Tom (representative of the dominant white society from which Huck has recently escaped), who engages Huck in an elaborate plan to free Jim. This exercise is, of course, an ironic effort, as Jim has already been freed by the terms of Miss Watson's will, and Tom knows it. If Huck had continued to see Jim as a friend, rather than a slave, he would not have participated in a demeaning and dehumanizing scheme. Valkeakari notes the effect of this betrayal: "Jim loses the only white ally he has ever had in the deep South . . . Now that Jim would need Huck, he has to watch the boy start a new phase in his life with restored white loyalties (39). Janet Gabler-Hover addresses this seemingly radical transformation in Huck. "As readers, we ask why we are lifted to such moral heights, inspired by Huck and Jim's great dream of escape and by Huck's moral awakening, only to be abandoned by a spurious conclusion where Huck and Jim appear to lose all dignity" (67). She notes that many critics (Leo Marx, in particular) attribute this change in Huck to Twain's inability to sustain what was shaping up to be a racially progressive heroic tale. Gabler-Hover absolves Twain of any narrative wrongdoing, however, arguing that Twain instead characterizes Huck *consistently* throughout the novel. Huck is, she argues, a character whose moral vision is seriously flawed and that his "passive submission to Tom's will at the novel's conclusion is a necessarily disturbing reminder that Huck's role in society is as victim, not savior" (74). Huck is not and cannot be a hero, because he is ultimately bound by the conventions and dictates of the slave-holding society represented by Tom Sawyer, who demands that Huck participate in his plan to "set a free nigger free" (324).

Huck Finn is, according to Nancy Cook, representative of a kind of American literary hero that does little to counter the struggles against racism (618). Atticus Finch is also representative of this type. She notes that both are heroes in the traditional sense (each receives a call to action, enters unfamiliar territory, and experiences revelations followed by a kind of resolution of the central conflict). Ultimately, through the redemption of others (i.e., Jim and Tom Robinson), these individuals become more accepting. These "heroic" tales ultimately reinforce the idea of white superiority, however. Cook explains that "Huck Finn, the white hero, is portrayed as rescuing the black victim from an enslaved condition that has been imposed by white society.... Significantly, however, the status of the black person has not changed" (626). Although Huck helps Jim escape, Jim (representative of the black population in general), essentially remains enslaved. This continued enslavement of former slaves reflects Twain's true purpose in writing the evasion sequence: to highlight the failure of Reconstruction by demonstrating that freed slaves are not in fact free. They are being systematically denied their civil rights.

One cannot read the "evasion" sequence without feeling frustrated (as does Huck) by the futility of Tom's plan, designed to be more complicated and take twice as long as Huck's simple strategy to free Jim. Although Huck objects when Tom lays out a "stylish" plan that requires tormenting the Silas family and humiliating Jim, Huck is silenced by Tom, who tells him, "Huck Finn, if I was as ignorant as you, I'd keep still" (268), and "It ain't no use to try to learn you nothing, Huck" (272). Huck has no choice but to comply; he resigns himself and follows Tom's orders. Jim, too, questions the wisdom in Tom's plan, but is quickly silenced by Tom, who accuses Jim, who "was just loadened down with more gaudier chances than a prisoner ever had to make a name for himself" (294) of being unappreciative. Like Huck, Jim gives up and accepts his fate. It is Huck's "fatalistic" attitude toward the ongoing degradation of blacks and failure to enact change (by asserting to Tom that the right thing to do is immediately free Jim at the Phelps farm) that diminishes the brave decision he has made earlier in the novel. As Cook notes, Jim's continued enslavement establishes that Huck cannot be understood as a hero. Even so, there is some hope at the novel's conclusion that Huck may ultimately revolt against the civilizing influences of society by "lighting out for the territory," thus establishing that perhaps a mature Huck might somehow rise above racism. Within the confines of his existing narrative, however, Huck was unable to do so. Although Jim has been freed, slavery, of course, continues.

Similarly, in *Mockingbird*, the status of Maycomb's black population following the trial and conviction of Tom Robinson remains unchanged; Tom is brutally murdered, and life in Maycomb ostensibly returns to "normal." As Scout recalls, "Things had a way of settling down, and after enough time passed people would forget that Tom Robinson's existence was ever brought to their attention" (243). Arguably, Maycomb pays little attention to *any* black person's existence, assuming that blacks are and will always be inferior to whites. Here Lee, like Twain, draws attention to the racial codes of Jim Crow—blacks continue to be denied their civil rights, and racial inequality persists. In the end, Huck and Atticus are not heroes, says Cook, because their main claim to heroism is their ability to "merely see the wrong that has been done to native peoples" but to do nothing to rectify that wrong. In other words, good intentions do not a hero make. Good intentions may, in fact, simply mask underlying racist attitudes. Such is the case with Atticus Finch.

The "First" Atticus Finch—*Mockingbird*

Atticus Finch, the moral center of *Mockingbird*, has long been revered as a character who stands for justice and equality in the face of racial discrimination. Upstanding citizen, honest man, and kind and loving father, Atticus has appealed to countless readers who are inspired by his noble actions. Would-be lawyers have looked to him as a role model. As Steven Lubet notes, "no real-life lawyer has done more for the self-image or public perception of the legal profession" than Atticus (1339). His reputation remained largely untarnished until the early 1990s, says Christopher Metress in his 2003 essay "The Rise and Fall of Atticus Finch." Metress provides an overview of "revisionary readings" from both legal scholars and literary critics calling Atticus's morality into question. He additionally points out how many contemporary readers are "like as not to emphasize Finch's complicity with rather than challenges to the segregationist politics of his hometown" (142). Metress's analysis is particularly significant, as it establishes that more than two decades before *Watchman* was published, Atticus Finch was being called a racist. In recognizing that Atticus's heroic status has long been the subject of debate, we will be better able to analyze *Watchman* Atticus.

An early Atticus detractor, according to Metress, can be found in Monroe Freedman, whose 1992 column in *Legal Times* titled "Atticus Finch, R.I.P." admonishes readers for their persistence in regarding Atticus (the purported hero) as someone to emulate. Acknowledging that Atticus does act heroically in representing Tom Robinson, Freedman points out that he does so under court appointment (therefore less honorably than if he had volunteered to take the case). Freedman's column was met with "total outrage" by the legal community, prompting the president of the American Bar Association to defend Atticus, asserting that he "rose above racism and injustice" (144). In 1994, Freedman reiterates his original claim in "Atticus Finch – Right and Wrong," arguing that Atticus Finch *never* demonstrated the moral integrity that admirers credit him, because when called upon to do his duty in representing Tom, he does so grudgingly. Freedman notes that Atticus never attempted to fight against racism and social injustice when he might have done so. Worse yet, Freedman accuses Atticus of "practicing apartheid every day" because he "tolerates, trivializes and condones the degradation of blacks in Maycomb" (477). Had he truly cared about racism, argues Freedman, Atticus would have voluntarily used his legal training and skills to make changes to the "pervasive social injustice of his own town" (481). Atticus is, after all, more than just a lawyer; he represents Maycomb County in the state legislature. Ultimately, says Freedman, while Atticus has many admirable traits, he is not a hero and is certainly not a role model for today's lawyers.

Metress continues his assessment of critical responses to Atticus, moving on to Eric Sundquist, who argues in "Blues for Atticus Finch" (1995) that Atticus engages in deception and evasion when he attempts to address Maycomb's racial hysteria. Atticus's attitude, says Sundquist—demonstrated in his warning to Scout, "This time we're not fighting the Yankees, we are fighting our friends"—reflects the novel's overall stance that the race crisis is a *Southern* problem. Because this attitude argues against the need for federal intervention in the South, "racial justice [will] never come to the black citizens of Maycomb" (147). Sundquist does not consider Atticus a hero who stands in opposition to his community, but as "an apologist whose moral vision embodies a subtle form of massive resistance to outside agitation" (147). Following his analysis of Sundquist's argument, Metress cites Rob Atkinson, who argues in his 1999 essay that Atticus is not a racial hero because his defense of Tom Robinson has less to do with Tom's fate than with his own need to be seen as honorable by those in his community. Atkinson points to Atticus's explanation to Scout about why he took the case: "If I didn't, I couldn't hold up my head in town, I couldn't represent this county in the legislature" (75). One wonders whether his failure to tell Jem and Scout that he was assigned the case rather than that he volunteered to take it stems from his desire to have his children hold him in equally high esteem.

A somewhat less harsh criticism can be seen in Katie Rose Guest Pryal's essay "Walking in Another's Skin: Failure of Empathy in *To Kill a Mockingbird*" published in a 2010 collection commemorating the novel's fiftieth anniversary. As empathy is central to Atticus's personal and professional philosophy and is, in fact, a strategy he encourages his children to implement in their interactions with others in community, it is important to understand whether Atticus "practices what he preaches" and whether his failure to do so ultimately diminishes his heroic status. Pryal believes that Atticus does not empathize with Tom, he sympathizes with him. This is a significant distinction, says Pryal, noting that empathy entails understanding the plight of another *from that person's point of view*, while sympathy only requires the feeling of pity for another's plight. She notes that it would be unlikely that a white lawyer in the Jim Crow South could actually *identify* with a black person because black people and white people were unequal in the eyes of the law. But does Atticus's failure to empathize with Tom make him less heroic? Perhaps not, yet it forces us to question whether whatever sympathy Atticus feels toward Tom's plight (and the plight of black people in Maycomb generally) refutes the idea that he is racist and does, in fact, believe that whites are superior to blacks. I do not think it does. Atticus clearly understands the *reality* of the law—that blacks and whites are *not* equal—and yet he instructs the jury in his closing that the courts are the one place where all are (in theory) treated equally. He contradicts this statement, however, when he later tells Scout following Tom's conviction by the jury, "They've done it before, they did it tonight and they'll do it again" (220), thus appearing to accept (and perhaps encouraging Scout to accept as well) that racism is simply an ugly aspect of Maycomb society. Pryal identifies Atticus's "inability or unwillingness to see racism as a large-scale problem [as] yet another manifestation of his failure of empathy" (181).

Gregory Jay addresses the issue of empathy in "Queer Children and Representative Men: Harper Lee, Racial Liberalism, and the Dilemma of *To Kill a Mockingbird.*" Jay offers a literary rather than a legal perspective in his 2015 essay published shortly after *Watchman's* release. He examines, in part, *Mockingbird's* popularity, noting that while it has traditionally been taught in schools primarily as a novel about empathy and moral courage, this interpretation is limited, as it prevents readers from confronting the history of white supremacy in America. While Jay does not suggest that Atticus is racist, he notes that Atticus fails to adequately address the issue of racial injustice, because he "constructs a world of privately nurtured and publicly displayed moral exemplarity and teaches it to his children through the discourse of empathy" (499). Atticus relates this lesson to Scout, in perhaps the most-oft quoted lines from *Mockingbird*: "You never really understand a person until you consider things from his point of view—until you climb into his skin and walk around in it" (30). Jay argues that because Atticus does not directly challenge the town's racial codes and white supremacy, his actions in defending Tom and preventing his lynching are "noble but futile." In his assessment, Jay, unlike Pryal, credits Atticus with the ability to "feel what it is like for the oppressed to suffer," but this capacity to empathize with Tom hardly confers heroic status upon Atticus. Rather, as Cook notes above, it reflects his ability to "merely see the wrong" without remedying the wrong.

Criticism against Atticus has been met, of course, with resistance. Abbe Smith, in particular, mounts an admirable defense against Atticus detractors (in particular Steven Lubet, Monroe Freedman, and Malcolm Gladwell) in her 2011 review of *Mockingbird* published in *Legal Ethics*. Responding to their claims that Atticus is not a hero, Smith makes a rather weak argument, however, that Atticus is "not a finished product when *Mockingbird* ends," citing Randolph Stone who calls Atticus "a work in progress" (152). Interestingly, this assertion anticipates the issue readers confront in *Watchman*—is this the "finished product" Atticus has become? I would argue that, ultimately, one can equate this completion with the "civilizing" process Atticus undergoes. In other words, he becomes more racist. In response to claims made by Freedman and Gladwell that Atticus is an apologist, Smith does concede that Atticus "displays a willful disregard of reality [and] *his own racism*" (emphasis added, 152). Smith's assertion that Atticus is a *product* of his time and place (1930s Jim Crow Alabama) clearly supports the idea that he is a racist, however. Smith argues that Atticus is "overly accepting of the prevailing social order, including aspects of Jim Crow [and] he could have done more to challenge it" (164). Smith believes that Atticus is nonetheless a hero, all the more appealing because of his flaws. It is these "flaws" that *Watchman* portrays through Jean Louise's revelations about Atticus upon her return home to Maycomb.

The "Second" Atticus Finch—*Watchman*

Having established that in recent years Atticus's reputation as a paragon of virtue has been questioned by a number of critics, it is not so difficult to align the Atticus of *Watchman* with the Atticus of *Mockingbird*. In the aftermath of *Watchman's* release, however, numerous writers have grappled with the apparent discrepancies between the two. In a July 10, 2015, *New*

York Times book review, Michiko Kakutani notes how the depiction of Atticus in *Watchman* makes for "disturbing reading" and is particularly "disorienting" for *Mockingbird* fans who are asking how the "saintly" Atticus of *Mockingbird* suddenly emerges as a bigot. Daniel D'Addario, writing for *Time Magazine,* relates that the idea of Atticus as a racist has alarmed many readers who are struggling to make sense of how "Atticus [who], more than any other character, has stood for justice and righteousness in the American imagination" is revealed as a racist. D'Addario responds to this confusion by arguing that Atticus's true feelings—expressed in a long debate with Jean Louise in *Watchman*—"actually squares neatly with the paternalistic attitude Atticus takes toward black people in *To Kill a Mockingbird*, and his occasionally overwrought compassion for his racist white neighbors."

Isabel Wilkerson eloquently characterizes the difference between *Mockingbird* Atticus and *Watchman* Atticus in her essay "Our Racial Moment of Truth." Rather than the Atticus who urges his daughter, Scout, to climb into someone's skin to understand him, this Atticus is an old-line segregationist, a principled bigot who has been to a Klan meeting and asks his grown daughter visiting from New York City: "Do you want Negroes by the carload in our schools and churches and theaters? Do you want them in our world?" (Wilkerson). It is interesting to note that Wilkerson, like Jay, identifies Atticus's insistence on empathy in *Mockingbird* as a defining feature and perhaps implies that he no longer attempts to practice empathy in *Watchman*. Even so, she has no trouble aligning the compassionate Atticus of *Mockingbird* with the bigoted Atticus of *Watchman*, noting that such qualities are not mutually exclusive and can, in fact, be present in the same person. Wilkerson explains that this kind of behavior, according to sociologist David Williams, is reflective of the actual racism that resides in many Americans today. This is a provocative claim likely to be met with resistance; while *Mockingbird* Atticus may not have been the hero we believed him to be, readers might have a hard time accepting that Atticus of *Watchman* is merely representative of "normal" Americans. To do so would seem to exempt both Atticus and ourselves from accountability.

Wilkerson suggests that Atticus is a "gentleman bigot, well meaning in his supremacy." While seemingly oxymoronic on the one hand (how can one treat members of another race with hatred and intolerance in an honorable or courteous way), this characterization reinforces the argument that 1950s Atticus is no different from 1930s Atticus. Certainly the

Atticus of *Mockingbird* was polite and well-mannered even as he practiced racism. He was, after all, held in high regard by Maycomb. It may be that Wilkerson's reference to Atticus' "gentlemanly" conduct echoes Jean Louise's sentiments upon witnessing the Citizens' Council meeting where her father was present. "The one human being she had ever fully and wholeheartedly trusted had failed her; the only man she had ever known to whom she could point and say with expert knowledge, 'He is a gentleman, in his heart he is a gentleman,' had betrayed her, publicly, grossly and shamelessly" (113). Jean Louise does not believe that a man who advocates that blacks be kept in their place and virulently opposes segregation can be the man she had once held in such high esteem. And we have trouble believing this as well. We, too, feel betrayed. Like Jean Louise, readers endeavor to accept this "new" Atticus. The problem with this acceptance, however, lies in the fact that neither Jean Louise nor readers understand (at least at this point in the narrative) that Atticus is not changed at all. It is through the process of mourning a loss (moving, as it were, through the stages of grief) that Jean Louise comes to realize that she has misread Atticus. In idolizing him, she has failed to see that he works "not to initiate progressive change but to maintain the status quo in terms of racial dynamics and barriers" (Brinkmeyer 219). It follows, then, that readers of *Mockingbird* have also misread Atticus.

Critical responses to *Watchman* are of course limited, as only a few years have passed since its release. In a recent essay, "Children Once, Not Forever: Harper Lee's *Go Set a Watchman* and Growing Up," Allen Mendenhall proposes that *Watchman* provides a "more complete (and, arguably, more historically accurate) picture of Atticus that, in fact, does not contradict the portrayal of Atticus in *Mockingbird*" (8–9). One might argue, then, that *Mockingbird* was historically *inaccurate*—a redacted text, sanitized to eliminate any reference to the painful reality of the racial inequality that persisted in 1950s America. In other words, Lee's contemporary readers were not ready for *Watchman* Atticus. Are today's readers? Yes, says Mendenhall, if we hold our judgment of Atticus in abeyance; if we understand that what we find paradoxical in Atticus merely reflects America at large. This idea closely mirrors Wilkerson's claim that Americans, in general, tend to be racist. As Mendenhall notes, "We are a country founded as much on principles of freedom and liberty as on the atrocities of human bondage, slave labor and racism" (12). The Atticus of *Watchman* therefore complements rather than detracts from the Atticus of *Mockingbird,* because it demonstrates that he is human; he has his failings. Yes, he is racist and has always seen the world in "black or white." Although he could not "transcend the evils of his time and place [he nonetheless] gave himself over to principles of justice and law that were, in fact, timeless" (14). In examining Atticus, we must consider that just as he exemplifies these principles in *Mockingbird*, he continues to do so in *Watchman*. The older Atticus does not reverse his position and does, in fact, remain steadfast in his belief that the law must be upheld. We, like Jean Louise, must recognize these consistencies even as we grapple with the disturbing reality that *Watchman* forces us to confront.

This confrontation occurs simultaneously through our interaction with the narrative; Jean Louise is, in effect, enacting the reader's own return to the landscape of *Mockingbird* and to a beloved character. Like Jean Louise, we are disgusted by what we find: Atticus has been reading *The Black Plague*, a pamphlet that espouses the idea that blacks are genetically inferior to whites. Atticus is on the board of directors of the Maycomb County Citizens' Council; at a meeting of this organization, Atticus sits at the table with a man who "spews filth from this mouth," thereby condoning the evil sentiments expressed by the speaker. Atticus once joined the Ku Klux Klan. Atticus does not want Negroes in his world. Atticus wants to preserve a way of life that discriminates against blacks and prevents them from gaining their full civil rights. Atticus is a hypocrite. Or is he?

We thus return to the question that motivates this analysis. If we admit that, like Jean Louise, we "confused Atticus with God and never saw him as a man with a man's heart and a man's failings" (265), we can then reassess his character, ultimately seeing him not as radically different from the Atticus of *Mockingbird*, but as a refinement of that character. He, like Huck Finn, has ironically become civilized to the "ways of white folks."

Perhaps the more difficult task for readers, however, is to accept that the young Scout of *Mockingbird* has become the Jean Louise of *Watchman* – a twenty-six-year-old woman who is, in fact, just like Atticus—"at heart a traditional white Southerner [whose] zealous commitment to what she mistakenly believed was Atticus' idealism has masked her own Southern allegiances and her acceptance of them" (Brinkmeyer 221). Such allegiances are reflected in her expression of the racist sentiments she originally appears to condemn. Like Huck and Atticus, Jean Louise has accepted indoctrination as an adult member of a white society. This may actually be the more disturbing aspect of *Watchman*. In this sense, it is not so much Atticus as it is Scout who is like Huck Finn—an innocent child who believes in the idea of equality and who thinks there ought to be "just one kind of folks" (227). It is this belief, presumably, that ultimately motivates Scout to flee the south for New York. But she grows up and returns to learn the truth—that in her world, there are white folks and there are black folks. And never the twain shall meet.

Works Cited

Brinkmeyer, Robert H. "Scout Comes Home Again." *Virginia Quarterly Review*, vol. 91, no. 4, 2015, pp. 217–21, www.vqronline.org/fiction-criticism/2015/10/scout-comes-home-again. Accessed 19 July 2018.

Chura, Patrick. "Prolepsis and Anachronism: Emmet Till and Historicity of *To Kill a Mockingbird*." *Southern Literary Journal*, vol. 32, no. 2, 2000, pp. 1–26, www.jstor.org/stable/20078264. Accessed 19 July 2018.

Cook, Nancy L. "A Call to Affirmative Action for Fiction's Heroes of Color, or How Hawkeye, Huck, and Atticus Foil the Work of Antiracism." *Cornell Journal of Law and Public Policy*, vol. 11, no. 3, 2002, http://scholarship.law.cornell.edu/cjlpp/vol11/iss3/5. Accessed 19 July 2018.

D'Addario, Daniel. *Go Set a Watchman* Review: Atticus Finch's Racism Makes Scout, and Us, Grow Up." *Time Magazine*, 11 July 2015.http://time.com/3954581/go-set-a-watchman-review/. Accessed 19 July 2018.

Freedman, Monroe. "Atticus Finch – Right and Wrong." 45 *Alabama Law Review* 473, 1994, http://scholarlycommons.law.hofstra.edu/faculty_scholarship/220. Accessed 19 July 2018.

Gabler-Hover, Janet. "Sympathy Not Empathy: The Intent of Narration in *Huckleberry Finn*." *The Journal of Narrative Technique*, vol. 17, no. 1, 1987, pp. 67–75. www.jstor.org/stable/30225168. Accessed 19 July 2018.

Jay, Gregory. "Queer Children and Representative Men: Harper Lee, Racial Liberalism, and the Dilemma of *To Kill a Mockingbird*." *American Literary History*, vol. 27, no. 3, 2015, pp. 487–522.

Katkutani, Michiko. "Review: Harper Lee's *Go Set a Watchman* Gives Atticus Finch a Dark Side." *New York Times*, 10 July 2015. https://www.nytimes.com/2015/07/11/books/review-harper-lees-go-set-a-watchman-gives-atticus-finch-a-dark-side.html/. Accessed 19 July 2018.

Lee, Harper. *Go Set a Watchman*. Harper Perennial, 2015.

———. *To Kill a Mockingbird*. 1960. Warner Books, 1982.

Lubet, Steven. "Reconstructing Atticus Finch." *Michigan Law Review*, vol. 97, no. 6, 1999, pp. 1339–62. doi: 10.2307/1290205.

Mendenhall, Allen. "Children Once, Not Forever: Harper Lee's *Go Set a Watchman* and Growing Up." *Indiana Law Journal Supplement*, vol. 91, no. 6, 2015. https://ssrn.com/abstract=2669553. Accessed 19 July 2018.

Metress, Christopher. "The Rise and Fall of Atticus Finch." *Modern Critical Interpretations: Harper Lee's To Kill a Mockingbird*, edited by Harold Bloom, Chelsea House, 2006, pp. 141–48.

Pryal, Katie Rose Guest. "Walking in Another's Skin: Failure of Empathy in *To Kill a Mockingbird*." *Harper Lee's* To Kill a Mockingbird: *New Essays*, edited by Michael J. Meyer. Scarecrow Press, Inc., 2010., pp. 174-192.

Smith, Abbe. "Defending Atticus Finch." *Legal Ethics,* vol. 14, no. 1, 2011, pp. 143–67.

Twain, Mark. *The Adventures of Huckleberry Finn.* 1884. Amazon Classics, 2015.

———. *The Adventures of Tom Sawyer.* 1876. Dover Publications, 1996.

Valkeakari, Tuire. "Huck, Twain, and The Freedman Shackles: Struggling with *Huckleberry Finn* Today." *Atlantis,* vol. 28, no. 2, 2006, pp. 29–43.

Wilkerson, Isabel. "Our Racial Moment of Truth." *The New York Times,* 18 July 2015 https://www.nytimes.com/2015/07/19/opinion/sunday/our-racial-moment-of-truth.html. Accessed 19 July 2018.

6

"I GOT SOMETHIN' TO SAY!"

Mayella Violet Ewell in Robert Mulligan's Film *To Kill a Mockingbird*

Kwakiutl L. Dreher

Without Sanctuary: Lynching Photography in America—that book wherein James Allen (collector), U.S. Congressman John Lewis, writer and theater critic Hilton Als, and Pulitzer Prize winner Leon Litwack meticulously document the visuals of lynchings in the United States. Their research widely circulates these national "treasures." *Without Sanctuary*, in addition, discloses the social engineer who made available these socio-cultural artifacts for the viewing public: the photographer. *Crisis* magazine reports in 1915 that "picture card photographers installed a portable printing plant . . . and reaped a harvest in selling postcards showing photographs of [Thomas Brooks,] the lynched Negro" (qtd. in *Without Sanctuary* 11). 5 ½" x 3 ½" postcards freeze-frame the jubilance of white men, women, and children who, after witnessing these national atrocities, addressed the postcards, and the United States Postal Service delivered them to their relatives and friends. Some white spectators, such as Joe, describe the lynching of Jesse Washington as a "barbecue" he attended in Robinson, Texas, on May 16, 1916 (Allen plates #25, #26). Then . . .

I. See. *Her.* In *that* volume. The white girl with the page-boy hairstyle dressed in her Sunday best. She stands tall in her ankle socks and Buster Brown shoes. Her hands are crossed in front of her bodice, and she gazes on with such pleasure as white men and women watch her from afar. The object of her joy? Ruben Stacy, a homeless Negro itinerant farmer hanging from a tree. Mrs. Marion Jones, a white woman, told the sheriff Stacy arrived at her house "to ask for food; [she] became frightened and screamed when she saw Stacy's face" (Allen plate #57). A mob of one hundred masked men lynched Stacy for his "crime" in Fort Lauderdale, Florida, July 19, 1935 (Allen 185). Neither confusion, fear, nor horror affects the girl at the scene; her pleasant stare, however, suggests the receipt of her right of passage into white female young adulthood.

Amy Louise Wood would assess the girl's smile as her reaction to the "tremendous symbolic power" of lynching "because it was extraordinary and . . . visually sensational" (1). Stacy's lynched body and the white girl's gaze upon the same, captured with eloquence by the picture card photographer in gelatin silver, indicate the legacies bestowed upon young white females. These legacies received a heft of currency as they traveled from real life to the postcard sold in the 5&10 store. In Robert Mulligan's film *To Kill a Mockingbird (1962),* that same girl came to my mind when Mayella Violet Ewell, the white plaintiff, cries out to say *something* in the courtroom of *her* white peers after her cross-examination by Atticus Finch, Esq. The unmitigated rage toward Finch, the court, and Tom Robinson, the Negro she accuses of assaulting her, prompted me to inquire about the gust of confidence on which her rage travels. "I know from where that kind of confidence comes," I thought, "and it is not just from *hearing* talk about Negroes in her community . . . something she saw . . . witnessed . . . sanctioned such self-assurance. It is she . . . that's the girl in the photograph . . . all grown up . . ."

Or it very well could have been.

"I Got Somethin' to Say" explores Mayella's court appearance in Robert Mulligan's film *To Kill A Mockingbird* (1962). The film brings to relief the potent visual of Mayella's full knowledge of white female power over the black male body in the South of the 1930s regardless of her class status. Harper Lee's character loses her case in the prequel, *Go Set A Watchman,* and Tom Robinson is acquitted. If we keep in mind that *Watchman* is the *prequel* to Lee's more famous novel, *Mockingbird,* then it is safe to hazard that, in Lee's creative imagination, Mayella, aged fourteen in *Watchman,* comes back with a vengeance five years later in *Mockingbird,* aged nineteen with *"somethin'"* *to say.* When Mayella Violet Ewell travels from the written word to the *silver screen,* her visual/discourse makes even more salient *poor* white femininity emboldened with a desperate *and* vicious intent. This essay locates the ways in which film forms deployed by Russell Harlan, the cinematographer, and Oscar-worthy character construal by Collin Wilcox Paxton, the actress cast as Mayella, yield agency to the young adult in the production of her testimony and closing argument. The attention to film forms such as the close-up and medium shot, and to character interpretation, counter the overall judgment by critics and scholars of Mayella as a corrupt, ignorant white and powerless poverty-stricken social outcast.

An understanding of the full dynamics of Mayella's testimony demands an overview of some of the criticism of her. I begin with the novel itself, and even though attention overwhelmingly comes from scholars who examine *To Kill a Mockingbird*, each analysis, nevertheless, generates insight into Mayella onscreen. Lee, in her own way, marginalizes Mayella within the novel; she has no narrative participation with any of the characters. Indeed, on Lee's description Mayella is the "loneliest person in the world" (218). The young woman's biography unfolds inside the courtroom—*not throughout* the novel—through the eyes of the narrator, an adult Jean Louise "Scout" Finch. Scout narrates Mayella's story on *reflection* once court proceedings commence, and reveals to the reader the socio-economic position of the Ewells in Maycomb. She says,

> People like the Ewells lived as guests of the county in prosperity as well as in the depths of a depression. . . . [The family] lived behind the town garbage dump in what was once a Negro cabin. . . . Against the fence, in a line, were six chipped enamel slop jars holding brilliant red geraniums, cared for as tenderly as if they belonged to Miss Maudie Atkinson. . . . People said they were Mayella Ewell's. (193-4).

On the community's treatment of Mayella, Scout says, "[w]hite people wouldn't have anything to do with her because she lived among pigs; Negroes wouldn't have anything to do with her because she was white" (218). The Ewell dwelling not only signifies squalor; Lee's description of it portrays two things. First, that the community withdrew its hands from Mayella indicts them for neglect and for being indirect participants in her marginalization. As for Mayella's family, Lee, more generally, describes Mayella's father, Bob Ewell, via Scout as a man with no work ethic who shirks responsibility to provide for his eight children. Scout tells the reader, Ewell "was the only man I ever heard of who was fired from the WPA [Works Progress Administration] for laziness" (284).

Secondly, and more important, Lee's description of Mayella's world via Scout illustrates the young woman's deafening silence. We neither hear nor read one line of dialogue spoken by Mayella prior to or after her courtroom testimony; she is an unseen, talked-about presence, but a shadow nevertheless hovering over the community. In Lee's prequel, *Go Set A Watchman,* for example, Mayella is just "the white girl" (109). Atticus wins his case against her, but then Lee associates the attorney with white supremacy—yet another deflection from Mayella's racism. In *To Kill a Mockingbird,* "the white girl" acquires a name, Mayella Violet, along with a few potted flowers and the contempt and pity of town residents. No one compliments Mayella on her gardening skills, and any demonstrations of concern by the "upstanding" Southern white women are nonexistent. Communal interactions with the family occur only at Christmas and on the first day of school. Sandra Churchwell notes, "Once Mayella has served her plot function, the book [*Mockingbird*] forgets all about her, sparing no further pity despite Atticus's constant injunctions to cultivate empathy." Each novel regards Mayella less as important in the popular imagination and more as an expedient critic of the sociocultural mores of Southern patriarchy.

Third, scholarship on the novel affirms Mayella's apparent delicate state of being. Alec Gilmore contends Mayella not only is "ignored" but also othered. He writes, "When Atticus asks her in court if she has any friends, Mayella seems not to know what he means. . . . [She has] had otherness thrust upon [her]" by the white citizens of Maycomb (239, 240). Bob Ewell, believes Robert C. Evans, "manages to pervert Mayella so thoroughly . . . he clearly helps to corrupt her ethics" (104). Holly Blackford calls her, among other things, "aggressive Mayella" (84). She is the "dark double" of Scout who has "frank sexual desires" (100, 106); a "pseudoromantic heroine entombed in her father's house" (115) who is "more object between Atticus and Ewell than subject in the trial" (139); and, she is a "motherless daughter" (207) with an "inordinately aggressive female body" (238), for whom the Negro Tom Robinson, her victim, expresses sympathy. Worth mentioning is the novel's currency in contemporary popular culture. In the educational comedy web podcast *Thug Notes*, Sparky Sweets, PhD (née Greg Edwards), praises Atticus's courtroom talent with a mere mention of Mayella as "Ewell's daughter." He comments, "At the trial, my boy Atticus spits mad game up in that courtroom." Sweets continues, "In fact, [Atticus] finds out it was Ewell's daughter who was puttin' the moves on Tom [Robinson]. Turns out, she wanted some of that dark chocolate, ya' know wha'I mean?" (Edwards).[1]

Critics fail to recognize, however, Lee's creation of one of the most formidable and *commanding* white female characters in modern fiction, yet she is an unsung literary/cinematic anti-heroine because of her class status. Lee's imagination endows Mayella with the potency of white womanhood, and the author charges her with the duty assigned to every white woman in Jim Crow South: to maintain *at all costs* the socio-legal order established by white patriarchs. Elizabeth Gillespie McRae would agree: "[White women] are at the center of the history of white supremacist politics in the South and nation. . . . [They] took central roles in disciplining their communities according to Jim Crow's rules" (4). Mayella disciplines her community within the court of law but the author cleverly throws the reader and the critic off guard as she casts the motherless teenager "among pigs" (218) and renders her invisible until the trial in the novel; Mulligan, *To Kill a Mockingbird's* director, follows suit. When Mayella does appear in court onscreen to have something to say, readers and film audiences have been so inundated with her father's blatant racism and hatred, his lack of a will to work, and his alcoholism and abusive behavior that sorrow and sympathy for Mayella divert attention from her skill in the courtroom in both mediums.

Consider Tom Robinson, the Negro whom Mayella accuses of assaulting her, and his white attorney, Atticus Finch. Robinson's choice of emotion for Mayella—sympathy—paradoxically, unleashes Mayella's power, however innocent she appears. In turn, Mayella's testimony in the novel and in the film (re)directs audience attention away from Atticus's catch of Mayella's lie about the assault; instead, Lee positions Mayella to use her closing argument to strategically point up the lawyer's lack of Southern gentility. Sociologist and Pan-Africanist W. E. B. Du Bois contends, "every white man became a recognized official to keep Negroes 'in their places'. Negro baiting and even lynching became a form of amusement" (as qtd in I. Evans 81). Atticus and every white male citizen in Maycomb fail miserably in their *duty* to advocate for Mayella's white womanhood *on her word*. That she is called to testify to defend herself against a Negro *in public*—that the *Negro* is given a trial—are low-down mockeries of every sociolegal system set up to govern the races. "True womanhood," asserts Amii Larkin Barnard, "provided the opportunity for the *taking* of Black life in the defense of a white woman's honor"; the veneration of white womanhood required, furthermore, an unwavering belief in the white supremacist theory that "white women [were the] cherished and admired jewels of a superior race" (10).

Lee exploits Mayella to restore these white supremacist norms. More significant, Lee's exploitation of Mayella broadcasts the unacknowledged impact of the rural poor white woman within the system of white supremacy. The class status and living conditions of Mayella (and the Ewells) drop her character into the group of "white trash," or poor whites, defined in eugenic family studies of the early twentieth century as being of "inferior heredity . . . considered the source of alcoholism, crime, . . . harlotry, . . . laziness, . . . and a host of other ills" (Rafter 1). Every member in this particular group is "a menace, the half-witted, Grendel-like stranger who likes to live in hollow logs and decrepit shanties" (Rafter 30). Lee apprehends all too well these definitions are but "a White Trash myth, but with the dimension of danger" (Rafter 30). The danger resides in the underestimation of Mayella Violet Ewell in scholarship, film reviews, and, I hazard, the classroom. Close readings of the novel and, central to this essay, the film adaptation of *To Kill a Mockingbird,* especially the work of Russell Harlan, the cinematographer, and Collin Wilcox Paxton (Mayella), reveal that Southern poor white femininity will leverage its own significance through the destruction of black masculinity.

In all, scholarship on Mayella pushes front and center a dirt-poor hyper-sexual young white woman without agency or communal correspondence. The film reviews as well move Mayella to the margins to spotlight the stories of Scout, Jem, and Atticus Finch. In the *New York Times* review, for example, Bosley Crowther writes that the film centers on "The charging of a Negro with the rape of a white woman"; the latter remains nameless. He cites the actress cast as Mayella, Collin Wilcox Paxton, only as playing one of the Southern bigots. Mayella, too, is absent from Larry Tubelle's review for *Variety.* James Powers, reviewer for *The Hollywood Reporter,* however, praises Paxton but only as "the accuser of Peck's client." Contemporary reviews of the film also make little mention of Mayella; any criticism of her lands on her class status and alleged victimhood. Calling her "Tom's purported rape victim," Mark Holcomb, for example, remarks "one can't help wondering about Mayella and the seven other Ewell children . . . Fatherless and with no means of support, what's to become of them?" (38). In addition, CNN's Katie McLaughlin gives no opinion on Mayella in her 2012 review entitled "Justice, Fatherhood Hold True." In an interview with Wilcox, Stephen Bowie surmises, as well, that Wilcox portrays Mayella as "the redneck teenager who falsely accuses a black man of rape".

Commentary from major players in the film adaptation also overlook Mayella's alarming significance. Paxton (Mayella), an avid civil rights activist, brings to boil her character's poverty and abuse as well as feelings of hatred, isolation and, more significant, white patriarchal disre-spect. She discusses her audition process and the costume and make-up she imagined for her character but offers no viewpoints on Mayella and her motivations. She attests to her perception of Mayella as dirty and unkempt: "I had known girls from that kind of background. I wore a sec-ondhand dress, tennis shoes with holes in them, and dirty little white socks. I rubbed cold cream through my hair—that's why my hair looked so dirty" (McLellan). Such was the veracity of her performance that Paxton received a less than warm reception when she attended an NAACP conference in Monterey, California. A conference official had to remind the participants, "Collin is here at this conference because she believes in the cause. She is not the character in the film" (McLellan).

The actor Gregory Peck (Atticus Finch), won the Academy Award for Best Actor in *Mockingbird*. Peck comments on his character in an in-terview, "I was very much in sympathy with the lawyer who risked his personal reputation, his law practice, his personal safety and that of his children in defending a Negro accused of rape in the south in the year 1931" (Peck). Again, Mayella is conflated in "accusation" and "rape."

In 1963, Horton Foote won an Academy Award for Best Writing—Screenplay for his adaptation of *Mockingbird*. Foote, too, offers no insight into the young woman. Wilborn Hampton, Foote's biographer, writes of how Foote's own life experiences in his hometown Wharton, Texas, mir-rored those in *Mockingbird* and influenced the screenwriter's fashioning of the characters of Atticus Finch and Boo Radley, the latter Maycomb's "bogeyman who becomes the savior" (145). He continues, "Like Atticus, Foote's own father had been held in high esteem by the town's black popu-lation. And like Atticus, he had grown up in a free-thinking Methodist family. Foote also knew first-hand the grim reality of redneck Southern justice—one of his older cousins had been the unwitting motivation for a lynching" (145). Mayella, along with her father, Bob Ewell, and Tom Robinson are conflated within the noun "lynching" and "redneck South-ern justice." More noteworthy, Hampton claims of all of the scenes writ-ten by Foote, "one of the poignant scenes in the film . . . [is when] Scout is being tucked into bed by Atticus" (146).

The novel/film reviews, cast interviews, and scholarship tend to toss Mayella to the side. Recent interviews, however, feature the playwright and actress cast as Mayella in the current broadway production of *To Kill of Mockingbord*. On November 1, 2018, *To Kill a Mockingbird* debuted at the Shubert Theater on Broadway in New York. The play's world premiere opened December 13 the same year. Written by Aaron Sorkin and directed by Bartlett Sher, the play stars Jeff Daniels as Atticus Finch, Gbenga Akinnagbe as Tom Robinson, and Erin Wilhelmi as Mayella Ewell. On her character's motivation to accuse Tom Robinson, Wilhelmi places the blame on maternal loss and domestic abuse. She says in an interview, "She lost her mother.... She's raising her seven siblings. She's living in a house with an abusive father—physically and sexually abusive. It's amazing she has the strength that she does ..." (Citizens of Mockingbird). Wilhelmi highlights Mayella's tragic familial circumstances with no reference to the character's own dare to wield the power of racism and white womanhood. Sorkin, as well, concurs, "Her rage at the end of her testimony where we hear her *parroting* things that we've heard her father say—*trying to grab onto a branch* any way that she can becomes as much about her circumstance as it is about her lying" (Citizens of Mockingbird my emphasis). Sorkin and Wilhelmi interpret Mayella as a desperate powerless character rather than a knowledgeable caretaker of her own agency as a young white woman coming of age within the system of racism.

Harlan's extreme and medium close-ups of Paxton firmly establish a visceral image of Mayella delivered with a callous ferocity by the actress. No sobbing Mayella here until she has said her piece. The eye of the camera catches only a strong and composed character. Before I proceed, it is instructive here to offer some theory of film forms, in particular the close-up and medium shot. In its strictest sense, close-ups "show details of a person or object, such as the face or hands ... perhaps indicating nuances of the character's feelings or thoughts" (Corrigan 109). American cinema conceptualizes the close-up as a film form aligned with the human face, and when closed in on, makes legible the interiority of the character. Crucial to the close-up is *reaction*. It is dictated by facial members (i.e., eyes, nose, mouth, jaws) transcribing the thoughts and feelings of the character—or those which make visible for the camera the cinematic unspoken. "Reacting," believes film director Jim Jarmusch, "is the essence of acting. And just tiny things can fleet across [the face] and say a lot more than probably pages of dialogue" (qtd. in Phillips 20–21). Susan Stewart maintains, "The face is a type of 'deep' text ... one of the great topoi of Western literature has been the notion of the face as book" (127). Harlan makes generous use of the close-up as his camera "reads" to the audience Mayella Violet Ewell, the shrewd and resourceful young white teenager just a half-year away from her twentieth birthday. As for the medium shot, Barsam and Monahan state, "the MS ... replicates our human experience of proximity without intimacy; it provides more detail with the body" (238). As is analyzed herein, Harlan's film form choices showcase a Mayella, who knows exactly on what sociocultural norm to rely upon to coax Maycomb citizens not only to believe her but also to *welcome* her as a viable member of the community.

Before Mayella takes the witness stand, Harlan's medium close-up gives us the first sight of the teenager as she sits with her father. Within the frame, Mayella's hatred and anger match her father's scowl. The court prepares to hear witnesses for the prosecution. The testimonies from these white males produce Mayella visually as battered body. Sheriff Tate swears Mayella was beaten "around the head . . . with bruising coming on her arms . . . and a black eye starting." Her father, Bob Ewell, swears to discovering Mayella "on the floor squalling" after seeing Robinson "with my Mayella." When the bailiff calls Mayella Violet Ewell to the stand offscreen, however, Harlan's close-up introduces the audience to a shy but ready young white woman who has healed from her wounds. The prosecuting attorney, Mr. Gilmer, gently guides Mayella to the witness chair. In medium shot, Mayella places her right hand on the Bible but not before rubbing her hand on her dress as if to clean it. Costuming, here, plays a pivotal role in the film's presentation of Mayella. Not only does her costume "suggest . . . self-image [as well as] the public image that the character is trying to project" (Basram and Monahan 182); more important, her clothing produces the corporeal site in direct contrast to Sheriff Tate's and Bob Ewell's testimonies of finding her mishandled and abused. In addition, her costume marks a young white woman who, in spite of her sociocultural and domestic circumstances, takes care in her appearance. She carries a hat decorated with a ribbon. The ruffled collar accentuates her printed dress; she wears loafers. She positions herself smoothly into the witness chair, being careful to keep her legs, ankles, and feet together. Her hat rests in her lap; a silk bow showcases her bangs. Mayella's sartorial choices sweep away from her the pigs and the garbage dump; they legitimize her presence. Even though Mary Cathryn Cain studies the aesthetics of whiteness among nineteenth-century, middle-class white women, her research applies to Mayella here. She writes, "operating under a cultural mandate to present fair faces to the outside world, [white] women transformed the obligation to look beautiful into a potent resource for *expressing their value* to the republic. This meant that the *very personal arts of the toilette became acts of racial identity construction*" (28; *my emphasis*). Mayella's dress, then, provides the means for her to pass as middle class *and* to demand the same protection afforded middle-class white women in Maycomb by Southern white patriarchs.

Harlan's high angle shot not only establishes the crowded environment of the courtroom; in addition, from a high angle, audiences sense and feel the atmosphere and intense emotions of the courtroom spectators fueled for weeks by Mayella's accusation. Theatre staging generates insight into the young woman's placement in the courtroom and serves as the leitmotif of her existence. Harlan's camera reveals a plaintiff engulfed legally within a white patriarchal structure. Within those structures, the camera positions her as a diminutive girl, alone and unprotected. Judge Taylor controls order upstage center. Mayella takes the witness chair front and center of him. The bailiff stands far upstage left over her shoulder. Center stage right is the all-white male jury; downstage right is the Negro defendant, Tom Robinson, and his white lawyer, Atticus Finch; Mr. Gilmer, the prosecutor and his associate watch downstage left. Mayella's father observes his daughter from the first courtroom pew also downstage left. Atticus's children, Scout and Jem, observe with the Negro spectators from the balcony.

The overwhelming power of white patriarchy within which Mayella lives comes through Harlan's camera. According to Julia Ernst, Mayella is a victim of a "gender biased legal system of that time" (1022). Mayella points up this bias, as we shall see, during her testimony to the prosecutor and her cross-examination. The medium high angle shot suggests a compassionate Prosecutor Gilmer who assumes a polite distance from Mayella as he questions her casually in front of the courtroom's desk. He sits on its edge throughout his entire examination of her, and Mayella, respectfully, talks eye-to-eye with him. This space affords Mayella confidence with which to make her statement. Prosecutor Gilmer directs her off camera, "Now Miss Mayella, suppose you tell us just what happened, huh?"

She tentatively begins:

> Well, [clears throat] Sir, I was sittin' on the porch and he come along . . . well there's this old chifferobe in the yard, and I said you come in here boy and bust up this chifferobe and I'll give you a nickel. So he come on in the yard and I go in the house to get him the nickel and I turn around and before know it he's on me and I fought him hard but he had me around the neck and he

> hit me again and again and the next thing I knew Poppa's in the
> room a'standing over me hollerin' 'who done it? Who done it?

An analysis of Mayella's story illuminates the Southern racial etiquette enacted by the young white woman. "Come in here boy,"[2] asserts her authority over Robinson, an adult married Negro man, husband, and father; custom requires Robinson to heed her command no matter the circumstances. To denote inferiority and a consideration of a Negro as a non-human being, some whites deploy the pejorative "boy." Its cousin is "nigger."[3] That Mayella addresses Robinson as "boy" signifies the power her whiteness grants over him despite her age.

Mayella, moreover, assures the white men and women in the courtroom of her strong-willed attempt to resist Robinson's "advances." Her assurances bid for white males to defend her purity and white femininity. According to Barbara Welter, "Purity was as essential as piety to a young woman, its absence as unnatural and unfeminine. Without it she was, in fact, *no woman at all, but a member of some lower order.* A 'fallen woman' was a 'fallen angel,' unworthy of the celestial company of her sex. To contemplate the loss of purity brought tears; to be guilty of such a crime . . . brought madness or death" (154; *my emphasis*).

Cain complements Welter's analysis. Mayella's boast of fighting the big black "strong" Negro suggests a perception of access "to a constituency that wrestled anxiously with questions of identity, dependency, status, and the true sphere of woman" (Cain 28). That she commands a Negro into her front yard to chop up a chifferobe for kindling affirms her position in the *constituency* of white women who depend on Negro domestics to relieve them of (heavy) labor. Mayella, a white female alone in her home offering to pay a Negro for work, signifies "female whiteness . . . actively equated with personal qualities of goodness, purity, innocence, and candor" (Cain 33). Mayella insists on the court's full understanding of her apparent bewilderment over Robinson's *being* on her and repeatedly assaulting her body. After all, her command to Robinson was innocent and, from her statement, Robinson took advantage of her "goodness [and] *innocence*" (Cain 33; *my emphasis*), an action she knows the white men and women in the courtroom will find horrifying. The accusation of Robinson pouncing on her while home alone marks Mayella's appeal to white male fear of the Negro or the "black buck,"[4] who, in the white imagination, hungers for white female flesh. But she also evokes every (white) woman's dread: to be violently offended in her own home by a Negro male defiles the sanctity of it.

The main terror rests on the "dirt," and in Maycomb, the Negro, Tom Robinson and his community constitute dirt in the segregated southern town. These four phrases/phases articulated by Mayella—"I go in the house," "I turn around," "before I know it," and "he was on me"—are expressed to strike panic onto hearts of white women and men alike. The dark specter has invaded the sacred white space/woman, Mayella reminds the court. Mayella's visual of Robinson's entry into the white domestic space hauls "dirt" within that sanctuary; it has been contaminated. Mayella's testimony is her cue to the all-white male jury and the white women spectators to visualize how Robinson upset social order. She verbally moves Robinson into the house and portrays him as "dirt out of place . . . in the systemic ordering and classification of [Negroes and Whites]" (Douglas 36). She bids the court to understand her vulnerability because she trusted the social order of segregation to safeguard her. Why should she look behind her to make sure Robinson stays in the yard? Robinson, she believed, knew his place because the patriarchal legal system ensures his conformity to them. Robinson, according to Mayella, transgressed the social and moral code.

If Mayella experiences calm and an assured testimony with Prosecuting Attorney Gilmer, Atticus produces no such feelings in her. In a medium tracking shot, Atticus stands and walks around the courtroom interrogating Mayella from different areas therein. During Atticus's cross-examination of her, Mayella shows signs of extreme discomfort. The medium low angle shots anoint Atticus with power and shore up his intimidating presence. These low angle shots force Mayella to look up at white patriarchal authority and follow him around the courtroom; each move by Atticus exacerbates her anxiety. What is more, Harlan's medium shot takes sides: it guides the audience's as well as Mayella's attention to the effect of Atticus's cross-examination; there is no intimacy between them. Mayella contradicts her statements as Atticus's cross-examination finally uncovers the truth: Tom Robinson did not assault her. For example, in medium shot, Atticus stands directly to Mayella's right and asks her if she remembers Tom Robinson "beating you across the face"; in Harlan's medium close-up, she leans away from Atticus confused. She shakes her head in the negative, blinks at the attorney through her bangs, and answers, "naw . . . uh . . . I don't . . . uh . . . recollect if he hit me." Her body suggests a drainage of energy, but her eyes betray her perjury.

Mayella, however, remembers her role in court; she turns away quickly from the camera to the center of the courtroom and counters, "I mean... Yes! He hit me. Hehehe hit me!" When Robinson testifies to the loss of use of his arm in a cotton gin accident, Harlan's medium close-up bares Mayella's awareness of being caught in a lie. Pandemonium erupts in the courtroom; Judge Taylor restores order. Mayella jumps at the pounding of the gavel. It is as if courtroom spectators are asking, "What are we to do now?" Mayella displays clear signs of nervous tension but Harlan's medium close-up flags her contemplation of her next move.

When Atticus asks her *how* Tom Robinson beat her, he stands side-by-side with his defendant. Harlan delivers this scene in medium shot to signify Atticus's belief in his client's innocence. Still in medium close-up, Mayella shrugs her shoulders and, through nervous laughter, testifies, "I don't know how . . . he done it . . . He just done it." Paxton's skillful performance unveils Mayella's puzzlement over why Atticus just does not take her word as had Prosecutor Gilmer. Her body language lets slip an annoyance over why she even *has to be* questioned. Robinson "just done it" is all Atticus needs to know.

Atticus moves away from Tom Robinson toward Mayella as he recounts her testimony: "You have testified that he choked you and he beat you. You didn't say that he sneaked up behind you and knocked you out cold but that you turned around and there he was. You want to tell us what really happened?" Mayella gasps and trembles; Harlan's camera remains in medium close-up to illustrate how the courtroom procedures have overwhelmed her. Even more emotionally detrimental, Atticus's cross-examination shatters the scenario she voiced to underwrite her own story. Curious of the effect Atticus's triumph has on Mayella, Harlan's camera tracks closer toward her, and the close-up edges Judge Taylor out of the frame to prominently feature Mayella's head. Audiences have "an exclusive view of the character's state of mind" (Barsam & Monahan 238). She announces with confidence, "I got somethin' to say an' then I ain't gonna say no more." It is powerful, her use of the "I" rather than a request for *permission* to speak. Mayella sets *her* parameters; in other words, she will refuse any further cross-examination of her.

In an act of defiance transcending the confines of her gender and socio-economic class, she continues as she pans the courtroom with her eyes, "He took advantage of me [turning to the jury] and if you fine fancy gentle-men [to Atticus] ain't gonna do something about it then [to the courtroom audience and back] you're just a bunch of lousy yellow stinkin' cowards and your fancy airs don't come to nothin'! Your "ma'amin' and your "miss Mayella'en" it don't come to nothin' Mr. Finch." Harlan's close-up makes legible in Mayella's face the monstrosity of her claim; her eyes and gritted teeth function as sites of fear, yes, but there is fierce determination to make her words count. As an aside, Mayella dares to cross the line of Southern decorum for Southern women. Not only does she speak, she speaks *loudly;* hers is a verbal aggression. In essence, Mayella countenances white *ladyhood* in the beginning with Prosecutor Gilmer (i.e., soft speech, cleanliness, neatness, politeness); however, she then conjures the Southern female confederate rebel who fights for self-respect via outrageous behavior (Ownby 6) in the private sphere of the courtroom. She gasps again (almost in a hiccup) at her statement's close, and runs toward the courtroom's door. She is stopped, however, by members of the patriarchal fold: her father and the sheriff. The soul and spirit of Mayella's testimony indicts the white men in the courtroom—in particular Atticus—for impugning her veracity. Within the frame of the close-up, Mayella skillfully delegitimizes the law on which Atticus brings to light her perjury. As Mayella deflects Atticus's "attack" on her story, she essentially speaks up for her right *to be* a white woman, and that right includes the practice of racism for a specific consequence. She may be an abused poor white daughter of an ingrate, but she *is* white, and well aware of the long-established culture of honor: white men are charged to protect the purity of white women *especially* when they speak of being sexually violated.

Harlan's medium/close-ups of Mayella as well as Paxton's character interpretation create for the viewer the "'steel magnolia' or the "superficially soft and melting woman who was quite capable of toughness and the wielding of power" (Nisbett and Cohen 88), and Harlan's close-up draws out the young woman's searing anger. Mayella conjures her power to hemorrhage out the potency of Atticus's cross-examination and that of the courtroom attendees' *insult* to her testimony, thus the "fancy fine gentlemen" statement. Why the uproar (when Atticus shines the light on her lie)? In Mayella's mind, the camera reads, Atticus breaks the code of honor. In the Southern culture of honor, "An insult implies that the target is weak enough to be bullied. . . . The individual who insults someone must be forced to retract. . . . A particularly important kind of insult is one directed at female members of a man's family" (Nisbett and Cohen 5). When she opens her mouth to speak, her words pour sarcasm over the mores cherished by Southern gentlemen. Mayella's challenge to white men to prove their manhood comes through one significant declaration in her testimony: "He took advantage of me." In Mayella's estimation, white manhood can be proven only via the conviction of the Negro, Tom Robinson, *on her word,* or they are "just a bunch of lousy yellow stinkin' cowards."

One other aspect of Mayella's testimony hinges upon her critique of Southern gentility, or the "fancy airs," in particular Southern speech practiced by white men to exhibit respect for the Southern white lady. Throughout the courtroom proceedings, Prosecutor Gilmer treats her tenderly; he attentively listens to her and then *thanks her* for her statement. Atticus calls her *Miss* Mayella before his cross-examination. Judge Taylor quiets the courtroom during its uproar. The "ma'am-ing" and "Miss Mayella'en" are supposed to set her firmly on the pedestal above her Negro counterparts; but, that she has to appear in court to *defend* her accusation of sexual violation deems these manners as social farces. Such is the command of Mayella's discourse, the state rests its case *without* a closing statement. Why? Because Mayella has charged the all-white male jury with its duty; she *is* the closing argument. Harlan's camera remains on Mayella; he only cuts to her father once, but Ewell's medium close-up reads as observation, *not* a coaching of his daughter—an important distinction because practically all scholarship subscribes to the belief that the father forces Mayella to tell and stand behind this lie.

The question remains, nevertheless, from where did Mayella find such courage to boldly and loudly speak out? I return now to the culture of lynching. The trouble with the photographs that open this chapter is the participation of parents and the school officials who made arrangements for children to gorge on these barbecued "meals." Allen writes, "hundreds of kodaks clicked all morning at the scene of the lynching. . . . *Women and children were there by the score.* At a number of country schools the day's routine was delayed until boy and girl pupils could get back from viewing the lynched man" (11; *my emphasis*).

Harlan's extreme/medium close-ups and medium shots, and Paxton's character interpretation provide some answers as well. In her performance, Paxton certainly channeled those "girls from [Mayella's] kind of background" (McLellan). Mayella's background: poverty stricken, uneducated, abused, motherless; girls Paxton knew who very well could have borne witness to a lynching and glommed on to the power of that spectacle. The story is set in the fictional town of Maycomb, Alabama in the early 1930s. In Alabama alone, 326 Negroes were killed from 1877–1950 (al.com). Paxton's Mayella might have seen the postcard of Neal Guinn's bullet-riddled sixteen-year-old body. Guinn was accused of an attempted attack on an eleven-year-old white girl in Haynesville, Alabama in 1931. The article in the *New York Times* reads, "Sheriff Meadows said the Negro accosted the girl this morning as she was walking from her home to a grocery store. *She fought him*, escaped and ran home" ("Negro Boy"; *my emphasis)*; or, she might have seen photos of Bunk Richardson, who was lynched in Gadsden, Alabama, in 1906 for rape and murder of a white girl (Allen plates #86, #87); or photos of George Meadows, lynched in 1889 in Birmingham, Alabama, on the accusation of an "assault on a lady . . . and brutal[ ] murder [of] her little son before her eyes . . . [and the] rape on a little negro girl" (Allen plates #95, #96); or the 1906 lynching of Dick Robinson in Pritchard Station, Alabama (Allen plate #17). Or maybe, just maybe, before she died, Mayella's mother passed down to her daughter those tenets of the Southern culture of honor. After all, someone taught the little girl viewing Ruben Stacy's body the value, prize, and power of being a white female in a segregated society. Perhaps Lee visualized Mayella scrutinizing that postcard.

The novel intimates, no doubt, that Mayella comes under the influence of an abusive father. Paxton's performance and Harlan's camera in the film, however, encourage the audience to (re)consider Mayella Ewell as the helpless subject of her father's iron will and to question her lack of agency due to her poverty. This examination of cinematography and actress portrayal establish how the visuals of lynchings could have validated the psyche of this poor white female, sanctioned her attitude toward adult black males, and empowered her to act with confidence on the compelling narratives widely circulated about them. Harper Lee's pen, Robert Mulligan's direction, and Russell Harlan' cinematography immortalize her defiance. It is time we paid attention.

Notes

1. The controversy over calling African American men "boy" has widespread currency in popular culture today. See Shaun King, "Bill Romanowski was blatantly racist even before he called Cam Newton 'boy' in post–Super Bowl tweet"; Roland Martin, "Understanding Why You Don't Call a Black Man Boy"; "How Racist is "Boy"?

2. Randall Kennedy writes, "*Nigger* has been a familiar part of the vocabularies of whites high and low. It has often been the calling card of so-called white trash—poor, disreputable, uneducated Euro-Americans" (7).

3. See Donald Bogle, *Toms, Coons, Mulattoes, Mammies, & Bucks,* wherein he defines the "black buck" as "big baadddd niggers, over-sexed and savage, violent and

frenzied as they lust for white flesh" (14). This stereotype was dramatized in D. W. Griffith's film *Birth of a Nation* (1915). Bogle continues, "Griffith played on the myth of the Negro's high-powered sexuality, then articulated the great white fear that every black man longs for a white woman. Underlying the fear was the assumption that the white woman was the ultimate in female desirability, herself a symbol of white pride, power, and beauty" (14).

Works Cited

Allen, James, Hilton Als, John Lewis, and Leon Litwack. *Without Sanctuary: Lynching Photography in America*. Twin Palms Publishers, 2000.

Barnard, Amii Larkin. "The Application of Critical Race Feminism to the Anti-Lynching Movement: Black Women's Fight Against Race and Gender Ideology, 1892–1920." *UCLA Women's Law Journal*, vol. 30, no. 1, pp. 1–10.

Barsam, Richard, and Dave Monahan. *Looking at Movies: An Introduction to Film*. 5th ed. W. W. Norton, 2016.

Blackford, Holly Virginia. *Mockingbird Passing: Closeted Traditions and Sexual Curiosities in Harper Lee's Novel*. University of Tennessee Press, 2011.

Bogle, Donald. *Toms, Coons, Mulattoes, Mammies, & Bucks: An Interpretive History of Blacks in American Films*. Continuum Press, 2007.

Bowie, Stephen. "An Interview with Collin Wilcox." 25 Mar 2009. www.classic tvhistory.wordpress.com. Accessed 27 Jan 2017.

Cain, Mary Cathryn. "The Art and Politics of Looking White Beauty Practice among White Women in Antebellum America." *Winterthur Portfolio*, vol. 42, no. 1, Spring 2008, pp. 27–50.

Churchwell, Sandra. "*Go Set a Watchman* by Harper Lee review: 'moral ambition sabotaged,'" 17 July 2015, theguardian.com. Accessed 19 Feb. 2018.

Citizens of Mockingbird: Erin Wilhelmi on Capturing the Rage of Racism in Mayella Ewell. 22 Apr. 2019. broadway.com. Accessed 5 Jun. 2019.

Corrigan, Timothy and Patricia White. *The Film Experience: An Introduction*. Fifth Ed. Bedford/St. Martin's, 2017.

Crowther, Bosley. 'To Kill a Mockingbird': One Adult Omission in a Fine Film 2 Superb Discoveries Add to Delight." 18 Feb. 1963, nytimes.com. Accessed 12 Jan. 2017.

Douglas, Mary. *Purity and Danger: An Analysis of Concepts of Pollution and Taboo*. Routledge, 2002.

Edwards, Greg. *To Kill a Mockingbird: Thug Notes Summary and Analysis*. 18 June 2013. youtube.com. Accessed 14 Jan 2017.

Ernst, Julia L. "Women in Litigation Literature: The Exoneration of Mayella Ewell in *To Kill A Mockingbird*." *Akron Law Review*: Vol. 47 : Iss. 4, Article 5, 2014.

Evans, Greg. "Jeff Daniels To Head Aaron Sorkin's 'To Kill A Mockingbird' On Broadway." 15 Feb. 18, deadline.com. Accessed 17 Feb. 2018.

Evans, Ivan. *Cultures of Violence: Racial Violence and the Origins of Segregation in South Africa and the American South*. Manchester University Press, 2011.

Gilmore, Alec. "*To Kill a Mockingbird*: Perceptions of "the Other." *Harper Lee's* To Kill a Mockingbird: *New Essays*. Ed. Michael J. Meyer. Scarecrow Press, 2010.

Hampton, Wilborn. *Horton Foote: America's Storyteller.* Simon & Schuster, 2009.

"How Racist is "Boy"? 1 Nov 10, economist.com. Accessed 4 Feb. 17.

Holcomb, Mark. "To Kill a Mockingbird." *Film Quarterly.* Vol. 55:4 (Summer 2002): 34-40. Print.

Kennedy, Randall. *Nigger: The Strange Career of a Troublesome Word.* Vintage, 2003.

King, Shaun. "Bill Romanowski was blatantly racist even before he called Cam Newton 'boy' in post-Super Bowl tweet." 8 Feb. 2017, nydailynews.com. Accessed 5 Feb. 2017.

Lee, Harper. *To Kill a Mockingbird.* HarperCollins, 2002.

Martin, Roland. "Understanding Why You Don't Call a Black Man Boy." 15 Apr. 2008, ac360.blogs.cnn.com, Accessed 5 Feb. 2017.

McLaughlin, Katie. "Justice, Fatherhood Hold True." 3 Feb. 2012, cnn.com. Accessed 12 Jan. 2017.

McLellan, Dennis. "Collin Wilcox Paxton dies at 74; actress was Mayella in 'To Kill a Mockingbird.'" 23 Oct. 2008, latimes.com. Accessed 27 Jan. 2017.

Meyer, Michael J. *Harper Lee's To Kill a Mockingbird.* Scarecrow Press, 2010.

"Negro Boy, 16, is Lynched." rarenewspapers.com. Item #569802. Accessed 1 Feb. 2017.

Nisbett, Richard E., and Dov Cohen. *Culture of Honor: The Psychology of Violence in the South.* Westview Press, 1996.

Ownby, Ted. *Manners and Southern History.* University Press of Mississippi, 2007.

Peck, Gregory. "Interview." N.d., youtube.com. Accessed 12 Dec. 2016.

Powers, James. "Pakula-Mulligan pic in line for honors." 11 Dec. 1962, hollywoodreporter.com. Accessed 12 Jan. 2017.

Rafter, Nicole Hahn. *White Trash: The Eugenic Family Studies, 1877–1919.* Northeastern University Press, 1988.

Tubelle, Larry. "To Kill a Mockingbird." 11 Dec. 1962, variety.com. Accessed 12 Dec. 2016.

Welter, Barbara. "The Cult of True Womanhood." *American Quarterly,* vol. 18, no. 2. Part 1, Summer 1966, pp. 151–74.

Wood, Amy Louise. *Lynching and Spectacle: Witnessing Racial Violence in America, 1890–1940.* University of North Carolina Press, 2009.

PART 3

MOCKINGBIRD CONTEXTUALIZED

7

"WITH ALL YOUR BOOK LEARNIN'"
Ignorance and Literacy in *Go Set a Watchman*
Adam Nemmers

On May 7, 2006, the reclusive Harper Lee broke a forty-six-year public silence to compose an open letter to Oprah Winfrey. Read aloud on Winfrey's program and later republished in *O Magazine*, the letter offers a paean to the power and promise of literacy, extolling the virtues of slow and diligent learning against the encroaching immediacy of technology. Anyone who has read Lee's *To Kill a Mockingbird* (1960) will encounter familiar touchstones in her address: a winsome narrator; depictions of a hardscrabble yet halcyon youth; a father reading newspapers every evening; and specific references to the Bobbsey Twins, *Anne of Green Gables*, and Tom Swift. In the letter, an eighty-year-old Lee reminisces about growing up in small-town Alabama during the Depression, where "books were scarce," and "there was nothing you could call a library," so children circulated books between the "long dry spells" broken by Christmas (Lee "Letter to Oprah" 152). Even so, Lee explains, "we were privileged" in comparison to African Americans and children from rural areas, who "had never looked into a book until they went to school" or "learned to read three-to-one—three children to one book" (152). As Lee and her friends grew older, however "we began to realize what our books were worth"—both in barter (for a doll buggy, a shotgun) and as valuable tools to improve their lives. Throughout her letter Lee looks fondly upon her lifetime of reading, wondering at the impossibility of an atavistic pre-literacy and ridiculing the notion of "curling up in bed to read a computer," affirming that "some things should happen on soft pages, not cold metal" (153). As Lee posits at the outset of the letter, "Do you remember when you learned to read, or like me, can you not even remember a time when you didn't know how?" (151) In this way, the letter, like *Mockingbird*, functions as a literacy narrative, offering an account of how the author came to read and write, and emphasizing the personal and societal importance of literacy.

Lee's missive found a natural benefactor in Winfrey, who identifies as a Southern woman and has emerged as latter-day sponsor and kingmaker of American literacy and letters. While Winfrey is an avid reader with an extensive library, her bibliophilia has been most prominently expressed through the vehicle of her Book Club, which, during its fifteen-year run (1996–2011), recommended seventy novels, the "Oprah editions" of which sold over 55 million copies. Beyond its tremendous sales, the Book Club has proven massively influential in establishing an international reading community and making literature a popular topic of conversation. In this regard, Oprah's Book Club functioned as an extension of the reading experience Winfrey had in the late 1960s:

> After reading *To Kill a Mockingbird*, I wished I had an accent, and I would go around trying to imitate Scout . . . just like I do now, I remember reading this book and then going to class and not being able to shut up about it. I read it in eighth or ninth grade, and I was trying to push the book on other kids. So it makes sense that now I have a book club, because I have been doing that since this book. It's one of the first books I wanted to encourage other people to read. (Winfrey "My Lunch with Harper Lee")

Because Lee declined Oprah's request for an on-air interview regarding her work, *To Kill a Mockingbird* was not officially included as a monthly Book Club selection. Yet Oprah has remained steadfast in advocacy of Lee and her novel, and to this day describes *Mockingbird* as her "favorite novel of all time."

In her fondness for *Mockingbird,* Oprah is far from alone; the novel rates as one of the most read and beloved works of American fiction. Claudia Durst Johnson reports that "*To Kill a Mockingbird* is unquestionably one of the most widely read, best-selling, and influential books in American literature" (*Understanding* xi); similarly, Alice Hall Petry writes, "One would be hard pressed to think of a novel besides *To Kill a Mockingbird* (1960) that has been more read, studied, loved and cherished in the United

States over the last forty years" (xv). On account of its simple prose and accessible themes, *Mockingbird* has become a staple of high school literature classrooms (no matter your current age, you likely read it during your sophomore year); it is the sort of novel that people who are not bookworms remember reading and remember loving. Like no other book *Mockingbird* has achieved enduring popularity across generations, to which the estimated thirty million volumes translated and printed into forty languages can attest (Betts 137). Though ostensibly about issues specific to the American South, the novel has become canonical even outside of the United States; Marian Spires reports that "almost forty years after Harper Lee's novel was first published, it still sits on many Year 10 English courses across Australia" (125).

Beyond the classroom, the broad appeal of *Mockingbird* has led to its adoption in various community literacy programs. As Deborah Vriend Van Duinen and Audra Bolhuis observe, the act of "reading and discussing literature in a communitywide reading program foregrounds its contextual aspect, taking literature out of a traditional school or academic context and placing it within a particular geographic community of people" (82). To this end, the All Pikes Peak Reads program selected *Mockingbird* to "promote literacy and encourage community dialogue about racial, cultural and generational issues" ("Pulitzer Prize-winner Gets First Read"). Similarly, in Jacksonville, the "JAX Reads!" group selected *To Kill A Mockingbird* not only "because of the many issues it deals with, such as discrimination, poverty, prejudice and single parenting," but also because "we want Jacksonville to get excited about discussing the book and to encourage individuals, families, businesses to focus on the need to read" ("City Forms City-Wide Book Club"). Mary Dempsey, Chicago's library commissioner, testified that she hoped reading *Mockingbird* for the city's One Book, One Chicago program "will encourage not just people who read books but those who don't to pick up this book" ("Library Wants Everybody to Read Book"). So it is that communities across the nation have increasingly turned to *Mockingbird* to launch their literacy programs because the novel's content and themes align with the gospel of literacy they seek to promote.

Given the resounding popularity of *Mockingbird*, it came as no surprise that the announcement of a "newly discovered" sequel was met with soaring expectations. Presale figures for *Go Set a Watchman* set a record for HarperCollins and Barnes & Noble, with many *Mockingbird* fans expecting a volume similar in content and tone. By and large, readers were disappointed to encounter an unpolished draft told from the third-person perspective of an adult, New Yorker Jean Louise, with the original's beloved characters altered: Jem dead, Calpurnia departed, and Atticus Finch, once the bastion of liberal enlightenment, a . . . racist? Reviews were mixed as well, with consensus marking it as poorly written and unevenly plotted, if valuable as a first draft and cultural artifact. Moreover, the controversy over its racial elements (*Watchman* is unlikely to experience similarly widespread adoption in schools and communities) has largely obscured its thematic content, specifically the novel's decidedly pessimistic attitude toward the promise of literacy. Indeed, Harper Lee's first-written "sequel" is entirely at odds with the celebration of reading and writing offered both by Lee's bestseller and her open letter nearly a decade earlier.

With this broad context established, the essay to follow explores the doubled-edged notion of literacy inherent to these novels, arguing that access to information is not the same as education, and that reading can often generate more heat than enlightenment. As presented in *To Kill a Mockingbird*, literacy is a vital and ameliorative force that, if extended to those benighted, would prove salutary for their lives and the problems of the world. Yet, as *Go Set a Watchman* demonstrates, literacy does not necessarily dispel ignorance, and its benefits do not always extend across lines of class, race, and gender—especially when such literacy is unevenly distributed or unshared by members of a community. From the mainstream classroom to the public imagination, this message complicates and darkens our cultural memory of *Mockingbird,* forcing us to reconsider the dogma we once believed. Indeed, the correction offered by *Watchman* has profound parallels to our current literacy landscape (especially with regard to media literacy), and invites further investment in the literature classroom and community literacy programs, through which students and citizens might learn and discuss crucial issues together.

"I Think It's How Long Your Family's Been Readin' and Writin'"

To Kill a Mockingbird can be read as a book-length literacy narrative, wherein Scout's "acquisition of increasingly complex forms of literacy figures prominently in how [she] understands . . . her life" (Dunbar-Odom 25). Across the novel Scout, serving as first-person narrator, emphasizes the value and relevance of reading, from the novel's opening scene, when Dill arrives and announces, "I can read," to its closing image, when

Atticus reads *The Grey Ghost* to Scout as she falls asleep. Indeed, literacy is the novel's most prominent motif. *Mockingbird* is suffused with references to the printed word, with books serving as currency for bets and barter, newspapers and magazines serving as the backdrop for everyday life, and literacy serving as a quick-and-easy determinant for one's class and morality.

In addition to its function as a literacy narrative, *Mockingbird* evinces Deborah Brandt's conception of literary sponsorship, offering examples both positive (Atticus and Calpurnia) and negative (Miss Caroline). In "Sponsors of Literacy," Brandt argues that literacy is never acquired without some sort of "sponsorship"; that such sponsors "are any agents, local or distant, concrete or abstract, who enable, support, teach, model, as well as recruit, regulate, suppress, or withhold literacy" (166), including parents, friends, bosses, or teachers. She maintains that these agents can sponsor "in the positive ways we normally recognize and expect, that is, we expect parents and teachers to encourage literacy," or in negative ways, such as by inhibiting or restricting literacy (Dunbar-Odom 34).

The novel's foremost sponsor of literacy is Atticus Finch, who serves as an exemplar of the Southern gentleman of letters. Though Scout claims "he hasn't taught me anything" (Lee *Mockingbird* 19) it is clear that Atticus's model has guided and inspired her toward reading and writing. As she recalls when attempting to plumb the depth of her literacy, "I had stared at [the lines above Atticus's moving finger] all the evenings in my memory, listening to the news of the day, Bills To Be Enacted into Laws, the diaries of Lorenzo Dow—anything Atticus happened to be reading when I crawled into his lap every night" (19–20). Indeed, reading is Atticus's sole pastime; Scout reports that "he did not do the things our schoolmates' fathers did: he never went hunting, he did not play poker or fish or drink or smoke. He sat in the living room and read" (102). Atticus's supposed bookish indolence and feebleness are belied by an episode wherein he kills the rabid dog Tim Johnson with a single rifle-shot; in a subsequent and related scene, Atticus confronts an armed lynch mob while reading a book. In this way, Lee establishes a connection between the power of a book and a firearm, both of which Atticus uses to control a chaotic situation—as Claudia Durst Johnson asserts, "Atticus's civilizing power comes from his reading, a power he has taken on in place of the power of the gun" (109). While Atticus was not himself formally schooled, he and his brother Jack were taught to read by their father, and he bestows this emphasis on responsible learning to his children, whether forcing Scout to attend classes or Jem to read *Ivanhoe* to Mrs. Dubose. Beyond his role as patriarch for the Finches, Atticus's role as literacy sponsor extends to the Maycomb community, to whom he has reputation as a "deep reader, a mighty deep reader" (186) and serves as both public defender and state representative. Given his consummate erudition and rectitude, Atticus figures as a champion of literacy for the Finch family and Maycomb at large, and has become a model citizen and inspiration for readers and viewers of *Mockingbird* as well.[1]

Atticus's steady and unassuming sponsorship is contrasted with the formal and disciplined pedagogy of Scout's first-grade teacher, Miss Caroline, who charges that Atticus "does not know how to teach" and that his efforts "interfere with [Scout's] reading" (19). Rather than allow children to approach reading organically, the college-educated Miss Caroline attempts to influence literacy through the educational theorems of John Dewey, or, as Scout calls it in her report to her father, the "Dewey Decimal System." That somehow Scout (and possibly Miss Caroline) has conflated the applications of John and Melvil Dewey becomes humorously apparent when Scout experiences Miss Caroline's "new way of teaching," which entails "waving cards at us on which were printed 'the,' 'cat,' 'rat,' 'man,' and 'you'"(20). While well intentioned, the practical result of Miss Caroline's effort bores her class and hinders their reading, writing, and individuality (Johnson *Threatening* 108); as Scout reports, "no comment seemed to be expected of us, and the class received these impressionistic revelations in silence" (20). Miss Caroline may possess more formal education than any other character in the novel (*Mockingbird* only mentions attending college in reference to Jem's football dreams), but her pedagogy is ineffective for lack of contextual awareness. It is clear, given her misunderstandings about Scout, Burris Ewell, and Walter Cunningham, that she has little knowledge of the folkways of Maycomb and its community. This ignorance and her geographic background (she hails from North Alabama, "full of Liquor Interests, Big Mules, steel companies, republicans, professors, and other persons of no background" [18]) mark Miss Caroline as an outsider. In this fashion, she serves as an incipient version of the clueless and carpetbagging Scout who returns to Maycomb in *Go Set a Watchman*.

Jem and Scout also encounter an unlikely sponsor of literacy in their maid, Calpurnia, who teaches Scout to write and has left a flowering legacy of literacy in Maycomb's African American community. Like Atticus, Calpurnia did not formally attend school, but was instead taught to read by old Miss Buford, Miss Maudie Atkinson's aunt, using a volume of Blackstone's *Commentaries* provided by Scout's Granddaddy Finch. She used the same volume, along with the Bible, to bring literacy to her son Zeebo, who in turn serves as unofficial cantor for Maycomb's First Purchase African M. E. Church, carefully "linin' " hymns so the congregation may sing in call-and-response fashion. In this way Lee demonstrates how a single seed of literacy can multiply across a community, providing the fruits of reading and writing to a large population that would otherwise have little or no access to printed material. Lee also promotes the notion of multiple literacies through Calpurnia, who lives a "double life" with "command of two languages": "colored-folks talk" and "white-folks' talk," an adroitness which astonishes Jem and Scout (143). Though her methods are decidedly nonstandard, Calpurnia serves as a surrogate for and sponsor alongside Atticus, fostering the children's literacy when he is at work or away from Maycomb.

Thus oriented toward literacy, the Finch children demonstrate a natural aptitude and penchant for writing and reading: Scout, whom "reading just came to" (19) and who read "everything I could lay my hands on" (36), and Jem, for whom "no tutorial system devised by man could have stopped him from getting at books" (36). Indeed, it is literacy, not breeding or wealth, that esteems the Finches in the eyes of Maycomb. The correlation between literacy and class is encouraged by Atticus, who moralizes about the responsibilities of literate citizens ("in your case, the law remains rigid" [33]) as well as by Aunt Alexandra, who cites a purple-covered book entitled *Meditations of Joshua S. St. Clair*—written by the Finches' deranged cousin, Joshua—as evidence that "you are not from run-of-the-mill people, that you are the product of several generations' gentle breeding" (152). Both comic and ironic, the episode has an enduring impact on Jem, who after weeks of rumination on the nature of literacy, class, and breeding, reaches the conclusion that: "Background doesn't mean Old Family . . . I think it's how long your family's been readin' and writin'. Scout, I've studied this hard and that's the only reason I can think of. Somewhere along when the Finches were in Egypt one of 'em must have learned a hieroglyphic or two and he taught his boy. . . Imagine Aunty being proud her great-granddaddy could read an' write—ladies pick funny things to be proud of" (259). Scout and Jem are both puzzled by the exact relationship between breeding and reading, but dearly value their early introduction to literacy. As Scout realizes, "If Atticus couldn't read, you and me'd be in a fix" (260).[2]

Throughout the novel the Finches' prized literacy is drawn in opposition to the lack thereof in rural whites such as the Ewells and Cunninghams, to say nothing of the nameless African Americans who populate Maycomb's Quarters. Though black and rural children are required to attend school (at least for the first day), they do not have access to the same literary networks, and thus are found lacking in intelligence, morality, and class. Brandt writes that, "throughout their lives, affluent people from high-caste racial groups have multiple and redundant contacts with powerful literacy sponsors as a routine part of their economic and political privileges. Poor people and those from low-caste racial groups have less consistent, less politically secured access to literacy sponsors—especially to the ones that can grease their way to academic and economic success" (170). *Mockingbird* expounds on the literacy privilege of affluent and high-caste groups. As Scout explains, regarding an assignment in her first-grade class, "few rural children had access to newspapers, so the burden of Current Events was borne by the town children"; the rural children are forced to bring clippings from "The Grit paper," which is "associated with liking fiddling, eating syrupy biscuits for lunch, being a holy-roller . . . all of which the state paid teachers to discourage" (280). Here the difference between the *Maycomb Tribune* and "the grit paper" offers a clear demarcation between the "class" of town children and lack of the country folk. The Ewells, in particular, dismiss the value of literacy, with young Burris's sneering at the idea of attending school; Mayella's having attended for just two or three years (208); and Bob's declaring he has use for writing only insofar as it allows him to cash relief checks. An alternate example of illiteracy is provided by the Cunninghams, who would like to send their children to school but are forced to recall them annually to help with farm work, thus perpetuating the cycle of ignorance and poverty. This disparity in literacy is directly related to the relative power of the characters; as Johnson asserts, "the more powerless Old Sarum residents and black citizens of Maycomb County are rarely literate; they are generally able only to sign their names" (110). Indeed, she continues, "the continuing powerlessness of the black and poor white people of Maycomb County is incidental to their inability to read, and their children, in contrast to Scout, are taken out of school, and thus denied their only access to power" (110). Though rural families may own land and guns, they have no access to books or education, and thus no access to the literacy that might offer personal edification or raise their station in Maycomb proper. The reverse is true of the novel's villain-cum-hero,

Boo Radley, who while a child won a spelling bee and stabbed his father in the leg while clipping articles from the newspaper—both markers of a burgeoning literacy. As an adult, however, Radley is closed off from the literary world and responds to the children's letters with objects rather than words. Johnson observes that Radley, "like other dispossessed people in the novel . . . is doomed to communicate without language" (*Threatening* 111). As in her letter, then, through *Mockingbird,* Lee offers a clear stance on the value of literacy, arguing that the command of language through reading, writing, and speaking is essential to high standing and success.

In all, *To Kill a Mockingbird* posits literacy as a salutary force that determines class and intelligence, in line with contemporary theories of literacy, such as a UNESCO statement that those who cannot read or write cannot learn new material (Dunbar-Odom 1). In the same vein, Sylvia Scribner's "Literacy in Three Metaphors" holds that literacy is "assumed to be necessary for a person's ability to think abstractly" and that "expansion of literacy skills is often viewed as a means for poor and politically powerless groups to claim their place in the world" (75). In *Mockingbird,* illiterate blacks and poor whites alike occupy Maycomb's abject sphere, while those who work with letters in the law or publishing—Atticus, Mr. Underwood, Judge Taylor—are the town's most politically powerful citizens, reinforcing Lee's message that literacy is the key to prosperity and power. To this end, Nancy Grimm posits that literacy is commonly viewed as an "unequivocally good thing, something that improves a person's position in life. The achievement of advanced literacy is supposed to make us better people, better citizens, and better workers" (39). Grimm's assertion is confirmed by the advancement of literacy in *Mockingbird,* where by novel's end the benighted (Walter Cunningham, Tom Robinson, Bob Ewell) have been vanquished and the enlightened (the Finches, Calpurnia) have triumphed. The dénouement features a poignant scene as if from a Rockwell painting: Atticus reading Jem's book to Scout as she falls asleep, struggling to hear every last word.

Lee, like Scout, counts as good fortune her being born into a family that placed a strong emphasis on literacy. In her letter to Oprah she reflects that:

> I must have learned from having been read to by my family.
> My sisters and brother, much older, read aloud to keep me
> from pestering them; my mother read me a story every day,

> usually a children's classic, and my father read from the four
> newspapers he got through every evening. . . . So I arrived in
> the first grade, literate, with a curious cultural assimilation of
> American history, romance, the Rover Boys, Rapunzel, and the
> *Mobile Press*. Early signs of genius? Far from it. Reading was an
> accomplishment I shared with several local contemporaries. . . .
> We were privileged. (Lee "Letter")

Mockingbird similarly functions as a literacy narrative for Scout, expounding upon the personal value of reading and writing based on a significant episode of her life. The message communicated by Lee through *Mockingbird* is straightforward, if unstated: if the "privilege" of literacy and literacy sponsorship were extended to everyone, each would become "better people, better citizens, and better workers"—in short, the world would be a better place.

"I Don't Reckon You Ever Really Had a Chance"

Go Set a Watchman begins with fundamental disjunction regarding the power of literacy. While travelling homeward by train, Jean Louise Finch (née Scout) ignores the posted warning about its equipment, accidentally "folding herself up into the wall" of her roomette (Lee *Watchman* 4). Though she is eventually rescued by a helpful porter, Jean Louise's embarrassment foreshadows the danger in her failing to read the obvious signs around her. The following page offers an example of the obverse: the danger that can result from reading too freely. Jean Louise recalls the literary pretensions of her cousin Joshua Singleton St. Clair who, as in *Mockingbird*, is revered by Aunt Alexandra as a poet and "splendid figure of a man" (Lee *Watchman* 5). Yet the narrator in *Watchman* further reports that St. Clair was placed in an asylum for the "irresponsible" after having pursued his studies too fervently (5). The institutionalized St. Clair occasionally had fits during which he acted like a whooping crane, but on good days he read extensively and wrote poetry that was "so ahead of its time no one has deciphered it yet" (6). In recalling his memory Scout laughs and recounts Atticus's mirth: the black sheep St. Clair has become a running family joke, his excessive literacy causing him to lose tether to reality.[3]

This initial framework highlights the difference between the novels' treatment of reading and writing. Whereas *Mockingbird* offers an ebullient declaration of literacy at its outset, *Watchman* frames literacy as a condition that makes the learned variously insipid and insane. Whereas in *Mockingbird* Scout falls asleep to an adolescent storybook in Atticus's lap, in *Watchman* Jean Louise falls asleep when trying to read *The Reason Why*, a volume of military history on the ill-fated Charge of the Light Brigade, in order to "bone up for Uncle Jack" (81). In *Mockingbird,* the term "deep reader" is applied to Atticus Finch and his keen understanding of the law and human nature; in *Watchman*, Bill Sinclair is described as a "deep reader"—the same Bill who believes "the niggers who are runnin' the thing up north are tryin' to do it like Gandhi did it, and you know what that is . . . Communism" (174). On a macro level, by 1955 Maycomb's usual institutions of literacy are either under siege or departed. The courthouse, once a seat of enlightenment under Judge Taylor, now serves as meeting-place for the "Maycomb Citizens' Council," a benighted cabal dedicated to preserving the Southern way of life. The Finches' house, once a site for vibrant reading and study, has now become an ice cream parlor, with Atticus's library of classic literature replaced by racist pamphlets. And the *Maycomb Tribune*, which once published editorials against racism, now disseminates white propaganda. So it is that the world of *Watchman* inhabits a paradox diametrically opposed to the proposition in *Mockingbird*: while more of Maycomb is literate, its literacy has not led to better workers and better citizens, but rather to a tribal ignorance cobbled from gossip, prejudice, and partial press coverage.

The demise of literacy institutions begins with Scout's erstwhile sponsors, who have either betrayed or abandoned her.[4] Far from his status as exemplar in *Mockingbird*, Atticus is a weak and diminished figure in *Watchman*. To begin, rather than extolled as the ideal, invested parent, Atticus is blamed for his irresponsible legacy of literacy. His loving practice of nightly oral reading is in retrospect odd and harmful, for Jean Louise realizes she and her brother gained erudite and obscure knowledge rather than learning material suitable for children (115). Atticus's retrogression extends to his social opinions, where his *Mockingbird* credo that "I believe in equal rights for all, and special privileges for none" has given way to racist bromides like "our Negro population is backward" (242); "when they vote, they vote in blocs" (243); and "we're outnumbered, you know" (246). Here Atticus evinces a hearty knowledge mixed with prejudice—the most dangerous strain of bigotry, as it operates under the patina of intelligence. His racist and paternalistic views have bled into his law practice, which in *Mockingbird* took on poor and black clients whom no one else would defend. When Zeebo's son accidently kills a white man in *Watchman*, Atticus likewise volunteers to take the case, this time not in order to offer a robust defense for the accused, but to keep the case away from the "wrong hands" of the NAACP-paid colored lawyers ("buzzards," in his words) who might "demand Negroes on the jur[y]" (148–49). The Atticus of *Watchman* uses the power of the law and his literacy to oppose progress and equality—a far cry from the man who defended Tom Robinson when no one else would. No wonder Jean Louise calls him a "double-dealing, ring-tailed, old son of a bitch!" (253).

Jean Louise also feels betrayed by her surrogate mother Calpurnia, who has left the Finches' employ and moved to the Quarters. After learning of Atticus's involvement in the Citizens' Council, Jean Louise flees to Calpurnia in search of reassurance and moral support. To her horror, she finds the gray and wizened Calpurnia a shell of her former self, using "erratic grammar" and "sitting in a haughty dignity that appeared on state occasions" (159). In all, Jean Louise realizes, Calpurnia is "wearing her company manners" (159)—the mode of "acting black" she utilizes in the presence of white strangers and black compatriots. Although Calpurnia could speak "Jeff Davis's English" perfectly, Jean Louise recalls, when a preacher visited the Finches' some years before, she "dropped her verbs," "haughtily passed dishes of vegetables," and "seemed to inhale steadily" (70). Such racial performances show Calpurnia putting distance between herself and her white "guest" (whether the preacher or Jean Louise)—in this case by refusing to use the kind of speech deemed "proper" by her audience. In desperation Jean Louise pleads " 'Talk to me, Cal. For God's sake talk to me right. Don't sit there like that!' "(160). Her plea to "talk to me" alludes to the intimate relationship they once had; in turn, her plea to "talk to me 'right' " surely refers to the Standard English Calpurnia previously used while living with the Finches. In other words, Jean Louise is asking Calpurnia to exhibit the high-class literacy to which she is accustomed; Calpurnia's refusal to do so figures as a rejection of the Finches' patronage and the high-class culture that enabled her to read, write, and speak as whites do.

The scene at the Quarters is linked via flashback to an episode during Scout's adolescence, when an exasperated Calpurnia scolds her: "With all your book learnin', you are the most ignorant child I ever did see . . . but I don't reckon you ever really had a chance" (137). Though applicable to Scout in general, the proclamation is offered specifically in reference to Scout's belief that she's pregnant because of a kiss she shared with

Albert Coningham. Calpurnia's remonstration is further indictment of Scout's failed education—not only Atticus's unorthodox parenting (he never took pains to educate his daughter about sexual intercourse), but also Maycomb's literacy sponsorship writ large, which emphasizes "book learnin'" without conveying the common knowledge that might render it useful.[5]

For the same reason, *Watchman* is critical of institutions of religion and higher education, which are portrayed as false and untrustworthy, having little practical value to anyone's life. The racist pamphlet *The Black Plague*, we are told, was written by "somebody with several academic degrees" (101); similarly, Henry reveals that the local Wizard of the Ku Klux Klan is a Methodist preacher (229). The learned Reverend Moorehead, while not openly a bigot, is instead a pedant and a windbag, delivering a sermon in which he endlessly splits grammatical hairs, drawing "distinctions of such profundity that not even Atticus Finch could tell what he was driving at" (61). *Watchman* depicts education alongside religion in negative light; higher education is particularly singled out as a fruitless pursuit bearing little profit for the real world. At her father's urging Jean Louise attended a desultory term at a women's college in Georgia before moving to New York (117); though she is well-educated, her degree has brought her neither wealth nor happiness. Her boyfriend, Henry Clinton, in turn "labored seven years in the vineyards of the University and the pastures of [Atticus's] office" for a chance at her hand in marriage (14)— an opportunity he will never receive. And, though Dr. Jack Finch earns an honorific along with his medical degree, the text does not show him practicing medicine or aiding the community, but rather reading poetry and dabbling with theory and philosophy—abstruse subjects that only he knows and cares about. Finch is at once the most educated and least useful character in the novel.

Indeed, Jack serves as the primary sponsor of literacy in *Watchman*, though his brand of esoteric literacy stands in stark contrast to the practical homespun wisdom of Atticus in *Mockingbird*. On account of his education and intellectualism, Jack emerges as "one of the most annoying 'characters' in Southern literature" (Henninger 622), the sort of man who confounds strangers and subjects friends seeking advice to extensive lectures on obscure poets. Though she petitions her uncle for insight regarding her predicament, Jean Louise cannot get a straight answer out of him, for his counsel usually devolves into a rambling reply whose reasoning makes sense only to him (186). Likewise, Jack's personal messiness, combined with his insistence on household neatness, causes him to "shak[e] a broom at a maid" who commits the crime of "losing his place in Tuckwell's *Pre-Tractarian Oxford*" (184). Like Cousin Joshua, Dr. Finch is stuck in the nineteenth century, embodying an inaccessible erudition that renders him out of touch with present-day reality. Unlike Atticus fanboys from *Mockingbird* who have taken up the law, few readers of *Watchman* will be inspired to join the medical profession on account of Dr. Jack Finch.

While Dr. Finch may figure as the acme of literacy in Maycomb, the practice of regular reading has trickled down to its grosser citizens, including Aunt Alexandra and her church circle, who fancy themselves well-versed in societal issues. As an elite New Yorker, Jean Louse cannot conceive of a woman like Hester Sinclair "having read anything other than *Good Housekeeping* save under strong duress" (174). Yet during their conversation about school integration Hester mentions a recent episode in which a black student was prevented entry by a group of vigilant "fraternity boys" (175). When Jean Louise responds: "Golly Hester. I've been readin' the wrong newspaper. One I read said the mob was from that tire factory—," Hester interjects to inquire: "What do you read, the *Worker*?" (175).

Jean Louise does not, in fact, read the Communist Party's *Daily Worker*, but instead peruses a variety of New York newspapers, each of which offers a different perspective on Southern racial upheaval: "to hear the *Post* tell it, we lynch 'em for breakfast; the *Journal* doesn't care; and the *Times* is so wrapped up in its duty to posterity it bores you to death" (24). According to her father, all Jean Louise gleans from the provocative New York papers is exaggeration and radical propaganda (238); in contrast, Hester gets her news from her husband and the *Maycomb Tribune*, both of which have a vested interest in upholding traditional Southern values (read: white supremacy) and the status quo. Though they both were born in Maycomb, went to the same schools, and were taught the same things, Hester and Jean Louise are at significant odds; their literacy, that is, has no commonality, and the conversation produces not enlightenment but discord. Literacy has not made Maycomb a better or more united community, except that its citizens are further united in ignorance and bigotry.

Finally, literacy no longer functions as a rough-and-ready determinant of class and morality in 1950s Maycomb. *Mockingbird* uses illiteracy to flag and isolate undesirables, similar to the discriminatory "literacy tests" that were used to keep poor whites and people of color from voting. As

Katherine Henninger argues, "By deploying the time-honored 'white trash scenario' of Southern racism at court … Atticus at once quarantines racist evil to poor whites and claims the moral high ground for his own class (himself and the 'many' Maycomb whites who secretly support his efforts)" (606). In *Watchman*, on the other hand, literacy is dispersed across the Maycomb community,[6] undermining class boundaries.[7] On the other side of the coin, literacy is no longer a guarantor of intelligence, morality, or class—to which the mixed company of bigotry attests. Jean Louise is disabused of this notion firsthand. After assuming that Southern Citizens' Councils were populated by "ignorant, fear-ridden, red-faced, boorish, law-abiding, one hundred per cent red-blooded Anglo-Saxons, her fellow Americans—trash" (104), she comes to realize the "trash" she read about in the New York papers includes all the highest-ranking members of Maycomb society. Among them are William Willoughby and Tom-Carl Joyner, the powerful men who run the county, and her own boyfriend and father, who boasts that "our council's composed of and led by our own people. I bet you saw nearly every man in the county yesterday, and you knew nearly every man there" (238). Far from the lynch mob of racist yokels that storms the jail in *Mockingbird*, the public council of *Watchman* is populated by literate and reputable men of all classes and professions.

Through the narrative maturation of Jean Louise, *Watchman* offers a corrective to the juvenile message Scout receives in *Mockingbird*—that the world is easily split into tribes of moral literate and immoral illiterate. As the adult Jean Louise discovers when returning to Maycomb, both categories include garbage men, lawyers, housewives, ministers, academics, and liberal carpetbaggers; judges, racists, doctors, and common folk. This discovery, along with her betrayal at the hands of trusted literary sponsors, sends her lurching, as she realizes that her entire worldview on literacy and morality has been upturned in the span of a weekend.

"I've Been Readin' the Wrong Newspaper"

Recent events have caused many Americans to conduct a similar reevaluation of worldviews they implicitly espoused. Though Harper Lee originally wrote *Go Set a Watchman* in the mid-1950s, the novel was serendipitously published in 2015, when it spoke not only to the racial upheaval that swept the United States that year, but also to the increasing balkanization of the media landscape that culminated with the election of Donald Trump in 2016. The tendency of Americans to rely upon isolated and partisan outlets for information drew even the notice of then-president Obama, who in an interview with Bill Maher remarked that "one of the things I'm most concerned about is the Balkanization of the media, where you've got 800 stations, you've got all these websites, and people have difficulty just sorting out what's true and what's not" (qtd. in Evans). Similarly, in a YouTube interview with Destin Sandlin, he observed that "some people are just watching Fox News; some people are just reading the *New York Times* . . . They almost occupy two different realities in terms of how they see the world" (qtd. in Nakamura). Obama touches upon one of the most pressing issues in American society today—not the breadth of literacy, but the commonality of it. As Jean Louise ponders in *Watchman*, regarding the disparity between her and Hester Sinclair's worldviews: "We were both born here, we went to the same schools, we were taught the same things. I wonder what you heard and saw" (175). In this case their ideological divergence does not owe to ignorance, but instead to media filter—that is, the line that separates them is not *that* they are reading, but *what* they are reading. Because Jean Louise reads the New York newspapers she occupies one version of reality; because Hester reads the *Maycomb Tribune* she occupies another, and never the twain shall meet.

Another topical episode arrives when Jean Louise confronts her Aunt Alexandra regarding the racist propaganda of *The Black Plague*. At first, reeling from the abhorrent material, Scout asks her aunt in disbelief whether she has actually read it and knows what is in it. But this is no matter of ignorance: Alexandra is well-read and well-informed. "Certainly," she replies, and asserts "There's a lot of truths in that book" (102). Jean Louise's further objections–regarding the pamphlet's endorsement of eugenics and innate white supremacy—are similarly met with replies of "Well?" and "That's true, isn't it?" (102–03). The latter question, positioned on the boundary between rhetorical and literal, serves as commentary both on the Jim Crow South and our current epistemological landscape: the "post-truth" world where "facts" are subject to the partisan lens through which they are viewed. While Alexandra uses the question to counter Jean Louise's opposition, it is clear that she herself doesn't know whether her understanding is actually true—she is simultaneously offering confutation and seeking affirmation. The conversation features two well-informed and literate citizens (from the same class, even) who disagree on account of their lived experience and media sourcing

(Alexandra concludes her piece by telling Jean Louise "I don't think you fully realize what's been going on down here" [103]).

One of the central messages of *Watchman*, then, is that the gospel of literacy has its limitations; we must take care not advance reading and writing as a simple panacea that will unilaterally make us "better people, better citizens, and better workers" (Dunbar-Odom 57). As Donna Dunbar-Odom argues, "Literacy can only give us the illusion of freedom as we remain weighted, inexorably, to our material lights. We want to believe that flight or escape is available through literacy, but when we look up from the page, we are the same people in the same bodies in the same circumstances" (1). This is to say that literacy, in and of itself, is not enough to transform or transport one's world; in fact, a parochial course of reading (as for Hester Sinclair) may both narrow one's worldview and expand blind spots and confirmation bias. Alternatively, even the most catholic course of reading (as for Jack Finch) may prove sterile if that literacy is disconnected from others and from reality. In the same vein, as Robert F. Arnove and Harvey J. Graff point out, at the community level "literacy does not automatically lead to anything by itself; to make social or economic change possible, it has to be part of a nexus of factors to have significant effect" (Dunbar-Odom 2). In the world of 1950s Maycomb, this "nexus of factors" includes race, education, culture, and opportunity—yet because these elements are unshared by members of its community, literacy does not create societal change, but rather leads to further entrenchment of existing disparity and division. In these instances and others, literacy can be a powerful force, but without a larger effort to build and ameliorate connections within a broader landscape, its value may not prove salutary for a given population, or indeed for the individuals therein. At heart, reading and writing are about acquiring and sharing knowledge. To realize the potential benefits of literacy, one must actively decide to make learning manifest—both in one's interior life and throughout one's community—as does Atticus Finch in *Mockingbird*.

Indeed, in casting down the tower of Atticus, Jean Louise may also be assailing the sacred cow of literacy itself—as Dr. Finch terms it, "letting your icons break one by one" (266). Though Jean Louise had made the round trip to Maycomb for five years annually, after her most recent homecoming episode she realizes she can no longer retreat into the liberal bubble of New York newspapers or escape the unpleasantness of the civil rights movement through the pages of a book. Despite her worthy misgivings Jean Louise decides to stay in Maycomb, reasoning that she can have a salutary impact on the community simply by "going to work every morning, coming home at night, [and] seeing [her] friends," who need her most when they are most wrong (272–73). She might struggle, and she will never marry Hank, who is "not of her kind," but she will always be a part of the Maycomb community. While *Mockingbird* serves as a bildungsroman for Scout, chronicling how she comes to learn there is evil and injustice in the world, *Watchman* is her second coming-of-age, when Jean Louise sheds the naivety of her youth and proceeds into well-informed adulthood. As Dr. Finch argues, "it takes a certain kind of maturity to live in the South these days" (273), to which I might add that it takes a "certain kind of maturity" to live anywhere these days.

The conclusion of Harper Lee's letter laments that "the village of my childhood is gone. . . . Now we are three in number and live hundreds of miles away from each other. We still keep in touch by telephone conversations of recurrent theme: 'What is your name again?' followed by 'What are you reading?' We don't always remember" (Lee "Letter" 153). In eulogizing her lost community of readers ("village"), who swapped books in youth and monitor each other's reading in age, Lee underscores the importance of the modern-day literature classroom and communal literacy program, which serve a similar function in our culture. *Mockingbird* has been often selected for such institutions on account of its uncontested values: its sepia-toned narration, its callback to a simpler time, and its endorsement of an (often literally) black-and-white view of the world. In concluding this survey of the works, I posit that we should also communally read works like *Watchman,* which may prove troublesome and thematically complex but also leave ample gray area for ambiguity and hearty disagreement among parties with divergent perspectives. Like Jean Louise, Atticus, and Dr. Finch, we may nearly come to blows when airing our views, but at least (and at last) we will be reading from the same newspaper.

Notes

1. Thane Rosenbaum reports that "Atticus Finch is invoked as a guiding influence more frequently in essays for law school admission than any other factor by far. His name is synonymous with moral perfection, his quiet dignity the standard of ethical conduct; he is the undisputed MVP of the [American Bar Association]," which "crowned him America's favorite fictional lawyer in 2010" (Rosenbaum).

2. Johnson notes that reading and writing are "means of empowerment. . . . Reading is inextricably connected with [Atticus] and with the civilizing, everyday business of this world, that it is somehow as natural as breathing" (*Threatening* 109).

3. This disposition may be genetic, as evinced by the later introduction of the similarly erudite and out-of-touch Uncle Jack Finch.

4. Her fellow-reading children are absent entirely: Jem has passed away and Dill is somewhere in Italy.

5. In an attempt to verify her belief, Scout consults the dictionary and an "ancient book . . . called *Devils, Drugs, and Doctors*, neither of which provide any illumination" (132).

6. With the notable exception of African Americans, whose "backwardness" Atticus uses to prove they cannot be trusted to vote or govern.

7. A flashback details twelve-year-old Scout's "invaluable service" in tutoring the low-class "slow thinker" Albert Coningham during six-weeks' tests. For their effort, he earns a C- in geography and she earns an appreciative (and appreciated) kiss (127).

Works Cited

Betts, Doris. "The Mockingbird's Throat: A Personal Reflection." *On Harper Lee: Essays and Reflections.* Edited by Alice Hall Petry. University of Tennessee Press, 2007, pp. 135–42.

Brandt, Deborah. "Sponsors of Literacy." *College Composition and Communication*, vol. 59, no. 2, 1998, pp. 165–85.

"City Forms City-Wide Book Club to Address Literacy Beginning with *To Kill a Mockingbird.*" *Jacksonville Free Press*, 7 August 2002, p. A5.

Dunbar-Odom, Donna. *Defying the Odds: Class and the Pursuit of Higher Literacy.* SUNY Press, 2007.

Evans, Greg. "Barack Obama & Bill Maher Slam 'Balkanization' of News Media, Warn of Dire Post-Trump 'Damage.'" 4 November 2016, Deadline.com, https://deadline.com/2016/11/barack-obama-bill-maher-donald-trump-real-time-with-bill-maher-1201848895/. Accessed 17 May 2019.

Grimm, Nancy. *Good Intentions: Writing Center Work for Postmodern Times.* Heinemann, 1999.

Henninger, Katherine. " 'My Childhood is Ruined!': Harper Lee and Racial Innocence." *American Literature*, vol. 88, no. 3, 2016, pp. 597–626.

Johnson, Claudia Durst. To Kill a Mockingbird: *Threatening Boundaries.* Twayne, 1994.

———. *Understanding* To Kill a Mockingbird: *A Student Casebook to Issues, Sources, and Historic Documents.* Greenwood Press, 1994.

Lee, Harper. "A Letter to Oprah." *Oprah Magazine*, vol. 7, no. 7, July 2006, pp. 151–53.

———. *Go Set a Watchman.* HarperCollins, 2015.

———. *To Kill a Mockingbird.* HarperCollins, 1999.

"Library Wants Everybody to Read Book." *Telegraph Herald* [Dubuque], 9 Sept. 2001, p. A13.

Nakamura, David. "Media Critic Obama is Worried that 'Balkanized' Media is Feeding Partisanship." *Washington Post*, 27 Mar. 2016, https://www.washingtonpost.com/politics/media-critic-obama-is-worried-that-balkanized-media-are-feeding-partisanship/2016/03/27/8c72b408-f1e3-11e5-89c3-a647fcce95e0_story.html?noredirect=on&utm_term=.c2eebf21db2c. Accessed 17 May 2019.

Petry, Alice Hall. Introduction. *On Harper Lee: Essays and Reflections.* Edited by Alice Hall Petry. University of Tennessee Press, 2007.

"Pulitzer Prize-winner Gets First Read." *The Gazette* (Colorado Springs), 8 Sept. 2002, p. M3.

Rosenbaum, Thane. "Atticus Finch is My Law Students' Hero." *Slate*, 9 February 2015. https://slate.com/news-and-politics/2015/02/atticus-finch-hero-worship-law-students-love-to-kill-a-mockingbird-anticipate-go-set-a-watchman.html. Accessed 17 May 2019.

Scribner, Sylvia. "Literacy in Three Metaphors." *Perspectives on Literacy*, Edited by Eugene R. Kintgen, Barry M. Kroll, and Mike Rose. Southern Illinois University Press, 1988.

Spires, Marian. "Developing a Critical Literacy Approach with *To Kill a Mockingbird*." *English in Australia*, 126, 2000, pp. 53–59.

Vriend Van Duinen, Deborah, and Audra Bolhuls. "Reading *To Kill a Mockingbird* in Community: Relationships and Renewal." *English Journal*, vol. 105, no. 3, 2016, pp. 81–87.

Winfrey, Oprah. "My Lunch with Harper Lee." *The Guardian,* 11 July 2015, https://www.theguardian.com/books/2015/jul/11/my-lunch-with-harper-lee-oprah-winfrey-go-set-watchman. Accessed 17 May 2019.

8

BUILDING CONTEXT TO READ THE RELATIONSHIP BETWEEN SCOUT AND CALPURNIA IN *MOCKINGBIRD* AND *WATCHMAN*

Audrey Fisch and Susan Chenelle

When Harper Lee's *Go Set a Watchman* was published in 2015, our national relationship with *To Kill a Mockingbird* faced a major challenge. "In many schools, *To Kill a Mockingbird* [served as] *that one book . . . the* race-relations book for the year" (Franks; our emphasis). If teachers used *Mockingbird* as *the* racial social justice text, *Watchman* upended that too-easy narrative.

Readers of *Watchman* discovered and were shocked by Atticus's connections to the Klan and his baldly racist ideas. We learned that *Watchman*'s Atticus joined the Klan a "long time ago," when it was, according to Uncle Jack, "respectable, like the Masons . . . every man of any prominence was a member" (229). Most pointedly, the *Watchman* Atticus offers up unequivocally racist ideas—that the "Negro population is backward" (242)—and deeply troubling questions— "Do you want Negroes . . . in [Maycomb's] schools and church and theaters . . . in our world?" (245). The mainstream media (see McClurg and Thorpe, for example) reacted with horror and disgust: Who is this new Atticus? How can the Atticus of *Watchman* be the Atticus of *Mockingbird*?

Careful readers of *To Kill a Mockingbird*, however, and an established body of scholarship (e.g., Franks, Pryal, Shaw-Thornburg, Gladwell, Margolick) have focused attention for some time on the complex racial politics of Lee's Maycomb and the flaws in Atticus's heroism. After all, Atticus takes on the defense of Tom Robinson involuntarily, telling his brother, "I'd hoped to get through life without a case of this kind, but [Judge] John Taylor pointed at me" (117). Atticus's integrity as a lawyer, here, comes into conflict with his tolerance of racism in Maycomb. He is, moreover, no civil rights activist before, during, or after the trial. When Tom is shot seventeen times in the prison yard for supposedly trying to escape, Atticus responds with care for Tom's family and for the African American community, but he does not initiate any legal appeal, investigation, or protest.

The Atticus of *Mockingbird*, who exists in relative equanimity within the gravely unequal and unjust world of Maycomb, is not equivalent to the Atticus of *Watchman,* who attends meetings of the Maycomb Citizens' Council. But the two versions of Atticus are closer than some uncritical champions of *Mockingbird* have been willing to admit. Indeed, the racism of *Watchman*'s Atticus is surely on a continuum with the accommodationism (see Shaw-Thornburg) of *Mockingbird*'s Atticus, who on the one hand defends Tom Robinson but on the other is fully part of a community in which African Americans live as wholly second-class citizens (see Margolick).

Mockingbird's Atticus may not express his racism quite so openly, but his character and ideas are, as we would expect, fully shaped by the racist views of his time. *Mockingbird*'s Atticus, for example, describes the Klan as "a political organization more than anything" (196). He also breezily dismisses an attack on a Jewish family: "They paraded by Mr. Sam Levy's house one night, but Sam just stood on his porch and . . . made 'em so ashamed of themselves they went away" (196). Clearly, *Go Set a Watchman* offers readers an opportunity to revisit and rethink our ideas about Atticus (many of which may derive as much from Gregory Peck as from Harper Lee) and the complicated dynamics of race in Lee's seminal American novel.

If the publication of *Watchman* forced readers across the United States to confront a more politically complicated Atticus than they remembered from the movie or English class, Harper Lee's new novel also offers an equally exciting opportunity to revisit the relationship between Scout and Calpurnia, and we take that relationship as the subject of our pedagogically focused essay below. As a young and sheltered child in *To Kill a Mockingbird* and as a privileged white young adult in *Go Set a Watchman,* Scout understands little about Calpurnia, and, particularly in *Mockingbird*, Scout's naïve and unreliable narrative voice makes Calpurnia a difficult character to access and the nature of Scout and Calpurnia's relationship difficult to assess or analyze.

In *Watchman*, however, Lee gives Calpurnia a moment of voice, agency, and anger that very much surprises Jean Louise (Scout). Just as *Watchman*'s Atticus draws our attention back to the complicated racism, paternalism, and privilege of *Mockingbird*'s Atticus, *Watchman*'s Calpurnia re-focuses our attention on the complexity of *Mockingbird*'s Calpurnia and of the caregiving but deeply unequal relationship at the center of *Mockingbird*. Examining the moment in *Watchman* when Calpurnia rejects and refuses her former charge allows readers to rethink Scout's limited and blinkered point of view about Calpurnia in *Mockingbird*. Teaching this moment demands that we unpack the social history of race that shapes the relationship between African American caregivers and their white charges so that our students are not, like Scout, blind and oblivious. More broadly, as teachers, when we help students analyze the complex tensions Lee builds into these two texts, we create spaces in our classrooms to engage in difficult but informed conversations about race.

This essay explores the use of clusters of texts focused on the representation of black women, particularly nannies, and the relationships between these women and the white children in their care. We begin with a photograph, titled "Quaker Oats's Aunt Jemima," which depicts the seemingly loving relationship between an older black nanny and her young white charge. Next, we offer students a brief excerpt from "Interview: A Perspective on the 1930s" (Johnson), in which three now-elderly white women who, like Scout, grew up with black nannies, discuss the loving, "wonderful" black people with whom they interacted. Finally, we turn to an audio excerpt of an interview with Dorothy Bolden, an African American woman who worked as a domestic in the 1930s South and founded the National Domestic Workers Union, focusing on the "system" of domestic labor in which those caregivers were respected, but only within the house, paid poorly, and forced to walk a fine line of acquiescence and silence.

Below, we detail how we selected the texts in our cluster, how we used them over two days in a classroom of ninth-grade students in a New Jersey high school, and how this cluster enabled these students to analyze the relationship between Scout and Calpurnia more critically, including key moments such as Scout's glimpse of Calpurnia's "double life" and "command of two languages" at church in *Mockingbird* and the hostile, remote Calpurnia in *Watchman,* who stiffly assumes "company manners" and rejects the now-adult Jean Louise.

Initial Thinking and Visuals

When Audrey visited the ninth-grade classroom of Amanda Racanati at Secaucus High School, an economically and racially diverse public school in Hudson County, New Jersey, the students had read through chapter 12 of *Mockingbird.* Audrey asked them to use one word to describe Calpurnia, and the answers were unsurprising but revealing: *helpful, thoughtful, caring, hardworking, reliable,* and *protective. Caring* was the word most commonly chosen. In other words, the students saw Calpurnia as Scout did.

Next, we turned to a visual representation of the black nanny/white child relationship. We found an accessible, relevant image on Michele Norris's website, "The Grace of Silence; The Power of Words." The image here features Joburness Kelso, one of several African American women employed by the Quaker Oats company to publicly enact the ritual of making and serving pancakes (see Norris). The image of this older African American woman, dressed in a uniform of some sort and offering food to a young white boy, reproduces in many ways Scout's perspective about Calpurnia and the students' characterization of her as caring and helpful.

Visuals are a great place to begin any lesson: our students are avid consumers of media, so working with multimedia texts builds on their strengths. Still, for all their multimedia fluency, students need practice applying their close reading skills to visual texts.

We began the conversation by asking students to write a quick narrative about the story this photograph tells, using these questions as prompts: *What conversation has occurred just before this moment? What conversation will occur after? What is the story behind this picture? What is the inner dialogue in the young man's mind? What is the inner dialogue in the older woman's mind?* Sharing and discussing these responses, we then moved to a general discussion about the relationship between white children and the black women who cared for them, and again the responses were typical and generally uncritical.

Next, we turned to more specific focus on the composition of the photograph. We asked the students: *What do you notice about the body positions of the two figures, and what effect does this have on your reading of this picture? Consider the gazes of the woman and the child. What ideas are conveyed by their facial expressions? Think about the clothing and/or physical characteristics of the two people. How do they add to your understanding of the message of this visual text?*

We had the students discuss these questions in small groups and then as a whole. They began to think about whether the African American woman figured as powerful in the photo, based on the fact that she was standing and was featured more prominently in the image. They noticed that she was positioned to serve the young boy, and one student pointed to the fact that the child was focused on the woman's face and not on the food he was receiving, suggesting that she, and not the food, was his real center of interest. The students also questioned how to read her facial expression but generally felt she was smiling and reflecting satisfaction. Answering these sorts of questions advances students in their practice of closely reading the visual text, moving between analysis of how the photograph works as a text to analysis of the ideas the photograph conveys.

From Pictures to Real People

At this point, we were ready to add the words and ideas of real people to our cluster of texts.

"Interview: A Perspective on the 1930s" (Johnson) offers a window into the attitudes of white women toward their black nannies or nurses. The interview was recorded in 1993 and features a discussion between Harper Lee scholar Claudia Durst Johnson and three women who, as Durst describes them, "grew up in the deep South of the 1930s . . . [and] were members of what could be described as prominent southern families" (145). As with the visual text, a very brief excerpt, like the one below, allows students to practice careful analysis.

> *Interviewer:* As members of prominent families, what was your relationship with black people when you were little girls of Scout Finch's age?
>
> *Mary Ann:* Your first experience with a black person was with your nurse. And the black people that took care of these little white children instilled in us the most wonderful traits. They stood for everything that was honest and Christian. . . .
>
> *Camille:* I loved to go down to Hale County . . . because I could spend the day with the little black children. And that's where I learned to love to dance.
>
> *Mary Ann:* We were incredibly attached to the black people we knew well.
>
> *Cecil:* But I read somewhere in a book on the South that while the white people felt very attached to the black people back then, the black people didn't feel that way about us. (149)

Again, we split our students into small groups, and each group took on one of the following questions: *What is Mary Ann's attitude toward black people? How does Mary Ann represent the feelings of white children toward their nurses/nannies? How do Mary Ann and Camille engage in stereotyping? How do Cecil's comments shape your overall understanding of the conversation among these white women?*

When we asked the groups to share their ideas, they began to move into a more nuanced, critical conversation about the white women's limited and stereotypical perspective on their relationships with their nurses or nannies.

At this point, we turned back to *Mockingbird* and Scout's experience at the First Purchase African Methodist Episcopal Church. We examined the passage in which Scout reveals her discovery: "That Calpurnia led a modest double life never dawned on me. The idea that she had a separate existence outside our household was a novel one, to say nothing of her having command of two languages" (167). The students were able to notice the connection between Scout's discovery of Calpurnia's double life and second language and Cecil's discovery, in a book, that black people may have had quite different feelings than the white women were aware of as young children.

We closed the session that day with some predictions about what would happen, years later, if an adult Scout and her former nanny Calpurnia were to reunite. Most students predicted the encounter would be loving. They had not, in other words, moved very far from Scout's perspective in their own critical analysis.

Day Two—More Complications

Moving from a discussion of the white women's perspective, we turned to an interview with Dorothy Bolden, an African American woman who had worked as a domestic in the 1930s and subsequently founded the National Domestic Workers Union. Before we turned to the interview, we spent a few minutes discussing the word "uppity." We talked about "uppity" as both a general reference to someone assuming airs or status above his/her place on the social ladder and as a slur typically directed against African American men and women, especially in conjunction with the word "nigger." Bolden uses both the words "uppity" and "nigger," so it was important for the students to be prepared for these words.

Bolden's interview is accessible in audio format at the *Voices of Labor Oral History Project* on the Georgia State University Library website.

Because she has a strong and distinctive voice, the audio recording, although difficult to decode aurally, is worth listening to. We had the students listen twice, once without the text transcription in front of them and once again, after a brief discussion, with it to read along.

> You could be a . . . household worker, which is a domestic worker. You didn't go into anything else . . . Everybody was uppity when you had five or six black peoples working for you, which was called Negro or niggers working for you, you was an uppity class white person, and you had all those peoples working for you because you could afford it – you weren't paying them anything – you weren't paying out a hundred dollars a week, and you had all those peoples working from sun-up to sun-down, and those was your house niggers. Peoples respected when they worked fine, but that's far as it go, respect you while you was in the house. So you had to survive on that. You think about it now. It was very sad. I'm not a person to get uptight over it 'cause I know it was a system built that way. We was locked into the system, and you couldn't get out. You had to walk a chalk line. And if you talked back in those days, you was an uppity nigger, you was sassy, and you was fired and put out and where would you go? [1]

To get students to unpack this dense and challenging excerpt, we focused on Bolden's use of specific phrases and targeted the students' analysis with questions or sets of questions. One set asked: *How does Bolden use the term "uppity"? When she talks about "everybody" being "uppity," whom and what does she mean? How does her use of the term "an uppity class white person" compare with her use of the term "an uppity nigger"?* The second set asked: *What point is Bolden making about the economics of domestic labor?* The third asked: *Why does Bolden describe domestic labor as a "system"? Why does she say, "We was locked into the system"?* And the fourth set asked: *What do you think Bolden means when she says, "You had to walk a chalk line"?*

The focused discussion based around these questions allowed students to navigate some politically challenging ideas. They were able to distinguish between what may or may not have been a relationship of attachment between black caregivers and white children and the "system" of domestic labor in which those caregivers were forced to walk a fine line of acquiescence and silence.

At this point, we asked the students to turn back to our initial Aunt Jemima photograph. We prompted them as follows: *Given what you read in the interview with the white women and what you've heard in the interview with Bolden, how might you revise your thinking about the photograph we examined earlier and the story it tells?*

This time, their critical thinking was in high gear. Some students held onto their initial storylines. For instance, one student wrote: "My interpretation of the picture is the same, that the woman is serving the boy because she's working." Most, however, were far more nuanced in their thinking. For example, one wrote: "Jemima is working for the young boy's parents. Although she cares for the kid, she is still working and has to obey his parents." Notice here that the student has incorporated a sense that the domestic worker's relationship to the child is shaped both by attachment and by her place in the labor economy. Another student was able to articulate this complexity using Bolden's own language: "It shows how black people were *locked into the system* of only being a household worker or cook" (our emphasis).

Calpurnia in *Mockingbird* and *Watchman*

Having built a solid context in which to consider the relationship between Scout and Calpurnia in Harper Lee's *Mockingbird*, we turned to *Watchman*. We focused on a brief selection (pages 158–60) in which Jean Louise (the adult Scout) encounters a hostile, remote Calpurnia. In these pages, we see Jean Louise's struggles to make sense out of Calpurnia's "company manners" (161) and the fact that the woman she calls "*my* Calpurnia won't have anything to do me" (167; our emphasis). Those of us who have read the whole of *Watchman* know that, at this moment, Jean Louise is looking to Calpurnia for reassurance, as her assumptions about the past and her childhood crumble and Jean Louise faces the reality of her family's racism and her own white privilege. The students read only these few pages, but they quickly realized that this was not the happy reunion they had predicted for Scout and Calpurnia.

Once again, we offered the students a series of very specific questions focused on moments in the text. First: *Jean Louise says that Calpurnia "was wearing her company manners" (159). What does Jean Louise mean? What do you think of Calpurnia's behavior?* Second: *Jean Louise says to Calpurnia, "I'm your baby, have you forgotten me?" (159). What do you think of Jean Louise's language here?* Third: *Why do you think Calpurnia remains silent in the face of Jean Louise's question about hating "us"? To whom do you think "us" in Jean Louise's question refers?* And fourth: *How do you understand the final gesture in this scene: "Calpurnia shook her head" (160)?*

From this specific analysis of the text of *Watchman*, we moved to broader questions that asked students to put everything from the cluster of texts into conversation. First: *How does Scout's brief recognition of Calpurnia's other, double life in Mockingbird parallel Jean Louise's unhappy realization in Watchman that she doesn't fully know the woman she thought was her Calpurnia?* Second: *Does Scout in Mockingbird have any sense that "black people" may not have felt "incredibly attached" to white people? Does this perspective allow you to think differently about the character of Lula and her reaction to the children at Calpurnia's church?* Third: *Are there moments in Mockingbird where we can see Calpurnia "locked into the system" and having to walk a "chalk line"? Think here about Aunt Alexandra's reaction to the children's trip to Calpurnia's church or Calpurnia's silence in Watchman.*

All of these questions allowed the students to recognize the ways in which Scout's limited perspective in *Mockingbird* obscures other realities in Maycomb. We can dig for those, and both Calpurnia, and especially Lula in the church, briefly de-center Scout's white privilege. *Watchman's* Calpurnia, however, who briefly steps outside the system and off the chalk line, suggests a far more fundamental challenge to the presumed attachment between white children and their African American caregivers and therefore to the young white woman at the heart of Lee's novels. Calpurnia may not hate Scout and the family, but Scout is not Calpurnia's "baby"—not her kin.

Difficult but Engaging Conversations

The pedagogy described above is one way to unearth for students the political complexity of *Mockingbird*. Indeed, as we argue at the outset, *Watchman* did not introduce troubling questions about race and injustice into the world of Maycomb that Lee creates. That world, as a reflection of our own world and our past, is full of problems. Its characters are flawed and problematic. It is, after all, a novel, full of ambiguity and nuance.

It might be worth asking, at this point, whether *Mockingbird* is still a text worth reading and teaching. Recently, Julia Franks, in a piece entitled, "Let's Stop Pretending *To Kill a Mockingbird* Is Progressive on

Race," bemoans, "Why, oh why, are we are still requiring this book in school?" Franks writes compellingly about how *Mockingbird*'s message about kindness and its refusal to question "the current social hierarchy" make it "very outdated." Moreover, she worries that this canonical text is "muscling out some other great books," some of which may be more pertinent and compelling to our students and to these important conversations about racial social justice.

Along the same lines, in a recent exchange in *English Journal*, Peter Smagorinsky asks whether it is time not just to stop reading but "to prohibit Mark Twain's *Huckleberry Finn*" (75). He worries that the Common Core State Standards, once adopted and still extant in some revised form in most states, has placed an undue "emphasis on reading within the four corners of the page while sublimating emotional responses in service of textual analysis" (80). Given this reading framework, he worries, in particular for students of color, about the emotional impact of reading *Huckleberry Finn*.

Jocelyn A. Chadwick, responding in the same issue, insists that teachers not turn away from either *Huck* or issues of race, class, and social injustice. She titles her rejoinder to Smagorinsky, "We Dare Not Teach What We Know We Must," and asks us to be led by the "curiosity and risk and daring and inquiry" (89) of today's students who are asking important new questions of Twain. For Chadwick, our task is to make our classrooms "safe and trusted spaces for . . . difficult conversations" (91).

Franks's and Smagorinsky's concerns resonate strongly with us, even if we don't necessarily want to turn students away from *Mockingbird* and *Huck*. Our project (Fisch and Chenelle, 2014, 2016, and 2018) has focused on using the impetus of the Common Core's focus on what is called informational text (or nonfiction) to broaden our students' reading, to move away from reading within the "four corners of the page" and particularly the four corners of only canonical pages, and instead to put a wider range of different kinds of texts into critical conversation with one another.[2] In this way, we reject an isolated focus on any one "great" text and emphasize instead reading clusters of texts, drawn from different genres and periods and curated by the teacher, so that students can have informed, difficult conversations about a range of issues.

For texts like *Mockingbird* and *Huckleberry Finn*, a focus on close reading as an isolated intellectual exercise in which the primary text is the source of all knowledge is particularly problematic: students struggle to make sense out of difficult issues without a broader context in which to frame their thinking. Using clusters of texts, what R. Malchow-Lloyd calls "text bouquets" and Coombs and Bellingham call "text sets," we can build in our students the capacity to engage in substantive, meaningful conversations. These text clusters allow us to rethink how we teach seminal literary texts; these clusters, as we have illustrated above, allow students to uncover and unpack the still "hidden transcript" (Lipari 120) of race in the United States. In this way, even as we undertake the work of revising our curricula, where appropriate, we can support "deeper and more meaningful inquiries than studying a single book" (Coombs 89) in isolation (see also Bintz).

Indeed, we surveyed the ninth-grade students, and they confirmed that our work with *Mockingbird* and *Watchman* helped make the texts more accessible, engaging, and easier to understand. Eighty-nine percent of the students indicated that they found *Mockingbird* "more interesting" based on our work; 63 percent of the students reported that our study had made *Mockingbird* somewhat or much easier to understand. Most encouraging, 58 percent indicated a desire to read more of *Watchman*, and 47 percent wanted to read more about the conditions of domestic workers. In other words, this two-day exercise promoted a greater level of intellectual curiosity in both history and literature in nearly half the ninth-graders.

Education has become focused, and with good reason, on cultivating so-called twenty-first-century skills like communication and collaboration, critical thinking, and media literacy. Recent scholarship, however, including a 2013 study from The New School for Social Research, indicates that literary fiction helps our students build empathy, particularly the ability to understand "others' subjective states . . . [and] allows successful navigation of complex social relationships and helps to support the emphatic responses that maintain them" (Comer Kidd 377). To navigate our increasingly contentious and divided twenty-first-century world, our students need literacy skills and knowledge—but they also need empathy.

Flawed as he may be, Atticus stresses the importance of empathy to Scout in *Mockingbird*: "You never really understand a person until you consider things from his point of view . . . climb into his skin and walk around in it" (39). Our study of *Mockingbird* and *Watchman* demonstrates how to put the seminal texts of the American canon in conversation with other texts in order to work to promote empathy and to engage in difficult conversations. Our students may, like Atticus, never climb into another person's skin, and perhaps that was never really a reasonable goal. But, hopefully, they can, as one student wrote after our lesson, learn "different point[s] of views and different ways to look at things. And there's always another side to a story."

Notes

1. The full audio of this interview, which stretches to more than an hour, is worth listening to with students, particularly because Bolden's voice and tone are so moving. Teachers are cautioned, however, that they should excerpt carefully. Some of Bolden's ideas and language are inflammatory and could be distracting to students. We used only the brief excerpt transcribed above.

2. The Common Core standards, for example, ask students to "Analyze how two or more texts address similar themes or topics in order to build knowledge or to compare the approaches the authors take." Explicitly, this standard and others articulate a reading practice in which students use multiple texts to build an "informative context" that expands beyond any singular close examination of a solitary text. Anchor Standard 5 also points to an intertextual focus that builds broader knowledge: "Analyze the structure of *texts*, including how specific sentences, paragraphs, and larger portions of the text (e.g., a section, chapter, scene, or stanza) relate to each other and the whole" (our emphasis). This standard invites analysis and comparison of multiple texts, particularly texts with differing structures. Anchor Standard 7 asks for a similar comparison of texts, with an emphasis on different types of texts: "Integrate and evaluate content presented in diverse formats and media, including visually and quantitatively, as well as in words."

Works Cited

Bintz, William. P. "Using Paired Text to Teach CCSS Anchor Standards in Reading." *Voices from the Middle*, vol. 22, no. 4, May 2015, pp. 39–43.

Bolden, Dorothy. "Oral History Interview with Dorothy Bolden." Interviewed by Earl Bernard West, December 7. *Atlanta History Center*, 7 Dec. 1978, http:// album.atlantahistorycenter.com/cdm/ref/collection/LAohr/id/247. Accessed 21 May 2019.

Chadwick, Jocelyn A. "We Dare Not Teach What We Know We Must: The Importance of Difficult Conversations." *English Journal*, vol. 106, no. 2, Nov. 2016, pp. 88–91.

Comer Kidd, David, and Emanuele Castano. "Reading Literary Fiction Improves Theory of Mind." *Science*, vol. 342, no. 6156, Oct. 2013, pp. 377–80.

Coombs, David, and Devery Bellingham. "Using Text Sets to Foster Critical Inquiry." *English Journal*, vol. 105, no. 2, Nov. 2015, pp. 88–95.

Fisch, Audrey, and Susan Chenelle. *Using Informational Text To Teach To Kill a Mockingbird*. Rowman and Littlefield, 2014.

———. *Using Informational Text To Teach A Raisin in the Sun*. Rowman and Littlefield, 2016.

———. *Using Informational Text To Teach The Great Gatsby*. Rowman and Littlefield, 2018.

Franks, Julia. "Let's Stop Pretending To Kill a Mockingbird Is Progressive on Race." *NCTE Blog*, 8 Nov. 2017, http://www2.ncte.org/blog/2017/11/lets-stop-pretending -kill-mockingbird-progressive-race/. Accessed 21 May 2019.

Gladwell, Malcolm. "The Courthouse Ring: Atticus Finch and Southern Liberalism." *The New Yorker*, 10 August 2009, https://www.newyorker.com /magazine/2009/08/10/the-courthouse-ring. Accessed 21 May 2019.

Johnson, Claudia Durst. *Understanding To Kill a Mockingbird*. Greenwood Press, 1994.

Lee, Harper. *Go Set a Watchman*. Harper Collins, 2015.

———. *To Kill a Mockingbird*. Hachette, 1982.

Lipari, Lisbeth. "Hansberry's Hidden Transcript." *The Journal of Popular Culture*, vol. 46, no. 1, 2013, pp. 119–42.

Malchow-Lloyd, Rachel. "Critical Encounters with Non-Fiction: A Literature Lover's Approach." Presentation at the National Council of Teachers of English Convention, Minneapolis, MN, November 19–22, 2015.

Margolick, David. "To Attack a Lawyer in To Kill a Mockingbird: An Iconoclast Takes Aim at a Hero." *The New York Times*, 28 Feb. 1992, https://www.nytimes .com/1992/02/28/movies/bar-attack-lawyer-kill-mockingbird-iconoclast-takes -aim-hero.html. Accessed 21 May 2019.

McClurg, Joycelyn. "'Watchman': Is Atticus Finch a Racist." *USA Today*, 10 July 2015, https://www.usatoday.com/story/life/books/2015/07/10/go-set-a-watchman -harper-lee-book-review/29980231/. Accessed 21 May 2019.

National Governors Association Center for Best Practices & Council of Chief State School Officers. *Common Core State Standards for English Language Arts and Literacy in History/Social Studies, Science, and Technical Subjects*. 2010.

Pryal, Katie Rose Guest. "Walking in Another's Skin: Failure of Empathy in *To Kill a Mockingbird*." *Harper Lee's To Kill a Mockingbird: New Essays*, edited by Michael J. Meyer. Scarecrow Press, 2010, pp. 174–89.

"Quaker Oats's Aunt Jemima." *The Grace of Silence: The Power of Words*, edited by Michele Norris, http://michele-norris.com/resources/. Accessed 21 May 2019.

Shaw-Thornburg, Angela. "On Reading *To Kill a Mockingbird*: Fifty Years Later." *Harper Lee's To Kill a Mockingbird: New Essays*, edited by Michael J. Meyer. Scarecrow Press, 2010, pp. 113–27.

Smagorinsky, Peter. "Huck and Kim: Would Teachers Feel the Same if the Language Were Misogynist?" *English Journal*, vol. 106, no. 2, Nov. 2016, pp. 75–80.

Thorpe, Vanessa, and Edward Helmore. "Atticus Finch is a Racist in *To Kill a Mockingbird*'s Sequel." *The Guardian*, 11 July 2015, https://www.theguardian.com /books/2015/jul/11/atticus-finch-racist-go-set-watchman. Accessed 21 May 2019.

9

"COMMAND OF TWO LANGUAGES"
Language Awareness and Acceptance
with Calpurnia
Brandie Bohney

Suppose you and Scout talked colored-folks' talk at home—it'd be out of place, wouldn't it? Now what if I talked white-folks' talk at church, and with my neighbors? They'd think I was puttin' on airs to beat Moses.

—Calpurnia, *To Kill a Mockingbird*

When I was a stay-at-home parent, I thought I might go out of my mind without the kind of intellectual stimulation I had gotten as a classroom teacher. Some friends and I started a book club to preserve our sanity. We were not a diverse group by any means: five (sometimes six) middle-class white moms with the good fortune to have spouses who supported our staying home with children as well as our monthly night out to discuss books and drink coffee. It turns out that our privilege did not end there, though. When we read Barack Obama's *Dreams from My Father*, we were shocked that Obama's black friends would be critical of his speaking "properly," according to our definition: using a mainstream, widely valued English dialect instead of a nonmainstream, less valued dialect of the black community. Looking back, I am shocked by and ashamed of my response: "Why would his friends not see that he wanted to better himself?" Ugh. Now I want to smack that privilege right out of my mouth; but then, as a speaker of the dialect of power and as someone who had rarely been outside the confines of very white communities, it simply did not compute: my language was the right one, and why wouldn't everyone else want to be right? I was far from understanding the extent of my privilege, from knowing that even within my mainstream dialect, I could use language in ways that would be considered "acceptable" because of my race and not necessarily because my use was mainstream enough. It would take a move to a more diverse community, work with more diverse students, and several graduate courses in composition pedagogy and linguistics before I would see the linguistic discrimination that accompanied my privilege.

Not every student speaks the same dialect, even among native English-speaking communities. While this should be a given understanding among writing and literature instructors, the reality of many English classrooms is that there is an acceptable version of English and many unacceptable ones. Considering the additional attention *To Kill a Mockingbird* has gotten in the wake of the publication of *Go Set a Watchman*, the opportunity to closely scrutinize language use in both texts is a good one. This chapter aims to use *To Kill a Mockingbird*—and specifically the conversation between Calpurnia and the Finch children referenced in the epigraph—as a vehicle through which to promote language understanding and to reduce linguicism: discrimination or prejudice based on language.

It is important to note here that in discussing English dialects, I use the term "mainstream" very purposefully. As I explain in greater detail in the next section and as is evidenced by various examples in *To Kill a Mockingbird*, there really is no "standard" English, and to treat students as if some speak a standard and others do not sets up a troubling dichotomy. Within mainstream varieties, there are many non-mainstream features, so even mainstream-English speakers are not always or even usually speaking a "standard." Awareness and legitimacy are at the heart of my approaches for both mainstream- and non-mainstream-speaking groups: the approach in the former hopes to provide mainstream speakers with an understanding of the legitimacy of "other" Englishes to promote acceptance, and the approach in the latter intends to promote understanding of their own language legitimacy and develop working strategies for identifying rhetorical opportunities to use their dialects. Either way, the text can be used to support students' understanding and acceptance of language differences, a difficult concept for many students as well as adults.

Context

So what is "correct" English? Is it the English dialect used most often by the mainstream? Is it the English of businesses? Is it the English teacher's

English? If so, whose English teacher do we listen to? Moreover, what are all the rules of "correct" English? Are the rules agreed upon universally, nationally, or even regionally? Why do the Brits use quotation marks differently than the Americans? Why did my high school grammar primer feel that was so important to detail? Perhaps most importantly, why are so many people hung up on details like *lay* versus *lie* or *less* versus *fewer* when confusing such distinctions does little to obfuscate meaning?

There are strong disagreements about many of the prescriptive rules of the English language, and while some people may feel indignant at the use of grocery-store checkout lanes marked *10 items or less*, the truth is we all know what the sign means, and there will always be jerks who get in that line with a cartful of groceries. So the meaning is intact, even if the usage may be "incorrect"—both in the sign phrasing and the actions of the shopper with more than ten items. In examining language in *To Kill a Mockingbird*, even when characters—regardless of race—use non-mainstream constructions and words, their meanings are still generally clear (with the only exception possibly being the Ewells, who use a few dialect features that are sometimes befuddling to students).

In reality, effective writers do not always follow all the rules or use only one "standard" English, so why do we ask of students what is not generally expected of our best writers? Joseph Williams explores this problem in "The Phenomenology of Error," and Peter Elbow outlines a variety of examples in *Vernacular Eloquence: What Speech Can Bring to Writing*. While the grammar mavens of the world may relentlessly judge and correct others for their use of language, there are also those who admonish the mavens for being so snobbishly focused on correctness rather than effectiveness. At some point, there is a balance to be struck in terms of language use: English speakers and writers cannot ignore widely accepted rules entirely, but neither should they be expected to use every stodgy, prescriptive rule that results in "fuzzy, clumsy, wordy, ambiguous, incomprehensible prose, in which certain thoughts are not expressible at all" (Pinker par. 8).

Further, every language is comprised of dialects, and no dialect is more correct or better than any other (Fromkin et al. 445). In fact, dialects "are systematic differences in the way different groups speak a language" (Fromkin et al. 445) and are therefore rule governed. No dialect is a wrong or bad version of a language; rather, they are each merely *different* versions of a language. Thus, English varieties such as African American English (AAE), Chicanx English, and Hawaiian Creole English (HCE) are no less correct or valid than any more mainstream dialect. As suggested by Rosina W. Lippi-Green in *English with an Accent,* rather than referring to the most widely accepted version of English as *standard,* in this chapter I primarily use *mainstream* and refer to it as she suggests: "For the sake of brevity, 'mainstream US English' will sometimes appear as MUSE, and its counterpart, 'non-mainstream US English,' as NMUSE" (62).

Still, the world is not made up entirely of linguists who understand dialect validity and respect the language differences among all English speakers. Much of the English-speaking world—especially in countries where English is the mother tongue—demands a certain fluency in the mainstream variety of English. Thus, certain dialects are granted prestige and legitimacy that others are not, as evidenced by my own evaluation of nonmainstream Englishes years ago with my book club. Unsurprisingly, the dialect granted consistent prestige and legitimacy in the United States (and therefore considered mainstream) is the dialect of middle- to upper-class white English speakers without a distinctive regional accent, and speakers of mainstream dialects tend to see NMUSE dialects as wrong, as is seen in Jem's criticism of Calpurnia using a dialect other than his: "why do you talk nigger-talk to the—to your folks when you know it's not right?" (Lee 167). Such distinction and devaluing of NMUSEs are not exclusive to MUSE speakers: interestingly—and unfortunately—many speakers of NMUSE also see their own dialects as incorrect, slangy, or inferior to the MUSE varieties.

Clearly, students' own dialects are an important consideration for writing and reading teachers; as English teachers, we need to recognize the validity of our students' varying dialects, help make them aware of the validity of their own and others' dialects, and help them use language in a way that is empowering rather than insulting. It may seem that these goals have little to do with *To Kill a Mockingbird.* After all, Jem—clearly a protagonist in the text—mentions the wrongness of Calpurnia's black language, describing it as "not right," and then responds to Cal's explanation of her being black with, "That doesn't mean you hafta talk that way when you know better" (Lee 167). How is a text so critical of an NMUSE English going to help students understand and accept language differences? The answer to that question lies in close reading and analysis of language use in the text. The analysis may be a bit different based on the student population examining the text, but ultimately what I recommend is looking carefully at how and why characters in the novel use various dialects to communicate.

Mainstream-Speaking Students

Since I identify as a middle-class mainstream-English-speaking white woman, and my experiences teaching *To Kill a Mockingbird* were in ninth-grade English classes in a wealthy suburban school filled with mainstream-English speakers, initially I felt there was little I could do to help the plight of speakers of devalued Englishes. Still, I felt empowered and impassioned by Vershawn Ashanti Young's piece "Should Writers Use They Own English?" in which Young performs the argument of the power of NMUSE in his writing: "What we need to do is enlarge our perspective about what good writin is and how good writin can look at work, at home, and at school. The narrow, prescriptive lens be messin writers and readers all the way up, cuz we all been taught to respect the dominant way to write, even if we dont, cant or wont ever write that way ourselves" ("Should" 112). It is clear in Young's words that the issue of linguicism and misunderstanding of one another's dialects is not a problem for NMUSE speakers alone. It is a problem for all speakers and writers. Acceptance of NMUSE dialects by MUSE speakers widens the margins of communication to include more voices, more perspectives. And until those margins widen enough to include speakers and writers of all dialects, they simply are not wide enough. Texts like *To Kill a Mockingbird* can serve as catalysts for discussion and understanding of language that may help the process of widening the margins.

I wanted to do more than just acknowledge writing in various English dialects, though. It was not enough for *me* to recognize the legitimacy: I needed to develop that understanding in my students as well. I knew that unless someone would intentionally intervene, my students were likely to end up believing—as I had in the past—that their language was correct and other Englishes were wrong. The key for me, I realized, was to develop in my MUSE students an understanding that not all good, powerful, effective writing had to be written in their mainstream dialect. And that's where Calpurnia, Vershawn Young, and Stanley Fish came in. The lesson I created was both powerful and effective, and in July 2016, I published an article about it in *The English Journal* with the hope of encouraging others in similar teaching situations to consider doing the same. I have since taught the lesson several more times, and the following is an updated and expanded description of that lesson.

In *To Kill a Mockingbird*, Cal takes Scout and Jem to her church. As they near the church, Scout notices a change in Calpurnia's speech: "I thought her voice strange: she was talking like the rest of them" (158). While the distinction of otherness Scout makes here is notable—black language is clearly not white language—it is also clear that Scout has not defined Cal as an Other; rather, she is used to Calpurnia speaking white language and has placed her in a position of belonging. Where I was most interested for my students to take note, though, was in the conversation the children and Calpurnia have as they return to the Finch house after the service. As Jem questions Cal about why she speaks like others in the black community, Scout ponders Cal's "double life": "The idea that she had a separate existence outside our household was a novel one, to say nothing of her having command of two languages" (167). Here, Scout realizes that the language Calpurnia uses in her own community—"colored-folks' talk"—was different enough from Scout's own language (the language Calpurnia uses in the Finch household)—"white-folks' talk"—to describe as another language. This was an excellent opportunity within the novel to discuss language difference with my students.

Before we discussed this chapter and the Finch children's recognition of Calpurnia's multilingualism, I used the students' blogs as a means to get them thinking about language—both Calpurnia's and their own. I briefly introduced students to the concept of code-switching, as it has come to be known in many educational circles. According to linguists, code-switching is "when bilingual persons switch from one language to another, possibly within a single sentence . . . [reflecting] both grammars working simultaneously" (Fromkin et al. 489). Many educators, however, have morphed the definition of code-switching into an intentional dialectal change depending on the rhetorical situation; thus, many educators see code-switching as a rhetorical choice regarding which language or dialect to use for a particular audience or purpose. Calpurnia's transition from "white-folks' talk" to "colored-folks' talk" and back again would fall under the wider educational definition of code-switching: she uses whichever dialect her audience and purpose require. Using this definition, my students were to respond to the following prompt in their blogs after reading chapter 12:

> Code-switching is widely understood as changing the way one speaks or writes based on audience or situational factors. This definition of code-switching includes the type of change in speaking that Calpurnia exhibits and explains in Chapter Twelve. For your blog entry, consider Calpurnia's rea-

> soning and explanation in one paragraph: how and why does
> she change the way she speaks? Then in a second paragraph,
> explain whether or not you think people code-switch in this
> way today. Offer examples where possible.

This type of code-switching is familiar to students—even those whose home dialect is very much the mainstream—because they change the way they speak for different audiences and purposes all the time. Each time I assigned this blog entry, the student responses were very similar: they recognized changes not only in Calpurnia's speech, but also in their own. Almost no students responded that code-switching did not occur anymore, and virtually all students used their own rhetorical choices as examples, citing everything from who they would and would not swear around to slang use to language formality. A few multilingual students discussed using a different language at home than at school, and some students even made distinctions between how they might change their speech habits around the same person in different scenarios.

When the students arrived in class for the discussion about their reading assignment and blog entries, we reviewed their responses first. Students offered their interpretations and experiences with code-switching, and I explained the difference between the linguistic definition of code-switching and the wider interpretation I offered them in the blog prompt. I asked students if they thought certain ways of speaking are considered more correct, more valid, or more important than others, and they agreed universally that some ways of speaking are more accepted than others. Then we transitioned into a discussion of devalued Englishes.

The sequencing of this lesson about language is very intentional: students need to discuss some of their opinions of language prior to the following mini-lesson about features of AAE and investigation of the following texts because they might not be as honest in their own judgments about language if the concepts or texts are introduced first. Part of the difficulty of this lesson is to get students to understand how linguicism informs societal perceptions of language. Students—especially MUSE-speaking students—often do not see judgment based on the way a person speaks as problematic. In fact, linguicism is widespread and often considered acceptable: "Many of us feel free to make judgments about others because of the ways that they use language . . . We act as though dialects and accents are windows to people's souls, and sometimes we dare to ignore or dismiss entire groups of people because of what we assume their linguistic habits reveal about them" (Zuidema 341). This lesson was designed precisely to point out that specific uninhibited prejudice and push students to recognize their subconscious judgments and thereby begin changing how they consider and treat speakers of NMUSE.

The mini-lesson on features of AAE took only ten minutes or so to present, but for most students, it was an eye-opening experience. I opened with an explanation that every language is comprised of various dialects—none more correct than any other. It is important to mention several English varieties: I introduced HCE, Chicanx English, Appalachian English, and AAE. I also asked students if they could think of other English dialects. Their responses usually included southern dialects, Boston or east-coast dialects, and British English, among others. It is also important to point out that just because someone is black or Hawaiian or from Appalachia does not necessarily mean they will be a speaker of AAE, HCE, or Appalachian English, respectively. I used my sister-in-law as an example: although she was raised in Hawaii, she knows little Hawaiian and does not speak HCE. Without this clarity, students often assume that every person of a particular race or nationality or from a particular region will be a speaker of the dialect associated with that race, nationality, or region. Then, I shifted specifically to AAE, but it would be possible here to use another English, if you choose. My explanation included the following purpose statement: more often than not, an NMUSE dialect will be widely understood by speakers of other dialects, but often certain features of dialects may be misinterpreted by outsiders of that dialect, and there are features of AAE that make this point quite beautifully. Neither of my examples is a feature of Calpurnia's speech in *To Kill a Mockingbird*, but I chose them because of the likelihood that students would be familiar with them rather than for their direct connection to the literature.

One of these features is the habitual *be*. Mainstream English has several ways to express the habitual aspect: *He often lies; he always lies; he is a liar.* In AAE, though, the habitual aspect is denoted with an invariant *be*: *He be lying.* My mainstream speakers were surprised to learn that constructions in AAE like *he be lying* or *she be late* are not erroneous conjugations of the verb *to be*, but instead rule-governed constructions indicating an action of habit. The other feature of AAE I explained to students is the zero copula. Zero copula is the elimination of the connecting *be*-verb between a subject and predicate in a sentence. So instead of *he is happy*, an AAE speaker might instead say *he happy*. The exception to this rule is the first-person singular, *I am*. When explaining this concept, it is easy to connect the zero copula to contractions, as AAE uses the zero copula for situations where a contraction might otherwise be used: *he's happy* becomes *he happy.* The first year I taught this lesson, one particularly astute student said, "Well, it makes just as much sense to get rid of it entirely as it does to make it a contraction." Exactly. In fact, the zero copula is simply a complete contraction of the verb rather than a partial one. By explaining the consistency and rule-based nature of just two aspects of AAE, students began to see that AAE and other Englishes are not wrong or bad versions of mainstream English, but rather different English varieties guided by their own rules and regulations.

Our next step was to read together the first thirteen paragraphs of Stanley Fish's op-ed "What Should Colleges Teach? Part 3" from *The New York Times.* When I taught *To Kill a Mockingbird,* it was during the third quarter of the school year, when we began to look closely at argumentation. Thus, I distributed copies of Fish's article and read it aloud three or four paragraphs at a time, and in each break in the reading, we discussed as a class what point Fish is trying to prove and what evidence he presents and rhetorical appeals he uses to prove his claims. We outlined on the board Fish's points:

> High schools are not preparing students for college-level writing.
> Colleges must teach unprepared students how to write well.
> Students should have to use standard English when writing college-level work.

Not every list looked precisely like this, but this is a representative sample of the points the students derived from the text. We also outlined the evidence and appeals Fish uses beneath each claim statement.

After completing the outline of Fish's argument, I then asked the class, "Do you agree with Fish? Should students who speak a variety of English that is not mainstream be forced to use the mainstream in school to be successful?" Invariably, almost every hand in the class went up for the positive response. This makes sense, of course: the students understood at this point that certain varieties of English are viewed by many as more valuable, more prestigious than others. They already spoke a mainstream variety, for the most part, so it required little of them personally to agree with Fish. Even among those who had started to put together the pieces of how some Englishes are devalued and discriminated against, it was very likely still unclear how writing and learning in the mainstream variety may be problematic for NMUSE speakers.

Enter Vershawn Young. Young's piece "Should Writers Use They Own English?" is a code-meshed piece written primarily in AAE in response to Fish's article. In the piece, Young introduces the term *code-meshing*. Because the meaning of *code-switching* is no longer universally understood in the linguistic sense (as descriptive rather than prescriptive), Young offers *code-meshing* as a replacement term. He explains, "Code meshing is the new code switching . . . [it] blend dialects, international languages, local idioms, chat-room lingo, and the rhetorical styles of various ethnic and cultural groups in both formal *and* informal speech acts" ("Should" 114).

I applied Young's concept by dividing my class into small groups of roughly four students each and presented the groups with copies of Young's article marked for them to stop reading after the tenth paragraph. The instructions I gave them were clear: read this piece two or three paragraphs at a time, similarly to how we read Fish's article. Every two or three paragraphs, stop to analyze the argument: what are the claims, evidence, and appeals presented? Write down your outline of Young's argument as you go. You must read the article out loud. You may take turns reading, or one person can read the whole thing, but it must be read out loud. I knew that very few of my students had enough familiarity with AAE to make the oral reading of Young's piece truly comfortable for them, and that is the point: they needed to experience trying to work through a piece of scholarly work written in a dialect other than their own. Another option here would be to use Lee Tonouchi's piece "State of da Pidgin Address," which I reference in the next section. Although Tonouchi's piece is not in direct reference to Fish, it does cover much of the same ground Young covers in a dialect (Hawaiian Creole English) that may be less familiar to mainland students than AAE.

As the students read, I circulated through the classroom, listening. The students struggled to read the piece fluently: they had trouble with the wording, the cadence. Some laughed and buckled down, getting the meaning of the piece to come clear. Others were visibly frustrated. In one class, a student said loudly, "This makes no sense! Why do we have to read this?" As the exercise continued, most of the students began to see not only Young's meaning and his purpose in using AAE to express it, but my reasoning as well. One student said, "If it's this hard for us to read this, what must it be like for students who speak like this to read everything in school?" Coming to understand the potential difficulties of being expected to do all one's work in a less-familiar dialect is an important realization in this lesson. The reality, of course, is that even MUSE-speaking students are not wholly unfamiliar with AAE, just like NMUSE speakers are rarely ever wholly unfamiliar with the mainstream variety, but fluency can and does affect understanding. In the end, none of the groups failed to interpret Young's meaning entirely, but some found more success than others. Perhaps some of this had to do with willingness and attitude: the student whose loud complaint I reference above decided early on not to continue to put effort into the activity, but the latter-referenced student was enthusiastic about the task. Were students' own prejudices influential in their interpretations of the text? When faced with information that challenges student beliefs or understandings, are they more or less likely to interpret the text fairly? Could challenges to their beliefs cause students to shut down?

When the small groups were mostly finished, we discussed the argument and wrote the outline on the board next to the outline of Fish's piece. The outline of claims usually looked something like this:

> A person's language is not responsible for prejudice.
> We should be learning as many dialects as we can in school.
> People should be allowed to write in the dialect that is most
> comfortable to them.

When we had gotten through the discussion and delineation of Young's claims, I asked the students the same question as before: "Do you still agree with Fish? Should students who speak a variety of English that is not mainstream be forced to use the mainstream in school to be successful?" This time, hands would still go up, but there were always far fewer than the previous time I asked.

Young's words clearly did more than merely empower me. They led me to develop a pedagogical strategy I hoped would open students' minds to the possibility that other dialects are just as valuable and legitimate as their own and that NMUSE varieties can be used in academic contexts with great skill and success. Not only did I hope to see students recognize the legitimacy of devalued Englishes, I hoped to create in them some empathy: it is not always easy to work with a language form that is not entirely familiar or comfortable to you. In considering this, I wanted to create understanding in the students so that they are less likely to make judgments of people based on the way they speak or write, thereby reducing linguicism. It is not, however, intended to be a standalone lesson without any further consideration of devalued Englishes in the classroom. To continue to bring MUSE speakers in contact with NMUSE writing, instructors should incorporate as many pieces of writing in various dialects as possible. A very small selection of pieces for consideration is included in the table below.

GENRE	DIALECT	AUTHOR AND TITLE
Poetry	HCE	Joe Balaz, various (I recommend "Da Last Squid")
Poetry	Scottish (Ayrshire)	Robert Burns, various (I recommend "To A Mouse")
Novel	AAE (early 20th-century Southern U.S.)	Zora Neale Hurston, *Their Eyes Were Watching God*
YA Novel	Some modern AAE	Kekla Magoon, *How it Went Down*
Short Story	Code-meshed Spanish and English	Junot Díaz, various (many are very good, but many also contain a lot of objectionable content; Díaz also became controversial in 2018 because of accusations of sexual misconduct and misogyny)
Short Story Collection	HCE	Lee Tonouchi, *Da Word*
Autobiography	Some Appalachian	Jeannette Walls, *The Glass Castle*

Nonmainstream-Speaking Students

Of course, reducing linguicism and creating greater understanding of language validity are lofty and worthy goals that lessons like the one above should help to achieve, but as much as it pains me to admit it, Stanley Fish has a point when he argues:

> It may be true that the standard language is an instrument of power and a device for protecting the status quo, but that very truth is a reason for teaching it to students who are being prepared for entry into the world as it now is rather than the

> world as it might be in some utopian imagination—all dialects
> equal, all habit of speech and writing equally rewarded. (456)

Reducing linguicism is only part of the solution so long as language discrimination causes a divide between MUSE speakers and NMUSE speakers. Unlike Fish, though, I do not think students should be asked to leave their home languages at home in order to gain familiarity with the MUSE variety of English in their writing. There is strong evidence that we are moving in a direction of greater acceptance of a broader variety of English. Peter Elbow contends that more serious writing in language that reads more like informal mainstream speech than formal, scholarly writing is being published and lauded (376–77). This chapter uses informal language and conversational tone periodically, for example. Even with that said, though, Elbow notes, "The speech that has begun to 'infect' writers in the *New York Times* and *The New Yorker* and other mainstream sites is mostly *mainstream* speech—a version of standardized White English" (377). So while the standard for respectable journalistic and scholarly writing may be relaxing, it still rarely includes marginalized varieties of English.

One significant problem in not recognizing the legitimacy of non-mainstream Englishes is that speakers of those dialects are given the impression that they are wrong or stupid for using their own dialect and that users of the mainstream are more correct or somehow smarter for using a mainstream dialect. This is certainly often true in the case of AAE, which is widely—and incorrectly—viewed as a bastardization of a standard English rather than a legitimate, rule-governed English dialect. Wheeler and Swords explain that "teachers and the public scorn the community language, believing it to be 'broken English,' 'corrupt,' and 'incapable of expressing complex ideas'" (56), and when, instead of acknowledging the community languages, teachers try merely to correct them, the students continue to struggle with the mainstream dialect, proving their difficulty through lagging test scores (Wheeler and Swords 57; "Racial").

Lee Tonouchi expresses a similar concern for speakers of HCE, or as he and other speakers of HCE often refer to their language, "Pidgin." Tonouchi writes in Pidgin and advocates strongly for the acceptance of the legitimacy of HCE, explaining that forcing students to try to write in a mainstream English is the primary cause of their forced, awkward, disorganized prose. When Tonouchi tells his students that he will not be collecting their work, though, their writing changes: "I walk around da room and I see lotta da kids stay writing in Pidgin like das da voice dat comes most natural to dem . . . and I'm all like WOW, dey get ideas. Stay organize. And can understand too" (76). Even though Tonouchi speaks and writes exclusively in Pidgin, his students are generally uncomfortable using Pidgin for any work they might submit because "da perception is dat da standard English talker is going automatically be perceive fo' be mo' intelligent than da Pidgin talker regardless wot dey talking" (75–76). Thus, like many students who speak AAE or other NMUSE dialects, the HCE speakers struggle to produce and organize ideas in a dialect that is uncomfortable to them, often resulting in similarly uncomfortable written work.

Tonouchi's point about writing in NMUSE still rings true: students need to use the English they are most comfortable with in at least the organizational stages of writing because forcing students to write only in the mainstream English, a dialect they may find uncomfortable and unnatural, does nothing to help them become good writers. To become good writers, to organize their thoughts and ideas, they need to be able to use the language that is most comfortable to them. Unfortunately, that language may not be widely accepted and valued. Many school districts and universities require that students submit their written work in mainstream English, and many standardized writing tests look more at language and punctuation "correctness" than clarity and expression of ideas. NMUSE dialects may not easily get students into college. It might not be as effective as MUSE in getting them the job they want. The stubborn prejudices of "a long-standing tradition of elitism in American life and language matters" (Smitherman 16) make it difficult for those outside the elitist language to succeed. These realities put English teachers in an awkward and difficult position, but just because our students are required to do academic writing in mainstream English does not mean that they cannot or should not be doing writing in their own Englishes.

First, students need to discover the legitimacy of their own dialects. Helping students recognize linguicism and the biased practices against certain dialects is a good step to help students find legitimacy in their own devalued languages and feel comfortable using their own language in their writing processes. Again, *To Kill a Mockingbird* can be a vehicle through which students might explore language diversity and discrimination. Because I have only recently entered more linguistically diverse classroom settings and because my courses no longer include *To Kill a Mockingbird*, this lesson segment is more hypothetical than experience based. Still, I believe the conversations and lessons will work in a diverse English language environment. Starting with the same passages from chapter 12 but focusing on Jem's judgment of Calpurnia's language use instead of Scout's recognition of her "command of two languages," the conversation with diverse NMUSE speakers has great potential. Keep in mind, though, this lesson assumes that students have had little instruction that validates non-mainstream Englishes. It could, of course, be easily adapted for students whose schools have encouraged and supported their home languages.

A blog or journal entry prompt based on the chapter 12 reading to start students thinking about language may be similar in some aspects to the one provided in the previous section. Instead of merely recognizing the change in language use, though, this prompt should consider more overtly Jem's judgment of Calpurnia's black English. The prompt should likely still consider Calpurnia's code-switching, but might then turn its focus to something like this:

> Think about how Jem reacts to Cal's language shift: on page 167, he says, "why do you talk nigger-talk . . . when you know it's not right?" and when Cal reminds him that she is Black, he responds, "That doesn't mean you hafta talk that way when you know better." What does his description of her language as "not right" reveal about what he thinks about "colored-folks' talk" versus "white-folks' talk"? Do people still think like this about different dialects of English today? Explain, using examples where possible.

Getting students to think about the judgments inherent in Jem's comments and in the expectations of the dominant society at large today will facilitate a good discussion in the coming class period. Bringing Scout into the judgment picture, the instructor may widen the prompt to include Scout's comment on Calpurnia's grammar in chapter 3: "when she was furious Calpurnia's grammar became erratic" (Lee 32). This evidence of Scout criticizing Calpurnia's community language could also be examined in the later conversation as evidence that Scout knew prior to her visit to Cal's church that Calpurnia could speak like the rest of the black community, but in chapter 3, Scout is equating Cal's black English to erratic grammar rather than another language. It is also strong evidence of the perceived value of one dialect and the perceived wrongness of another.

In the class period or periods that follow the reading assignment and journal, opening with discussion of the students' thoughts on the prompt provides a good opportunity to introduce the idea of linguicism as well as the legitimacy of various dialects. In the conversation, the instructor explains dialects as rule-governed variations of a language and makes clear that every dialect is as valuable and correct as any other. In a diverse classroom, an explanation of widely misunderstood rules of one or more varieties of English is helpful, but just as helpful would be a brief investigation in which students research and explain—either individually or in groups—a few varieties of English and their most widely misunderstood rules. One group researches AAE, and another investigates Chicanx English, and another HCE, and so on, or the instructor opts to allow each group or student to select a dialect that interests them personally. At the high school level, the instructor should provide appropriate resources for students to read to develop their understanding; at the post-secondary level, students may be more capable of finding their own sources. Regardless of the setup of the investigations, allowing students to come to a greater understanding of the rules that govern their own or another devalued dialect is empowering and validating. Then, students present their findings, and the instructor keeps a log of linguistic features of various dialects on the board or in a class book or the students record them in their notes. Having a way to record the rule differences may become important later if the instructor discusses translating between the students' community languages and MUSE.

It is possible, in introducing the validity of students' community dialects, that some students may feel awkward or even embarrassed by such discussion. These are conversations that should wait until a point in the course where the instructor and students trust one another enough to work through uncomfortable conversations. One tactic to develop some groundwork to avoid discomfort would be to start with a dialect unfamiliar to all of the students as a sample so that no one student or student group feels singled out by the initial discussion. I have successfully employed this tactic with HCE in classrooms where I have speakers of several Englishes, but no speakers of Pidgin. Another strategy if you, like me, are not a speaker of a devalued English, is to allow the students to take the lead in explaining their own dialects; by your becoming their student and they your instructors (and by pushing them to define how their language works), you reduce the risk of appearing to talk down to them about their own language. Such a discussion requires the students to be able to both consider and explain how their language works, and that linguistic awareness is difficult for many students to articulate. This strategy must give students time to consider their dialect and how to explain it to others; it is not an on-the-spot activity. Another tactic could be using humor aimed specifically at breaking down stereotypical understandings of language. Comedy duo Keegan-Michael Key and Jordan Peele (of Comedy Central's *Key & Peele*) address language differences in their sketch "Phone Call," which centers on black men changing their language use based on their proximity to other black men; it is a good conversation starter or way to continue the conversation on another day to discuss stereotypes centered in language use.

After researching the features of various Englishes, return to *To Kill a Mockingbird* for further investigation. First, students work in small groups with perhaps two or three chapters each to cover, and the class reviews the previous eleven chapters, looking for non-mainstream features in Jem and Scout's language. Examples students find could include use of *ain't*, constructions like "Can't anybody tell what I'm gonna do," as found in Jem's dialogue on page 78, use of *me* as a subject pronoun, or shortened or combined words like *hafta, gonna, who'da, an',* and *'fore.* These non-mainstream usages can serve to show students that speakers of MUSE use words and constructions that do not fit the definitions of "standard" use. By showing the students that Jem and Scout—who see the features of Calpurnia's black English as strikingly different at best or just plain wrong at worst but fail to see their own divergence from "proper" English—do not speak a perfectly standard English, they may continue to see that their own dialects are not faulty.

As they read the rest of the book, ask students to make note of non-standard speech features, collect the examples in a class notebook, and discuss them regularly. Which elements are specific to children? Which are specific to white characters? To black characters? It would also be interesting to analyze the language used by the Ewells in the trial scene, and especially to look at the warning by Judge Taylor to Bob Ewell to "keep [his] testimony within the confines of Christian English usage, if that is possible" (233). What does Judge Taylor mean by "Christian English usage"? Is the judge's language discriminatory? Do the students see patterns in the speech of Bob and Mayella Ewell? If so, what are those patterns? What speech features do the Ewells use that the Finch children also use (or do not use)? Are the speech characteristics of the Ewells consistent or rule-governed? What rules do they follow (if any)? What impression are the speech characteristics of the Ewells intended to give the reader?

Is it problematic to impress upon the reader certain stereotypes based on language?

To supplement the ideas the students explore and discuss in *To Kill a Mockingbird,* several articles, chapters, and additional texts might be useful. Of course, exposing students to literature written in NMUSE is critical, but using strong pieces of scholarly work written in dialect or code-meshing like Young's "Should Writers Use They Own English?" or Lee Tonouchi's "Da State of Pidgin Address" or Gloria Anzaldúa's "How to Tame a Wild Tongue" or any of Geneva Smitherman's *Soul 'n Style* columns from *The English Journal* is another excellent way to introduce students to the powerful influence possible in academia through NMUSE. Further, as mentioned earlier, Joseph Williams's smart and funny article about "standard" usage, "The Phenomenology of Error," is an interesting piece for students to examine as evidence of both the ridiculousness of certain rules of correctness and the unnecessary nature of following all the rules all the time. And by using Williams's examination of error, students should begin to understand that the creation of "errors" does not necessarily equate to poor writing, and perhaps find themselves less likely to create the awkward prose Tonouchi describes because of trying to press their ideas into a set of awkward and often illogical rules. (Care should be taken with the Williams piece, though, so that students do not view it as a reflection of their language as erroneous.)

But equally important to allowing students to read NMUSE dialects and discuss language differences is not just *allowing* but *encouraging* them to write in their familiar dialects. Selecting texts written in various devalued Englishes is comparatively easy next to the task of getting students to write in their community languages. As John Ogbu found in his study in Lafayette, CA, in the 1990s, it isn't that the students don't know how to use their dialects; it's that their communities as well as their schools often expect students to learn and use "proper" English at school (Ogbu 169). This expectation can make it complicated and difficult to encourage students to use NMUSE in their work, even if by doing so your intention is to help them eventually translate to and use MUSE more effectively in their writing in order to meet requirements of your district or standardized tests. And encouraging students to write in their home or community languages is also a highly charged political endeavor as evidenced by the widely misinterpreted Ebonics resolution in Oakland, CA, in the 1990s. In my own practice, I started with encouraging students to use their languages and dialects in smaller, formative assignments that they use for thinking through topics that will be available for the larger summative assessments The expectation of mainstream English may be there in the later piece (as is often required), but students may use whatever language they are most familiar with for their brainstorming, organization, and drafting processes.

Teachers do not need to learn all dialects in order to communicate with their students solely through each student's own dialect; teachers of English language learners are rarely well-versed in the languages of all their students, and it would be a ridiculous undertaking to expect teachers of NMUSE-speaking students to learn all their students' dialects. It is advisable, though, for teachers to show genuine interest in their students' Englishes and how they use their languages. One retired instructor I know kept a notebook on his desk for students to share their language patterns with him; both he and his students wrote in it and discussed its contents regularly, forming a collaborative, two-way learning environment Paulo Freire—the Brazilian educator widely known for his work *Pedagogy of the Oppressed*—would have been proud of. Recognition of students' languages, reading pieces written in various dialects, and allowance for students to do at least their thinking and organizing in their own Englishes goes a long way in acknowledging language legitimacy and encouraging greater clarity of thought. In classes I taught at a technological institute, I encouraged students to write in whatever language or dialect they felt most comfortable with in their journals and discussion posts. The journals or posts then became think-pieces for their larger writing assignments, so they were able to do a lot of thinking and organization in whatever language came most naturally to them and then work toward translating—code-switching—into the mainstream English in their formal essays (which was required by that institution).

I recommend here some strategies suggested by Wheeler and Swords, as I find their dedication to helping teachers discover the linguistic legitimacy of non-mainstream Englishes a step in the right direction (as opposed to, for example, simply correcting "errors" in NMUSE writing and speaking rather than validating the rule-governed nature of every dialect). There are significant disagreements about Wheeler and Swords' approach to language, though. Young argues that teaching NMUSE-speaking students to translate or code-switch still divides home and school languages as wrong and right or worse and better, perpetuating a linguistic hegemony (Young "Nah"). It is not my intention—nor is it, I believe, the intention of Wheeler and Swords—to encourage hegemony.

Rather, my intention is to help teachers think about language differently. I've met and known many teachers who consider "otherness" in language as error rather than difference, much as Scout does in chapter three and Jem does in chapter twelve of *To Kill a Mockingbird*. I think for many teachers who see language difference in terms of right and wrong, translation with a focus on rhetorical situation instead of "correction" is a step in the right direction even if it is not as strong or complete a step as code-meshed texts would be. In addition, many teachers work with administrators, school boards, and communities who would be strongly resistant to any methods that did not require mastery of "standard" English. Wheeler and Swords' suggestions meet the needs of such teachers and are a better approach than simply "correcting" students.

To address the balance between producing ideas, organization, and writing in NMUSE and producing finished works in MUSE when required, Wheeler and Swords encourage code-switching—in the wide educational definition—as a means of helping students write using the language they are most familiar with and then translating to MUSE only *when appropriate or necessary*. My approach with linguistically diverse students at a previous institution was loosely based on the suggestions in their text, *Code-Switching: Teaching Standard English in Urban Classrooms*. Their approach pushes students to consider the rhetorical context of their work, an important skill for all writers. It treats NMUSE dialects as valid languages and has seen success in both preserving students' community languages and helping students develop stronger MUSE communication skills (Wheeler and Thomas). In this way, students should not, as Smitherman laments, "become unwitting accomplices in their own linguistic and cultural demise" (16), and instead become more aware of their own rhetorical choices and able to write according to purpose and audience. In addition, Wheeler and Swords' approach uses a shift in treatment of and educator language referring to students' community languages: rather than "correcting errors," students are "translating" or "code-switching"; rather than labeling language as "good or bad," Wheeler and Swords encourage teachers to discuss whether the language is "effective or ineffective" in a particular rhetorical situation (57). Such shifts in language about language lend further validity to students' home dialects rather than labeling it as broken or substandard.

Your school may require that students write in "standard" English, and standardized tests certainly expect the MUSE variety; those realities do not mean that students cannot or should not be able to use their own language varieties in their writing. Students should still be encouraged to use language that is comfortable to them at the very least in their brainstorming and drafting, and then, if it is appropriate and necessary, use strategies like code-switching to revise later drafts. As Tonouchi notes, students who write in the dialect that is most natural to them do a better job expressing their ideas and organizing their thoughts. If the MUSE variety is required, Wheeler and Swords argue that students can learn to use MUSE more effectively through translating their own language patterns to the mainstream than they may be able to learn to do all their thinking and writing in a dialect that is not natural to them (Wheeler and Swords 55–57, 61–62). By allowing students to do their thinking and writing in the dialect that is natural to them and then translate certain portions or entire assignments to MUSE, they maintain the integrity of their own language while developing skills using the mainstream when required.

Learning to use language based on the rhetorical situation is critical for all students. Using mentor texts—both literature and scholarly work—that include code-meshing allows students to evaluate the rhetorical choices made by others, as well. Such evaluation could occur with *To Kill a Mockingbird*: Why does Calpurnia change the way she talks for the Finch family? How does her code-switching allow her to be an accepted part of two different communities? Does her ability to speak white-folks' talk grant her access to all the same privileges as the white community in Maycomb? Would it today? Does her ability to speak white-folks' talk cause her problems in her black community? Would it today? Because language is very much a part of identity in most communities, it is important to discuss what is and is not acceptable among the various communities in which students interact. It is also important, especially if you speak only a widely valued, mainstream variety of English, to let the students do the talking. It is their voices, after all, that need to be heard.

Works Cited

Anzaldúa, Gloria. "How to Tame a Wild Tongue." *Borderlands La Frontera*. 4th ed., Aunt Lute Books, 2012, pp. 75–86.

Bohney, Brandie. "Moving Students toward Acceptance of 'Other' Englishes." *English Journal*, vol. 105, no. 6, July 2016, pp. 66–71.

Elbow, Peter. *Vernacular Eloquence: What Speech Can Bring to Writing*. Oxford University Press, 2012.

Fish, Stanley. "What Should Colleges Teach? Part 3." *Opinionator*, The New York Times, 9 Sept. 2009, opinionator.blogs.nytimes.com/2009/09/07/what-should -colleges-teach-part-3/.

Fromkin, Victoria et al. *An Introduction to Language.* 7th ed., Thomson/Heinle, 2007.

Key, Keegan-Michael, and Jordan Peele. "Phone Call." Comedy Central, 2011, www .youtube.com/watch?v-JzprLDmdRlc.

Lee, Harper. *To Kill a Mockingbird.* Grand Central Publishing, 1960.

Lippi-Green, Rosina. *English with an Accent: Language, Ideology and Discrimination in the United States.* Routledge, 2012.

Obama, Barack. *Dreams from My Father: A Story of Race and Inheritance.* Crown Publishers, 1995.

Ogbu, John U. "Beyond Language: Ebonics, Proper English, and Identity in a Black-American Speech Community." *American Educational Research Journal*, vol. 36, no. 2, 1 July 1999, pp. 147–184, www.jstor.org/stable/10.2307/1163537?ref=search -gateway:20bddac1e17c7bebb24fabf866fo8d11.

Pinker, Steven. "Grammar Puss: The Fallacies of the Language Mavens." *New Republic*, 30 Jan. 1994, newrepublic.com/article/77732/grammar-puss-steven -pinker-language-william-safire.

"Racial and Ethnic Achievement Gaps." *The Educational Opportunity Monitoring Project*, Stanford Center for Education Policy Analysis, cepa.stanford.edu /educational-opportunity-monitoring-project/achievement-gaps/race/.

Smitherman, Geneva. "Soul'n Style." *The English Journal*, vol. 63, no. 2, 1 Feb. 1974, pp. 16–17, www.jstor.org/stable/10.2307/813674?ref=search- gateway:8311431a0a1dafe7 ac994d6d8fe18d37.

Tonouchi, Lee A. "Da State of Pidgin Address." *College English*, vol. 67, no. 1, Special Issue: Rhetorics from/of Color, 1 Sept. 2004, pp. 75–82, www.jstor.org/stable /10.2307/ 4140726?ref=search-gateway:be59fadec22d19914fbb9fe9442f472a.

Wheeler, Rebecca S., and Rachel Swords. *Code-Switching: Teaching Standard English in Urban Classrooms.* National Council of Teachers of English, 2006.

Wheeler, Rebecca S., and Julia Thomas. "And 'Still' the Children Suffer: The Dilemma of Standard English, Social Justice and Social Access." *JAC*, vol. 33, no. 1/2, 2013, pp. 363–96, https://www.jstor.org/stable/43854557.

Williams, Joseph M. "The Phenomenology of Error." *College Composition and Communication*, vol. 32, no. 2, 1981, pp. 152–68. Rpt. in *Writing About Writing: A College Reader*, by Elizabeth Wardle and Doug Downs, Bedford/St. Martin's, 2011, pp. 37–55.

Young, Vershawn A. "'Nah, We Straight': An Argument against Code Switching." *JAC*, vol. 29, no. 1/2, 2009, pp. 49–76. http://www.jstor.org/stable/20866886.

———. "Should Writers Use They Own English?" *Iowa Journal of Cultural Studies*, vol. 12, no. 1, 2010, pp. 110–17. ir.uiowa.edu/ijcs/vol12/iss1/10.

Zuidema, Leah A. "Myth Education: Rationale and Strategies for Teaching against Linguistic Prejudice." *Journal of Adolescent and Adult Literacy* 48.8 (2005): 666– 75. Rpt. in *Students' Right to Their Own Language: A Critical Sourcebook*, edited by Staci Perryman Clark, David E. Kirkland, and Austin Jackson, Bedford, 2014, pp. 341–52.

10

QUEER ABSENCES
Christian Polemics and Boo Radley
Cheli Reutter

1. Where Have All the Polemics Gone? Long Time Passing!

As a coda to his lengthy physical, emotional, and verbal assault, the catalyst of which is purportedly Jean Louise's bigotry, Dr. Finch, better known as "Uncle Jack," pontificates thus: "Prejudice, a dirty word, and faith, a clean one, have something in common: they both begin where reason ends" (270–71). In arguments involving Jean Louise, Atticus and Uncle Jack, *Go Set a Watchman* introduces race polemics of its time. The resolution of their arguing constitutes apologetics for the status quo of Southern society. Yet, despite its forceful exertion of a single point of view, this novel, unlike its better-known counterpart, *To Kill a Mockingbird,* is contemporaneous, and at least recognizes the existence of the pivotal current events, topics, and constituencies.

When Uncle Jack compares prejudice and faith, readers might expect him to engage Christian polemics as well. It is too bad, though, that in the next moment, he is putting out his cigarette and demanding that Jean Louise drive him home. This drawing back from the brink of critical inquiry into social and moral platitudes may feel like déjà vu. *To Kill a Mockingbird* is simply a more beautifully rendered and symbolically veiled retreat from polemics involving issues including race relations, gender and sexuality norms, and applications of religious beliefs than is the recently published *Go Set a Watchman.* Both novels use metaphors of race, sexuality, disability, sin, and sacrifice—and yet they fail to produce cogent polemical arguments about the social and cultural issues they address.

It is worth considering the implications of Harper Lee's metaphors, including her religious ones. In both novels, the titular metaphors are religious. *Go Set a Watchman* and *To Kill a Mockingbird* are also rife with church scenes and religious talk. They highlight the institutional significance of the Methodist Church in particular, and Christian popular thought more broadly. Harper Lee's titles appeal to this Christian popular imagination, and suggest a seamless connection between the sacred and the secular.

Lee's *To Kill a Mockingbird* uses religious symbols to imbue sacred significance into a few pivotal characters, most significantly, Atticus in *To Kill a Mockingbird* and Uncle Jack in *Go Set a Watchman*. Harper Lee was a younger contemporary of existential religious philosopher Paul Tillich, who encapsulates an idea about the power of the religious symbol: "Man's ultimate concern must be expressed symbolically, because symbolic language alone is able to express the ultimate." Lee uses religious symbols in both novels, but most effectively in *Mockingbird,* where references to birds and sin "express the ultimate" in Scout Finch's life. In this more famous Harper Lee novel, Atticus's single commandment for the children, to remember that "it's a sin to kill a mockingbird" (*Mockingbird* 49) infuses godly authority into the iconic Atticus. Then, when, in *Go Set a Watchman,* Uncle Jack says that "every man's watchman, is his conscience," he captures the authority of the prophets through the symbol of the watchman. Chapter seven of *Watchman* cites Isaiah 21:6: "For thus hath the Lord said unto me, Go, set a watchman, let him declare what he seeth." The moniker of Harper Lee's 2015 novel is a simple abbreviation of this verse.

Tillich differentiates between signs and symbols, with signs being easily removable and not (as he suggests with symbols) cogently connected to "express[ing] the ultimate." In *Go Set a Watchman,* signs of church life are ubiquitous, and religion and the church loom large in Jean Louise's memories of her everyday experience in Maycomb. In the church scene in chapter six, Jean Louise is greeted by her Uncle Jack. The church service in chapter seven then presents Jean Louise's perspective on Reverend Stone and his "liberal tendencies" (*Watchman* 95). Reverend Stone, Lee suggests, is merely signposting religion. The chapter is raucously entertaining, and, like the critique of Miss Caroline's "Dewey Decimal System" in *To Kill a Mockingbird,* demonstrates Harper Lee's scorn for what she apparently regards as pretentious new ideas. This signing and the characters she associates with it are subject to mockery, while those associated with religious symbols are revered.

A religious *symbol* enters *Go Set a Watchman* early on—but only as anathema to the central symbol of the watchman and the authorities it is associated with. Chapter five flashes back to Jean Louise playing baptism with Jem and Dill. They are surprised by the appearance of Atticus and the visiting minister, as Scout stands naked and drenched with the water of this play baptism. This confrontation is Jean Louise in the Garden of Eden realizing she is naked, and she is ashamed. She is recognized by the twin representatives of "the ultimate"—a preacher and her father. Here, her shame may not have been about her corporeal nakedness, but her symbolic nakedness, playing sacrilegiously with a religious symbol.

This sense of symbolic shame, and its interaction with paternal and pastoral authority, may further account for why Jean Louise is unable to leave her "home." The church is an integral part of the Maycomb Jean Louse claims she wants to leave behind. After her fight with Atticus, Jean Louise declares, "Aunty . . . I am going so far away from Maycomb that it will take me a hundred years to get back! I never want to see it or anyone in it again, and that goes for every one of you, the probate judge, the undertaker, and the chairman of the board of the Methodist Church!" (*Watchman* 258).

Yet, despite how "sick and damn tired" she is of "listening to the lot of you" (*Watchman* 260), Jean Louise does *not* run away from *any* of the representatives of the social or religious institutions representing Maycomb, Alabama. Even if at first, she says it is because she "can't fight them anymore" (*Watchman* 260), Jean Louise still comes "home." By the end, she does so willingly. Uncle Jack has convinced her that Maycomb "needs" her (272), and she is willing to believe him, perhaps in good part at least because she encounters the symbolic "watchman."

From a secular viewpoint, Jean Louise's choice is a clear failure. For those of us who wonder how she could have been so taken in, it helps to remember that a broad swath of mainstream Americans, "churchgoers" or not, vest the religious symbol with interpretive power exceeding that of narrative logic. For example, "Christ imagery" or prophetic wisdom may outweigh other themes and ideas, whether the reader is conscious of this privileging or not. They are affected by the power of the religious symbol at the level Tillich describes. In this context, Harper Lee's claim in her 1966 letter that *Mockingbird* is "Christian in its ethic" may not be so wrong.

I admit that when I first read *Watchman,* I could not believe that Uncle Jack had the gall to talk to Jean Louise about a "conscience," when, on so many levels, it appeared to me he did not have one. For example, he smacked his adult niece in the mouth, and then behaved as if this were perfectly acceptable. I realized, then, that my idea of a "conscience" involves a principled social consciousness, cognizant of race equity, gender equity, and respect for physical boundaries, among other matters.

Jack Finch's idea of conscience, however, involves a conceptualization of absolute truth rather than social consciousness. "There's no such thing as a collective conscious" (*Watchman* 265), he claims. He then indicates to Jean Louse that her own and her father's conscience had to part ways, and that the Finch men saw it coming. With this in mind, Harper Lee's decision prior to 2015 to only publish her 1960 novel seems especially curious. Wouldn't Harper Lee have wanted to highlight the achievement of her character's independence of thought, and thus published *Watchman* much earlier? Yet Jack clarifies when he says that Jean Louise's conscience had merely "fastened ... like a barnacle, onto [her] father's" (*Watchman* 265). It's not Jean Louise's disagreement with her father that Jack approves of. It is that Jean Louise is no longer a "barnacle," and can become an agent in perpetrating the absolutist ideas the Finch men believe in.

In *Mockingbird*, Harper Lee introduces an especially potent central symbol suggesting the primacy of some sort of absolute truth. Atticus's singular imperative, "it's a sin to kill a mockingbird" (49), emphasized by its use in abbreviated form as the novel's title, ultimately absolves readers of all other sins of social practice and of moral application of religious belief. After all, before speaking the titular line, Atticus tells Jean Louise that she can "shoot all the bluejays you want" (49). That Atticus gives Scout explicit permission to shoot bluejays suggests, metaphorically, that she might be careless in her regard for the many, providing she treats select objects of reverence with respect.

"Shoot all the bluejays you want" (*Mockingbird* 49) is an imperative coming from Atticus's own authority. Yet, his next statement, dramatically underscored with his own imperative—"but remember, it's a sin to kill a mockingbird"—nevertheless appears to evoke an authority higher than himself. In *Watchman,* Jack makes a point of telling Jean Louise that Atticus is not a god, however great he thinks his brother is. Yet the Atticus of Scout's memory in *Mockingbird* draws on a well-established Judeo-Christian tradition of understanding that a "sin" is a breaking of a law established by none other, and thus Atticus is a sort of prophet.

This morally authoritative dictum "it's a sin to kill" is evoked only three times in *To Kill a Mockingbird*: two of which seem to protect (after a fashion) the queer Boo. The third decries the lack of protection for Tom Robinson, not as a human being, and certainly not as a black man, but as a "cripple":

> To Maycomb, Tom's death was typical . . . just run blind first chance he saw . . . that Robinson boy was legally married, they say he kept himself clean, went to church and all that, but when it comes down to the line the veneer's mighty thin. N——— always comes out in 'em . . . There was a brief obituary in the Colored News, but there was also an editorial. Mr. B. B. Underwood . . . didn't talk about miscarriages of justice, he was writing so children could understand. Mr. Underwood simply figured it was a sin to kill cripples, be they standing, sitting, or escaping. He likened Tom's death to the senseless slaughter of songbirds by hunters and children, and Maycomb thought he was trying to write an editorial poetical enough to be reprinted in The Montgomery Advertiser. (*To Kill a Mockingbird* 128)

It is "a sin to kill cripples," Mr. Underwood believes, "be they standing, sitting, or escaping." It is unclear here how much distance there is between the "Maycomb" point of view and the narrator's own. The narrator leaves some doubt in the readers' minds whether Tom's shooting would have been considered wrong if he was not also "crippled." The narrator suggests an alignment of the narrator's own sentiment with that of the Maycomb community. Underwood's comparison of Tom, a "cripple," to a "songbird" that children should not shoot, has no similar moral authority, in Maycomb's eyes, to that which Atticus's imperative about Boo has in Scout's.

When Underwood speaks of songbirds, Maycomb will simply indulge his soft heart, purchasing subscriptions even when they don't believe him or when he waxes too "poetic" for their taste. Scout, on the other hand, defers entirely to Atticus's authority after Boo defends Jem and her from Bob Ewell. When telling the truth about Boo's involvement in the incident, Scout says to her father, "It would be sort of like shootin' a mockingbird, wouldn't it?" (147), and he affirms her answer. While the town mocks Underwood's comparison of Tom to a songbird, the narrator makes it clear that Boo Radley is to be regarded as a mockingbird, symbolically sanctified and protected, even to the degree that the novel's icon of legal justice endorses lying. Still, though the queer Boo gets to *live* while Tom (symbolically, a "bluejay") is mortally sacrificed, it is not entirely clear that Boo's symbolic protection makes his condition exactly free.

When we consider that *Go Set a Watchman* was likely written in the same six-month period as *To Kill a Mockingbird,* Lee's choice on behalf of Boo *and* the adult Jean Louise seems especially poignant. According to Oprah, Harper Lee told her: "You know the character Boo? Well, that's me!" If true, it seems the symbolic immolation happened twice. It seems as well that Harper Lee had to head back in time twenty years to romanticize a decision forged from self-abnegation: "He would be there all night, and he would be there when Jem woke up in the morning" (*Mockingbird* 149). Despite Jean Louie's declared commitment to racial justice and despite the omnipresence of the church in Maycomb, the heroine cannot work through her disagreements with the men in her family with the tools of social or religious polemics, and instead retreats into self-abnegation and nostalgic memory. By the end of *Go Set a Watchman,* Lee's "Christian . . . ethic" leads to repression of both self and principle.

Even in the era in which Lee wrote her novels, there was available an intermediate narrative strategy which might have navigated between religious symbol and secular metaphor. That strategy is the polemical. By the 1960s, before Lee wrote her letter, many religious leaders were actively engaging Christian social justice polemics. These Christian polemics were highly visible in the United States in the 1960s civil rights movement but had originated much earlier. When American author Pearl S. Buck wrote her "Is there a Place for Foreign Missions?" letter in 1932, the well-known civil rights leader and theologian Dr. Martin Luther King, Jr., was a preschooler, and Harper Lee an elementary school child. Both Lee and King were clearly affected by consideration of "Christian . . . ethic[s]," but responded to very different degrees to the charge to engage polemics.

To Kill a Mockingbird, like its recently published book-kin, brings up the subjects but only superficially engages controversies concerning social applications of religious thought. When Scout pokes fun at the women in the missionary circle who come to tea, she seems to be critiquing a religious controversy of the 1930s, the decade in which the novel was set. Harper Lee writes: "Mrs. Grace Merriweather sat on my left, and I felt it would be polite to talk to her . . . Mrs. Merriweather's large brown eyes always filled with tears when she considered the oppressed. 'Living in that jungle with nobody but J. Grimes Everett . . . Not a white person'll go near 'em but that saintly J. Grimes Everett'" (234). Mrs. Merriweather is apparently a good old-fashioned Christian bigot.

Yet Lee's depiction of Mrs. Merriweather's condescending hypocrisy does not extend beyond mockery. It stops far short of the critique of Pearl S. Buck. In the 1930s, some of the leadership in the Methodist Church went well beyond this superficial criticism. In the early 1930s, some of the leadership in the United Methodist Church supported a critical review of Christian missions in practice. They, along with supporters in four other Christian denominations, joined Presbyterian intellectuals including William Earnest Hocking on the Commission of Appraisal, collectively publishing *Re-Thinking Missions: A Laymen's Inquiry after One Hundred Years* in 1932.

Buck sometimes collaborated with Hocking, reflecting on what she had seen up close and personal as the child of missionaries. She poses a polemical question about the role and relation of missionaries to non-US citizens in her 1932 speech "Is there a Case for Foreign Missions?" She opens her argument as follows:

> I have seen the missionary narrow, uncharitable, unapprecia-
> tive, ignorant. I have seen missionaries . . . so lacking in sympa-
> thy for the people they were supposed to be saving, so scornful
> of any civilization but their own, so harsh in their judgments
> upon one another, so coarse and insensitive among a sensitive
> and cultivated people, that my heart has fairly bled with shame
> . . . apologies to the Chinese people that in the name of a gentle
> Christ we have sent such people to them.

That should have struck a chord in Harper Lee, and does, for a fleeting moment. When Jean Louise is most upset with Atticus in *Watchman,* she brings up a Buck-esque critique, yelling "why didn't you make it very plain to me that God made the races and put the black folk in Africa . . . so the missionaries could go tell them that Jesus loved 'em but meant for 'em to stay in Africa?" (249). Yet she drops her position. In *Mockingbird,* she would have to look no further than the outskirts of Monroeville, where the black community lived, to discover a comparable situation. Yet Lee is unwilling to critique the peculiar brand of racism of her own family and the community in which she cut her own teeth. Other "isms" including heterosexism and ableism are tucked into the narrative as well. If anything, Lee's truncated polemics, overpowered as they are by symbolic argument, undercut the sort of polemical argument Buck and Hocking introduce.

In 1966, Harper Lee said of her 1961 Pulitzer Prize–winner that it was "Christian in its ethic," and that it "the legacy of all Southerners." The letter in which these words appear is in response to the Fairfax, Virginia Board of Education, which had banned her book. She was defending herself against the charge that her novel was "Marxist." Lee's epistle is deliciously snarky: the author told the Hanover County, Virginia, in 1966, that "the problem is one of illiteracy, not Marxism," and she enclosed ten dollars, that the School Board members might educate themselves in a "first-grade classroom of their choice."

Witty as the author was in her own defense against the communist charge, though, she and an ever-growing band of supporters had also shuttered the novel from a more reasonable scrutiny. Her novel may have been "Christian" in its ethic, at least in the sense of the existential Christian symbology of Paul Tillich, but it did not, in fact, engage the Christian polemics of its day and was also not equitable in its treatment of black or queer characters. She was no Dr. Martin Luther King, Jr.

In 1968, Dr. King, like Harper Lee's Tom Robinson seven or more years earlier, was shot to death. With his death, he was no longer a threat. He became noble and loving, an icon of passion and peace. He was reduced to a few paragraphs, in which black children and white children played together. He became, as Susan L. Mizruchi might have it, an icon of suffering and sacrifice. Essentially, he became a character in a white-authored American narrative—maybe even Tom Robinson.

Before his assassination, Martin Luther King was considered "dangerous" and, at times, "an enemy of the people." Since his death, he lives in the popular imagination with a repackaged image, emphasizing his idyllic paragraph in "I have a dream." This was the integrationist dream, the

American dream, not King's own Poor People's Campaign. After King's death (and subsequent lack of power to provide a corrective), King himself could be granted posthumous accolades while mainstream leaders appropriated the dream.

White literati, meanwhile, could congratulate themselves for racial progress. Though we might admire Harper Lee's rhetorical brilliance in her 1966 letter, we see no real evidence that she had earned the hostile charges against her concerning "Marxism." (It might have been interesting if she had.) As it is, even Link Deas, who sympathizes with Helen Robinson enough to walk her to work, does not suggest a change in the economic relations between black and white Maycombers.

This absorption of Christian polemics and the polemical legacies of such thinkers as Pearl S. Buck and Martin Luther King, Jr., into an absolutist religious-secular symbology should give readers pause. As Jonathan Cullick notes elsewhere in this volume, King reminds us that the white moderate was the enemy of the everyday African American. King famously writes, "I have almost reached the regrettable conclusion that the Negro's great stumbling block in the stride toward freedom is not the White Citizens Council or the Ku Klux Klanner, but the white moderate who is more devoted to order than to justice." This is from his well-known "Letter from a Birmingham Jail" in 1963—less than three years after the publication of *To Kill a Mockingbird*.

Jean Louise—more so than her father—represents the white moderate. More precisely, in *Watchman*, she clearly adopts the stance of a white moderate. Jean Louise's choice is influenced by the condescending kindness of her father Atticus, and the violent passion of her Uncle Jack, but it becomes her own through shame. Though she starts out trying to take a progressive stand back home with her, she instead learns to regard herself as a "turnip-sized bigot" (267). She is a Finch, at the end of the day, and follows Finch logic rather than pursuing social justice ideals, even Christian ones.

Harper Lee is curiously silent, in the decade in which both her book and Martin Luther King, Jr, rose to fame, about this famous black theologian. She wrote her "Christian ethic" letter in 1966, at a time when King was a household name. Yet she followed a trend common among members of the six major Christian denominations associated in the early 1930s with the Commission on Appraisal. After the publication of the *Re-thinking Missions,* most of the leadership in the six denominations distanced themselves from the findings of the report, and, more generally, from polemical social justice arguments like those of Dr. King. King also writes in his "Letter from a Birmingham Jail":

> I have the honor of serving as president of the Southern Christian Leadership Conference ... Several months ago the affiliate here in Birmingham asked us to be on call to engage in a nonviolent direct action program if such were deemed necessary. We readily consented, and when the hour came we lived up to our promise ... I am here because I have organizational ties here.
>
> But more basically, I am in Birmingham because injustice is here.

King makes clear that his reason and purpose are explicitly religious and explicitly polemical, born out of an obligation and commitment to Christian social justice as he sees it. Yet Harper Lee's diversion of religious discourse in the popular imagination from social polemics to the strictly symbolic is helpful for the reassertion of American mainstream cultural dominance threatened by both Hocking's report and the writings and speeches of Dr. Martin Luther King.

Harper Lee's mockingbird, whom Atticus tells us it would be a "sin to kill," lives at the intersection of the religious and the secular imagination. The mockingbird is the dove of the secular world, just as bluejays are its pigeons. When in her own meta-criticism, she says that her novel is "Christian in its ethic," many readers are happy to take Harper Lee's word on what constitutes *social* sin.

We might wonder about the extent to which Harper Lee's choice to sacrifice or protect her *Mockingbird* characters was motivated by self-preservation. Recall, only the mockingbird is protected by Atticus's authority. Perhaps by protecting Boo (and herself?) with Atticus's decree, she staves off the moral judgment of none other than Reverend Jerry Falwell. It may still be troubling to consider that she was willing to sacrifice "bluejays," but her desire to protect "mockingbirds" makes sense in context of both secular and religious conversations of her day. As the next section explains, LGBTQ writers have had to create safe spaces in light of religious and secular rhetoric that has denied that they are "human."

2. Where Did Boo Go, Anyhow?

When, in December of 1962, Robert Duvall appeared larger-than-life on-screen as Boo Radley, he animated some of Harper Lee's textual metaphors. He is shadow and light. In the *Mockingbird* novel, Scout recounts her meeting with Boo thusly: "Feeling slightly unreal, I led him to the chair farthest from Atticus and Mr. Tate. It was in deep shadow. Boo would feel more comfortable in the dark" (144). In the years since, talk of Boo Radley or of Duvall has faded, while Gregory Peck, as Atticus, seems to loom as large as ever. Even as parades are thrown (literally) for Atticus Finch, and while celebrities including Stephen Colbert continue to sing the praises of Gregory Peck, Duvall and Boo are relegated to one-liners or footnotes.

I grew up when Boo mattered. In the early 1980s, owning a VCR was still rare in middle-income U.S. households (a tech company litigation issue, but I digress). Public viewings of major box office hits, including old standards like *To Kill a Mockingbird*, were thus regarded as special treats. I watched the *Mockingbird* film as a sophomore in high school. All two thousand girls at my high school were invited to attend. On a giant screen, where even Scout was three times taller than any of us, in the dark auditorium in which we had been threatened that we would all be marched out if we even whispered to our friends next to us, we *felt* the queer spaces of the *Mockingbird* narrative.

One of my senior colleagues, about the same age of Mary Badham the year the *Mockingbird* film came out, recalls the story of a "queer young girl in dungarees, just like me." She related, she said, to sassy, sharp-shooting, cussing Scout, but she also enjoyed the kids' neighborhood expeditions and Scout's encounter with the camera-shy Boo. Yet as the size of the screen shrank and the shadows disappeared, *Mockingbird* became more likely to be encountered in mainstream and regulated pedagogical venues. Boo himself and the ambiguity he represents almost disappeared, to be replaced more singularly by a pedagogical discourse of Atticus the icon.

Boo's intriguing and liminal space has been described in scholarship earlier in this decade, including Holly Blackford's *Mockingbird Passing* (2011). Yet by the time of the publication of *Go Set a Watchman,* Boo's champions were harder to find. Several readers I knew were upset, upon reading *Go Set a Watchman,* by a purportedly changed Atticus. One said she felt "cheated" that Jem was dead. None mentioned the disappearance of Boo.

The diminution of the historical memory of William J. "Bill" Kraus, gay rights activist and community advocate who stepped into the political spotlight as congressional aide for a time, perhaps resembles Boo's literary demise. When Kraus spoke to the Democratic Party Platform Committee in Washington, DC, in 1980, he said:

> I am Bill Kraus, liaison between Congressman Phillip Burton and the gay community of San Francisco. The Gay Rights plank I am asking to be included does not ask for special privileges, it does not ask anyone to like us, it doesn't even ask that the Democratic Party give us many of the legal protections which are considered the right of all other Americans. What this amendment asks is that the Democratic Party recognize that we, the gay people of this country are also . . . human. (Shilts 339)

When, back in 2004, I first heard Bill Kraus's speech, I thought of Boo Radley, even though I had not read Harper Lee's text for over twenty years. I conceived of Bill Kraus as an educated and professional version of Boo Radley. Since learning of Kraus's background, I even wondered about the angst he might have felt in reconciling his identity with his Catholic upbringing, just as a "real-life" Boo Radley would surely have struggled with his feelings in relationship to the evangelical Methodist community in which he was raised.

This moment of Bill Kraus's life, when he stepped into the political spotlight and talked back, even in his very restrained way, to the normative establishment, can be compared to Boo Radley's killing of Bob Ewell in defense of the Finch children. The context of this moment in Kraus's life is represented at length in the 1993 film *And the Band Played On*. The narrative takes some artistic license with character development but is largely based on Randy Shilts's expository tome. Kraus, who died in 1986 at only 38, is written for screen as the tragic hero, and played with commendable thoughtfulness by the much-older Sir Ian McKellan. Aware of possible oversimplification, McKellan still hoped his portrayal would do good in a world where AIDS patients were not even regarded as human. The renowned Reverend Jerry Falwell, after all, was to famously proclaim also in 1993 that "AIDS is the wrath of a just God against homosexuals . . . [and] the society that tolerates homosexuals" (35). Perhaps, a self-effacing public speaker was the most disarming way to answer such strident bigotry.

Since then, though, Bill Kraus, Kentucky-born and Jesuit-educated at St. Xavier high school in greater Cincinnati before he joined the exodus to San Francisco, has faded from public memory. For a time, he was known because he was controversial: was his safe sex campaign on some level a renunciation of his gay identity? Contextual evidence supports the interpretation that Kraus's self-deprecating plea to be considered "human" in such a limited sense was utilitarian—as a means for procuring for his community some modicum of medical and health care. We do know that, by 1982, AIDS, dubbed "the gay plague" or "the gay cancer," was still as stigmatized as it was misunderstood—and that research funding, public information, and research were all slow in coming, even while the epidemic quickly spread. Kraus himself and Ian McKellan might both have been considered heroic in their efforts, but perhaps made a relatively small impact.

Sadly, Kraus's real-life role, like Boo's fictional one, was timely, not timeless. His role was to be a conduit for change only to be forgotten: the story's pivot, not its hero. Like Bill Kraus, Boo Radley exists in a space perhaps best characterized as a closet of queer innocence. It is a space defined by access to a certain privilege of status despite queer identity. If Bill Kraus was a protégé of the charismatic Harvey Milk, Boo Radley was the son of the second most well-established man in Maycomb, and the neighbor of the first. Theirs are spaces of limited and self-effacing agency. In the film version of *And the Band Played On*, Kraus's AIDS diagnosis is a shock, a collision of pathos and ethos, the moment when the saint is revealed as still yet a sinner. Then, in the film at least, the straight white doctor Don Francis saves the soul, even if not the queer body, of his friend Bill. Don Francis, it is implied, learns to love Bill *despite* his queer identity, and thus bestows social grace. In *Mockingbird,* meanwhile, it is Atticus who performs metaphorical last rites over Boo Radley just before Scout engages Boo in the queer masquerade Gary Richards describes.

At the end of *Mockingbird,* Jean Louise herself escorts Boo Radley home after Atticus's definitive dismissal, "thank you for my children, Arthur" (146). Boo goes back to the dialogical closet forever, never to emerge, even when Jean Louise returns to Maycomb as a young adult. Acting under authority of Atticus, Jean Louise escorts her friend out of the political life of Maycomb forever after. He has been treated with dignity, but he will never reappear. Yet despite this eternal closeting, Boo might still silently call, especially to millennials and post-millennials, who live in a world where queer identity and Christian polemics may again become public conversations.

As a queer son of a ranking family, Boo Radley of *To Kill a Mockingbird* is certainly a misfit among misfits. He accompanies other Maycomb boys in various shenanigans (including dancing and locking the town's beadle in an outhouse), but after they are called up before the judge, all but Boo are sent to the state industrial school:

> Mr. Conner said he knew who each and every one of them was, and he was bound and determined they wouldn't get away with it, so the boys came before the probate judge on charges of disorderly conduct, disturbing the peace, assault and battery, and using abusive and profane language in the presence and hearing of a female ... it was no prison and it was no disgrace. Mr. Radley thought it was. If the judge released Arthur, Mr. Radley would see to it that Arthur gave no further trouble. Knowing that Mr. Radley's word was his bond, the judge was glad to do so. (*Mockingbird* 6)

Boo, it seems, is caught between a rock and a benevolent place. He, like Bill Kraus, occupies a fluid relationship with the mainstream community. Bill Kraus, it seems, could pass through a portal into heteronormative society through his position as a political spokesperson. Boo, meanwhile, seems to occasionally squeeze through the keyhole of his Maycomb home. Somehow or another, Boo Radley makes it beyond from time to time, never to be seen but simply to give—a marble here, a carved wooden toy there—and, once, to offer his personal security and risk his very life. Yet, surely, if Boo's ineffable stabbing of his father in the leg is any indication, he lived with more than a modicum of unspeakable pain in that closet space. Meanwhile, Kraus ends up suffering through the unspeakable pain of AIDS, a pain sentimentalized in Randy Shilts's narrative and in Roger Spottiswoode's film, before he faded out of the narrative of historical memory.

Unlike Bill Kraus, though (in his real-life speeches or in Ian McKellan's representations of his suffering), Boo neither verbalizes not dramatizes his pain at any point. Boo keeps his mouth shut about his sufferings and asks for absolutely nothing. It is as if Scout's childish assertion that Boo is "real nice" is supposed to be enough for him. It is his short-term reward for his longsuffering. Relying on the benevolence of his father, "the meanest ever God blew breath into" (*Mockingbird* 7), on the justice of the town's sheriff, and on the wisdom of the town's ultimate hero, Atticus Finch, may not have profited Boo Radley much, but it seems he had no other available course of action.

In the course of the *Mockingbird* novel, Scout wants to discover the space of her friend Boo. It is a space of alteriority but not of interiority, as its single full-time inhabitant is essentially both mute and unable to act on his own behalf. There are hints of an aesthetic interiority, as Boo makes his narrow world tenable by making or finding objects of beauty, and sharing them, as he does, with the children—though he hides his efforts from the public eye in the hollow of a tree. And yet the only time he attempts to go beyond the merely decorative in his social interaction (not counting the ineffable stabbing of his father), it escalates to murder.

Yet even then, he does not get to gain authority over his own action. His justifiable murder of Bob Ewell is quickly over-written by a gentleman's agreement between the town sheriff and the town pillar: "Bob Ewell fell on his knife" (145). These exact words are repeated three times, as if to make it magically true. The queer ethos Boo develops to live by is replaced by a normative pathos when Scout proclaims that he is "real nice" (149).

The angst engendered, with the publication of *Go Set a Watchman*, about revisiting this space of Scout's childhood is arguably as much neoliberal as conservative. In *To Kill a Mockingbird,* queer characters find the sort of niches and benevolent safe spaces Bill Kraus implicitly requests; however, they are in basements, in dark, Gothic nights, and in brief, queer encounters. Readers searching vicariously find an imaginary space, a Gothic playground if you will, to use the language of George Haggerty. This space is timeless, and beyond the range of social debate.

Yet these safe spaces are not self-sufficient or sustainable spaces, even within the fictional Maycomb of Harper Lee's novels. It is not just one, but three town pillars who allow for the existence of this tiny alternative queer space, as that means all three of them get to determine the conditions of it. Atticus, Sheriff Tate, and Mr. Radley represent family loyalty, everyday racism, and generalized paternalism, respectively. Mr. Radley, Boo's father, for all his "meanness," houses the queer son he cannot abide or comprehend. The sheriff, the keeper of the law, nevertheless turns a blind eye and deaf ear to Boo's law-breaking behavior. Yet he is motivated by racism: "The sheriff hadn't the heart to put him in jail alongside Negroes, so Boo was locked in the courthouse basement" (6).

Later, when Atticus accepts his story that "Bob Ewell fell on his knife," Sheriff Tate once again provides Boo with special privileges. Bob Ewell is white trash, the sort who makes the racism of the town's average whites too apparent; and, thus, this "trash" (metaphorically rendered by his residence by the town dump) needs to be thrown out. If "Bob Ewell fell on his knife," the status quo of race relations in Maycomb can continue. Tom's death had already been forgotten in white memory after only a few days, so when the narrator brings him up again, it is to remind us that other threats to the status quo remain: "If Mr. Ewell was as forgotten as Tom Robinson, Tom Robinson was as forgotten as Boo Radley" (132). Bob's extremism and Boo's queerness were the remaining threats. But then, once Bob Ewell is irrevocably gone, the sacred object has no more use in this story, and he is eternally stuck inside.

The shadow that hangs over Bill Kraus's memory is that in working to create the safe space for himself and for other gay men, he brings his community into the light of scrutiny by an ignorant and mob-minded public—represented most vociferously by the Reverend Jerry Falwell. This is the same sort of public scrutiny Atticus Finch tells Scout that Boo Radley could not bear. When Scout asks Atticus whether the light of public scrutiny of Boo would be "like shooting a mockingbird" (147), Atticus confirms that it would be.

Yet readers should know that in a cosmic court of justice, it would not be Boo, but the entire town of Maycomb that would deserve scrutiny. Similarly, the bathhouses were not (despite Shilts's own misinformation and misrepresentations and his use of Kraus as the internal champion against them) the causal source of AIDS. Neither is it the case, we now know, that there really was an aggressively deliberate patient zero who was singularly responsible for AIDS.

In Boo's story, the fact that he murdered Bob Ewell is not an issue. No one—except, perhaps, his daughter, in some distorted and pitiful way—cares much that Bob Ewell was murdered. The reason Boo Radley cannot bear public scrutiny is not on his own account but that his image is fragile. He is the neighbor the townspeople *need,* in order to feel like their hearts are in the right place. The town needs to be kept ignorant of this, and to conceive of him as harmless and helpless. Boo Radley, regardless of his identity, is the son of one of Maycomb's genteel poor elite. The town would not know how to even conceive of a narrative in which this queer, quiet Radley is a murderer, however justified.

Perhaps the angst engendered among mainstream readers by the publication of *Watchman* is our own guilt that we readers have accepted the false resolutions of *Mockingbird.* What is unsettling about *Watchman* is not really that Atticus is changed; it is that Boo is absent and that we forget to miss him. Perhaps we cannot miss him because Tom and Bob are gone, and he was always only the foil to the innocent black man and the guilty white extremist. His space was carved out of a race-hate that outweighed the distrust of the queer among us, and when the pressure valve on racist society has been relieved with a good sacrificial purge, queer innocence has no purpose. In *Mockingbird,* Scout aligns with her father, and when in *Watchman,* she throws Henry over with the claim that he is not her "kind," we might also wonder whether Jean Louise has been willing to accept a lie about herself, stamping out possibilities of her own queer identity.

Lately, sexual orientation and identity issues have emerged in a pithy way in the very denomination in which not only Lee, but also Hilary Rodham Clinton and George W. Bush, have been lifelong members. Methodists, the heirs of America's "circuit riders," may not seem particularly relevant, based on statistics alone, to the conversation about Harper Lee's novels in the popular religious imagination. Methodism ("United Methodism" since 1968) is not the largest single Christian denomination in the United States (that distinction belongs to Catholicism), nor even the largest Protest denomination (as that would be the Southern Baptist Convention). United Methodism ranks third. Yet, it is in many ways as "middle-of-the-road" as one can get among the various Christian denominations. It is liturgical in its worship style (like Catholicism), while being classified as *both* "evangelical Protestant" *and* "mainline Protestant" in its theology.

Furthermore, its involvement with (and against) LGBTQ issues and persons places it among mainstream Christian denominations. Before and since the ordination of the first openly gay and non-celibate bishop in the United States, Gene Robinson, of the Episcopal Diocese in New Hampshire in 2003, sexuality has been discussed—whether openly or angrily—in each major Christian denomination, including United Methodism. Methodism can be viewed as either an early starter or a late bloomer in these conversations, depending on whether one is looking at the body politic or the niche group.

Methodists became "United" Methodists based on inclusive but *unequal* mergers involving smaller and less influential denominations. At the end of the decade in which *Mockingbird* was released, the United Methodist Church discussed the issue of race and segregation in the church. During the 1960s, annual conference discussions occurred, until various denominations—African Methodist Episcopal, Christian Methodist Episcopal, United Brethren, and Methodists—largely merged with the Methodists to form the "United Methodist Church" in 1968—the very year King was assassinated. The AME and CME denominations were black, while the other two were white denominations. With the 1968 merger forming the United Methodists, all clergy from the AME and CME who choose to merge lost their ranks—even the bishops.

Then, in 1972, at the next General Assembly of the United Methodists, the body of delegates voted for a specific *exclusion:* language was added to the *Book of Discipline*, the Methodist constitution, a book-length text updated every four years. In 1972, Methodist delegates to the national convention voted to add, "While persons set apart by the Church for ordained ministry are subject to all the frailties of the human condition and the pressures of society, they are required to maintain the highest standards of holy living in the world. The practice of homosexuality is incompatible with Christian teaching." In language best characterized as antagonistic, amid otherwise dry clauses, the United Methodist Church built in, within four years of formation as a "united" denomination, a polemical tension which has taken almost fifty years to reformulate as open argument.

In 1983 and 1984, a small group of Methodists organized as "Reconciling Methodists," "affirming" people regardless of their sexuality. But then, in 1984, delegates to the United Methodist annual conference voted to add more strident language to the 1972 clause: "Therefore, self-avowed practicing homosexuals are not to be certified as candidates, ordained as ministers, or appointed to serve in The United Methodist Church."

Since 1984, requests to bring changes to a vote have been denied—until 2016. Just one year after the publication of *Go Set a Watchman,* the United Methodist delegates elected to hold a Special Session of the United Methodist Convention exclusively for considering LGBTQ members' ministry in the church.

If you thought that the language of the clauses in the *Book of Discipline* resembled Atticus's language in *Go Set a Watchman* about black people, you are not alone. In Jean Louise's anger with Atticus, she offers this scathing criticism of her father: "You deny that they're human. You deny them hope. Any man in this world, Atticus … was born with hope in his heart. You won't find that in the Constitution, I picked that up at church somewhere" (251). The parallel is that Jean Louise sees "hope in [one's] heart" as a religious principle of symbolic significance, and Atticus, whom she "looked up to" (250), as failing to live up to that standard. Meanwhile, the *Book of Discipline* of the United Methodist Church, amendable at the will of its annual conference delegates, seems to commit the same breach of authoritative trust. Jean Louise continues: "You are telling them that Jesus loves them, but not much. You are using frightful means to justify ends that you think are for the good of most people" (251).

One thought-to-be progressive mega-church UMC pastor, Matthew Rawle, has developed a Sunday School program called *The Faith of a Mockingbird,* presumably to nurture inclusivity on matters of racial and sexual identity. Yet this sort of "Sunday school primer" approach does not have a mechanism to deal with the revealed hypocrisy of Atticus, who says, "They were coming along fine, traveling at a rate they could absorb … Then the NAACP stepped in with its fantastic demands and shoddy ideas of government—can you blame the South for resenting being told what to do about its own people?" (241). It seems, at this point, that understanding of policy and polemics *must* be layered over symbolism and sentiment alone.

I wonder where it will all go for the Methodists. I wonder whether they will ever collectively take on the task of reading both *Mockingbird* and *Watchman* critically, beyond the Abington Press guide *The Faith of a Mockingbird.* I wonder where it will go for the six mainstream denominations whose body of leadership, not just its rogue dissidents, seemed, for just a moment in the 1930s, collectively interested in applications of religious polemics for the purposes of self-critique and new developments in racial and social justice, local and global, but who seems, at this juncture, largely interested in the preservation of extant polity and social practices. But mostly, I wonder where it will all go for the large community of American readers who rely, consciously or not, on at least symbolically religious interpretations.

Yet there is that mustard seed of faith that those many Americans who indulge the religious popular imagination, whether "churchgoers" or not, might be persuaded to shift their approach. This change cannot help Bill Kraus, who is already deceased, nor Boo Radley, who is not real—yet there are more than a few real Boo Radleys in American culture. Surely it is time to peel back the layers of religious symbolism and realize that the Boo Radleys of the world cannot be saved at the expense of the Tom Robinsons. Surely it is time to realize that the status quo of Maycomb—and, indeed, many policies in political and religious institutions—damage in intersectional ways. Perhaps it is time to talk *Grand Theft Jesus* with Robert McElvaine. Perhaps religiously interested readers will engage the polemics of Bishop Karen Oliveto, who has been at the center of the controversy in the United Methodist Church; though a significant division in the United Methodist Church appears inevitable since the 2019 special session, her reasoned polemics may be influential in future developments. Without a doubt, though, it is time to consider the extent to which religious popular thought, void of polemical reasoning, has perpetrated less than socially responsible readings of Harper Lee's novels.

Works Cited

Anderson, Benedict. *Imagined Communities: Reflections on the Origins and Spread of Nationalism. Revised edition.* Verso, 1983.

Blackford, Holly. *Mockingbird Passing: Closeted Traditions and Sexual Curiosities in Harper Lee's Novel.* University of Tennessee, 2011.

Conn, Peter. *Pearl S. Buck: A Cultural Biography.* Cambridge University Press, 1998.

Haggerty, George. *Queer Gothic.* University of Illinois Press, 2006.

King, Martin Luther. "Letter from a Birmingham Jail." Aug. 1963, https://web.cn.edu/kwheeler/documents/Letter_Birmingham_Jail.pdf. Accessed 30 Jan. 2019.

Lee, Harper. *To Kill a Mockingbird.* J.P. Lippincott, 1960.

———. *Go Set a Watchman: A Novel.* HarperCollins, 2015.

McElvaine, Robert S. *Grand Theft Jesus: The Hijacking of Religion in America.* Random House, 2009.

Mizruchi, Susan L. *The Science of Sacrifice: American Literature and Modern Social Theory.* Princeton University Press, 1998.

Oliveto, Karen P. *Together at the Table: Diversity without Division in the United Methodist Church.* Louisville: Westminster John Knox Press, 2018.

"Oprah Reflects on her Private Lunch with Harper Lee. *The Oprah Winfrey Show.* 9 Aug. 2015. https://www.youtube.com/watch?v=prS5072tOEs. Accessed 30 Jan. 2019.

Rawle, Matt. *The Faith of a Mockingbird: A Small Group Study Connecting Christ and Culture.* Abingdon Press, 2015.

Richards, Gary. "Harper Lee and the Destabilization of Heterosexuality." *Lovers & Beloveds: Sexual Otherness in Southern Fiction, 1936–1961.* Louisiana State University Press, 2005, pp. 117–57.

Shilts, Randy. *And the Band Played On.* St. Martin's Press, 1987.

Tillich, Paul. *Dynamics of Faith.* Harper & Row, 1957.

PART 4

MOCKINGBIRD REIMAGINED

FEAR/VULNERABILITY/ANGER
Teaching *To Kill a Mockingbird* and *Go Set a Watchman* in the Era of Black Lives Matter

Monica Carol Miller

"They shot him," said Atticus. "He was running. It was during their exercise period. They said he just broke into a blind raving charge at the fence and started climbing over it. Right in front of them—"

"Didn't they try to stop him? Didn't they give him any warning?" Aunt Alexandra's voice shook.

"Oh, yes, the guards called to him to stop. They fired a few shots in the air, then to kill. They got him just as he went over the fence. They said if he'd had two good arms he'd have made it, he was moving that fast. Seventeen bullet holes in him. They didn't have to shoot him that much. They didn't have to shoot him that much."

—*To Kill a Mockingbird*

This scene, in which the respected, white Southern lawyer Atticus Finch reports the death of Tom Robinson, a black man wrongfully convicted of the rape of a white woman in 1930s Maycomb, Alabama, is generally considered a significant turning point in Harper Lee's 1960 novel, *To Kill a Mockingbird.* In the film adaptation, the scene is similarly tragic, although Atticus reports that the guard was shooting to wound and missed.

When I taught *To Kill a Mockingbird* in the spring of 2016, however, these reports of Tom Robinson's death read as a different kind of tragedy to my students and me. Although the general popular and academic consensus about this scene has been that expressed by scholar Andy Crank, who describes Tom as being "unceremoniously killed while trying to escape from police custody," reading this scene felt different this time, with so many reports of police violence against black men fresh on our minds. The spring of 2016 saw the continued growth of the Black Lives Matter movement, a response to a stream of high-profile killings of people of color, beginning with the 2012 death of seventeen-year-old Trayvon Martin, shot and killed by his neighbor George Zimmerman, who was ultimately acquitted of the murder. The year 2014 alone was relentless in stories of violence against young black men and boys, including Eric Garner, John Crawford, Michael Brown, and Ezzell Ford. By the spring of 2016, accounts of black men being killed by police and vigilantes seemed so ubiquitous that it affected our understanding of Tom Robinson's story.[1]

To many of my students, the reports of Tom's attempted escape seemed to be a cover story for police retaliation against a black man whose obvious innocence brought attention to the sins of a white man in the public space of a courthouse as well as made apparent the lies told by a white woman to hide her father's crimes against her. Tom was not an escaping prisoner; as a potential threat to the system, he required neutralization. Our discussions echoed Mark Bauerlein's essay about *Mockingbird,* written about the Ferguson protests after the death of Michael Brown, in which he analyzes the press's treatment of Brown in comparison to the portrayal of Tom Robinson in *Mockingbird:* "No matter how sympathetic, Tom is a flat and contrived figure. He is Harper Lee's instrument through which moral instructions in race and justice works. But the drama is artificial: a transcendence of white guilt and American wrongs through the sacrifice of an unfallen black soul" (72). We are so used to focusing on Scout and Atticus that it is easy to overlook the flatness of Tom. My class's suspicious reading of *Mockingbird* was reinforced by subsequently reading Lee's *Go Set a Watchman* and Ta-Nehisi Coates's *Between the World and Me* in the class along with the more canonical novel and film. Indeed, considering *To Kill a Mockingbird* against the backdrop of *Go Set a Watchman, Between the World and Me* as well as current events forced us to confront the contradictions so often overlooked in conventional readings of *To Kill a Mockingbird,* which celebrate it as a model of racial social justice. Atticus's automatic acceptance of what—from our vantage point—seems a suspicious story highlights the ways in which white privilege can blind us from understanding the whole story.

In this chapter, I will discuss the opportunities and challenges presented by teaching these newly published texts by Lee and Coates not only as commentary and scholarship about them was being written, but also during the growing Black Lives Matter movement. Not only was the critical discourse surrounding Harper Lee and her newly published text unfolding over the course of the semester, but the death of Harper Lee in February 2016 as well as the renewed national attention to race-based violence, police brutality, and civil rights gave the course a relevance that is rare in a first-year composition class. My students were creating scholarship concurrent with that of professional scholars, which gave students a strong sense of ownership and relevance in their own work.

I will also discuss the ways in which the multimodal aspects of the class facilitated student engagement with scholarship as it unfolded. Finally, I will discuss the relevance of Lee's work within the context of contemporary race-based violence and civil rights, and the ways in which the multimodal composition classroom allowed students to create knowledge concurrent with the development of academic and popular scholarship on the same topics they were researching and analyzing.

English 1102: From *Mockingbird* to *Watchman*

English 1102 is one of two core courses in Georgia Tech's Writing and Communication Program (WCP) that satisfies the Georgia Board of Regents requirements for writing and communication in English. After taking or receiving credit for English 1101, which focuses on writing, communication, and critical thinking skills, students enrolled in English 1102 continue to "learn how to communicate more effectively, but with a greater emphasis on research, argument, and applied theory" ("Composition Courses"). English 1102 courses often take as their focus topics in literature or popular culture.[2]

I began planning this *Mockingbird*-centered class the summer before, when Lee's *Go Set a Watchman* was released, in July 2015. Having preordered both it and Ta-Nehisi Coates's *Between the World and Me,* I was struck by their overlapping themes and potential for comparative reading. Among the myriad commentaries upon the release of *Go Set a Watchman,* a frequently overlooked aspect of its publication is that it was released the same day as *Between the World and Me,* a book-length, first-person account of racism in contemporary America that takes the form of a letter from the author to his son, an homage to James Baldwin's similar essay to his nephew in his 1963 *The Fire Next Time.* The ways in which the racism of the mid-twentieth-century South portrayed in Lee's work (including the film adaptation of *To Kill a Mockingbird*) resonate with the racism of the early-twenty-first-century America presented in the Coates memoir were so striking that I felt I must address them in the classroom.[3]

While literature and cultural studies are important aspects of English 1102, the primary focus is to provide these texts with a focus on analysis, argument, and research. So, while I began the course with *To Kill a Mockingbird* (both the novel and the 1962 film adaptation) and *Go Set a Watchman* and ended with Coates's *Between the World and Me*, I broke the course up into units, which provided several different analytical and thematic approaches to these texts, reflected by the unit themes, readings, and assignments. In the first unit, students read *To Kill a Mockingbird*, watched the film, and read *Go Set a Watchman*; they then wrote a comparative analysis of these works, incorporating visuals from the film to support the arguments they made about the ways in which the three texts interacted, informed, and complicated each other. The next major unit was to culminate in a visual composition project, and took as its major themes the Southern gothic (with Truman Capote's *Other Voices, Other Rooms* as its major text) and second wave feminism (with Sylvia Plath's *The Bell Jar*). Originally, this unit's primary assignment was going to be a researched book cover assignment; as I will discuss in the next section, however, Harper Lee's death in February convinced me to change this assignment to one that more directly engaged with the author's work and life. And, for the final assignment, students worked in groups to research a theme, historical context, or conflict related to Lee's work or life; they used this research to produce ten-to-fifteen-minute podcasts that addressed their chosen topics. [4]

Much of my students' responses started with the different perspectives we see in the two Harper Lee texts. Though both *Mockingbird* and *Watchman* are narrated by the adult Jean Louise from the distance of the 1950s, the twenty-year gap between the narrator and the events of the 1930s allows for some disavowal of the racism and sexism of the past; *Watchman*, narrated by the adult Jean Louise in the present of the 1950s, does not allow such distance. At times, *Watchman* comes close to intersectional analysis, such as when Jean Louise's beau Henry chides her for being blind to the privilege that her socioeconomic status—and particularly, the privilege of her family name—affords her in Maycomb. Despite the potential for such insights, however, scholar Amy Clukey's observation that, "Lee's critique of southern femininity is one of the novel's strongest points, but she stops frustratingly short when it comes to investigating southern racism, even as she compellingly links it to white masculinity"

(710), ultimately applies to any number of points of potential intersectional analysis present in *Watchman*. Clukey argues that, "for *Watchman* to have an aesthetically and politically coherent end, Jean Louise needs to recognize her own privilege and complicity in Jim Crow segregation, if not meaningfully challenge the racist, classist, patriarchal authorities of Maycomb. . . . Lee draws connections between gender, class, and race to expose Atticus's racist liberalism but shrinks from making Jean Louise recognize her own" (713). And though, as Katherine Henninger observes, what Jean Louise "cannot see, even though Lee includes abundant evidence in each flashback, is that the gender role (and attendant 'proper' female embodiment) to which Jean Louise has struggled her whole life to adapt to goes hand in hand with a specific race and class performance" (616), it is imperative that we, as readers, identify these gaps and find ways of continuing such analysis beyond the text.

It is Jean Louise's ultimate failure to understand the nature of racism in both Atticus and herself that undercuts the novel's possible achievements. As Clukey points out, "Jean Louise associates racism with white poverty, such as the gauche racism of Bob Ewell (whose full name is Robert E. Lee Ewell), who rapes his own daughter, beats her, and blames Tom Robinson for it in *To Kill a Mockingbird*" (710). Indeed, Jennifer Murray's pre-*Watchman* extended consideration of critical assumptions about Calpurnia's role in the Finch household along with the distinct lack of critical curiosity about Calpurnia's life outside of the Finch household—her lack of last name, the vague terms of her employment—seems to presage the existence of *Watchman*, which lifts the veil on Calpurnia's life and her relationship to the Finches much more than *Mockingbird*'s more idyllic (albeit limited) vision of Calpurnia's life.

Although *Mockingbird* is more often assigned in junior high and high school classes than it is in college, reading it at a college level with other texts allowed us to consider it in much broader cultural and historical contexts. My class was a mix of students—some who adored the novel and its phenomenon, some who had read it in junior high and had vague memories of it, and some who were not familiar with it at all. Such a mix of affective attachments and regional knowledge often occurs when I teach courses with Southern themes—and I find that having a range of responses makes for a dynamic class environment. Even for students who identify with the South, learning the details of twentieth-century governmentally sanctioned racism and racist violence is often new to them, as so many of these details are glossed over in high school history classes as well as popular culture. And for all of the students, providing clarifying details about the current historical moment was equally important.

I assigned my students to read sections of the Black Lives Matter website along with a blog post by Berkeley Professor Jerome Karabel from the *Huffington Post,* "Police Killings Surpass the Worst Years of Lynching, Capital Punishment, and a Movement Responds," which provides a summary of the events that gave rise to the movement. The Arabel piece was particularly surprising to students, who were angered to learn that multiple investigations have determined that there was no clear record of the many police-involved shootings across the country: "Though the FBI annually issues a report that provides figures on 'justified police homicides,' reporting from local police forces is voluntary and thousands of them turn in no information" (Karabel).

Such incredulous anger did not begin with the Black Lives Matter unit, however. When we read *Go Set a Watchman,* I lectured on the historical context of the novel, providing a timeline of events that included Jim Crow segregation, major boycotts, assassinations, and important pieces of legislation and court cases of the civil rights era, focusing on the 1950s and 1960s. I also provided background information on White Citizens' Councils; in *Watchman,* Jean Louise finds Atticus's brochures about them and follows him to a meeting, where she discovers that not only Atticus but also Uncle Jack and Henry attend. As these organizations are less well-known to students than the more dramatic KKK, it was important for students to understand that such groups met openly and were seen as what historian Charles M. Payne characterizes as "pursuing the agenda of the Klan with the demeanor of the Rotary Club" (35). I wanted students to understand that these socially acceptable councils were wholly in favor of violence, and that they were often supported by local and state governments. Many students (and many Americans in general) think of racists exclusively as white-hooded KKK members firebombing houses and lynching black men. And, while it is important to remember that such vigilante racist violence was (and continues to be) perpetuated, there were also government-sanctioned structures and institutions to enforce racist codes, such as the WCC. In *Mockingbird,* the face of racism belongs to the evil Bob Ewell, who is not only racist but also rapes his own daughter. It is easy to place the evils of racism upon evil men. What makes *Watchman* more emotionally complex—and what Jean Louise struggles with—is its recognition of racism in the hearts of supposedly upstanding men such as Atticus.

Multimodality and Student Analysis

Going from the novel of *Mockingbird,* to the film adaptation, to *Watchman,* the class saw how a core story could be conveyed from different perspectives and the ways in which these differences convey very different messages. In addition to the radical differences between the noble Atticus Finch in the original novel (and especially in the film adaptation) and *Watchman,* as well as the very different understandings of Scout/ Jean Louise in these texts, there are less-dramatic differences across the texts which provided a fertile ground for classroom discussion and student analysis. Comparative analysis led students back to the *Mockingbird* text to reconsider Atticus's legacy in light of not only his character in *Watchman* but also the ways in which the film adaptation refocused his character and established his legacy.

For example, the *Mockingbird* novel is primarily a bildungsroman about both Scout and Jem. Though narrated by the adult Jean Louise and seen through the eyes of the child Scout, the novel begins with Jem's broken arm and ends with Atticus keeping watch over him after the attack that caused the injury (3, 376). While Scout wrestles with the changing expectations of herself as a maturing Southern girl child, Jem struggles with his growing awareness of the hypocrisy between what he has been taught about fairness and justice and what he sees in his growing awareness of the world around him, particularly in the trial of Tom Robinson.

The trial itself seems to be an application of Atticus's famous teaching that, "You never understand a person until you consider things from his point of view . . . until you climb into his skin and walk around in it" (39). Importantly, though this line has been quoted and repeated ad infinitum as an exemplary foundation for morality, reading it with the *Watchman* Atticus in mind, we were struck by the context in which it is introduced: "[I]f you can learn a simple trick, Scout, you'll get along a lot better with all kinds of folks. You never really understand a person until you consider things from his point of view" (39). The more critical reading of *Mockingbird*'s Atticus that *Watchman* encourages calls into question even Atticus's famous teaching: Atticus doesn't present this advice as a foundation for morality, but rather a simple trick for getting along with people.

Unlike *Mockingbird*'s bildungsroman form, *Watchman* conducts a more complex generic feat, as it pushes beyond a traditional coming-of-age novel to an adult reconsideration of Scout's education and those who served as models. As Henninger describes, *"Mockingbird's* child Scout must come into an Atticus-like racial innocence after a hard awakening to the injustices of Southern society; she passes through a period of double consciousness in which she learns to respect and emulate her father's performative not-noticing" (608). In *Watchman,* then, the "adult Jean Louise arrives on the page fully formed by Atticus's performance, though apparently without the slightest consciousness of its performativity" (609). In other words, while *Mockingbird's* Atticus provides a conflicted and conflicting adult role model for Scout, of how to be aware of the South's hypocrisies and yet ignore them well enough to live sanely, *Watchman's* Jean Louise has enough distance from such double consciousness that she finds it difficult to perform (or even stomach) such feats.

Henninger observes that Jean Louise's "flashbacks to childhood often occur while Jean Louise is dozing. . . . But these episodes of somnolence are accompanied by increasingly urgent calls to wake" (614). These works together provide an interesting literal precursor commentary on what has lately come to be known as "being woke"—or rather, the asleepness that requires wokeness. Significantly, Jean Louise seems to have difficulty both staying awake and "staying woke," in the contemporary sense of the phrase. As Pulliam-Moore explains, "Among black people talking about Ferguson, 'stay woke' might mean something like: 'stay conscious of the apparatus of white supremacy, don't automatically accept the official explanations for police violence, keep safe. In this usage, 'woke' indicates healthy paranoia, especially about issues of racial and political justice." Indeed, much of *Watchman* involves Jean Louise's struggle to stay awake and become woke, despite the seductive appeal of Maycomb and her position as Atticus's daughter and Henry's girlfriend.[5]

Not only is Jean Louise often asleep in *Watchman,* but also Jem's characterization of the town's hypocrisy and failure to insist upon justice prevailing in *Mockingbird*—and his argument with the neighbor, Miss Maudie—presages the arguments that Jean Louise has in *Watchman.* After Tom Robinson's guilty verdict, Jem explains, "'It's like being a caterpillar in a cocoon, that's what it is,' he said. 'Like somethin' asleep wrapped up in a warm place. I always thought Maycomb folks were the best folks in the world, least that's what they seemed like'" (*Mockingbird* 288). Jem then questions who besides Atticus did a thing to help Tom, and Miss Maudie replies that there were quite a number of people on Tom's side, even Judge Taylor: "Did it ever strike you that Judge Taylor naming Atticus to defend that boy was no accident? That Judge Taylor might have had his reasons for naming him? . . . I thought, Atticus Finch won't win, he can't win, but he's the only man in these parts who can keep a jury out so long in a case like that. And I thought to myself, well, we're making a step—it's just a baby-step, but it's a step" (289). In *Watchman*, Atticus advocates for a baby-step approach as well, albeit one with a more overtly racist explanation: "Now think about this. What would happen if all the Negroes in the South were suddenly given full civil rights? I'll tell you. There'd be another Reconstruction. Would you want your state government run by people who don't know how to run 'em? . . . Honey, you do not seem to understand that the Negroes down here are still in their childhood as a people" (246–47).

Uncle Jack, too, expresses support for a gradual approach in *Watchman*, what he characterizes as a "bloodless Reconstruction" (197), articulating more clearly than Atticus that the South is surely changing, and in ways that his generation of men are loath to see: "The South's in its last agonizing birth pain. It's bringing forth something new and I'm not sure I like it, but I won't be here to see it" (200). In the end, Uncle Jack tries to lure Jean Louise back to Maycomb by encouraging her to see herself as part of this long game, telling her, "You'd be amazed if you knew how many people are on your side, if *side* is the word. You're no special case. The woods are full of people like you, but we need some more of you" (272).

While we saw *Mockingbird* and *Watchman* both showing Scout/Jean Louise and Jem struggling to make sense of justice, the world of Maycomb, Alabama, and their place in it, my class observed that the film adaptation of *Mockingbird* changes the focus from their coming-of-age stories to the nobility of Atticus. For example, in the novel, we learn of Atticus's appointment to defend Tom through his conversation with Scout, after Cecil Jacobs announced in the school yard that "Scout Finch's daddy defended niggers" (99). When Scout asks Atticus about this, his first response is to correct her use of the word "nigger," followed by a conversation about why he was defending Tom Robinson. In the novel, Atticus first explains that Tom is a member of Calpurnia's church, emphasizing that Tom is of "clean living folks" (100), which makes it that much easier for Atticus to defend him. Atticus explains to Scout that "there's been some high talk around town to the effect that I shouldn't do much about defending this man" (100), but that there are important reasons why Atticus should defend Tom: "The main one is, if I didn't I couldn't hold up my head in town, I couldn't represent this county in the legislature, I couldn't even tell you or Jem not to do something again" (100).

Many of my students wrote essays about the ways in which the film adaptation of *Mockingbird* shifts the focus from the children to Atticus. Much of *Watchman*'s effects has been to call attention to the change in Atticus from the original novel to the film adaptation. As Amy Clukey observes in the review article she wrote for *Contemporary Literature* in response to the publication of *Watchman*: "Although there's plenty of scholarship on *To Kill a Mockingbird*, most of it isn't suspicious of the novel's approving depiction of the white savior complex" (705). My students concurred with Clukey, who argues that "The first thing we need to reconsider is Atticus's centrality to discussions of Lee's work" (706). New scenes were added in the film, such as Scout overhearing Atticus being asked to take Tom's case. Indeed, Atticus of the novel reads as much less noble than Atticus of the film and has much more in common with *Watchman*'s Atticus. In the film, Sheriff Taylor comes to visit after Atticus has put Scout to bed; he tells Atticus that he is thinking of appointing Atticus to take Tom's case. After the sheriff acknowledges that Atticus is busy with his law firm and his children, Atticus is silent for just a moment, and then simply says, "I'll take the case." New scenes such as this bring Atticus's integrity to the center of the film and explain much of the Atticus-adulation that *Watchman* upset.

Commentaries on teaching the novel tend to shy away from more complicated readings of racism and instead focus on what Murray has observed as an interpretation that "focuses on the moral lesson of empathy as the cardinal virtue and urgent program of racial liberalism" (488). Indeed, the HarperCollins teacher's guide has only two questions about Robinson's death, neither of which engages with very weighty issues: "Why does Atticus return home early? What does he say is especially tragic about what has happened?" (17). The teacher's guide published by the National Endowment for the Arts' 2014 "Big Read" program doesn't even reference Tom's death directly—it only suggests a writing prompt, "Rewrite the novel's ending as if Tom Robinson was acquitted. If he were acquitted, would the novel be as powerful? Would it be more powerful?" (8).

In addition to the more complex analyses of the college classroom, teaching these texts in English 1102 at Georgia Tech had the added advantage of the course's multimodal dimension. Multimodality—both in the texts the students examined and the projects the students create (as well as digital tools such as Google docs and Audacity software for podcasting which we employed) allowed for more in-depth, relevant, and sustained analysis. Central to our class was a Google sheet the class constructed over the course of reading *Mockingbird,* watching the film, and then reading *Watchman*. The sheet had a row for each character in each text—as the excerpted example below demonstrates, there were rows for Scout and Atticus in the two novels and the film; we also included Jem, Dill, Uncle Jack, Calpurnia, Boo Radley, Tom Robinson, the Ewells, the Cunninghams, and Aunt Alexandra. In addition to the themes of violence, truth and justice, gender roles, and race, the Google sheet included community, family, history, class, the Gothic, the South, and learning.

	Violence	Truth/ Justice	Gender Roles	Race
Mockingbird Scout				
Film Scout				
Watchman Jean Louise				
Mockingbird Atticus				
Film Atticus				
Watchman Atticus				

In class, students worked in small groups to fill in the matrix with direct quotations from the texts and a brief explanation of each quotation's significance. For example, one entry for *Mockingbird* Scout/Violence quoted from the scene in which Scout punches her cousin Francis after he refers to Atticus as a "nigger-lover" (*Mockingbird* 112). Students explained that that quotation demonstrates Scout's allegiance to her father, despite not fully understanding the nature of Francis's insult.

In the course's final unit, we read Coates's *Between the World and Me* along with readings on Black Lives Matter. The central conceit of Coates's work, a letter to his son, allowed us to consider the role that audience plays in these works even more than the earlier works did. For example, when one white student complained that Coates was unfairly lumping all whites together, another white student responded that the context of the book was a letter to his son, which brought the rhetoric-related question of audience to the center of the class. Who is the audience of the book? How do we read a text if we are not the audience being addressed? What is the purpose of writing a book for a larger audience with this strategy? Class discussions led to the realization that there are many possible audiences for various texts—and that there are ways of reading texts for whom one is not necessarily the primary audience.

The points of intersection between the texts in this unit and the Lee texts were quite productive. For example, when Coates asks, "The question is not whether Lincoln truly meant 'government of the people' but what our country has, throughout its history, taken the political term 'people' to actually mean" (6), we were able to connect this with *Watchman,* when Atticus insists that Jean Louise understand and agree with his vision of Jeffersonian democracy: "Jefferson believed full citizenship was a privilege to be earned by each man, that it was not something to be given lightly nor to be taken lightly. A man couldn't vote simply because he was a man, in Jefferson's eyes. He had to be a responsible man. A vote was, to Jefferson, a precious privilege a man attained for himself" (244). Unfortunately, Jean Louise lacks the ability to criticize a Founding Father. However, reading Coates's critique alongside Lee's allows Coates to meet Atticus's arguments where Jean Louise fails.

True, Jean Louise does meet Atticus's overt racism head on at times—when Atticus asks her, "Do you want Negroes by the carload in our schools and churches and theaters? Do you want them in our world?" she is at least able, at first, to respond, "They're people, aren't they?" (245–46). However, her own unexamined prejudices keep her from fully combatting Atticus, which is why pairing Lee's work with Coates was critical. Coates explicates the racial prejudice that Atticus fully espouses and Jean Louise expresses in a conflicted way: "Americans believe in the reality of 'race' as a defined, indubitable feature of the natural world. Racism—the need to ascribe bone-deep features to people, and then humiliate, reduce, and destroy them—inevitably follows from this inalterable condition" (Coates 7). What Atticus is arguing for both with Jean Louise and at the White Citizens' Council is what Coates describes as "the notion that these factors can correctly organize a society and that they signify deeper attributes, which are indelible—this is the new idea at the heart of these new people who have been brought up hopelessly, tragically, deceitfully, to believe that that are white" (7). And, bluntly, Coates explains:

> In America, it is a tradition to destroy the black body—*it is heritage.* . . .There is no uplifting way to say this. I have no praise anthems, nor old Negro spirituals. The spirit and soul are the body and brain, which are destructible—that is precisely why they are so precious. And the soul did not escape. The spirit did not steal away on gospel wings. The soul was the body that fed the tobacco, and the spirit was the blood that watered the cotton, and these created the first fruits of the American garden. (104)

Coates's explanation is not that different from Jean Louise's conclusion to her argument with Atticus, in which she remarks (albeit with heavy sarcasm): "We've agreed that they're backward, that they're illiterate, that they're dirty and comical and shiftless and no good, they're infants and they're stupid, some of them, but we haven't agreed on one thing and we never will. You deny that they're human. . . . You deny them hope" (251).

What *Watchman* struggles with and what Coates calls out is the falseness of the nostalgic visions of racial innocence to which whites fiercely cling. As Henninger explains, "For *Mockingbird*'s Scout, as for many readers of that text, memories of her childhood in the South are a source of security, a founding fantasy of racial innocence and authenticity at the core of her Southern—and our American—identity" (620). As Jean Louise accuses Atticus of denying blacks hope, so *Watchman* refuses to allow Southern and American whites the hope of denying their own implication in our continuing history of race-based violence and massive resistance to civil rights.

Harper Lee and Black Lives Matter

I will end with some final thoughts on Lee's legacy at the end of 2017 going forward, in the context of the Black Lives Matter movement, the 2016 election, and the rise of what the popular media has termed the "alt-right." According to *New York Times* journalist Amanda Taub, "alt-right" refers to "an attempt to rebrand racism and white nationalism into something palatable enough for mass consumption" ("'White Nationalism'"). Ultimately, the commentary that *Mockingbird* and *Watchman* together enact on civil rights, racism, and racial violence continues to have a tragic relevance in America today. When Taub reports that, "Whiteness means being part of the group whose appearances, traditions, religion and even food are the default norm. It's being a person who, by unspoken rules, was long entitled as part of 'us' instead of 'them'" ("Behind 2016"), she could be commenting on the struggle that Jean Louise has in calling out Atticus's racism without recognizing her own assumptions of privilege.

I am one of many scholars who argue that we should look to Lee's work for elucidation of our present moment. Reconsidering Tom Robinson's death, the changing legacy of Atticus Finch after the publication of *Watchman,* and the historical moment for civil rights all seem to have in common the demystification of cultural myths. As Crank explains about the release of *Watchman:* "In the South, a region in which parents routinely name their children after the fictional father . . . there was a sense of disappointment, betrayal even, in Lee's perceived attack on southern culture; specifically on the myth of the white-savior as the crux of the Civil Rights Movement. Atticus could no longer be the scaffolding on which they built their narratives of relevancy."

Previously, *Mockingbird* had been used to acknowledge the South's racist past but also to find a way of carving out a space for "good" Southern whites. *Watchman* calls this exercise into question: "Where *Mockingbird*, following American literary tradition, offers childlike racial innocence as a solution, *Watchman* excoriates it as the problem" (Henninger 608).

In the classroom, the most I can hope for is to ultimately encourage myself and my students to strive for what Coates explains is the impetus behind his title: "I have spent much of my studies *searching for the right question* by which I might fully understand the breach between the world and me" (115; my emphasis). Indeed, Clukey makes similar connections in her analysis of *Watchman,* observing that, "many readers will use *Watchman's* troubled depictions of southern liberalism to ask difficult questions about white privilege, power, and responsibility" (716). However, while *Watchman* calls so much of *Mockingbird* into question, it reaches no conclusions.[6]

This is not to say, however, that there aren't answers—only none to be found directly in Lee's work. Rather, *Watchman* highlights what Henninger observes as "the extent to which racial and class innocence is central to Jean Louise's image of Atticus, and thus to her image of herself" (616), and, as she ultimately argues, "dismisses any moral argument for a nostalgic preservation of racial innocence as immorally childlike" (620). If we are critical readers, we should follow Coates's lead and focus on the questions that Lee's work raises and seek out the answers ourselves. *Watchman* makes us aware of Henninger's observation that, "While clearly conscious of contemporary racial discrimination and African American resistance, Jean Louise appears almost willfully oblivious of the role of 'her kind'—a race and class status apotheosized by Atticus—in perpetuating injustice" (609). Both those who mourn for their idealized Atticus and those who mourn for *Watchman*'s failure to fully destroy his pedestal should take the opportunity to examine what their own community identities make them complicit in.

Reading these texts from the past and today together allows for the kind of analysis that Jessmyn Ward describes in the introduction to the 2016 collection she edited, *The Fire This Time*: "First, it confirmed how inextricably interwoven the past is in the present, how heavily that past bears on the future; we cannot talk about black lives mattering or police brutality without reckoning with the very foundation of this country." In an online piece for *Buzzfeed* in December 2016 titled, "This was the Year America Finally Saw the South," Ward observes that the election of Donald Trump as the president of the United States, a "presidential candidate who spewed openly racist, homophobic, xenophobic, misogynist rhetoric, who hosted rallies where people of color and women were actually physically assaulted," had what she characterizes as one "bright spot": that "it's become a bit harder for Americans to disavow their willful ignorance." Specifically, Ward says, "Now, no one can deny it: The rotten underpinnings of the South anchor the whole damn country, like the swampy bottom of the Mississippi River delta. And now we are all sinking in it" ("This Was the Year America Finally Saw the South"). In contrast to Malcolm X's famous 1964 statement that we should stop talking about the South because everything south of the Canadian border should be considered "the South" for blacks, Ward, instead, sees the contemporary South as instructive for the rest of the country to realize its own racist evils.[7]

Reading Harper Lee in the era of Black Lives Matters may, as Crank suggests, encourage "a painful but needed national conversation." When Crank claims that *Watchman* "teaches the same lessons *Mockingbird* privileges: examine your perspective; be critical of your investments; be wary of the fantasies you dream and how far they take you from the truth," I am reminded of Ward's meditation on the death of Trayvon Martin:

> I realized most Americans did not see Trayvon Martin as I did. Trayvon's sable skin and his wide nose and his tightly coiled hair signaled something quite different for others. Zimmerman and the jury and the media outlets who questioned his character with declarations like *He abused marijuana* and *He was disciplined at school for graffiti and possessing drug paraphernalia* saw Trayvon as nothing more than a wayward thug. ("This Was the Year America Finally Saw the South")

Ward explains that white America's perception of Trayvon Martin was a myth she knew well, a myth with a pernicious hold on the South:

> A place where the old myths still hold a special place in many white hearts: the rebel flag, Confederate monuments, lovingly

> restored plantations, *Gone with the Wind*. A place where black
> people were bred and understood to be animals, a place where
> some feel that the Fourteenth Amendment and *Brown v. Board
> of Education* are only the more recent in a series of unfortu-
> nate events. A place where black life has been systematically
> devalued for hundreds of years. ("Introduction" 4–5)

By calling attention to and calling into question the myth of Atticus and Southern white racial innocence, *Watchman* forces us to do the work of questioning and undoing the racist myths that support institutionalized privilege.

The title for this chapter originally came from the reoccurring themes that emerged from my class. During one class discussion about *Between the World and Me,* the reoccurring reference to these themes—and the ways in which they work together in the text—led to my writing, "FEAR/VULNERABILITY/ANGER," across the top of the board to summarize the day's discussion. What I didn't realize was how, by the end of the year, these themes would seem even more relevant and descriptive of America. Perhaps the ultimate challenge of Harper Lee's is to take Atticus at his word and try to put ourselves in *his* shoes: whether at the White Citizens' Council or arguing with Jean Louise, he is doing what he thinks is best to protect and preserve his community. The themes that emerge from the Coates work—fear, vulnerability, and anger—are in fact what drive Atticus as well. For those of us who may be feeling especially vulnerable, angry, or afraid in this unprecedented era under Trump, perhaps this is Atticus's true legacy: that it is critical to walk a mile in another's shoes, and in doing so to realize that our motivations perhaps are not as different from each other as they may seem. When Scout finally makes it to the Radleys' porch in *To Kill a Mockingbird*, she sees her house—and herself—from Boo's perspective for the first time. In *Watchman,* she sees even more, but finds it difficult to articulate what she sees.

The title *Go Set a Watchman* is a reference to Isaiah 21:6, quoted during a church service by the minister Mr. Stone: "For thus hath the Lord said unto me,/ Go, set a watchman, let him declare what he seeth" (qtd. in Lee, *Go Set a Watchman,* 95). And I believe that it is this message, when combined with Atticus's, which is the most productive lesson from reading Harper Lee today. Not only should we seek out perspectives other than our own, but we should also "declare what we seeth," regardless of how difficult our visions are or how different they are from the stories we are used to telling ourselves. What these texts ultimately advocate for is walking in another's shoes to understand not only the other but also ourselves, that we see our unexamined biases and privileges, and work to become—and stay—woke.

Notes

1. See "Timeline: The Black Lives Matter Movement."

2. An important aspect of English 1101 and 1102 in Georgia Tech's Writing and Communication Program is its emphasis on multimodality and what is referred to as its "WOVEN" (Written, Oral, Visual, Electronic, and Nonverbal) curriculum. I will discuss what I see as the significant role that multimodality played in this class in the next section. For example, I have taught English 1102 courses with themes of "American Gothic" and "Region without Nostalgia: The Georgia Surreal."

3. Katherine Henninger's 2016 article "'My Childhood is Ruined!': Harper Lee and Racial Innocence" in *American Literature* is one of the few articles so far which does make this connection.

4. The entire course syllabus may be found online at http://www.monicacmiller.com/syllabi.

5. Online columnist Pulliam-Moore explains the origin of "wokeness" as a political status: "In her 2008 song 'Master Teacher,' Erykah Badu (along with Bilal and Georgia Anne Muldrow) sing about how they dream of a world where here are 'no niggas' but instead 'only master teachers.' They immediately clarify that they 'stay woke.' (Meaning that they recognize that, although it would be nice, their dream of racial equality is far from reality.) Badu's song is generally considered the first major usage of the phrase" (Pulliam-Moore).

6. Henninger reflects the general critical consensus that, "Deprived of the comforts of racial innocence, however, both Jean Louise and the novel flounder for a response" (618).

7. See Malcolm X, "The Ballot or the Bullet."

Works Cited

"About the Black Lives Matter Network." 20 Nov. 2016, *BlackLivesMatter.com.*
Baldwin, James. *The Fire Next Time.* 1963. Vintage, 1992.
Bauerlein, Mar. "Angels in Ferguson." *First Things,* Nov. 2015, pp. 72–73.
"Citizens Council, The." 1956. *CitizensCouncils.com.* Accessed 20 Nov. 2016.
Clukey, Amy. "The Sexual Politics of Massive Resistance." *Contemporary Literature,* vol. 56, no. 4, Winter 2015, pp. 705–16.
Coates, Ta-Nehisi. *Between the World and Me.* Random House, 2015.
"Composition Courses." *Georgia Tech Writing and Communication Program.* Accessed Nov. 21, 2016.
Crank, Andy. "Unkillable Mockingbird." *Los Angeles Review of Books,* Sept. 2, 2015.
"ENGL 1102." http://www.usg.edu/academic_affairs_handbook/section2/C738. Accessed 20 Nov. 2016.

Henninger, Katherine. "'My Childhood is Ruined!': Harper Lee and Racial Innocence." *American Literature*, vol. 88, no. 3, Sept. 2016, pp. 597–626.

Karabel, Jerome. "Police Killings Surpass the Worst Years of Lynching, Capital Punishment, and a Movement Responds." 4 Nov. 2015, *HuffingtonPost.com*. Accessed 20 Nov. 2016.

"Learning Outcomes for English 1101 and English 1102." http://blogs.iac.gatech.edu /wcppolicies/engl-1101-and-engl-1102-common-policies-spring-2016/#Learning _Outcomes_for_English_1101_and_English_1102. Accessed 20 Nov. 2016.

Lee, Harper. *Go Set a Watchman*. HarperCollins, 2015.

———. *To Kill a Mockingbird*. 1960. Grand Central Publishing, 1982.

Murray, Jennifer. "More than One Way to (Mis)Read a *Mockingbird*." *The Southern Literary Journal*, vol. 43, no. 1, Fall 2010, pp. 75–91.

National Council of Teachers of English. "NCTE Position Statement on Multimodal Literacies." 2005. In *Multimodal Composition: A Critical Sourcebook*, edited by Claire Lutkewitte, Bedford/St. Martin's, 2014, pp. 17-21.

Payne, Charles M. *I've Got the Light of Freedom: The Organizing Tradition and the Mississippi Freedom Struggle*. University of California Press, 2007.

Pulliam-Moore, Charles. "How 'Woke' Went from Black Activist Watchword to Teen Internet Slang." 8 Jan. 2016, *SplinterNews.com*. https://splinternews.com /how-woke-went-from-black-activist-watchword-to-teen-int-1793853989. Accessed 9 Dec. 2016.

Taub, Amanda. "Behind 2016's Turmoil, a Crisis of White Identity." *The New York Times*, 1 Nov. 2016, http://nyti.ms/2ffJlnF. Accessed 21 Nov. 2016.

———. "'White Nationalism,' Explained." *The New York Times*, 12 Nov. 2016, http:// nyti.ms/2ffJlnF. Accessed 21 Nov. 2016.

"Teacher's Guide to Harper Lee's To Kill a Mockingbird, A." *HarperAcademic*. 20 Nov. 2016, http://www.abc.net.au/news/2016–07–14/black-lives-matter-timeline /7585856.

"Timeline: The Black Lives Matter Movement." 22 July 2016. *ABCNews*. https:// www.abc.net.au/news/2016-07-14/black-lives-matter-timeline/7585856. Accessed 21 Nov. 2016

Ward, Jessmyn. Introduction. *The Fire This Time: A New Generation Speaks about Race*. Scribner, 2016.

———. "The Year America Finally Saw the South." 6 Dec. 2016, *Buzzfeed*. Accessed 7 Dec. 2016.

Wortham, Jenna. "Black Tweets Matter." *Smithsonian*, vol. 47, no. 5, Sept. 2016, pp. 21–24.

X, Malcolm. "The Ballot or the Bullet." 1964. Digital History. http://www.digital history.uh.edu/ disp_textbook.cfm?smtid=3&psid=3624. Accessed 7 Dec. 2016.

12

IN SPITE OF WATCHFUL MEN
Harper Lee, Zora Neale Hurston, the Limits of Orderly Regionalism, and Feminist Hope
Jericho Williams

Harper Lee's *Go Set a Watchman* (2015) is as much a necessary, valuable story of the present as it is now a preserved treasure from the past. The novel—although much different in point of view and plot—served as the genesis for *To Kill a Mockingbird* (1960), the book that single-handedly propelled Lee into the literary fame that continues beyond her recent passing. *Mockingbird* would become Lee's only published novel for more than fifty years, until the manuscript for *Watchman* resurfaced and received Lee's approval for release. Originally drafted in 1957, *Watchman* would likely have precluded the writing of *Mockingbird* had it been published at that time, and it certainly would have elicited different public responses because of its blunt depiction of Southern racism through Atticus Finch, *Mockingbird*'s hero. Also, because *Watchman*'s anecdotal structure is very loosely centered around a young woman's alienation from attitudes within her hometown, the novel may not have merited as much critical attention as *Mockingbird*. Yet, *Watchman*'s twenty-first-century publication provoked a different reaction. It appeared to readers of a different era with both the benefit of Harper Lee's reputation and the difficulty of unrealistic expectations as Lee's second novel. Consequently, even though its portrait of the social underpinnings of a dominant and fearful white Southern society may find a larger audience now, *Watchman* cannot escape inevitable comparisons to *Mockingbird* and the resulting host of criticism. Some of its readers angrily decried Atticus Finch's change in character; other detractors proclaimed *Watchman* inferior and dismissed it as a first draft. As more time passes and the hype around its publication fades, the novel may also be at risk of designation as a lesser work of a major artist, a cultural curiosity conveniently categorized as an example of literary regionalism of the American South.

This essay posits that a swift regionalist label is unnecessarily reductive and dangerously dismissive, especially if one considers *Watchman* in conjunction with another misunderstood and previously maligned literary classic, Zora Neale Hurston's *Their Eyes Were Watching God* (1937). In some ways, Harper Lee's second work risks suffering from a similar plight as Hurston's rich and unshapely portrayal of the Southern United States in the first half of the twentieth century. In Hurston's novel, a woman named Janie Crawford struggles to find acceptance when she returns to her hometown after turbulent relationships with three men. Like Hurston, Lee espouses a coarser and less ideologically tidy view of race relations and domestic violence in *Watchman* than in *To Kill a Mockingbird*. She presents a view that is not always appealing or just, but still illuminating. In *Watchman*, she moves beyond Scout's childhood to share a story of a woman who is not in line with the dominant ethos of her community, yet still returns annually and treasures parts about it; who must make difficult, infuriating choices in the face of other community and family members she has known, respected, loved; who must suffer and react against abrupt violence at the hands of at least one town patriarch. As both Scout and Janie confront the inequities that engulf the lives of people around them, Hurston and Lee develop stories that transcend the expectations and avoid the pitfalls of literary regionalism. Instead, they remind readers that the violent realities of women's lives are not merely regional, but instead occur throughout rural cultures governed by clear-cut examples of patriarchy and saddled with ignorance and the hovering presence of poverty. Furthermore, Hurston and Lee suggest that efforts toward progress and lasting forms of change begin with inner enlightenment and forgiveness from strong women who undermine political allegiances, shock their peers, and remain courageous amid dangerous situations.

The Problem of American Literary Regionalism

American literary regionalism, a designation that emerged to help explain the popularity of region-specific publications after the Civil War, encompasses a vast array of writings about people's lives within a fractured and widely dispersed country. In *Cosmopolitan Vistas: American*

Regionalism and Literary Value, Tom Lutz notes that literary regionalism came about as a means to account for the "radical transformation of American society preceding and following the Civil War, and because it took as its prime subject the conflicting interests of specific populations during these changes" (14). The movement also recognizes writers who accurately rendered the lives of certain groups of people from different eras, revealing how factors such as geography, values, and religious or philosophical beliefs fostered variations of American life. Often, though not always, regionalist works are non-cosmopolitan, and they capture the lives of citizens in rural towns or villages, and thereby share the lifestyles of underrepresented pockets of people. In American literature, Mary E. Wilkins's New England, Sarah Orne Jewett's Maine, Sherwood Anderson's small-town Ohio, and William Faulkner's Yoknapatawpha County are among the enduring geographical areas routinely categorized as regionalist-oriented texts.

Nonetheless, while regionalism may enable schools of literature and writers' legacies to extend beyond their lifetimes, it sometimes mars, maligns, or constricts locales, such as the American South. For more than a century, Southern writers have expressed anxiety about how their distance from New York, "the site of literary power," impacts what becomes published and thereby misrepresents fiction from the southern states (Gray 35). They came to believe that the great separation between the major publishing companies and Southern writers resulted in regional associations of certain tropes or fixations that characterized Southern literature, such as the Southern Gothic. Throughout Harper Lee's lifetime, some of the South's more prominent women authors endeavored to address criticisms of Southern life from outsiders. Marjorie Kinnan Rawlings, for example, encouraged southern writers to ignore how distant critics framed the South. In 1940, she wrote, "The South also reads books about the South . . . [because], while not too much concerned with what outsiders say about us, we are all agog to know what we say about one another" (275). By 1957, Flannery O'Connor began warning others of the great drawbacks of being imagined as simply a Southern writer. She notes, "The woods are full of regional writers, and it is the great horror of every serious Southern writer that he will become one of them" (803). While Rawlings asserts that writers should ignore the critical establishment outside of southern boundaries and write how they wished, O'Connor became convinced that a regionalist designation could limit writers simply by how they wrote about their homes, undoing great efforts to attract larger audiences and garner respect from established literary titans throughout the United States.

For Zora Neale Hurston and Harper Lee, the threatening limitations of regionalism prove especially problematic as both writers focus on fictionalized versions of their own respective hometowns of Eatonville, Florida, and Monroeville, Alabama. In an essay about Hurston's great influence on her writing, Alice Walker describes Hurston as unique among many African American writers because the Eatonville of her youth was comprised of a "community of black people who had enormous respect for themselves and for the ability to govern themselves" (166). Hurston's father was a central figure in Eatonville, a mayor who helped to write some of the town's laws, and so she displays great pride in her depiction of African American life there. Similarly, Harper Lee's father occupied a pivotal role as a town lawyer in her hometown of Monroeville, and like Hurston, she sets her two novels in Maycomb, a fictionalized version of it. In a 1964 interview, she describes her feelings about Monroeville: "I would simply like to put down all I know about this [town] because I believe there is something universal in this little world, something decent to be said for it, and something to lament in its passing" (Newquist 412). As a result of their familiarity with their communities, Hurston and Lee each portray complex settings that extend beyond regionalist limitations—for Hurston, the idea that a predominantly African American town can flourish by its own design amid a great sea of oppression and exclusion, and for Lee, the notion that the quaint, Southern small town can harbor both horrific racial oppression among its elders and the potential for change among their descendants. In each situation, Hurston and Lee fictionalize Eatonville and Monroeville as succumbing to, but also potentially transcending, simplistic, black-and-white notions of life in the American South.

The Political Quagmires of Kinfolk

One characteristic of regionalism is the presence of an overbearing, dominant culture that often defines people and their livelihoods. One might think of the crushed Midwestern farmers in Hamlin Garland's *Main-Travelled Roads* (1891) or the quiet but desperate lives strewn across coastal Maine in Sarah Orne Jewett's *The Country of Pointed Firs* (1896). In some cases, how a writer questions or pushes back against this dominant culture can determine the critical success of his or her work and drive it beyond the geographical area of its composition toward wider appreciation. For example, *Their Eyes Were Watching God* begins and ends in Eatonville, Florida, with a woman named Janie, who recounts her life story to her friend Pheoby. As Janie speaks, her friend—who knows what the local community gossips have said about Janie's peculiar decisions and circumstances, from her former tumultuous marriage to the town mayor to her decision to leave town with a younger man within a year of her ex-husband's death—listens and seeks to understand Janie's choices instead of falling in line with the prevailing local viewpoint of her behavior. As Janie finishes relating her life, Pheoby exclaims, "Ah done growed ten feet higher from jus' listenin' tuh you, Janie. Ah ain't satisfied wid mahself no mo'" (192). Janie's story inspires and moves a friend from within her own region to think beyond what she has previously known and assumed, a point that Hurston suggests as an important validation of one human's ability to influence the perspective of another and as evidence that people living within a region should not so easily be reduced to regional categories or stereotypes.

In regards to politics and representations of African-American life, Hurston's approach in *Eyes* quickly prompted others to criticize her novel as an inferior regional text. Richard Wright, who would later publish *Uncle Tom's Children* (1938) and *Native Son* (1945), wrote, "Hurston seems to have no desire whatsoever to move in the direction of serious fiction … her prose is cloaked in a facile sensuality … [and the] sensory sweep of her novel carries no theme, no message, [and] no thought" (25). In hindsight, not only is this a gross misreading of the novel's accomplishments, but it is also an ideological assault on works of literature that do not accord with particular sociopolitical modes of expression. Hurston understood the plights of African Americans, but she sought to portray their lives in *Eyes* as part of a community like what she had known in Eatonville. She documents their oppression more subtly through stories of human lives rather than exploiting pointed, politically charged rhetoric. For example, not long before Janie marries her first husband, her grandmother implicitly criticizes the lack of opportunities for African-American women while simultaneously celebrating their individuality: "You can't beat nobody down so low till you can rob 'em of they will" (16). She pushes Janie into marriage because, from her vantage point within a deeply racist and patriarchal culture, it might provide a reasonably good life for her granddaughter. The frustration that Hurston conveys exists in what an elderly woman feels is her best choice: to orchestrate her granddaughter's marriage with the community member she believes will best help her live a satisfying life. What Wright deems as pandering to a white audience is in fact a history of pain transmuted, but in no way muted, through an oral storytelling tradition. Hurston shows that as wrongheaded as Janie's grandmother's choice may be, it provides a possible avenue for Janie to form a more successful life of her own and to ascend to a life beyond the confines of poverty. Her grandmother's desire for Janie is not limited by her dialect, speech, insistence, or simplicity; rather, it speaks to the social politics among families in difficult conditions, and in this way, it extends beyond a regional association of what Wright calls the "Negro folk-mind" (25).

Likewise, more than seventy-five years later, Harper Lee's *Watchman* disappoints some readers for what appears to be a far less unified or uplifting political message than *Mockingbird*. Most notably, it condemns Atticus Finch, Scout's father and childhood hero, who is the novel's paragon of justice. Too, the heightened racism of the 1950s cools Scout's relationship with Calpurnia, the African-American caregiver who reared Scout during her childhood in the 1930s. While Atticus and Calpurnia may be treasured figures who influence Scout in *Mockingbird*, they also remain important in *Watchman*, albeit in new ways. Here, Atticus and Calpurnia appear to be weathering and revealing signs of more difficult physical and social circumstances. More than fifteen years have passed since *Mockingbird*'s conclusion, and both are now elderly. Atticus is seventy-two and suffers from rheumatoid arthritis, while Calpurnia is "old . . . [and] bony" (158) with failing eyesight. For Scout, interactions with the two provoke rage (in the case of Atticus) and surprise (in case of Calpurnia), but pointedly, Lee insists that these feelings are inseparable from Scout's deeper appreciation for each of them. As Lee reveals, neither Atticus nor Calpurnia are ideological constructs, but rather are humans with complicated histories caught in the middle of a national debate about desegregation that reverberates from Washington to Alabama and then into Maycomb. The ways that Lee depicts Atticus and Calpurnia are especially jarring in conjunction with the great lapse of time since the publication and the half-century celebration of *Mockingbird*. Since Lee largely stopped speaking to the press after 1964, the older versions of Atticus and Calpurnia may convey Lee's impressions of her aging hometown during the 1950s for the first time (Petry 145). The updated versions of Atticus and Calpurnia suggest a more complex, warts-and-all portrayal of politics during this era, and they energize Scout, who wrestles to comes to grips with the racism in Maycomb while at the same time delighting in her childhood and young adult memories there.

Lee embeds much of the political upheaval beneath the surface in both Maycomb and its African-American community in *Watchman*, focusing more on Scout's disillusionment than a collective sense of injustice. She also exacerbates the effect by depicting a much smaller snippet of time than in *Mockingbird*. Instead of a three-year period of Scout's childhood, *Watchman* offers little more than a three-day weekend of Scout's life when she returns for her "fifth annual trip home" as an adult (1). This compressed period in Maycomb contributes to the novel's claustropho- bic, frenetic atmosphere just after Scout realizes that many of the people closest to her uphold the destructive racial divisions there. It also implies that the opinions and minds of the local residents might or might not eventually change, but that for the present, Scout must remain isolated in her views about what she knows to be morally just. Unlike *Mockingbird*, there is an absence of some of the characteristics that make that novel a classic, what Holly Blackford sums up as a "focus on child conscious- ness, racial exclusion, social passing, and individuals in the closet" that allows the book "to unite various crusades for rights" (314). *Watchman* suggests that change comes much more slowly, and it captures what Lee understood as the difficulties rural people face when being left behind by the tide of national progress. It also mirrors what she witnessed in Monroeville, which remained segregated long after Lee completed both novels, and where "public schools did not integrate until 1970" (Murphy 36). Rather than stressing the potential for change and revering pivotal leaders as she would in *Mockingbird*, Lee highlights the inner frustration of a young woman spearheading the need for change, while also yearning to maintain some degree of rootedness with her childhood community. For Lee, this meant having the courage to interrogate family members and companions about their beliefs rather than glossing over or attempt- ing to quickly revise the sins of the past. In this way, Lee highlights the evolving social intricacies among Maycomb's citizens without simplify- ing the town by portraying it as a static, regionalized place.

Navigating Sensibility

Their Eyes Were Watching God and *Go Set a Watchman* are also novels that push beyond regionalized visions of the rural South in their em- phasis on women who must traverse and engage with the mire of the past, and who accomplish their journeys with feelings of love and affection for troubled people in socially uncomfortable places. When she composed *Their Eyes Were Watching God*, Hurston realized that much African American literature and art still stemmed from the influence of the Harlem Renaissance, which she experienced during its height in the 1920s. She also knew that many of the associated artists from this era hailed from cities and different backgrounds; and that consequently, rural African Americans often "had their representations reconfigured in an art form that was not for them," an unfortunate situation that she sought to change (Corkin and Frus 205). To do so, however, meant that she had to write about what she knew, which entailed representing the heart of a region that African American writers had envisioned being defined either "by the horrors of racism" or "the flight from those horrors" within the prior century (Patterson 33). In her depiction of Janie, Hurston presents a strong, forward-thinking woman who must respond to a community of people who reject her non-traditional lifestyle. Janie's immediate challenge, presented at the beginning and at the end of the book, consists not of reacting to the difficult circumstances of her past relationships with men, but of dealing with the impressions that Eatonville women glean or create, and then seek to spread, upon her arrival. As soon as Janie returns home after the tragic passing of her third husband, Tea Cake, the watchful women in the town judge her: "The women took the faded shirt and muddy overalls and laid them away for remembrance. It was a weapon against her strength and if it turned out of no significance, still it was a hope that she might fall to their level some day" (2). Here, Hurston shows Janie as naturally distinguished figure within the all African American community, but she also implies the potential danger of a mob mentality that seeks to define and oppress.

Instead of having Janie begin another life in a new location, Hurston returns her to Eatonville, where she attempts to find and negotiate a new social position with the local women she once left behind. For Janie, the town is neither so unbearable that she must flee, nor is it imbued with overwhelming memories of the past. Surrounded by other African Americans, the physical terrors of slavery and racism are absent. This unique situation enables Hurston to probe the "internal aspects of identity" rather than "external behavior" (West 122). She does this through the framing of Janie telling her story to Pheoby, who provides her support and who will help her reestablish a place in the community. When Pheoby questions her about Tea Cake, Janie replies, "Yeah, Pheoby, Tea Cake is gone. And dat's de only reason you see me back here—cause Ah ain't got nothing to make me happy no more where Ah was at . . . we been kissin'-friends for twenty years, so Ah depend on you for a good thought" (7). Hurston implies that even strong women such as Janie need community in the event of tragedy, but she also illuminates the difficulty of reconciling oneself within a small and insular group of people known for their skepticism and ridicule toward outsiders. As Janie shares her story with Pheoby, she slowly renews an alliance that flourishes from sharing her experiences rather than labeling, defining, or skewering other women in town. With at least one ally, Janie resituates herself within Eatonville and attempts to make the town she abandoned in a hurry a place for reconciliation, healing, and a future.

Harper Lee also emphasizes an outsider's attempt to return and find a place within a local culture at odds with her experiences and beliefs. Like Janie, Scout makes the long return trip with hope and renewed appreciation for her former home. As she is aboard a train from New York to Maycomb, Lee writes, "she could see nothing but pastureland and black cows from window to horizon. She wondered why she had never thought her country beautiful" (6). Yet, Scout's home county is deeply isolated, "a wilderness dotted with tiny settlements . . . so cut off from the rest of the nation that some of its citizens, unaware of the South's political predilections over the past ninety years, still voted Republican" (7). As a progressive, college-educated woman in her mid-twenties who spent much of her adult life in New York, she finds it more difficult to situate herself among her childhood companions who subscribe to "backwards" views. This clash is more vivid than in *Mockingbird*, where youth and innocence shielded Scout. In that book, as Kathryn Seidel notes, Scout must learn behaviors as a child that will enable her to "resist the worst prejudices and behaviors" that might position her as "a member of a mob, rather than a member of the good" (81). In *Watchman*, she comes face-to-face with those adult behaviors and must decide how to react.

Like Janie, Scout struggles to relate to any women in the novel—in Scout's case, to the point that she cannot find anyone sympathetic to her opinions and perspective. She lacks a Pheoby, and the closest woman she engages with is her Aunt Alexandra. They are separated by age and their relationships to Maycomb, as Alexandra is much older and deeply rooted within the town she cannot leave. Even if Alexandra's allegiances are impossible for Scout to accept, they both want to hold to values that Lee privileges in both novels. Yet, as an adult, Scout realizes that racism, ignorance, and poverty—all legacies from the prior century—undermine the very ideals that Alexandra and others desire to uphold. This becomes apparent when Alexandra holds a coffee meeting for her niece, where Scout attempts to have conversations with women older and younger than her. She grapples with the fact that there is a greater separation between white and African American citizens than ever before and feels isolated from her fellow women, who rely on their husbands for their news and opinions. However, Scout conversely thinks, "Everything I have ever taken for right and wrong these people have taught me—these very people" (167). She thinks of Atticus sending her to a woman's college in Georgia and then about her time in New York, where internally she reprimands what the city has taught her to think:

> I can say only this—that everything I learned about human decency I learned here. I learned nothing from you except how to be suspicious. I didn't know what hate was until I lived among you and saw you hating every day. They even had to pass laws to keep you from hating. I despise your quick answers, your slogans in the subway, and most of all I despise your lack of good manners, you'll never have 'em as long as you exist. (178)

Like Janie, Scout does not fully forsake her hometown because to do so would be to abandon the foundation of some of the more important moments of her life; however, she is torn and, for the time being, must keep some of her opinions to herself. Scout defies some of her aunt's beliefs and expectations, but she also acknowledges a deep sense of love and remembrance for her childhood in Maycomb. Her intensely split adult perspective elevates *Watchman* to a realm beyond mere regionalism, as Lee's heroine must grapple with how both the familiar and the foreign have shaped her into a unique individual. Instead of adamantly positioning herself on either the Maycomb or New York sides of a fence, Scout attempts to control herself among the women and to impart some of what she has learned in the respectful and restrained public way that characterizes Maycomb culture. She negotiates her entrance, and presents herself as a model for any readers who return to their abandoned hometowns or cities with different ideas than when they left.

Weathering Brutal Storms

Even as the social pressures of community, politics, and family present formidable challenges for both Janie and Scout, they must overcome the violence that encompasses women's experiences not only in the American South, but also throughout the United States and other parts of the world. Much like their creators Hurston and Lee, these women refuse to be pigeonholed as subordinate figures within their respective subcultures. Coming face-to-face with violence, Janie and Scout both deal with masculine wrath; Janie pushes back while Scout simply tries to argue her viewpoint. The empowerment of women and strengthening of conscious resolve are such central concerns in *Eyes* and *Watchman* that Janie and Scout encounter not one or two, but three men whose dominance potentially threatens who they may become. In *Eyes*, Janie marries three times. Though her first—arranged—marriage is not tempestuous, she feels constrained and does not love her husband, Logan. After her grandma dies, she runs away and marries Jody, the first of two violent men in her life. In Eatonville, as Jody becomes the most well-known and important man in town, he attempts to define Janie's life. Both husbands succumb to the temptation to control Janie, seeking to "rewire [her] thoughts into beliefs of helplessness and dependency" (Simeon-Jones 30). Whereas Logan simply attempted to tell her what chores she ought to complete, Jody tried to fully control Janie, hitting her multiple times, the last a beating in town before his subsequent decline and death. After being publically insulted, Janie snaps, mocking the appearance of her husband's genitalia and subsequently "rob[bing] him of his illusion of irresistible maleness" that according to the narrator "all men cherish" (79). When Janie dares to raise her voice at Jody in front of others, it is more than he can abide. This is perhaps Hurston's strongest overt statement against a codified form of masculinity that delimits women's aspirations and goals, and one that she confronts in Janie's final marriage to Tea Cake.

Any form of prescribed ideology about behavior between women and men, in both a regional or worldly sense, dissolves in the context of Janie and Tea Cake's relationship. On the one hand, when she abandons Eatonville with the much younger man, Janie enters a relationship that is more mutually participatory and fulfilling than she has ever known. Living in the Everglades after a stint in Jacksonville, she and Tea Cake garden and gather food together. When Janie confesses to being proficient at hunting, traditionally a more masculine activity, this skill does not impact Tea

Cake's opinion of her. Hurston depicts them working together on what seem like equal terms. And yet, the violence reappears. Controversially, Hurston writes:

> Before the week was over he had whipped Janie. Not because her behavior justified his jealousy, but it relieved that awful fear inside him. Being able to whip her reassured him in possession. No brutal beating at all. He just slapped her around a bit to show he was boss. Everybody talked about it in the fields. It aroused a sort of envy in both men and women. The way he petted and pampered her as if those two or three face slaps had nearly killed her made the women see visions and the helpless way she hung on him made men dream dreams. (145)

It is easy to recoil at this description of a woman who seems so accustomed to physical abuse to the point that she accepts it, but Janie must later act violently herself when she must kill her husband after he contracts rabies during a hurricane. Even though she may tolerate the domestic violence rampant in her culture, she is strong enough to shoot Tea Cake as he descends into madness and attempts to kill her. As Janie confronts violence with violence, Hurston suggests that her ability to act accordingly when at risk likely saves her from an early death.

In a similar situation, Scout reacts against the patriarchal dominance, verbal aggression, and physical violence that are often a hidden part of women's lives in Maycomb. At different points in *Watchman*, she counters three adversaries: her father, Atticus, her suitor, Hank Clinton, and her uncle, Dr. Jack Finch. Her principal disagreement with all three men derives from their beliefs about racism and social progress in town. The heart of each conflict consists of Harper Lee's own experiences oscillating between her hometown and New York. As Marja Mills notes, Lee was "a collection of contradictions . . . an Alabama native whose love for the state's back roads was matched only by her love of New York City streets" (4). Scout's greatest disappointment is with Atticus, who during a Maycomb County Citizens' Council meeting seems to abandon all that he has taught her about justice. In this scene, Atticus knows that Maycomb needs to change but cannot get beyond his inherently racist views. When Scout presses and accuses him of "moral double-dealing," Atticus retorts, "Have you ever considered that you can't have a set of backward people living among people advanced in one kind of civilization and have a social Arcadia?" (242). Like Lee's own father, Atticus appears in *Watchman* as a gradualist who, adhering to a Jeffersonian line of logic, claims that the social changes Scout demands will come only after a longer period, presumably beyond his lifetime, but perhaps within hers (Shields 79). Katherine Henniger argues that for many of *Watchman*'s twenty-first-century readers, this moment is indicative of the larger process of how "childhood racial innocence is allowed to be ruined" (600) in the novel. Hence, the uncovering of the great cultural sore that afflicts Maycomb astounds and stuns Scout, who must reconceive what her hometown has become. However, her pain also extends beyond race, as the one person she deeply respects and relies on appears to be as offensive as some of the other town members, having seemingly abandoned the values he taught her. If physical violence is absent in this situation, Lee implies that Atticus's disappointing defense of his involvement in the Maycomb Citizen's Council may be the harshest blow Scout has yet received. While she tries to counter her father's views, she is unable to break away from him as Janie does the men in her life.

In addition to challenging Atticus, Scout must come to terms with the social pressure to marry Hank Clinton. As soon as he arrives at the train station to pick her up, Hank assumes that Scout's coming home is a precursor to their inevitable marriage and their settling in town. However, Scout's great inner awakening to Maycomb's racial politics sours her opinion of Hank as a partner, and she rethinks and rejects the idea. Toward the end of the novel, after Hank argues that women should defer to men, Scout clarifies his definition of what "loving your man" is with regard to its unfair cost for women: "You mean losing your own identity [as a woman], don't you?" (227). When Hank replies yes, she immediately says she will never marry him. However, in announcing this decision, Scout commits herself to potential isolation as a woman in Maycomb, as Hank is the only person around that she imagines she could marry.

A disappointed Hank accepts her wishes, but Scout faces a harsher response to her beliefs from Maycomb's most distinguished intellectual, her uncle, Dr. Jack Finch, who attempts to belittle her perspective with an overview of Southern history. As he defends Atticus and the slow progress of change, Jack admits, "Men like me and my brother are obsolete and we've got to go . . . [but] when a man's looking down the double barrel of a shotgun, he picks up the first weapon he can find to defend himself, be it a stone or a stick of stovewood or a citizens' council" (200). Scout refuses to accept Jack's historical justification or resignation as an excuse; when she continues to resist his views in a later scene and threatens to leave Maycomb, he loses control of his temper and slaps her (260). Unlike Janie, Scout remains stunned and does not counter her blows verbally or physically. As in the case of Atticus, she respects his age and their kinship. Although Jack immediately apologizes and expresses regret for hitting Scout, and although Scout herself actually *thanks* her Uncle Jack afterwards, readers' own discomfort with the scene is likely to cause them to challenge the idea that formal education makes a difference in the fight against racism. It also demonstrates how groupthink and the refusal to adapt and treat others as equals in any setting or region can corrupt even the most ostensibly polite and refined people.

Conclusion

In time, Scout makes amends with Atticus, Hank, and Jack, and, like Janie, appears to accept a hometown she still cherishes despite her desire for swifter social progress. By choosing to remain in Maycomb, as Atticus and Jack prompt her to do, Scout has a chance to make a greater local impact than if she absconded back to a comparatively anonymous life in New York for the greater part of the year. After discussions with Jack and Atticus, she appears to accept their differences in experience, perspective, and belief. As Atticus walks toward the car in the novel's closing scene, for example, Scout rethinks her perspective of her father. Lee writes that as she "followed him to the car and watched him get laboriously into the front seat," Scout "welcomed him silently to the human race" (278). Then, she adds that this "the stab of discovery made her tremble a little" (278). Grasping that Atticus is aging and flawed, Scout reassesses her impression of him, and she elects to remain in Maycomb, unmarried for the present time. By the end of Hurston's novel, Janie has also experienced a storm of change and finds a place in Eatonville with the belief that her former home provides the best opportunity for healing. Both novels come to similar conclusions about the empowering nature of positively influencing communities from within as their heroines experience dangerous storms. In the process, Zora Neale Hurston and Harper Lee suggest that strong women from the South are to be confined neither by regional expectations nor by violence; and that through the processes of navigating and reacting to stymieing circumstances, women impact the lives around them for the better. If *Their Eyes Were Watching God* and

Go Set a Watchman offer uncompromising, controversial, and less-than-polished idealistic visions of progress, they also suggest that stronger and more just communities begin with the determination, strength, and bravery of women who do not fit regionally-sanctioned molds and who seek to broaden their neighbors' ways of understanding.

Works Cited

Blackford, Holly. *Mockingbird Passing: Closeted Traditions and Sexual Curiosities in Harper Lee's Novel.* University of Tennessee Press, 2011.

Corkin, Stanley, and Phyllis Frus. "An Ex-centric Approach to American Cultural Studies: The Interesting Case of Zora Neale Hurston as a Noncanonical Writer." *Prospects,* 21, 1996, pp. 193–228.

Gray, Richard. *Southern Aberrations: Writers of the American South and the Problem of Regionalism.* Louisiana State University Press, 2000.

Henninger, Katherine. "'My Childhood is Ruined!': Harper Lee and Racial Innocence." *American Literature, vol.* 88, no. 3, September 2016, pp. 597–626.

Hurston, Zora Neale. *Their Eyes Were Watching God.* Harper Perennial, 2006.

Lee, Harper. *Go Set A Watchman.* HarperCollins, 2015.

Lutz, Tom. *Cosmopolitan Vistas: American Regionalism and Literary Value.* Cornell University Press, 2004.

Mills, Marja. *The Mockingbird Next Door: Life with Harper Lee. New York:* Penguin, 2014.

Murphy, Mary McDonagh. *Scout, Atticus, and Boo: A Celebration of Fifty Years of To Kill a Mockingbird.* HarperCollins, 2010.

Newquist, Roy. Interview with Harper Lee. *Counterpoint.* Rand McNally, 1964, pp. 403–12.

O'Connor, Flannery. "The Fiction Writer and His Country." *Collected Works.* Library of America, 1988, pp. 801–6.

Patterson, Tiffany Rub. *Zora Neale Hurston and a History of Southern Life.* Temple University Press, 2005.

Petry, Alice Hall. "Harper Lee, the One-Hit Wonder." *On Harper Lee: Essays and Reflections.* Edited by Alice Hall Petry. University of Tennessee Press, 2007, pp. 143–64.

Seidel, Kathryn. "Growing Up Southern: Resisting the Code for Southerners in *To Kill a Mockingbird." On Harper Lee: Essays and Reflections.* Edited by Alice Hall Petry. University of Tennessee Press, 2007, pp. 19–34.

Shields, Charles J. *Mockingbird: A Portrait of Harper Lee, from Scout to Go Set a Watchman.* Henry Holt, 2016.

Simeon-Jones, Kersuze. "Masculinity in Hurston's Texts." *"The Inside Light": New Critical Essays on Zora Neale Hurston,* edited by Deborah Plant, ABC-Clio, 2010, pp. 23–32.

Tarr, Rodger L, and Brent E. Kinser, editors. "Regional Literature of the South." *Uncollected Writings of Marjorie Kinnan Rawlings.* University of Florida Press, 2007.

Walker, Alice. "Zora Neale Hurston: A Cautionary Tale and a Partisan View." *Friendship and Sympathy: Communities of Southern Women Writers*. Edited by Rosemary M. Magee. University of Mississippi Press, 1992, pp. 164–71.

West, M. Genevieve. *Zora Neal Hurston and American Literary Culture*. University of Florida Press, 2005.

Wright, Richard. "Between Laughter and Tears." *New Masses*, 5 October 1937, pp. 22–25.

13

TEACHING *MOCKINGBIRD* IN THE POST-*WATCHMAN* CLASSROOM

Jonathan S. Cullick

Part I: Disrupting the Pedagogy

Harper Lee's classic, *To Kill a Mockingbird,* is a mainstay of middle school and high school classrooms throughout the United States. For reluctant teenage readers, the novel offers an accessible narrative and relatable childhood characters. For engaged readers, it offers historical and social resonance. For a general audience of young adult readers, it offers an inspiring story with a seemingly unambiguous hero and reassuring parent figure. The Common Core State Standards even lists *To Kill a Mockingbird* as an exemplar text for grades nine through ten alongside works of Ovid, Homer, and Shakespeare. Yet the author's controversial *Go Set a Watchman* confronts teachers with a more rounded portrait of the hero of *To Kill a Mockingbird.* Jean Louise, now twenty-six years old, discovers to her horror that her father expresses blatantly racist views that include membership in a local White Citizens' Council. As Cheli Reutter argues in the introduction to this volume, *Go Set a Watchman* threatens the iconic status of respected characters and even the literary status of *To Kill a Mockingbird* itself. *Go Set a Watchman* seems to cast shadows on the landscape of the imaginary Maycomb and potentially the landscape of the classroom.

For grades seven through twelve English teachers, students in university education programs, and university educators who prepare those future teachers, the publication of *Go Set a Watchman* raises compelling pragmatic questions. How does *Go Set a Watchman* complicate the inclusion of *To Kill a Mockingbird* in the middle school or high school curriculum? Could we—or should we—teach both novels together as a pair? Should we ignore *Go Set a Watchman* altogether? Should *Go Set a Watchman* be a required text or an optional supplementary text in English teacher preparation courses? The broader theoretical question is, does the publication of *Go Set a Watchman* change the way teachers can—or must—approach *To Kill a Mockingbird*? Teachers will need to confront this issue as they introduce their young readers to Scout and the other characters in her world.

In my methods courses for English secondary education students, since the publication of *Go Set a Watchman,* responses have been mixed. A few of the soon-to-be teachers and some of the currently teaching graduate students have expressed reluctance to read *Go Set a Watchman* precisely out of fear of witnessing the iconic Atticus Finch toppled from his pedestal. Still, many of them express curiosity or a sense of obligation that a future English teacher ought to be familiar with this recently released novel (and I urge them to feel that sense of obligation). *Go Set a Watchman* is a flawed text, but it directly addresses issues that remain silent in *Mockingbird;* or, as Howell Raines says, "*To Kill a Mockingbird,* while it is the superior storytelling book, wobbles morally in comparison to *Watchman.*" *Go Set a Watchman* can make teachers and students more aware of the margins, the blanks, the silences, the absent voices, and absent scenes in *To Kill a Mockingbird.*

In our discussions of ways to design lesson plans for *To Kill a Mockingbird,* my education students and I have already been pushing into the silences of the text. Using an *English Journal* article by teacher Brooke Richelle Holland, which describes how Atticus's speaking styles reveal types of classical rhetoric, we have discussed inviting high school students to analyze appeals to *ethos, pathos,* and *logos* in his closing argument. After considering the voice of Atticus in the courtroom, we have considered the silences in the courtroom—in other words, the closing argument that Atticus *does not give.* A popular inferential approach in middle school and secondary classrooms invites young readers to imagine their own additional or "missing" chapters of a text. Students can be invited to create their own closing arguments, to speculate or perhaps to wish for what Atticus might have said, or even to write a "missing chapter" of the jury deliberations. We ask ourselves, *What happened in that jury room? Did the members of the jury believe in the truth of their own verdict? Did they deliberate in bad faith? Did they rationalize the unjust verdict to themselves out of fear for the social consequences of finding a black man not guilty?*

Inspired by an animal cartoon that features a mockingbird on a tree branch typing into its iPhone ("To Tweet a Mockingbird" by "Fritz"), we have even considered the now popular teaching strategy of having students analyze literary characters by creating online social media profiles. A bit of irreverent, undergraduate humor sometimes emerges as groups in the class transpose this classic literary work into the shorthand slang and emojis of Twitter. Atticus has been given the handle @AtticusBadassicus, and another character's tweet has described him as the GOAT (Greatest of All Time) of all lawyers. But mostly somber expressions have emerged from the tweets. One had @TheRealMaycombCountyJudge observing: #NotaGoodFeeling. Another had Dill tweeting his disbelief: "What is going on in this place on this day?"

A responsibility that I face as the professor is to encourage these future teachers to include the perspectives of the black characters in their lesson plans. Calpurnia and Tom Robinson particularly represent the speeches that remain unwritten and the chapters that remain missing. In a 1998 article she wrote for *English Journal,* titled "When the Mockingbird Becomes an Albatross," high school teacher Carol Ricker-Wilson describes her black students reporting their discomfort to her, as her teaching and the novel itself has "positioned them as objects of a lesson on racism for white students." She observes, "It did not seem to be their classmates' stares or comments, but their very act of reading which caused these black students, in their identification with the black characters in the novel, to feel demoralized. In short, the mockingbird had become their albatross, just another burden hung around their necks" (Ricker-Wilson 69–70). For Roxanne Gay, *To Kill a Mockingbird* seems to matter only to "white people who inexplicably still do not understand the ills of racism, and seemingly need this book to show them the light." Rather than representing the experiences of black characters, however, those experiences end up being shallow. Calpurnia and Tom Robinson "are vehicles for Scout's story instead of their own" (Gay).

Those absent or underrepresented voices have limited representation in the resources that teachers depend upon the most: the teachers' guides. A brief survey of popular teachers' guides will bear out this assessment.

The Big Read (BR) project of the National Endowment for the Arts is a community reading program that brings presentations and book discussions to local schools and public libraries. The project offers a Teacher's

Guide for the classroom and a Reader Resources booklet for book clubs. Though not mentioning *Go Set a Watchman* in the lessons or in the brief biography of Harper Lee, the BR Teacher's Guide for *To Kill a Mockingbird* does offer background information, discussion questions, and writing exercises for many key topics such as Harper Lee's biography and the cultural and historical context of the novel (including Jim Crow laws and a recording of Billie Holiday's 1939 "Strange Fruit"). It also addresses the teaching of narrative point of view, character development, figurative language and symbolism, plot development, and themes—all leading up to a final lesson, titled, "What Makes a Novel Great?" The preface to the BR Reader Resources booklet introduces the novel with this statement: "Harper Lee's *To Kill a Mockingbird* is the rare American novel that can be discovered with excitement in adolescence and reread into adulthood without fear of disappointment." Intended for adult readers, this booklet mentions *Go Set a Watchman* in its background section. The brief list of discussion questions focuses on Scout and Atticus.

The BR Teacher's Guide lesson on character development invites students to consider a black character's point of view in asking them to "write a paragraph explaining who they believe is the most heroic character," with Tom Robinson offered among the options. Yet when the Teacher's Guide lesson on narrative and point of view suggests that teachers have students retell the story from character perspectives, only Dill and Boo are offered as options. Students are asked to explore and do group presentations on the roles of "secondary characters" such as Calpurnia and Tom Robinson, but each group is told only to answer the question, "How do their unique personalities help Scout learn about herself?" Notice that the question emphasizes only how the black characters serve the character of Scout. Along that line, the lesson on characters asks students to discuss what Scout and Jem learn from going to church with Calpurnia; Calpurnia's perspective is not an option.

The teachers' guides published by Harper Perennial (HP) are impressively comprehensive and useful documents that provide the teacher with chapter-by-chapter vocabulary and discussion questions, topics for writing and research, and additional multi-media resources for student research. All of the sections are helpfully aligned to specific standards in the Common Core. These guides are written for teachers of two distinctly different reading audiences for each novel: a younger readership for *Mockingbird* and an older readership for *Watchman*. The "Note to Teachers" in the HP Teacher's Guide for *To Kill a Mockingbird* states, "Since the novel is most commonly taught in middle school, this guide is aligned to the Common Core standards for grade 8." The "Note to Teachers" in the HP Teacher's Guide for *Go Set a Watchman* states, "Thematically complex and highly allusive, it *[Go Set a Watchman]* is a text that demands active and close reading. It is best suited as a text for college and upper-level high school students."

The HP Teacher's Guide for *To Kill a Mockingbird* offers useful research topics related to cultural, historical, and thematic contexts. Among the writing prompts, some compelling questions about racial perspectives appear. Topic #4 addresses the Finch children visiting Calpurnia's church, asking students to research and write about code-switching, "the linguistic term for adapting speech to different contexts" (26). (Elsewhere in our essay collection, Brandie Bohney explores this issue fully in the article, "Command of Two Languages": Language Awareness and Acceptance with Calpurnia.") Topic #8 in the HP Teacher's Guide suggests that students "research the civil rights movement's link to Alabama history" (26). Topic #10 offers, "There are numerous real-life examples of African-American men being falsely accused and convicted of crimes. Research a real-life case of someone who was falsely convicted" (26). (This kind of contemporary connection is explored by Monica Carol Miller in this essay collection, in the chapter "Fear/Vulnerability/Anger: Teaching *To Kill a Mockingbird* and *Go Set a Watchman* in the Era of Black Lives Matter.")

The HP Teacher's Guide for *Go Set a Watchman* picks up these themes and takes them much further. Every chapter-by-chapter list of discussion questions is followed by annotated lists of the many allusions—Biblical, literary, historical, cultural, and otherwise—that appear throughout the novel. In total, an impressive list of more than seventy-five annotations appears, indicating the intense allusiveness of the novel. Each annotation includes the URL to a web page that offers definition and background information about each term. The first page of the HP Teacher's Guide further explains that "students may approach *Go Set a Watchman* with trepidation or preconceived ideas based on their experience with *To Kill a Mockingbird*. It may be helpful to address these issues before you start to teach the text." It suggests that teachers begin *Watchman* with their students by considering topics such as the history of the NAACP, the Great Migration, Jim Crow, the Civil Rights Movement, race and social class, public school integration, and current challenges in racial equality and social justice.

The argumentation writing prompts in the HP Teacher's Guide invite investigation into these kinds of topics. Prompt #3 asks, "What causes prejudice?" Prompt #4 invites consideration of *Brown v. Board of Education*. Prompt #5 suggests research into how pervasive slavery was in the South. Prompt #8 asks, "Is there such a thing as 'heritage not hate'?" (17). Prompt #9 asks students to "research the history of race and equality in our judicial system" (19). Prompt #10 notes the presence of "racial language" in the novel and asks students to research the terms (19). Prompt #12 notes that "Jean Louise states that she is who she is in part because she was 'raised by a black woman and a white man'" and then directs students to "examine the impact that Calpurnia and Atticus had on Jean Louise's development" (19). Prompt #13 asks students to research the struggle for interracial marriage rights (19). With respect to the perspectives of black characters, the most compelling argumentation question is Prompt #12: "Other than the section in which Jean Louise visits Calpurnia, there are only a few glimpses of an African-American perspective in the novel . . . How does the novel deepen or complicate your understanding of the racial landscape of the 1950s?" (18).

Related to the underrepresented perspectives of the black characters, a nuanced approach to Atticus is equally missing from the teachers' guides. He is understood to be the ideal father, lawyer, and conscientious citizen who stands as an icon for racial justice. The interpretation of Atticus in the "white savior" role is precisely dependent upon the subordinate position of the black characters in the narrative. But recent criticism has complicated that view. Atticus is an advocate for law and order, but he is no progressive advocate for justice. His view ranges from moderate to conservative. As Howell Raines writes, "Atticus's pedantic reverence for the rule of law communicates to Scout and Jem a message that has misled generations of 'honorable white Southerners.'"

Naa Baako Ako-Adjei even argues that "it's time schools stopped teaching *To Kill a Mockingbird*." Ako-Adjei makes the compelling argument that the sentimental portrayals in *Mockingbird* feed "the collective and peculiar American delusion" (185) that racism is not historically systemic but is rather located only in the lowest socio-economic classes of whites. White moderates in the 1950s wanted to distance themselves from the violence and negative news coverage that followed the *Brown vs. Board of Education* decision (192). Harper Lee herself "was keenly aware of how the South was being portrayed by the Northern Press" and thus depicted the

South's problem "as something that could be addressed slowly and internally by thoughtful and sober whites in the mold of Atticus Finch and not something that needed to be addressed by the intervention of the federal government" (Ako-Adjei 193–95). Both *Mockingbird* and *Watchman* thus argue for a gradualist approach to ending white supremacy. Ako-Adjei concludes that both educators and school systems "seem unprepared to question Lee's motives" in *To Kill a Mockingbird,* because our country's "engagement with history has been about reifying the idea that racism, and the paroxysms of violence that it produced, were aberrations in its history" (197). Ako-Adjei does not believe that *Go Set a Watchman* will change the way we read a novel that has an "enduring place on middle and high school reading lists" because of "its sentimentalized account of America's racist history" (200). The solution, then, is to stop teaching *To Kill a Mockingbird.*

I agree with Ako-Adjei's argument, but only up to the point of suggesting that *Mockingbird* should not be taught. I would propose that we take Ako-Adjei's reading not as a rationale to pull the novel from our classrooms but instead as a timely challenge to give students a more nuanced engagement with the novel's historical context. Ako-Adjei awakens us to that task. If educators are not prepared to teach the novel, then as a teacher-educator, I consider it my responsibility to prepare my education students. While I would not suggest that we stop teaching the novel *Mockingbird*, I do propose that we update our teaching of the conventional, white, middle class cultural experience known as *To Kill a Mockingbird.* We must bring *Go Set a Watchman* into our classrooms to guide our students to acknowledge and enlarge the imagined community in which they have been learning about *To Kill a Mockingbird.*

As both Ako-Adjei and high school teacher Carol Ricker-Wilson have realized, traditional pedagogies are not filling in the blanks. The solution is bringing something new into our pedagogy; the publication of *Go Set a Watchman* provides teachers with that material. Atticus's explicit racism and the larger role that Calpurnia takes in *Go Set a Watchman* are precisely what get us into those spaces. As the brief survey of teachers' guides above shows, the best one for calling out those issues that inhabit the spaces and margins of *Mockingbird* is the Harper Collins Teacher's Guide to *Go Set a Watchman.* Far from casting a shadow, *Go Set a Watchman* can shine a pedagogical light.

Part II: Renovating the Pedagogy

To imagine new classroom approaches, we must consider *To Kill a Mockingbird* as something more than a text subject to the kinds of learning objectives listed in the Common Core State Standards. This novel is an imagined community; many readers have grown up with *Mockingbird.* No one yet has grown up with *Watchman.* Consequently, the anti-*Watchman* camp has been anxious to leave intact conventional readings of *Mockingbird.* As the experience of teachers such as Carol Wicker-Wilson demonstrate, those readings are not necessarily consonant with the experiences of contemporary readers. Accordingly, teachers can embrace new pedagogical strategies that destabilize the mainstream reading of *Mockingbird* with student voices and other resources that do not align with the "consensus" reading.

Part of *Mockingbird's* classroom popularity has derived from the seemingly clear lines it draws between villains and heroes—racist segregation on one hand and inclusive integration on the other. We teach and learn about historical moments, such as the civil rights movement, as binary conflicts in which we imagine ourselves on the side of the angels. *Go Set a Watchman* will help the teacher complicate those literary and historical perspectives. While the battle line between racism and justice is clearly drawn in our reading of *Mockingbird,* in *Watchman* the lines are blurred by the middle class white conservatives and moderates who explicitly advocate gradualism. This is where *Watchman* is most forceful and has its greatest potential as a text complementary to *Mockingbird:* the sentimentality of the latter is replaced by the polemics of the former. In addition, *Watchman* introduces a black voice—the voice of Calpurnia—briefly but powerfully enough to illuminate *Mockingbird* in a new way. I suggest that teachers pair *Go Set a Watchman* with *To Kill a Mockingbird,* incorporating complementary passages from *Watchman* into the teaching of *Mockingbird,* or if instructional time permits for more advanced students, teaching both texts side by side. Below I offer examples of passages from *Go Set a Watchman* that can supplement class discussion by giving voice to Calpurnia and complicating the student's reading of Atticus.

Calpurnia's Voice

Both novels present scenes in which Scout notices that Calpurnia addresses her differently as she grows up and speaks differently in social situations. Scout notices Calpurnia's double voicing. The Scout-Calpurnia relationship is especially accessible to young readers because of its parental qualities. In *Mockingbird,* Calpurnia's role in the family is central yet marginal. Calpurnia is such a part of the household that Jean Louise introduces her at the same time she introduces the family, yet Calpurnia's role remains in the margin of that introduction because she is the employee. Yet, with Scout's mother deceased, Calpurnia functions in a maternal role. The narrating Jean Louise introduces Calpurnia at the same time she mentions the death of her mother, by default putting Cal in the maternal role. Emphasizing the point, Jean Louise notes that Atticus takes Calpurnia's side in disputes between Scout and Calpurnia.

Calpurnia takes the same maternal role toward Scout in *Go Set a Watchman.* When Scout has her first period, it is Calpurnia who assists and teaches her. When Scout worries that she has become pregnant because a boy kissed her, it is again Calpurnia who explains sexual maturity to her (see *Go Set a Watchman* chapter 11). When Scout has a school dance, it is Calpurnia who assists her with her dress, and when Scout unwisely inserts conspicuous falsies into the dress, it is Calpurnia who provides terse critique. We see a level of familiarity that is reflected only in a mother-daughter relationship.

In *Go Set a Watchman,* Jean Louise recalls that, as she entered adolescence, Calpurnia shifted toward addressing her with formality, as if she were an adult. In addition to formality, Scout observes a change in Calpurnia's manners and speech from "Standard American" to "African American Vernacular" when company comes to the house, shifts that parallel those that appear in the church scene in *Mockingbird* (*GSW* 139, 70).

Calpurnia's linguistic nuance is addressed at length in *To Kill a Mockingbird* when she takes the Finch children with her to the First Purchase African M.E. Church in the Quarters. A congregant named Lula challenges Calpurnia for bringing the white children as guests into the church. Scout and Jem feel discomfort during this exchange, but they also notice the shift in Calpurnia's speech, which strikes them as strange. Scout realizes that Calpurnia has a life as well as a language outside the Finch household. Later, the children ask Calpurnia about her bad grammar—as they call it—in the church. They ask Calpurnia why she talks that way, and Calpurnia explains that if she spoke in her church the same way she spoke in the Finch household, people would think she was trying to raise herself above others. In this exchange, Scout discovers a separateness that is represented by their differences in language (See *TKM* 135-36, 135, 143-44, 143, 27, 142-43).

In *Go Set a Watchman,* these shifts rise to a crisis when the 26-year-old Jean Louise visits Calpurnia after her grandson has fatally struck a pedestrian with his car. Atticus will serve as his attorney. Calpurnia's manner and speech are distant, treating Jean Louise as a guest. In this emotionally powerful scene, Jean Louise pleads with Calpurnia to stop talking to her formally, as if she is company, to recognize her and remember their relationship. Back in her car, Jean Louise tries to reassure herself that Calpurnia surely must have loved her and the Finch family, but now when Cal looks at her, she sees only a white person, a racial divide. (See *GSW* 159–61).

These scenes offer ample opportunity to explore more deeply these two characters, their relationship, and the pressures of racial codes on that relationship. An exploration of multi-voicing can be highly relevant to contemporary students because they are already engaging in multi-voicing for different audiences and modes of technological communication. Because of its parental nature, the Scout-Calpurnia relationship is one that can connect with young readers. Individually and in groups, students can read the scene at Calpurnia's church in *Mockingbird* and the scene at Calpurnia's home in *Watchman.* They can describe how the characters react to each other and make inferences to explain those reactions, using reference to specific words and phrases to support their responses. Then they can be invited to respond creatively by imagining themselves in the role of each character writing to herself or to the other character. These activities can encourage greater empathy or sensitivity to the separateness that is imposed upon these characters by Southern racial codes. Taught together as a pair, *To Kill a Mockingbird* and *Go Set a Watchman* offer students an opportunity to discover how social attitudes about race put pressure on interpersonal relationships. The results could be illuminating.

Atticus, *Brown v. Board of Education*, and the White Moderate

The other parental relationship, of course, is between Scout and Atticus. The concluding conversation between Atticus and Jean Louise in *Watchman* chapter 17 offers a provocative pairing with the father-daughter dialogues in the early chapters of *Mockingbird.* The gradualist viewpoint that *Mockingbird* only hints at is represented directly as the paternalistic Atticus conducts this father-daughter conversation in the manner of a Socratic dialogue in a law school seminar. He poses leading questions to Jean Louise, who obediently provides the responses as prompted. When

Atticus leads the conversation with reference to the *Brown vs. Board of Education* decision, Jean Louise dutifully criticizes the Supreme Court (even calling the Court "hateful") for overstepping its authority and imposing its will on the state (GSW 241). "'I know it's got to be slow, Atticus, I know that full well," Jean Louise says with reference to integration and social change (GSW 252). As Ako-Adjei points out, *Watchman* "reveals the ideological foundation on which *To Kill a Mockingbird* was built" and that foundation is "the agenda of trying to plead the case for a very gradualist approach to ending white supremacy" (Ako-Adjei 199).

As students are assigned to read this dialogue in *Watchman* chapter 17, they can be presented with key sections from the *Brown vs. Board of Education* decision, which ruled, "Segregation of white and Negro children in the public schools of a State solely on the basis of race ... denies to Negro children the equal protection of the laws." Reminding the students that the *Brown* decision of 1954 preceded the writing of *Watchman* and *Mockingbird* only by a few years, the teacher can then introduce the Southern Manifesto, a 1956 statement signed by 101 members of Congress from the deep South. Authored by segregationist Senator Strom Thurmond, the Manifesto declares, "We regard the decisions of the Supreme Court in the school cases as a clear abuse of judicial power. It climaxes a trend in the federal judiciary undertaking to legislate, in derogation of the authority of Congress, and to encroach upon the reserved rights of the States and the people." The Manifesto puts into context questions that Atticus rhetorically poses to Jean Louise, "Can you blame the South for resenting being told what to do about its own people by people who have no idea of its daily problems?"(GSW 247).

The teacher can supplement these *Watchman* passages further with biographical information from Joseph Crespino in *Atticus Finch: The Biography*. Harper Lee's father, A. C. Lee (upon whom Atticus Finch was modeled) was one of the many white moderate Southerners who was a Democrat but turned away from the party as it embraced the labor and civil rights movements; the result was political differences between A.C. Lee and his daughter (Crespino xviii). In Crespino's thesis, Harper Lee wrote *Go Set a Watchman* to work through her own struggle with the conservativism of white Southerners such as her father. In a reaction against a Northern press that represented Southern reactions to the *Brown* decision only through the most extreme voices, "it would be *Mockingbird*, with its more careful, selective, and allusive evocation of a principled, decent white southerner, that coincided with and provided cultural reinforcement for a quiet oppositional politics in the white community, one that defied the essential, foundational myth of the militant segregationists" (xviii). Crespino's "biography" of Atticus intensifies the light that *Watchman* shines upon *Mockingbird*. Crespino concludes that, with the publication of *Watchman*, "We know now not only that the Atticus of *Mockingbird* was always too good to be true, but that Harper Lee knew it as well. She knew all the things that Jean Louise discovers in *Watchman*: that Atticus's kindly paternalism covered ugly beliefs about racial difference," and "that what as a child she had assumed was genuine, reciprocal love and devotion across the color line was more like an elaborate act intended to ease, for whites, the guilt and, for blacks, the burden of racial injustice" (173). What *Go Set a Watchman* brings to our classrooms is the discovery that the student-reader shares with Jean Louise: that Atticus Finch, like Harper Lee's father, was not ahead of his time but rather, in Joseph Crespino's terms, a man "*of* his time and *of* his place" (19). The teaching potential of *Watchman* is evident in its power to transform Atticus Finch from a literary hero to a flawed man situated within a time and place that is equally flawed.

The connections that Crespino and Ako-Adjei make to Martin Luther King recommend "Letter from Birmingham Jail" as another essential primary text to pair with Harper Lee's novels in the classroom. Because of its superb appeals to ethos and pathos and its mastery of parallel and periodic sentences, King's "Letter" is a frequently used text for rhetorical and stylistic analysis projects in college-level writing courses. King's "Letter" also appears, like *Mockingbird,* on the list of exemplar texts of the Common Core State Standards. "Letter from Birmingham Jail" identifies the white moderate as a source of frustration greater than that posed by extremists. The moderate "who is more devoted to order than to justice . . . who paternalistically feels that he can set the timetable for another man's freedom" insidiously undermines the entire civil rights project. For King, "Shallow understanding from people of good will is more frustrating than absolute misunderstanding from people of ill will." Martin Luther King becomes an essential voice to bring into the classroom when teaching Harper Lee. Crespino identifies A. C. Lee and Atticus Finch as the very type of Southerner—the white moderate—whom King was criticizing in these statements. "Letter from Birmingham Jail" is "the quintessential statement of how well-meaning whites can often get in the way of genuine racial progress" (Crespino xix). Ako-Adjei calls

To Kill a Mockingbird "the literary expression of the position of the white moderate" whom King was addressing in the "Letter" (195).

Having assembled *To Kill a Mockingbird* with *Go Set a Watchman,* the text of the *Brown* decision, the Southern Manifesto, and Martin Luther King's "Letter from Birmingham Jail," the teacher can refocus on the passage from *Mockingbird* that is probably the object of the greatest amount of classroom discussion commentary, and assessment: Atticus Finch's famous advice to Scout to get along more with other people by walking in their shoes and seeing things from their perspectives (33). Informed by a reading of *Go Set a Watchman* and King's "Letter," Atticus Finch's "[there are] some very fine people on both sides" approach becomes a moral flaw in his character—and here I am shamelessly using the term *character* as a pun in both its moral sense (*a person of character*) and its narrative sense (*a fictional character*). An equanimity toward racist whites is what high school teacher Carol Ricker-Wilson is referring to when she explains, "Somewhat troubling to my students was how, in *Mockingbird,* Lee invited her readers to have an informed and sympathetic understanding for several of the white characters who kept racism alive and well" (72). When Atticus tells Scout that she will have better relationships with many other people by taking their perspectives into consideration, significantly the people whom Atticus is telling Scout to understand are racist whites. Atticus is frequently depicted as helping Scout and Jem navigate—with patience and civility—a world of taunts and threats from Cecil Jacobs in the schoolyard, Miss DuBose in their neighborhood, and a lynch mob at the local jail. Critics such as Monroe Freedman in the *Legal Times* (1992), Malcolm Gladwell in *The New Yorker* (2009), and Randall Kennedy in the *New York Times* (2015) have noted that Atticus practices equanimity to a fault. Atticus, an educated attorney who is surely not unfamiliar with the activities of the Ku Klux Klan, describes the KKK as merely a harmless social or political group that can be embarrassed into good behavior with a stern talking-to from a Jewish shop keeper. Atticus tells his children to regard Walter Cunningham, the lynch mob leader, as a decent person who is merely making mistakes like anyone else. As Monroe Freeman has said, "It just happens that Cunningham's blind spot (along with the rest of us?) is a homicidal hatred of black people'" (qtd. in Gladwell).

As a result of such observations, Adam Gopnik, writing about *Go Set a Watchman* in the *New Yorker,* points out, "The idea that Atticus in this book, 'becomes' the bigot he was not in *Mockingbird* entirely misses Harper Lee's point—that this is exactly the kind of bigot that Atticus has been all along." As harsh as this assessment of Atticus may sound, visiting the Atticus Finch of *Watchman* better positions the student to make contemporary connections. The language of the Southern Manifesto—the accusation that civil rights–minded judges are overstepping their authority, legislating from the bench, and encroaching upon the rights of states—persists in contemporary political discourse.

The language of false equivocation also persists. It certainly applied in August of 2017, when members of the so-called "Alt-Right" gathered in Charlottesville, Virginia, to join a protest against the removal of a statue of Confederate general Robert E. Lee. With signs and voices, they shouted slogans dating back to 1930s-era Nazism. Counter-protestors were violently assaulted. In the most well-known incident, a counter-protestor was killed and several others were injured when a white supremacist deliberately drove his car into the group (he has since been convicted and sentenced). Two police officers patrolling from above were killed when their helicopter crashed. For the next several days, leaders in government offered undiluted condemnation of the neo-Nazi violence; however, President Donald Trump delayed making any such statement, and then delivered conflicting statements. His infamous equivocation, "You also had some very fine people on both sides," was typical of his hesitation to make any undiluted criticism of the pro-Confederate protestors. (See Rosie Gray for a timeline of the president's statements.)

The events of Charlottesville proved to be informative for the stage adaptation of *To Kill a Mockingbird,* which opened on Broadway at the Schubert Theatre on 13 December 2018. Playwright Aaron Sorkin has noted in interviews and in an essay for *New York* magazine that, after an unsuccessful first draft, he realized that he needed to construct the character of Atticus in a way different from the novel: "A protagonist has to change. A protagonist has to be put through something and be changed by it. And one more thing: A protagonist has to have a flaw. How did Harper Lee get away with creating a flawless protagonist who's the same person at the end of the book as he is at the beginning? Simple. In the book, Atticus isn't the protagonist—Scout is." Sorkin and producer Scott Rudin agreed that Scout would not be the only protagonist; Atticus would be a protagonist as well. This decision led to Sorkin's realizing that there must be a flaw in the character of Atticus Finch—a flaw both moral and structural. Sorkin's realization is very useful for helping teachers introduce innovative readings. As the narrator of the novel, Scout is the subjective consciousness; Atticus is her object. But this simple observation can evade our attention because—undoubtedly influenced by the screenplay and portrayal by Gregory Peck—we have transformed Atticus into the protagonist. Surely, he is the hero of the story in the sense that he is *Scout's* hero; but, in terms of literary analysis, Atticus is not the narrative hero. Scout serves that role. She is the one who journeys from home to the court house and the Radley house and then returns home, transformed at the end of the narrative. In her consciousness, however, Atticus is the symbolic hero, the source of paternal morality and stability, unchanged from the beginning of her narrative to the end. As Jean Louise says in the final line of *Mockingbird,* Atticus "would be there all night, and he would be there when Jem waked up in the morning" (323). Atticus would *be there* still, a steady, reliable presence. That is who he was when she was a child, and he remains that figure in her consciousness as an adult narrator. Her point of view becomes the reader's point of view; consequently, we, too, idolize Atticus. This must be the reason some *Mockingbird* readers have been reluctant to read *Go Set a Watchman*: it changes that which we hope is unchanging.

Acknowledgement of that flaw—the flaw that Sorkin speaks of—is what changes Atticus for us. But, as Adam Gopnik notes: that flaw was there all along. Sorkin concurs: "I didn't have to give Atticus a flaw because, to my mind, he already had one; it's just that we'd always considered it a virtue . . . He believes in the fundamental goodness in everyone, even homicidal white supremacists. He believes . . . that there are fine people on both sides"? As Casey Cep observes, Sorkin realized that Atticus sounded "a little like President Trump [saying] that there are good people on both sides of a lynch mob. It was Trump's comments after the counter-protester was killed by a white supremacist in Charlottesville that, Sorkin has said, helped him see the contemporary resonance of the play." Thus, "in this new production, the empathy for which Atticus has always been celebrated . . . would be his fundamental flaw." Sorkin's resolution of this central playwrighting challenge can be instructive for teachers addressing the pedagogical challenges. Additionally, this contemporary transformation of *To Kill a Mockingbird* to the stage returns us to the question of those silent voices. Teachers may find also that Aaron Sorkin's 2018 stage adaptation of *To Kill a Mockingbird* will serve as an important resource in providing voices for the unvoiced characters. The play gives Tom Robinson "the dignity of voicing his own predicament" and Calpurnia "serves in the play as Atticus's foil and needling conscience" (Green).

Underrepresented Perspectives

Consider the margins of the final pages of *To Kill a Mockingbird*. High school teacher Carol Ricker-Wilson has expressed concern that the happy ending of *Mockingbird*—with its "catharsis" and "loose ends all neatly tucked away —is "most readily available" only to the novel's "white readers" (69–70). In the final scene after Scout accompanies Boo Radley to his front door hand-in-hand, our narrator (Jean Louise) recalls feeling older than her years. (My earlier essay in this collection, "Mockingbird's First Draft: How *Go Set a Watchman* Was Made to Come Out," begins with an examination of this scene.) That line about feeling old is an unusual statement coming from a child, suggesting an innocence that has been challenged by all that this young girl in the courthouse balcony has learned about social and physical violence in her hometown. But, once home, her father tucks her into bed. In the movie, she is sleeping in her father's arms. The final scene reflects Jean Louise's memory of domestic security against all that lies exterior to her home.

Whose domestic tranquility is that? Certainly not the Robinson family's. Tom Robinson is dead. He was convicted for a rape he did not commit and shot for attempting to free himself. He will not be sitting up all night watching over his sleeping children. But the Robinson family does not appear on the page. That family is denied the scene of domestic tranquility that Scout is privileged to enjoy. The narratives of the black residents of Maycomb remain unwritten. The teacher can refer to Calpurnia's voice in chapter 12 of *Watchman* as a reminder of that missing voice in *Mockingbird*.

The court house scenes in *Mockingbird* and *Watchman* offer parallel innocence-lost moments that can be taught alongside each other. In *Watchman*, rather than observing the trial, Jean Louise at the age of twenty-six surreptitiously observes her father attending a conservative (white) Citizens' Council meeting—after she has discovered racist pamphlets in his living room. Similar to those final pages of *Mockingbird*, Jean Louise realizes that everything now looks different to her. This time no tranquility waits for her at home when she confronts Atticus. She is shocked, wants out, packs her bags to catch the next train getting out of town.

Again, whose shock is that? The black citizens of Maycomb are certainly unsurprised that racist individuals and organizations inhabit their town and court house. In *Threatening Boundaries,* Claudia Durst Johnson traces the motif of threatened-and-defended boundaries throughout *To Kill a Mockingbird.* The crossing of boundary is where the gothic emerges, she argues; it is horror made familiar, the discovery of the other within the self (Johnson 71, 73). *Mockingbird's* Scout discovers racism in her community, but *Mockingbird* provides both Scout and her readers a mechanism to address that horror within the familiar. That mechanism is Atticus with his ever-ready parental advice and reassurance of security. *Watchman's* Scout and her readers lack that mechanism, making the gothic discovery of racism in her own home more complicated. In *Mockingbird,* her father is her protector against monsters. In *Watchman,* the father becomes the monster. For the black characters, however, the monsters are there all along. The black characters require no introduction to the horror of racism, as it has always been part of their lives. They experience the gothic differently from the white characters. As Roxanne Gay notes, "I don't need to read about a young white girl understanding the perniciousness of racism to actually understand the perniciousness of racism. I have ample firsthand experience."

Against that perniciousness, *To Kill a Mockingbird* offers solace; *Go Set a Watchman* does not. *Mockingbird* concludes with reassurance; *Watchman* concludes without closure, a sense that the struggle is far from over. The two ending scenes—Scout at home and Jean Louise leaving home—offer some compelling and perhaps uncomfortable material for class discussion. To address the student's unease, I offer two recommendations. First, in Gerald Graff's sense of teaching the conflict, we can invite students to explore the controversies surrounding the publication of *Go Set a Watchman:* questions about its provenance, its artistic quality, and its destabilizing of conventional readings of Atticus Finch. These controversies are addressed in book reviews and articles appearing in the bibliography of my essay earlier in this collection, "Mockingbird's First Draft: How *Go Set a Watchman* Was Made to Come Out." An additional teaching strategy would be to invite the students to bring their own voices into the controversy in their personal journal writing.

The central question that has emerged from the publication of *Go Set a Watchman* is how to reconcile Atticus's different perspectives. "The Atticus We Always Knew," by Dale Russakoff the *New Yorker* might help students negotiate the narratives. Russakoff recounts a conversation with Diane McWhorter, historian of the civil-rights movement in Birmingham, and Mary Badham, who as a child played the role of Scout in the

1963 movie *To Kill a Mockingbird.* These three women grew up together as Camp Fire Girls in 1962 Birmingham Alabama. "We talked for hours about the vexed state of readers who had loved and revered the original Atticus," Russakoff remembers. "Along with them, we mourned the loss of an icon, but we were not shocked. In nineteen-sixties Birmingham, as in Scout's Maycomb, the two Atticuses could coexist, and did." She continues, "The whole truth about white people in the segregated South, even in the best people, is invariably disappointing." Even those who did not like the system, such as Russakoff's father, "made an uneasy peace with it." She concludes, "My parents, like most white people in Birmingham, sat out the marches that MLK led on our downtown streets. They decried our racist police commissioner, Eugene 'Bull' Connor, but from the safe distance of home."

The safe distance of home: that is the image at the conclusion of *To Kill a Mockingbird.* The safe distance of self-exile is the image at the conclusion of *Go Set a Watchman.* Jean Louise leaves Maycomb just as Nelle, as she was called in Monroeville, would "keep the railroad tracks hot between Alabama and New York" (Raines 15). Each woman's struggle with her father—Harper Lee's, Jean Louise's, Dale Russakoff's—is the kind of honest personal connection that might be the most unsettling result of reading *Go Set a Watchman.* Every white Southerner has had an experience with an Atticus Finch in their neighborhoods, in their families, and even in themselves. While *To Kill a Mockingbird* soars with high aspirations, *Go Set a Watchman* hits close to home. This reality might be the reason for the visceral objections to reading and teaching *Go Set a Watchman.* It is also the strongest argument *for* teaching it.

Works Cited

Ako-Adjei, Naa Baako. "Why It's time Schools Stopped Teaching *To Kill a Mockingbird.*" *Transition,* 122, 2017, pp. 182–200. https://www.jstor.org/stable/10.2979/transition.122.1.24. Accessed 24 Sept. 2018.

Cep, Casey. "The Contested Legacy of Atticus Finch." *New Yorker,* 17 Dec. 2018, https://www.newyorker.com/magazine/2018/12/17/the-contested-legacy-of-atticus-finch?fbclid=IwARozGrKJ3tLQgTovQ-REZaLGZBzC4_biDvP1EI_Q1NHIn-wh2u61oGcqtX8. Accessed 29 May 2019.

Chadwick, Jocelyn. "Harper Lee Tribune: What Students Today Think about *To Kill a Mockingbird.*" *Chicago Tribune,* 3 Mar. 2016, http://www.chicagotribune.com/news/plus/ct-what-students-think-of-to-kill-a-mockingbird-htmlstory.html. Accessed 29 May 2019.

Crespino, Joseph. *Atticus Finch: The Biography.* Basic Books, 2018.

Facing History and Ourselves. *Teaching Mockingbird.* The Facing History and

Ourselves National Foundation, 2014. https://www.facinghistory.org/mockingbird. Accessed 29 May 2019.

Freedman, Monroe. "Atticus Finch, Esq., RIP." *Legal Times* 24 (1992): pp. 20–21.

Fritz. "To Tweet a Mockingbird." 22 Dec. 2018, http://www.rackafracka.com/2010/07/15/to-tweet-a-mockingbird/. Accessed 29 May 2019.

Gay, Roxanne. "*Mockingbird* Reconsidered." Review of *Why To Kill a Mockingbird Matters* by Tom Santopietro." *New York Times Book Review,* 24 Dec. 2018, https://www.nytimes.com/2018/06/18/books/review/tom-santopietro-why-to-kill-a-mockingbird-matters.html. Accessed 29 May 2019.

Gladwell, Malcolm. "The Courthouse Ring: Atticus Finch and the Limits of Southern Liberalism." *The New Yorker,* 10 Aug. 2009, https://www.newyorker.com/magazine/2009/08/10/the-courthouse-ring. Accessed 29 May 2019.

Gopnik, Adam. "Sweet Home Alabama: Harper Lee's *Go Set a Watchman.*" *The New Yorker,* 27 July 2015, https://www.newyorker.com/magazine/2015/07/27/sweet-home-alabama. Accessed 15 Sept. 2017.

Graff, Gerald. *Beyond the Culture Wars: How Teaching the Conflicts Can Revitalize American Education.* Norton, 1992.

Gray, Rosie. "Trump Defends White-Nationalist Protesters: 'Some Very Fine People on Both Sides.'" *The Atlantic,* 15 Aug. 2017, https://www.theatlantic.com/politics/archive/2017/08/trump-defends-white-nationalist-protesters-some-very-fine-people-on-both-sides/537012/. Accessed 15 September 2017.

Green, Jesse. "Review: A Broadway *Mockingbird* Elegiac and Effective." *New York Times Book Review,* 13 Dec. 2018, https://www.nytimes.com/2018/12/13/theater/to-kill-a-mockingbird-review-jeff-daniels.html. Accessed 29 May 2019.

Harper Perennial. *A Teacher's Guide to Harper Lee Go Set a Watchman.* http://www.HarperAcademic.com. Accessed 29 May 2019.

Harper Perennial. *A Teacher's Guide to Harper Lee To Kill a Mockingbird.* http://www.HarperAcademic.com. Accessed 29 May 2019.

Holland, Brooke Richelle. "Classical Rhetoric in Atticus Finch's Speeches." *English Journal,* vol. 105, no. 6, 2016, pp. 78–82.

Johnson, Claudia Durst. *To Kill a Mockingbird: Threatening Boundaries.* Twayne Masterwork Studies. Twayne, 1994.

Kennedy, Randall. "Harper Lee's *Go Set a Watchman.*" *New York Times,* 14 July 2015, https://www.nytimes.com/2015/07/14/books/review/harper-lees-go-set-a-watchman.html. Accessed 29 May 2019.

King, Martin Luther. "Letter from a Birmingham Jail." Aug. 1963. https://web.cn.edu/kwheeler/documents/Letter_Birmingham_Jail.pdf. Accessed 27 Dec. 2018.

Lee, Harper. *Go Set a Watchman.* HarperCollins, 2015.

———. *To Kill a Mockingbird.* HarperCollins, 1960.

National Endowment for the Arts. *Reader Resources: To Kill a Mockingbird.* The Big Read. https://www.arts.gov/partnerships/nea-big-read/to-kill-a-mockingbird. Accessed 29 May 2019.

National Endowment for the Arts. *Teacher's Guide: To Kill a Mockingbird.* The Big Read. https://www.arts.gov/partnerships/nea-big-read/to-kill-a-mockingbird. Accessed 29 May 2019.

Raines, Howell, "Mockingbird Reconsidered." Review of *Atticus Finch: The Biography* by Joseph Crespino. *New York Times Book Review,* 24 June 2018, 1, 15, https://www.nytimes.com/2018/06/18/books/review/atticus-finch-joseph-crespino-ac-lee-biography.html. Accessed 29 May 2019.

Ricker-Wilson, Carol. "When the Mockingbird Becomes an Albatross: Reading and Resistance in the Language Arts Classroom." *English Journal,* Mar. 1998, pp. 67–72.

Russakoff, Dale. "The Atticus We Always Knew." *New Yorker,* 17 July 2015, https://www.newyorker.com/books/page-turner/the-atticus-we-always-knew. Accessed 29 May 2019.

Sorkin, Aaron. "Bringing *To Kill a Mockingbird* to Broadway was Nearly Impossible." *New York Magazine.* 25 Nov. 2018, https://www.vulture.com/2018/11/aaron-sorkin-to-kill-a-mockingbird.html#comments. Accessed 29 May 2019.

Southern Manifesto. March 1956. http://americanradioworks.publicradio.org/features/marshall/manifesto.html. Accessed 27 Dec. 2018.

United States Supreme Court. *Brown v. Board of Education of Topeka*, 347 U.S. 483 (1954). https://supreme.justia.com/cases/federal/us/347/483/. Accessed 29 May 2019.

REVISITING MONROEVILLE, ALABAMA, AND MAYCOMB, USA

Cheli Reutter

It is more than a notion that lives depend on fairly representing the narrative connecting the real town of Monroeville and the imagined community of Maycomb, Alabama. It is also more than a notion that lives have been lost or nearly lost on account of getting it wrong. "Getting it wrong" is a joint endeavor, not a matter of author-blaming Harper Lee, but rather, of recognizing a shared refusal of a collective and mainstream readership to take responsibility for the implications of context, interpretation, and pedagogy on the daily lives and security of all of Monroeville's and the country's citizens in the center of the community and on its margins.

Specifically, we can point to the life of Walter McMillan, who was wrongfully convicted of the murder of eighteen-year-old Ronda Morrison in Monroeville, Alabama on November 1, 1986. McMillan was convicted in 1987 by—no joke—a "Sheriff Tate," who placed him immediately on Alabama's death row, where he remained for fifteen months while awaiting his trial. A pulp worker in his early fifties from a black community outside Monroeville with no history of violence or prior felonies, McMillan was ordered to appear for said trial in the 86 percent–white Baldwin county—not his own 40 percent-black Monroe County. There, the eleven white jurors and one black juror convicted him of the murder of the young white store clerk.

Though McMillan testified that he was at a fish fry at the time the murder took place, and though a dozen black witnesses confirmed his alibi, Sheriff Thomas Tate told him, "I don't give a damn what you say or what you do. I don't give a damn what your people say either. I'm going to put twelve people on a jury who are going to find your goddamn black ass guilty." McMillan's conviction was apparently a foregone conclusion.

Unlike Tom Robinson, Walter McMillan did get "just mercy," if we can call it that. He did not have seventeen bullets pumped into his back. Thanks to Bryan Stevenson, an excellent and persistent young Harvard-educated African American lawyer, and to the Equal Justice Initiative, Walter McMillan was released from death row in 1993. He lived almost another generation as a free man—yet died in 2012 after experiencing severe dementia, likely provoked by his extended incarceration.

But for Bryan Stevenson, Walter McMillan's life would have ended in 1993 as Tom Robinson's did in the world-renowned Maycomb narrative published thirty-three years earlier—that is, with his execution. Only, McMillan's would have been state-sanctioned, while Tom's was just what we today like to call an "unfortunate incident," or an "officer-involved shooting."

Walter McMillan's case more than a generation later was eerily similar to Tom Robinson's in the 1960 novel, even down to two major points: (1) the very *accusations* against the fictional black man in 1930s Maycomb and the real-life black man in 1980s Monroeville were all but death sentences. And, (2) the wrongful convictions did not hurt the town's leading white men or challenge their authority and popularity in the least. Ultimately, neither Atticus nor either of the Sheriff Tates, fictional or real, was to come out worse for the wear. While Atticus has parades and a hashtag movement in his honor, the real-life Sheriff Tate would be elected several more times.

Bryan Stevenson won his fight for McMillan's release, but it did not change the national conversation concerning *To Kill a Mockingbird*. High schoolers are still reading *Mockingbird,* and, through it, they are taught to appreciate and pity a black man characterized by his voluntary servitude to and deferential respect for white women and men, and to admire a white man who is willing to defend him in court. Given the events in Monroeville in 1986 and 1987, we might wonder whether *To Kill a Mockingbird* has done anything at all for racial social justice—or whether it simply feeds a cultural appetite for the sacrifice of black men.

After all, the primary value of Tom Robinson's character in the novel is the personal catharsis and cultural redemption his death provides. Susan L. Mizruchi critiques the central role of sacrifice narratives in American realism and its contemporaneous sociological narratives in her 1998 study *The Science of Sacrifice*. However, Tom Santopietro's 2018 book represents the broader conversation on *Mockingbird*. *Why To Kill a Mockingbird Matters* essentially dismisses even the limited challenge of Harper Lee's own *Go Set a Watchman*. In a popular argument which does not acknowledge Bryan Stevenson's work, Santopietro validates the *Mockingbird* narrative as exemplary of racial social justice. Yet just because we can default to this facile interpretation does not mean we should. In fact, life tells us we should not.

In latter-twentieth-century Alabama, the black sacrifice narrative presented itself in fiction and then in nonfiction. Perhaps when we are convinced of the truth of art, life is likely to imitate it. From 1987 when McMillan was charged to 1993 when he was exonerated, life in Monroeville was to imitate the literary art produced more than a quarter century earlier. By the late 1980s and early 1990s, *Mockingbird* had reached a fevered pitch of popularity even before the Common Core mandate, and the end of the story for the real-life Walter McMillan was already written. He was guilty. And, if he were innocent and got killed anyhow, it was just an unfortunate error, as it had been with Tom Robinson.

Aaron Sorkin's version of the play *To Kill a Mockingbird* is thoughtfully updated and involves brilliant actors and actresses, including Tony-Award-Winning Celia Keenan-Bolger. Yet while certain characters, such as Calpurnia, are more extensively developed, it has become clear that even this modern adaptation still prizes voluntary white benevolence, not structural reform. Yet the flip side of the power of literary art to affirm and perpetuate the status quo is its power to challenge it. That is to say that what we assume about the nature, the history, and the ideological implications of the Maycomb story can change if we are to engage the multiple narratives connecting contexts for Monroeville, Alabama, and Maycomb, USA. And there are such narratives available.

Pete Earley's 1995 *Circumstantial Evidence: Death, Life and Justice in a Southern Town* featuring Walter McMillan and Bryan Stevenson was perhaps the first broadly available nonfiction story of Monroeville beyond Harper Lee biographies. In October of 2014, Stevenson published his own narrative, *Just Mercy: A Story of Justice and Redemption*. In it, he intertwined Walter McMillan's story, reflections on his own experiences with race in his childhood, and other stories of racial and other injustices in the criminal and legal systems. Stevenson's book, brilliant and complex as is Lee's classic Maycomb story, offers a counter-narrative of rural and small-town Alabama.

Stevenson's narrative has reached a different audience than what Toni Morrison calls "the White literary imagination." Stevenson's narrative is more likely to resonate in the "African American hush harbor" Vorris L. Nunley speaks of than in the traditionally "white" spaces of the classroom, libraries, book clubs and mainstream scholarship Adam Nemmers critiques in this volume. African American community spaces including barbershops are havens of safety and free speech, and these places are well-springs of cultural knowledge. As readers learn in his book, many of Stevenson's own experiences, both growing up and getting to know Walter McMillan, come from the hush harbor.

A few reviewers have claimed since the publication of Bryan Stevenson's own *Just Mercy* that it is "the new *To Kill a Mockingbird*." Yet, at this juncture, even to the extent that Stevenson is known or appreciated, his story is not generally integrated into scholarship, popular thought, or any of hundreds of classroom discussions each year on *To Kill a Mockingbird*. There are unspoken racial barriers limiting engagement. We might think of *Go Set a Watchman*'s Jean Louise, who becomes angry with Calpurnia for not speaking "Jeff Davis' English"—and who is either unwilling or unable to grasp the meaning of the older woman's dialect or her silence. Yet this argument is not only about dialect; it is about white failure to value epistemology of the hush harbor.

While I do not suggest that hush harbor texts must therefore be translated, mainstream texts approaching similar issues can be valuable in tandem with them, as Monica Carol Miller suggests in this volume. Jericho Williams's comparison of Janie Starks and Jean Louise Finch guides us through a regional example of this endeavor. Yet we have an extraordinary opportunity to make an even closer comparison. The publication of *Go Set a Watchman* less than a year after *Just Mercy* was fortuitous. Through it as well as *Just Mercy*, broad audiences might question the values of the entrenched national narrative even through a counter-narrative involving the very town around which an imagined community has thrived for over half a century.

In the 2015 release of *Go Set a Watchman,* we learn of an important difference between Atticus as he was originally conceived in 1957 or thereabouts and Atticus as he was represented only a few years later with the publication of *To Kill a Mockingbird*. In *Go Set a Watchman,* Jean Louise recalls that Atticus actually *won* the trial back in the early 1930s on behalf of a "black boy accused of murdering a white girl" (p. 207). We also learn that he did so reluctantly, and merely because it was his duty.

We also learn that Atticus allows himself to shirk his duty when the black man under consideration is not perfect in the eyes of the white community. When in the present time of *Go Set a Watchman* (the early 1950s), the elderly Calpurnia seeks his support as the attorney for her grandson, Atticus is loath to come visit her, let alone to support her grandson. We do not know and can only speculate as to why Harper Lee merged the two legal stories involving Atticus and black residents of Maycomb in *Watchman* into a single story in *Mockingbird*; we only know that when *Mockingbird* emerged, the rift between the 1950s Atticus and the black community was transformed into a memory of the black community's unabashed appreciation of the white attorney. Whether Harper Lee made this change to comfort herself, the white community, or both, we may never know. We only know that the narrative of this binary relationship of black dependency and white nobility is the story mainstream readers want to remember and retell.

Rather than becoming angry or dismissive of the more realistic Atticus, readers, teachers and scholars should come to terms with him. Disappointment with the Atticus of *Go Set a Watchman,* in contrast with the truly admirable real-life Bryan Stevenson of *Just Mercy,* should provoke us to revisit the *Mockingbird* Maycomb. It changes things when we remember that the Atticus of *Mockingbird* did not want to defend Tom Robinson, and was arguably motivated by his defiance of Aunt Alexandra's more overtly racist and protective arguments. It comes as a shock, perhaps, to realize that it was the mainstream imagination (with some help from Horton Foote's film adaptation), not Harper Lee independently, which created an unambiguous hero and a Southern icon.

Though *Go Set a Watchman* is also fiction, the relative extent to which it even recognizes examples of false egalitarianism and exposes secret channels for white power is challenging. Through the Atticus in *Watchman,* whose imperfection is rendered obvious even to white readers reluctant to notice, Harper Lee herself provides an opportunity for deeper examination. The contrast between the real-life lawyer who defended Walter McMillan and the fictional Atticus Finch who defends Tom Robinson in *To Kill a Mockingbird* is striking. Mainstream readers (my own high school teacher included) often uphold Atticus as a model of courage, admirable for his efforts despite his failure to protect Tom Robinson. Yet all Atticus had to say about Tom Robinson's death is that "they didn't have to shoot him that much" (*To Kill a Mockingbird* Chapter 24). The Atticus of *Go Set a Watchman,* who defended a "black boy" is not, after all, so different. Meanwhile, Bryan Stevenson pushed through years of improper evidence and repudiated requests for *habeas corpus* relief for his client, and he attended to other problems in order to win his client's freedom. Then, after Walter McMillan's death, *his* attorney, Bryan Stevenson, was to eulogize him.

I will put it this way: on October 2014, something extraordinary and, to the best of my knowledge, unprecedented occurred in the literary world. An unsung hero, perhaps this nation's greatest attorney, released a true story about Monroeville, Alabama. If it, together with Harper Lee's 2015 novel *Go Set a Watchman,* receives attention from dozens of high school teachers, hundreds of popular readers, reviewers, scholars, and even Oprah, it could change a great deal. The timing of *Just Mercy's* release—fifty-four years after the publication of Harper Lee's 1960 *To Kill a Mockingbird*—reminds us that neither the pity of a Scout nor the going-through-the-motions of an Atticus—nor yet the hollow claims of such high school English teachers who teach their students to idealize Atticus—nor even the cautious retreat of the niche reader who extols its other virtues such as its gender bending or disability inclusivity— will save the real-life Walter McMillans of our very own generation any more than they did the fictional Tom Robinsons of the 1930s of memory- narrative. The facts of the case of African American pulp worker Walter McMillan, falsely convicted of murdering a young white woman in Monroeville, may be disturbingly similar to Harper Lee's classic novel, and yet McMillan had one thing and one thing only that Tom Robinson did not: he had a genuinely good and noble lawyer. And we might begin to question the implications of that different in imagined community of Maycomb, Alabama.

In the twenty-first century, we must read Harper Lee's *To Kill a Mocking- bird* differently. We, the twenty-first-century students, scholars, teachers, and readers collectively should allow the 1995 *Circumstantial Evidence,* the 2014 *Just Mercy,* and the 2015 *Go Set a Watchman* to work in the liter- ary imaginations of a huge cross-section of readers, pedagogues, artists and scholars—inspiring film and documentaries, book clubs, author interviews, and multiple media venues to produce the sort of justice that is required to keep the Helen Robinsons of the world safe without a white escort and to ensure that the Walter McMillans of the world are not condemned to death at the moment of accusation.

While I am all for celebrating an annual Bryan Stevenson day, perhaps even organizing a parade in his honor, and while it would be my hope that such a hero as this might be named Attorney of the Year, it is even more so my hope that we, collectively, recognize Maycomb for its *failure* to produce racial justice in its own time and in ours. And may Maycomb be the place where the Jean Louise Finches of the world—the white young people, and women in particular—might realize they should not worry about white fragility—their fathers' or their own—and that the world will still turn even if they go out on a limb, disinheriting the legacy of Andrew Jackson or even Simon and Atticus Finch. May it be the place where white boys and men, gay or straight, do not have to grow up to be confined by their fathers or die in war if they do not become their fathers. And may it be the place where black children can grow up without their fathers and mothers being taken from them—that they might become the doctors, teachers, and, heck, even the lawyers of their community. #WhatWouldBryanStevensonDo.

The reader who comes to *Go Set a Watchman* without a thorough immersion in the narrative of *to Kill a Mockingbird* may follow a different path in consideration of racial social justice. As Laura Fine points out in this volume, *Watchman* is ultimately not about Atticus, but about Jean Louise. We may have a host of complicated feelings toward heroine who fails, in her own adult years, to empathize with the worry and grief of the woman who raised her, whose own uncle hits her, and who then offers apology to both him and her father. We might have complicated feelings toward the heroine who throws over the young man who is in love with her not, as we might have hoped, because of her own independence or alternative approaches to gender and relationships, but because he is not her "kind." Kwakiutl L. Dreher's essay in this volume may provoke us to wonder whether Jean Louise Finch has become an exhausting young white woman. We might nevertheless understand why Jean Louise makes her choices, even if we believe (as I hope we do) that she is wrong. Perhaps we might wonder whether she felt she needed the support of her family, and a sense of belonging, and felt that her humiliation at the hands of her Uncle Jack was a price she had to pay. These reflections might yield further insight into the mechanisms of gender and white privilege.

One of my own students, who read *To Kill a Mockingbird* in spring of 2015, and who pounced on her library's first available copy of *Go Set a Watchman* in July of 2015, had just this experience. By her account, she fought with her father, whom she had always adored, for about six months after finishing *Go Set a Watchman*. She saw too much of what she calls "respectability racism" in him. And yet, she says, in the end, *Go Set a Watchman* helped her acknowledge her father's willingness to participate in systems of oppression, and to discover boundaries for herself to keep from adopting them, even while recognizing that he is human.

In tandem with *Just Mercy* and other contextual pieces, *Go Set a Watchman* is the American story for our times. It is our collective maturation novel. It will never generate the same feelings as *To Kill a Mockingbird,* given that we cannot idealize a patriarch who hangs out with white supremacists. It might not give us values to live by, but, perhaps more importantly, it will give us failures to learn from.

We might consider that *To Kill a Mockingbird* is a valuable portrait by an author who engaged the national narrative not once, but twice, and that she might have something worthwhile to contribute to the conversation through her "other" published text, and through the aggregate of her two novels. We might see how interesting *Go Set a Watchman* is in context of its much more renowned Maycomb twin and other texts in our literature, popular, film, and new media engaging the national narrative. And we might ask the questions about whether our contentment with the classic Maycomb narrative is a contentment with dangerous half-truths and comforting lies.

Bryan Stevenson cannot be everywhere. But if we engage a comprehensive revision of our interpretation of Monroeville, Alabama, and Maycomb, USA—and, by "we," I mean readers in the mainstream as well as in the hush harbor—we might get into the joints and pivots of social justice reform. Lives—in Monroeville, Alabama, and Maycomb, USA—still depend upon it.

Works Cited

Anderson, Benedict. *Imagined Communities: Reflections on the Origins and Spread of Nationalism. Revised edition.* Verso, 1983.

Earley, Pete. *Circumstantial Evidence: Death, Life, and Justice in a Southern Town.* Bantam, 1995.

Hurston, Zora Neale. *Their Eyes Were Watching God.* J.P. Lippincott, 1937.

Lee, Harper. *To Kill a Mockingbird.* J.P. Lippincott, 1960.

———. *Go Set a Watchman: A Novel.* HarperCollins, 2015.

Mizruchi, Susan L. *The Science of Sacrifice: American Literature and Modern Social Theory.* Princeton University Press, 1998.

Morrison, Toni. *Playing in the Dark: Whiteness and the Literary Imagination.* Harvard University Press, 1992.

Nunley, Vorris L. *Keepin' it Hushed: The Barbershop and African American Hush Harbor Rhetoric.* African American Life Series. Series Editor Melba Joyce Boyd. Wayne State, 2011.

Santopietro, Tom. *Why To Kill a Mockingbird Matters: What Harper Lee's Book and the Iconic American Film Mean to Us Today.* St. Martin's Press, 2018.

Stevenson, Bryan. *Just Mercy: A Story of Justice and Redemption.* Spiegel and Grau, 2014.

CONTRIBUTORS

HOLLY BLACKFORD is professor of English at Rutgers University-Camden, where she teaches and publishes literary criticism on American and children's literature. Her books include *From Alice to Algernon: The Evolution of Child Consciousness in the Novel* (University of Tennessee Press, 2018), *Out of This World: Why Literature Matters to Girls* (Teachers College, Columbia University, 2004), *Mockingbird Passing: Closeted Traditions and Sexual Curiosities in Harper Lee's Novel* (University of Tennessee Press, 2011), *The Myth of Persephone in Girls' Fantasy Literature* (Routledge, 2011), edited volume *100 Years of Anne with an 'e': The Centennial Study of* Anne of Green Gables (University of Calgary, 2009), and edited volume *Something Great and Complete: The Centennial Study of My Ántonia* (Fairleigh Dickinson University Press, 2018). Her newly released monograph titled *Alice to Algernon: The Evolution of Child Consciousness in the Novel* (University of Tennessee Press, 2018) demonstrates the influence of early developmental psychology, evolutionary theory, and sexology on "child study" in modern novels. She is an associate member of the Childhood Studies doctoral program at Rutgers-Camden. Her next project is *The Animation Mystique: Sentient Toys, Puppets, and Automata in Literature and Film.*

BRANDIE L. BOHNEY, currently a PhD student in Rhetoric and Writing at Bowling Green State University, has a decade of high school English teaching and university composition instruction experience. She received her MA in English from Indiana University's School of Liberal Arts. A teacher consultant with the National Writing project, she specializes in working with reluctant and remedial writing students. Her research interests include pre-service teacher preparation in writing instruction, devalued Englishes in the writing classroom, and using discovery learning for mechanics and usage instruction. Her work "Moving Students Toward Acceptance of 'Other' Englishes," for which she received an award from Indiana University-Purdue University Indianapolis, appeared in the July 2016 issue of *English Journal.*

SUSAN CHENELLE is Supervisor of Curriculum and Instruction at University Academy Charter High School in Jersey City, New Jersey, where she taught English and journalism for nearly ten years. She holds a master's degree in education from New Jersey City University and is a doctoral student in teacher education and teacher development at Montclair State University. She and Audrey Fisch have published three volumes in the Rowman and Littlefield series, *Using Informational Text*. The fourth volume in the series, *Using Informational Text to Teach* The Great Gatsby, is forthcoming in 2018. Their work has also appeared in *English Journal* and *English Leadership Quarterly*.

JONATHAN S. CULLICK is professor of English, past chair of the Department of English, and past director of the Writing Instruction Program at Northern Kentucky University. A former middle school language arts teacher, he supervises student teachers and teaches courses in the methods of teaching of high school writing, literature, and young adult literature. With scholarly interests in literature of the American South, he is the author of *Robert Penn Warren's All the King's Men: A Reader's Companion* (University Press of Kentucky, 2018), *Making History: The Biographical Narratives of Robert Penn Warren* (Louisiana State University Press, 2000), and peer reviewed articles on Warren, William Faulkner, Walker Percy, and other American writers. He is a co-author of *Writing in the Disciplines* (Bedford/St.Martin, 2013) and *Teaching With Hacker Handbooks* (Macmillan, 2014), and author of *Religion in the 21st Century* (Pearson Longman, 2009). The journals in which his work has appeared include *Studies in American Fiction, Southern Literary Journal, Southern Quarterly, Mississippi Quarterly, American Literary Realism, Studies in Popular Culture,* and *Journal of Dramatic Theory and Criticism* as well as several regional journals. The Kentucky Council of Teachers of English selected him to be the recipient of the 2019 College Teacher of the Year Award.

PATRICIA F. D'ASCOLI teaches academic writing at the University of Hartford. She received her MS in English education at Southern Connecticut State University, where she received a graduate research fellowship and was the winner of the 2011 graduate commencement speech contest. Her essay "Coming Up Empty: Exploring Narrative Omissions in Huckleberry Finn" is included in *Twain's Omissions: Exploring the Gaps as Textual Context* (Cambridge Scholars Publishing, 2014). She has also contributed an essay to an edited collection titled *Teens and the New Religious Landscape* (McFarland, 2018).

KWAKIUTL L. DREHER is associate professor of English and Ethnic Studies at the University of Nebraska-Lincoln specializing in African American literature, auto/biography, film, visual and popular culture, and mass-marketed popular literature. She published *Dancing on the White Page: Black Women Entertainers Writing Autobiography* (SUNY, 2008). Her work has appeared in the edited collections *Screening Motherhood in Contemporary World Cinema* (Demeter P, 2016), *Movies in the Age of Obama: The Era of Post-Racial and Neo-Racist Cinema* (Rowman & Littlefield, 2015), and *African Americans on Television: Race-ing for Ratings* (Praeger Press, 2013). An actor/playwright, her one-woman show, "In A Smoke-Filled Room, Color Matters," was a playlab selection at the *Great Plains Theater Festival* 2013 in Omaha, Nebraska. She is a film reviewer for the *Mary Riepma Ross Media Arts Center* in Lincoln.

LAURA FINE, associate professor of English at Meredith College in Raleigh, North Carolina, teaches American and world literature. With areas of interest in southern literature and contemporary American female writers, she has published articles in such journals as *Biography*, *The Southern Literary Journal*, and the *South Carolina Review*. Articles on *To Kill a Mockingbird* appear in *The Southern Quarterly* and in Alice Petry's edited volume On *Harper Lee: Essays and Reflections* (U of Tennessee P, 2008).

AUDREY FISCH is professor of English at New Jersey City University; for more than fifteen years, she also served as Coordinator of Secondary English Education. She has published a wide variety of academic work, including *American Slaves in Victorian England* (Cambridge 2000) and the *Cambridge Companion to the African-American Slave Narrative* (2007). Fisch and Susan Chenelle have published three volumes in the *Using Informational Text* series for Rowman and Littlefield; their fourth is due out shortly, *Using Informational Text to Teach* The Great Gatsby (2018). Their work has also appeared in *English Journal* and *English Leadership Quarterly*.

MONICA CAROL MILLER is assistant professor in the Department of English at Middle Georgia State University. She is author of *Being*

Ugly: Southern Women Writers and Social Rebellion (Louisiana State UP, 2017), and has written chapters for *Small Screen Souths: Interrogating the Televisual Archive* (LSUP, 2016), *Seeking Home: Marginalization and Representation in Appalachian Letters and Song* (U of Tennessee P, 2017), and *Neil Gaiman in the Twenty-First Century* (McFarland, 2015). Her work has appeared in *Mississippi Quarterly, South Atlantic Review, Flannery O'Connor Review, Eudora Welty Review, Journal of Transatlantic Studies, Studies in Gothic Fiction,* and *Journal of Appalachian Studies.*

ADAM NEMMERS is assistant professor of American Literature at Lamar University in Beaumont, Texas. He is coeditor of *With Filial Regards: The Civil War Letters of a Texan Family* (TCU Press, 2015) and associate editor of *Transatlantic Anglophone Literatures 1776-1920* (under development with Edinburgh University Press). His work has recently appeared in *Popular Modernisms: Then and Now* (Bloomsbury Academic, 2016); forthcoming publications include essays on William Faulkner, Richard Wright, *Passing, American Tragedy,* settler colonialism, and rural women. He is currently working on a monograph project about the American modernist epic novel.

LELAND S. PERSON is professor of English at the University of Cincinnati. He is the author of *Aesthetic Headaches: Women and a Masculine Poetics in Poe, Melville, and Hawthorne* (U of Georgia P, 1988), *Henry James and the Suspense of Masculinity* (U of Pennsylvania P, 2003), and *The Cambridge Introduction to Nathaniel Hawthorne* (2007). He is the editor of the Norton Critical Edition of Hawthorne's *The Scarlet Letter and Other Writings* (2005) and *A Historical Guide to James Fenimore Cooper* (Oxford UP, 2007), and co-editor of *Hawthorne and Melville: Writing a Relationship* (U of Georgia P, 2008) and *Roman Holidays: American Writers and Artists in Nineteenth-Century Italy* (U of Iowa P, 2002). He teaches courses in nineteenth-century American literature, gender, and sexuality, and literature and the environment.

CHELI REUTTER is associate professor-educator of English and affiliate faculty member in the Department of Women's, Gender, and Sexuality Studies at the University of Cincinnati; she has also taught in UC's Africana Studies department and at the University of Louisville and Northern Kentucky University. A Fulbright scholar in Freiburg, Germany, in 2006, she co-edited *Criss-Crossing Borders in Literature of the American West* with Reginald Dyck in 2009 (Palgrave). Research interests include race, gender, and nation. Her articles have appeared in *Papers on Language and Literature,* the College English Association (CEA) *Critic,* the CEA *On-Line Forum,* and *Swiss Papers on English Language and Literature,* with reviews appearing in the *Journal of the Society for Multi-Ethnic Literature (MELUS)* and *Antipodes.* Reutter guest lectures and involves students in local outreach projects, including with Cincinnati Public Schools. She teaches courses in American and African American literary traditions, African American poetry, ethnic women's literature, and medical humanities. Her current project is on Harriet Beecher Stowe and Frances E. W. Harper.

JERICHO WILLIAMS earned a PhD in English from West Virginia University. He is an independent scholar whose current research interests include American, African American, and Southern literature. He has published essays about educational debates in the fiction of Claude McKay and Wallace Thurman in *Critical Insights: The Harlem Renaissance* (Salem Press, 2015) and environmental education in the writings of Henry David Thoreau (*The Thoreau Society Bulletin,* 2014) and in American slave narratives in *Ecogothic in Nineteenth-Century American Literature* (Routledge, 2017). His entry for *To Kill a Mockingbird* appears in *Race in American Film: The Complete Resource* (ABC-Clio, 2017), and he is preparing forthcoming essays about African American historical fiction and Nella Larsen.

INDEX